14.99

MODERN IRAN

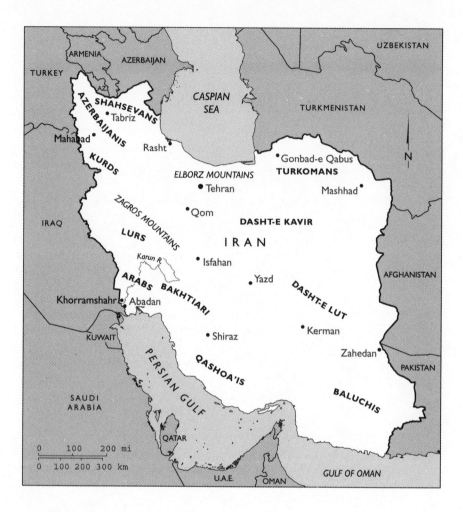

Modern Iran

Roots and Results of Revolution

Nikki R. Keddie
with a section by Yann Richard

Yale University Press New Haven & London

Designed by James J. Johnson and set in Stemple Garamond type by Keystone Typesetting, Inc.

Printed in the United States of America.

Library of Congress Cataloging-in-Publication Data

Keddie, Nikki R.
Modern Iran : roots and results of revolution / Nikki R. Keddie ; with a section by Yann Richard.
p. cm.
Rev., updated ed. of: roots of revolution. 1981.
Includes bibliographical references (p.   ) and index.
ISBN 0-300-09856-1 (alk. paper)

1. Iran—History—20th century. 2. Iran—History—Revolution, 1979. I. Richard, Yann. II. Keddie, Nikki R.
Roots of revolution. III. Title.
DS316.3.K42 2003
955.05—dc21
2003052543

A catalogue record for this book is available from the British Library.

The paper in this book meets the guidelines for permanence and durability of the
Committee on Production Guidelines for Book Longevity of the Council on Library Resources.

10   9   8   7   6   5   4   3   2   1

To the people of Iran

2003—A year of major anniversaries
- *50 years since the coup overthrowing prime minister Mohammad Mosaddeq.*
- *25 years since the main events of the 1978–79 revolution.*
- *6 years since the landslide election of president Mohammad Khatami.*
  - *The struggle continues*

. . . could thou and I with Fate conspire
To grasp this sorry Scheme of Things entire,
Would not we shatter it to bits—and then
Re-mold it nearer to the Heart's Desire!

An eleventh-century Iranian scientist

Religious distress is at the same time the
expression of real distress and also the *protest* against
real distress. Religion is the sigh of the oppressed
creature, the heart of a heartless world, just as it is the
spirit of spiritless conditions. It is . . .

A nineteenth-century European socialist

Contents

List of Illustrations   ix

Preface   xi

Preface to the 1981 edition of *Roots of Revolution*   xv

1. Religion and Society to 1800   1
    Background   1
    Islam and Society   3

2. Foundations of Nineteenth-Century Iran   22

3. Continuity and Change under the Qajars: 1796–1890   37

4. Protest and Revolution: 1890–1914   58

5. War and Reza Shah: 1914–1941   73
    1914–1921   73
    1921–1925   80
    1925–1941   88

6. World War II and Mosaddeq: 1941–1953   105
    World War II, 1941–1945   105
    Postwar Socioeconomic Problems   110
    The Oil Crisis and Mosaddeq   123

7. Royal Dictatorship: 1953–1977   132
    General Character of the Period   132
    1954–1960   135
    1960–1963   140
    Reform, Boom, and Bust: 1963–1977   148

8. Modern Iranian Political Thought   170

     Intellectual and Literary Trends to 1960 by N. Keddie   170
     Contemporary Shi'i Thought by Yann Richard   188
     Conclusion by N. Keddie   212

9. The Revolution   214

     Secular and Guerilla Opposition Forces   214
     The "Religious Opposition" and the Revolution   222

10. Politics and Economics under Khomeini: 1979–1989   240

11. Politics and Economics in Post-Khomeini Iran   263

12. Society, Gender, Culture, and Intellectual Life   285

Conclusion   317

Notes   323

Select Bibliography   355

Index   367

Illustrations

Map of Iran   *frontispiece*

Following page 169

The 1905–11 Revolution (photos from the collection of Nikki Keddie)
    Sattar Khan, leader of the Tabriz freedom-fighters
    Mirza Jahangir Khan, editor of *Sur-e Esrafil*
    Sayyed Jamal ad-Din Esfahani, popular preacher of the Revolution
    Malek al-Motakallemin, another leading popular preacher

Peoples of Iran (photos by Nikki Keddie)
    Shahsevan tribeswoman of Azerbaijan, 1975
    Baluchi, near the Afghan border, 1973
    Kurd at a town market, 1974
    Arab family, Ahwaz, Khuzistan, 1974

The Qashqa'i of Fars province: old and new ways
(photos by Nikki Keddie)
    Qashqa'i tribespeople on autumn migration, 1977
    Qashqa'i factory worker, Marvdasht, 1977

Carpet weaving: Iran's primary non-oil export
(photos by Nikki Keddie)
    Family weaving at home, Kerman, 1974
    Carpet workshop, Ardebil, Azerbaijan, 1974

Comic and tragic popular theatre (photos by Nikki Keddie)
    Blackface clown of the popular theatre, Shiraz, 1977
    Ta'zieh (passion play) on the death of Ali, the first Imam,
    Taleqan valley, 1979

Leading figures in Iran's revolutionary movement
(photos from collection of Nikki Keddie)

Ali Shariati
Ayatollah Mahmud Taleqani
Abolhasan Bani Sadr, Mehdi Bazargan, and Ayatollah Khomeini
Ayatollah Kazem Shariatmadari (photo by Nikki Keddie)
Political prayer meeting at the University of Tehran, 1979,
addressed by Ayatollah Taleqani (photos by Nikki Keddie)
    Women's section
    Men's section, Mehdi Bazargan (at right) and Sadeq Ghotbzadeh
    (second from left) in front row
Oil workers, Abadan, 1974 (photo by Nikki Keddie)
Silk reeling factory, Gilan, 1974 (photo by Nikki Keddie)
Women physicians in operating room. Abbas/Magnum Photos
Couple in contemporary Tehran. Abbas/Magnum Photos

Preface

This year, 2003, is the twenty-fifth anniversary of 1978, the year in which most of the struggles of the Iranian Revolution took place, though its final victory came in Feburary 1979. That revolution spurred worldwide interest in Iran and a large variety of theoretical and empirical writings that continues until now. The year 2003 is also, as of April, a crucial one for the whole Middle Eastern region and an appropriate time to try to summarize in one volume both the historical background of the Iranian Revolution and the evolution of Iran since 1979.

Roots of Revolution: An Interpretive History of Modern Iran was published in 1981, twenty-two years ago, and it continued to have a considerable readership both in the West and more recently in translation in Iran, even after more than two decades have passed since its closing date. The editors of Yale University Press in 2002 asked me if they should undertake a new printing, or would I be willing to write a revised, updated book. I opted for the latter, especially as Yale did not want a complete rewrite of the text, but rather what I have provided in this book: three new chapters covering events since 1979, correction of a few points in the old text that now seemed wrong, and a new conclusion, preface, and revised bibliography and footnotes. This approach has meant that some points in the text that required either no revision or minor change could be supported by notes and brief quotations from books published after 1981, though to have done so for all relevant books would have meant extending the footnotes beyond reason. For new note entries my editors kindly agreed to include full first names of authors, which is not the case for prior note entries.

In rereading my text I was struck by a point that was first brought to my attention by Perry Anderson, namely, that the chapter on Reza Shah was unbalanced. It was largely a critique of his economic programs, based on my own research—a critique that I have now greatly shortened and balanced by a discussion of achievements and problems in other domains. This does not mean that I am renouncing my economic criticisms, which are still available in fuller form in the first edition.

Iran as well as the United States and the entire world is, in early 2003, in an extraordinarily complex situation in which it is impossible to predict what will happen even by the time this book appears, much less later. The continuing political struggles in Iran and among the Iranian diaspora have resulted in opinions about that country being both fragmented and passionately held, and holders of a variety of opinions support them with differing interpretations of the Iranian past. Any history of Iran is bound to incorporate interpretations and emphases, and in the current climate there may be more disagreement over my interpretations than was true of the first edition. This, however, would be true no matter what I wrote. I try for balance but make no secret of my dislike of clerical rule but also of any plan for outside intervention to overthrow it. I have confidence in the Iranian people's abilities to manage their own affairs in the long run.

Writing in the United States in 2003, I am struck that many of the features this book notes as significant in either the Pahlavi period or since in Iran are now more prevalent in the United States than they were when I wrote the first edition—huge and increasing income distribution gaps; special favors to the rich and powerful and neglect of the poor; hubris about one's own country's past and future, about its virtues in domestic and foreign policy and its divine guidance; ideologically driven government leaders; attacks on civil liberties; and major corruption involving business and government. Some of these are less true of today's Iran than they are of the United States, although we have many better features not found in Iran today. Criticisms of such aspects of Iran, which are mainly directed at governmental policies rather than the people, do not mean that one is writing from a viewpoint of superiority or unawareness of partially similar, and also different, problems at home.

Since 1981 there has been a flowering of largely monographic studies and of journalistic books concerning modern Iran. Over the years I have read many of these books and articles, and they greatly inform what I have written here. As Yale University Press set tight deadlines for this revised book, I did not have time to reread books and articles, which means that specific footnote references are far from reflecting the range of my reading, or of valuable works, which are better reflected (as regards books in English) in the Select Bibliography. I should note, especially in view of the assertion by the Campus Watch website that scholars of Middle Eastern origin are hurting Middle Eastern studies via biased research, that the flowering of significant publications in Iranian studies in recent decades has come mainly from scholars of Iranian origin, whose works are in no way inferior to, or more biased than, those of Western scholars. My enormous debt to such scholars, some of whose dissertations I supervised, is clear from the new items in the footnotes and bibliography.

The following persons are due heartfelt thanks for reading all or part of the new manuscript and for giving me a variety of helpful suggestions: Jahangir Amuzegar, Maziar Behrooz, Mark Gasiorowski, Eric Hooglund, Charles Kurzman, Afshin Matin-Asgari, Rudi Matthee, and Nayereh Tohidi. Azita Karimkhany carefully checked the notes and bibliography. My Yale University Press editors, Larisa Heimert and Lawrence Kenney, suggested the project and kept me (and themselves) on time on a demanding schedule. Several publishers and individuals were very helpful in sending me books and articles, among whom I should single out Golnar Mehran in Tehran, Houchang Chehabi in Boston, Janet Afary in Chicago, and friends in France—Bernard Hourcade, Farhad Khosrokhavar, Azadeh Kian, Yann Richard, and Olivier Roy—some of whose very useful works appear in my notes.

A few new facts about the 1953 coup, added in May 2003, are not footnoted but are based on new books in the bibliography Supplement.

As before, transliteration follows a simplified system without diacritics, and names well known in the West in other forms than those adopted here are given in those forms, though selection of which are well known is necessarily arbitrary. Some religious and legal terms that have entered English mainly in their Arabic, not Persian, transliteration are given that Arabic form, for example, fatwa, Ramadan.

Addendum

In June 2003, after this book was in proof, several U.S. leaders made a variety of threatening statements about Iran, with occasional assurances that no military action was now being planned. Reports of strong disagreements regarding Iran policy within the U.S. administration said that some favored military action to overthrow or fundamentally destabilize the regime, while others favored various alternatives ranging from negotiation to supporting various antiregime groups. There were also several nights of major student-led antiregime demonstrations that were internally caused and generated but augmented by Iranian exile satellite television beamed in from Los Angeles. Many demonstrators called for an end to the current regime, not just reforms in it. Most of the demonstrators and their supporters quoted in the international press and in private sources said they did not want U.S. interference in Iran but had confidence the Iranian people would in the long term achieve their aims. These events further developed trends discussed in this text, where earlier demonstrations and threats against the regime are described and documented.

Santa Monica, California
June 2003

Preface to the 1981 edition of *Roots of Revolution*

This book embodies elements of research and study on Iranian history and politics done over more than two decades, beginning with my Ph.D. dissertation and continuing until today. So many persons, Iranian and Western, have helped me in this long-term research and writing that it would be impossible to list and thank them all. Most of them have been thanked in my past books and articles. Here will be mentioned only those who helped significantly and specifically with this book, omitting those whose presence might cause them embarrassment.

First, heartfelt thanks are due to my outstanding, omnicompetent, and efficient graduate assistants, Brad Hanson and Julia Clancy. The entire manuscript was read and usefully criticized by Gene Garthwaite, John Gurney, Fred Halliday, John Perry, M. H. Pesaran, and Stanley Wolpert. Parts of the manuscript were read and helpful suggestions made by Shaul Bakhash, James Bill, Juan Cole, Richard Cottam, Brad Hanson, Yann Richard, Barry Rubin, and Andrew Whitley.

Also to be thanked are Nancy Lane of Oxford University Press for giving me an advance copy of Barry Rubin's *Paved with Good Intentions,* and to the following persons who gave me advance copies of their book manuscripts or proofs to read and utilize: Mangol Bayat, Gene Garthwaite, Eric Hooglund, Homa Katouzian, Michael Ledeen, and John Stempel. Yann Richard was especially helpful through all the metamorphoses his section had to undergo to make it fit meaningfully into the book.

Several fellowships for work in Iran, Europe, and the United States have sustained my research on Iran over the years. In chronological order, there have been fellowships from the American Association of

University Women, the Social Science Research Council, American Council of Learned Societies (two), the John Simon Guggenheim Foundation, the American Philosophical Society, research units at UCLA and, directly for this book, from the Rockefeller Foundation, to all of whom, especially the last, thanks are due.

Last but in no way least, my gratitude to my Yale editor, Charles Grench, is overwhelming. He has made what is sometimes a difficult or mixed experience into a wholly pleasant one and has uniformly showed excellent sense, liberality with his time and efforts, and constant good humor. Others at Yale University Press have also been most helpful and efficient, as have my copyeditor, Robert Brown, and all who typed the manuscript, and Juan Cole and Eric Hooglund.

Transliteration follows a simple system, without diacriticals even in cited works. In this system *o* and *e* are used for Persian short vowels, except in a few, mostly religious, terms well known with the transliteration *u* and *i*. Some names and places widely known in the West under spellings not conforming to my system are left in their more familiar form, including some, generally self-chosen, spellings of Iranians' names. Before Reza Shah many Iranians had both names and titles; herein titles are italicized when they follow names.

In a book embodying research and reading in many languages over a long period it was impractical to list in the notes or bibliography every source used. Hence, except in Yann Richard's section, only selected works, mainly in English, are listed. Most of the listed books and articles have notes and bibliographies that should give enough information to those who want to pursue research on specific topics. The select bibliography of books in the English language is not a listing of works in the notes but is intended to help guide those who want to pursue a more detailed study of particular topics, or of modern Iranian history and culture in general. Part of this book is based on interviews or on observation during eight stays in Iran, 1959–79.

Nikki R. Keddie
Los Angeles, California
March 1981

The second printing incorporates a few necessary corrections, but generally retains the original final cutoff dates.

MODERN IRAN

I

Religion and Society to 1800

Background

The 1978–79 Revolution and its aftermath awakened for the first time in twenty-five years widespread public interest in Iran—and, to a large degree, bafflement and incomprehension. This revolution did not fit the patterns and expectations of even the relatively well informed. Where before had one seen a leader of an established religion emerge as the widely popular, charismatic head of a revolution against a royal ruler who stressed his own legitimacy, his ties to the national past, and his reformist plans? And where before had one seen a state bristling with armaments worth billions of dollars, armed forces, secret and open police, all supposedly ready for use, crumble in the face of periodic, rising, peaceful mass demonstrations and strikes? Scholars in the field of Middle Eastern studies are now accustomed to being asked: Was this revolution religious, political, social, economic,—or what? The only good answer seems to be that it was all of these; as will be discussed in this study, economic, social, and political discontents had developed over the decades and coalesced in the late 1970s, while added to the central Islamic identity felt by the majority of the popular classes were new interpretations of religion that justified revolutionary ideas and became widespread in society.

Several long-term factors in Iranian history have contributed to political and social development down to the present. Among these are geographical characteristics that, as in much of the Middle East, favored the early development of settled agriculture (as the clearing of massive forests and use of the heavy plow so vital in Europe were not necessary).

On the other hand, as in much of the Middle East, irrigation led to salination of the soil and deforestation to erosion, so that agricultural difficulties and aridity almost surely increased over the centuries, which encouraged a pastoral nomadic adaptation to arid conditions. Economic fluctuations based in part on geographic conditions also gave rise to rebellions, and in recent times inappropriate imitation of Western agricultural methods led to further ecological deterioration.

Iran's location has for centuries been important to international trade and strategy. It borders on Azerbaijan and Armenia to the north, Iraq and Turkey to the west, the Persian Gulf to the south, and Afghanistan and Pakistan to the east. Iran encompasses about 628,000 square miles, a far larger area than that of any Western European country, but much of this is now desert, including the two huge eastern deserts, the Dasht-e Lut and the Dasht-e Kavir. Most of Iran is a high plateau strewn with mountains, the two major ranges being the Alborz in the north and the Zagros from the northwest toward the southeast. Seasonal extremes of hot and cold prevail throughout most of the country, and Iran is predominantly dry. The regions touching the Caspian Sea in the north, however, have high rainfall; the province of Gilan has among the highest in the world. This allows for a dense and organized peasant population, which encourages a more rebellious peasantry than where peasant population is sparse and scattered.

Since very ancient times, many different peoples have lived in Iran. The word "Iran" is a cognate of "Aryan"; these words were used by that branch of the Indo-European peoples who migrated southeast before 1000 B.C., the Iranians staying in Iran and the Aryans going on to India. (Persia was the Greek name for Iran, taken from the southwestern province of Fars; Reza Shah did not change the name of the country in the 1930s; rather he asked foreigners to use the indigenous name.) Iran had an important history and culture before the rise of Islam, with two major dynasties, the Achemenian, 559–330 B.C., and the Sasanian, A.D. 224–651, the latter lasting until Iran's conquest by the Muslim Arabs from A.D. 637 to 651. (In this book "Iran" denotes a land with about Iran's current boundaries; after the Muslim conquest, only the Mongols, the Safavids (1501–1722), and rulers since 1796 united this territory as one kingdom.)

Pre-Islamic Iran was fruitful in the development of religions, some of whose ideas and social content continued into Islamic times. The complex and varied religion called Zoroastrianism was characterized by a dualistic struggle between a good deity and an evil power in which the good was to win; and it also encompassed beliefs about rewards and punishments in the afterlife and interceding angels. Many scholars think Zoroastrianism influenced Judaism, Christianity, and Islam. Another type of dualism, viewing matter as evil and spirit as good and praising renunciation of this world, characterized Manichaeism founded in Iraq (then an Iranian culture area) by the third century A.D. prophet Mani. The negative Manichaean attitude toward this world has been seen by some scholars as reflecting economic decline and inequities and the growth of a rigid class system. Manichaeans both before and after the rise of Islam were considered dangerous heretics and were often persecuted by rulers. A more radical Iranian offshoot of Manichaeism in the fifth and sixth centuries was founded by Mazdak, who is said to have preached communism of goods and, along with his large body of followers, revolted against the class rigidities, poverty, wars, and economic decline that characterized his period (and ultimately rendered the Muslim conquest of Iran relatively easy).

Themes of righteous battles between the forces of good and justice and those of evil and oppression, of the economically oppressed and their oppressors, thus go far back into pre-Islamic as well as Islamic times, as does emulation of martyr figures, who are found in the great pre-Islamic Iranian religions. Because of the nature of the documents that have survived, and also of the doctrinal interests of scholars, we know much more about religious doctrines than about the details of socioeconomic life in the past. Even religious documents carefully studied, however, can tell a great deal about the injustices and inequalities that sometimes aroused people centuries ago, much as they do today, to risk their lives for a better world. In the early Islamic centuries several social revolts combined pre-Islamic with Islamic ideas in Iran.

In some ways Iran's recent "Islamic Revival" is very new, with ideas never voiced before. In other ways it follows a long tradition in both Iran and in the Muslim world of expressing socioeconomic and cultural grievances in the only way familiar to most people—a religious idiom arraying the forces of good against the forces of evil and promising to bring justice to the oppressed.

Islam and Society

In Iran as elsewhere, the so-called Islamic Revival does not mean that most people are more religious than they used to be: for the majority the degree of religiosity shows no sign of significant change. Rather, it means that Islam is reentering politics and government in a stronger and more militant way than it had in most areas for many decades. Within this general trend, however, Iran is, to date, a special case, in having rule by a leader of the regular Islamic *ulama* (a word that in Twelver Shi'ism can be rendered by "clergy" as all believers must follow the rulings of one of their leaders). This difference between Iran's religiopolitical movement and that of other Muslim countries is based in part on the contrast between the way the two main divisions in Islam, the Shi'is of Iran and the Sunnis who rule most of the rest of the Muslim world, have developed. We speak here of development because there has been much more change and development in both Sunni and Shi'i theory and practice than is usually realized, and specifically because many points often made about Shi'ism are really only, or mainly, true during the past century or two. Although not nearly enough research has been done to allow any scholar to give a complete history of the relations between religion and politics in either Shi'ism or Sunnism, enough has been done to allow a general outline that suggests the directions of change in Sunnism and in Shi'ism. Some elements in recent Shi'i politics hark back to the earliest period of Islam, and so some understanding of that period, as well as of later Shi'i history, is necessary to the understanding of more recent events.

The intertwining of religion and politics, found in several religions, began in Islam with the Prophet Mohammad himself. Among his revelations, later gathered together in the Quran, were a large number that would generally be called political and/or legal. Particularly after the Prophet's migration from his home city of Mecca, where he met opposition, at the invitation of notables of the nearby Arabian city of Medina, which he increasingly ruled, Mohammad received governmental and legal revelations. He led his community politically as well as religiously. After his death in A.D. 632, most of his adherents followed the rule of the first three caliphs, or successors, who had in theory no power to alter the revealed religion. A minority felt that succession belonged to Mohammad's cousin and son-in-law Ali (Mohammad having had no living sons), and this originally political claim within a few generations took on religious content. The group who recognized elected caliphs but without granting them religious powers beyond the protection and spreading of Islam came to be called Sunnis (followers of the practice or *sunna* of the Prophet). The party or "Shi'a" of Ali insisted on the charismatic leadership of the male descendants of Ali and were called the Shi'is (adjective) or Shi'a (noun) and developed a variety of doctrines. At first the split was not as clear-cut as it was later made to seem. Ali was chosen as the fourth caliph, and is still revered by the Sunnis, but he succumbed, through battle, arbitration, and assassination, to the founder of the Umayyad caliphate (661–749). This was the first Sunni caliphate to adopt, in practice, hereditary succession, and was castigated by many pious Muslims, both Sunni and Shi'i, as an illegitimate despotism.

Behind these and later doctrinal developments were sociopolitical changes discussed by recent scholars. The most plausible theory regarding the seventh-century rise of Islam notes that Mecca and Medina, as relatively advanced trading and agricultural cities outside the direct sphere of the Byzantine and Sasanian Empires, were at the point of state formation and needed an ideology to help unify the urban populace and the nomadic tribes around them into a state. Within Mecca and Medina class divisions were replacing tribal solidarity and tribes no longer provided for their weak members. In Mecca the rise and fall of merchant fortunes and the development of a complex, class-divided economy demanded the creation of a legal and welfare system. A full explanation would be more complex, but these factors help explain the rise of Islam and its rapid conquest or winning over of Arabian tribes. In addition, the weakening of both Byzantine and Persian Empires through exacerbated class divisions, persecution of religions considered heretical, and frequent mutual warfare left Arab areas unusually free of their influence.[1] Once Arab tribes adopted Islam they were bound no longer to engage in the raids that had kept population down and helped support many tribes. Tribes were still equipped for warfare and sought to make up what they had lost in raids. Mohammad's spreading of his religion and rule through wars against nearby tribes and the Meccans gave Islam a warlike precedent and theory, suggested by the word *jihad* or holy war. Contrary to what many believe, jihad was not meant to force conversion, and it appears that the concept of non-Arab Muslims did not occur to the earliest Muslims. Rather jihad aimed at extending the territory ruled by Muslims, while allowing inhabitants who were "People of the Book" (monotheists with a scripture) to keep their own religion in return for a special tax. This policy allowed the Arab Muslim armies to offer religious freedom to large Christian groups in greater Syria and Egypt treated as heretics by the Byzantine rulers, and hence to attain peaceful surrender from many Near Eastern cities. This, along with the internal conflicts and problems in the great empires, and the tactical superiority and enthusiasm of Arab armies, helps explain the expansion of these armies in a few decades as far as Spain in the west and Pakistan in the east.

The Arab armies' camp cities soon attracted local populations, whether Iranian, Egyptian, Iraqi, or other, and among them the demand arose for conversion to Islam. Along with conversion and contact there entered into some Muslim groups ideas with Iranian, Christian, Jewish, Manichaean, or other provenance. The Shi'is, who originally had few doctrinal differences with the Sunnis, were, as an oppositional group, more open to outside influences.

After the death of Ali and the resignation of a claim to rule by his first son, Hasan, Ali's second son, Hosain, put forth claims to leadership, but, with a small band of followers was massacred by an armed force under the orders of the Umayyad caliph Yazid in A.D. 680. This event, occurring on the tenth day (Ashura) of the first month (Moharram) of the Muslim year, became the great day of mourning and commemoration of the martyrdom of Hosain, with the previous nine days building up to it. One of Hosain's sons who survived was able to carry on the line of Shi'i leaders (imams), who were increasingly regarded by their followers as infallible.

Under the Umayyads began the religiopolitically sectarian character of Shi'ism. Various groups paid allegiance to different branches of Ali's descendants, or to men who invoked their name in leading revolts, often against the Umayyad caliphs. Certain ideas entered into Shi'ism more than Sunnism that Sunnis and moderate Shi'is labeled as "extremist," such as the incarnation of divinity in the imams, transmigration, and especially messianism. The *Mahdi* or "rightly guided one," who is not found in the Quran, entered particularly into Shi'ism, and Sunnism to a lesser degree, as the figure who will come at the end of time "to fill the world with justice and equity as it is now filled with injustice and oppression." This tag line suggests the social base of messianism: it appealed especially to the uprooted masses and lower middle classes who longed for the equity promised by the Quran but not realized under imperfect governments ruling for one or another social elite. A series of small Shi'i and semi-Shi'i revolts was crushed but Shi'i ideals remained.

The growing unpopularity of the Umayyads, who were closely tied to an early Arab aristocratic group and did not meet the needs of either the middle or the popular classes, led to an underground anti-Umayyad (Abbasid) movement in the first half of the eighth century that included

Shi'i elements. Its propaganda was carried out so as to make Shi's believe
that Ali's descendants would come to power if the movement succeeded,
but when the Abbasids overthrew the Umayyads in A.D. 749, the new
caliphs were not in any Shi'i line and many Shi'i movements were
suppressed.

Under the Abbasids (749–1256) the three different lines of Shi'ism
that are considered its main divisions took shape. The smallest, moderate group, today predominant only in North Yemen, are the Zaidis or
"Fivers," who revere their Fifth Imam. They follow a legal system similar to the Sunnis' and do not claim infallibility for their imams, which
could bring conflict with the Sunni caliphs. The larger groups are the
"Seveners" or Isma'ilis, and the "Twelvers" or Imamis. These two lines
reflect a split in opinion over the legitimate successor to the great Sixth
Imam, Ja'far as-Sadeq. The Isma'ilis, who opted for one son, Isma'il, do
not believe that he was the last imam, but rather have a continuous line of
living imams (although there are disagreements about which is the true
line); and in one large group of Isma'ilis the line is alive in the person of
the Agha Khan. In the early centuries the Isma'ilis were often radical,
especially the Carmathian group of Isma'ilis who had a semicommunist
ideology that served for a time as the basis of a state. Another Isma'ili
group set up the Fatimid caliphate, which conquered Egypt in 969 and
became a rival of the Abbasids. Emerging from the Fatimids was a group
known in Europe under the pejorative nickname of "Assassins," although their attempts to reshape Muslim society in the eleventh to thir-
teenth centuries went beyond the idea of killings as a way to gain power.
They lost much power after they were suppressed by the Mongols after
the thirteenth-century Mongol invasions.[2]

The Twelver Shi'is followed the descendants of a more moderate son
of Ja'far as-Sadeq. The Twelvers believe that the infant son of the Eleventh Imam went into "occultation" in the ninth century leaving behind
four successive interpreters of his will. After the death of the fourth,
during the "greater occultation" (which continues to the present), there
is no infallible interpreter of the Twelfth Imam's will until he reappears
as the Mahdi to institute the realm of perfection and justice. Twelver
Shi'is and many Western scholars have generally believed that before the
occultation there was a unified Shi'i community following the imams,
and many also believe that from the time of the occultation trained
theologians have been recognized as the best interpreters of the Twelfth
Imam's will during his absence. Recently both these views have been

challenged. Regarding the preoccultation period, W. M. Watt sees no evidence of a united Twelver community or doctrine, but finds rather a variety of views, with no large unified group giving politicoreligious allegiance to the successive imams.[3] Various views existed even after the disappearance of the infant imam. The doctrine of occultation, which became orthodox, was first put forth by a wealthy Shi'i leader in the Abbasid court in Baghdad. At first this doctrine may have been a way to avoid the consequences of the idea that the imam was both visible and infallible, implying that the imam's orders took precedence over the caliph's. The doctrine of occultation may, in its first phases, have been a way for Shi'is to compromise with the reality of Sunni power, and in this first period Twelver Shi'is in fact tended to be politically quietist and to compromise with Sunni governments. The belief that any orderly government was about equally acceptable (or unacceptable) in the absence of the Twelfth Imam could, however, become a two-edged sword.[4] In more recent periods of hostility between the Shi'i ulama and rulers it was used to assert the illegitimacy of any temporal government, and over time claims began that the ulama were more qualified than temporal rulers to interpret the will of the Twelfth Imam, and hence had superior political claims.

In Abbasid times, however, the blunt side of the sword generally was felt. Not only was the doctrine of occultation put forth by Shi'is in Abbasid service, but the main religious split for most of the Abbasid period was more between the Isma'ilis, who in their various political incarnations often tried to undermine or overthrow the Abbasids, and the Sunni Abbasids allied with the Twelver Shi'is on the other. The one significant dynasty of the Abbasid period with Twelver Shi'i leanings, the Buyids (945–1055), held the Abbasid capital of Baghdad but never tried to abolish the caliphate or to establish Twelver Shi'ism. Hence, Twelver Shi'ism during this period was very different from the militant movement that came to power in Iran under the Safavid dynasty in 1501.

It should be stressed that the idea common among some Muslims and Western Orientalists, that Shi'ism is peculiarly Iranian, has no basis before 1501. Before then, although there were many Iranian Shi'is, the great majority of Shi'is were non-Iranian and the majority of Iranians were Sunni. The Zaidi, Isma'ili, and Carmathian Shi'is are still found mostly outside Iran; the great majority of Shi'i dynasties were outside Iran, with only the Buyids as a major partial pre-1501 exception; and the great majority of Iranian dynasties have been Sunni. This is not to deny the profound modern identification of Iranians with Shi'ism, but only to note that this, like many other "traditional" phenomena, is more recent than is usually imagined. The legendary marriage of Imam Hosain with a Sasanian princess, which has no historical basis, was useful in cementing the identification of Iran with Shi'ism, but such legends are usually available when needed.

In the centuries of the greater occultation there was considerable development of Twelver Shi'i thought and law which, prior to the establishment of Twelver Shi'ism as Iran's state religion in 1501, was carried out mostly outside Iran. For relations between religion and politics perhaps the most important development was that of the *mujtahid.* In Sunni Islam it was widely held that after an early date all fundamental legal principles had been decided on the basis of the Quran, the reported words and practices of the Prophet (*hadith*), and the consensus of scholar-jurists, and that there was no more room for new judgments based on the effort (*ijtihad*) of a qualified jurist. New decrees and interpretations continued to be made, but they remained within the traditional framework and had not the same status as the early lawbooks or hadiths. In Twelver Shi'ism the early centuries had not, in theory, seen the need for juridical effort and interpretation that was felt in Sunnism, as only the imams could give correct, indeed infallible, opinions on all subjects. With the disappearance of the imams, however, the Twelvers were in a position roughly parallel to that of the very early Sunnis; the source of infallible legal judgment had disappeared and yet issues continued to arise on which some trustworthy judgment, even if fallible, was desired. To meet this need there gradually developed mujtahids: legal and theological scholars whose intelligence, training, and following qualified them to make judgments on a range of questions. Although their judgments were fallible, and they lacked the divine qualities of the imams, by their learning and response to popular needs they commanded a respect that increased over time.

While these developments were taking place within the body of learned Twelver Shi'ism, particularly in Asian Arab states, there were different developments with a Twelver Shi'i tinge in Iran, Anatolia (Turkey), and Syria, which ultimately had an impact on "orthodox" Twelver Shi'ism. If from Abbasid times on it was often hard to draw a political line, and certainly not one of enmity, between Twelver Shi'ism and Sunnism, their intermixture appears in a new way among several fourteenth- and fifteenth-century movements, usually with a strong mystical or "extremist" bent. Among these are the Hurufi movement originating in Iran and based largely on a mystical letter-number symbolism; the Bektashi religious order, which became the order of the Ottoman Jannisary crops, and incorporated respect for the twelve imams, Hurufi symbolism, and some Sunni, Turkic, and Christian elements.[5] A number of other orders combined Shi'i and Sunni elements, often along with some of local popular origin, and such groups still exist in various Muslim countries. Such groups were growing in Iran, the Ottoman Empire, and Syria in the fourteenth and fifteenth centuries, even though all these areas were officially Sunni. The intermixture and political cooperation between some Twelver Shi'is and Sunnis before 1501 facilitated the growth of groups combining Shi'i and Sunni ideas. The transformation of some of these diverse groups, many of which expressed popular grievances and provided ideologies for nomad and peasant revolts, into a powerful political movement took place under the leadership of a popular Iranian Sufi (mystic) order, the Safavids. Originally a quietist Sunni order centering in Ardebil, East Azerbaijan, and with ties to the fourteenth-century Mongol rulers, its leaders became militant warriors following a kind of Twelver Shi'ism in the mid-fifteenth century after travels among Anatolian nomadic tribes. The Shi'ism of these Safavids was of the militant "extremist" type reminiscent of the earliest Shi'is; a belief in divine incarnation was important, the Safavid leaders were considered divine, and egalitarianism was strong. Like other Muslim dynasties that came to power at the head of religious "extremists" (such as the Abbasids and Fatimids), the Safavids, soon after gaining power in Tabriz, began to moderate their views and search for orthodox Shi'i books and leaders. An early account relates that the first Safavid ruler of Iran, Isma'il, after entering Tabriz in 1501, ordered a search for an orthodox Shi'i religious book, but that in all Tabriz only one such book could be found.[6] Although this must be exaggerated, as other reports say there were many Shi'is in Tabriz, it suggests how little Isma'il, his followers, or most Tabrizis had contact with official Shi'ism. The Safavid rulers soon turned their doctrine, which they may not have known was different from learned Twelver Shi'ism, from one suitable for popular, enthusiastic, egalitarian revolt and conquest into one suitable for stable, conservative rule. They turned their backs increasingly on their tribal followers, seen with some reason as anarchic (armed nomadic tribespeople have often hindered centralized control), and succeeded in enlisting men from the old Persian bureaucracy, and imported some of the official Twelver theologians from nearby Arabic-speaking lands.

Under the first Safavid rulers such theologians, who were paid directly or indirectly by the government and had few ties with the local population, were a firm pillar of political support. Extremist ideas were increasingly suppressed, and by late Safavid times the word *Sufi*, which had once designated a supporter of the Safavids, became a term of opprobrium as Sufi orders were suppressed as a danger to the state and the official religion. More than most Islamic dynasties the Safavids worked for conversion to their branch of Islam and for ideological conformity. Isma'il demanded that all preachers and mollas publicly curse the first three (Sunni) caliphs, usurpers of the place of Ali, and this "loyalty-oath mentality" remained characteristic of many Safavid rulers. One of the main reasons for such rigor by Isma'il and his followers was to give Iran ideological distinction and identity vis-à-vis its (Sunni) military-political enemies, the Ottoman Empire and, for a time, the Central Asian Uzbeks. Isma'il came to power on the eve of Ottoman expansion into the Near East by Sultan Selim. The Anatolian tribes who helped the Safavids were hostile to the Ottoman government both because they resisted centralization and for religio-ideological reasons. Isma'il must have considered a new affirmation of the differences between Twelver Shi'ism and Sunnism to be important in creating ideological identity in Iran as a rampart against the Sunni Ottomans. (Some speak of the Safavids as setting up a national state but this is anachronistic; not only were the socioeconomic preconditions of modern nationalism not present, but there was no national or ethnic content to the Safavids' ideology. Isma'il, for example, habitually wrote in Turkish and his enemy, Sultan Selim, in Persian.)

In 1511–12 Selim launched a violent campaign against the Shi'i "fifth column" in Anatolia, killing thousands and resettling many more. Then he sent armies to invade Iran, defeating Isma'il at the Battle of Chaldiran in 1514, but then turned back, partly because of overextended supply lines and a hard winter, but perhaps also owing to disaffection among his janissaries who might have felt some identity with Twelver Shi'is. This was only one of several wars between the Iranians and the Ottomans, a long struggle providing continual encouragement for the Safavids to strengthen the Shi'i identity of Iran. Although conversion was not as rapid as Isma'il's forcible policies might suggest, the vast majority of Iranians did identify strongly with Shi'ism by the end of the Safavid era in 1722 (an end brought on by Afghan Sunni invaders).

Little socioeconomic research has been done on the Safavids, but it appears that by the fourteenth and fifteenth centuries Iran was beginning to recover from the ravages of prior invasions and to find a system of accommodation to a large nomadic population that could be termed "tribal feudalism," if one uses the term broadly, recognizing the absence of serfdom and a manorial system. Under this system military power was largely in the hands of tribal leaders, who also held revenue rights to and often administered large peasant and sometimes even urban populations. Most of the nomads spoke languages other than Persian, either as descendants of invaders or as longstanding autonomous groups (like the Kurds). Ever since the eleventh-century Seljuq conquest of Iran, Turkic languages were predominant among rulers, who were all of nomadic origin or, in the Safavid case, brought to power by nomads. Nomadic or nomad-backed dynasties included two fifteenth-century Turkmen dynasties who preceded the Safavids; the Safavids themselves; various eighteenth-century rulers; and the nineteenth-century Qajars. However, all major dynasties made use of a Persian-speaking bureaucratic class with long experience in administration and tax collection. One secret of Safavid success was their early enlistment of this class and of Persian landlords and merchants, which involved moving away from the egalitarianism of their early tribal followers.

The Safavids also benefited from the desire of several European states for any ally against the Ottomans, which encouraged diplomatic and trade relations. Even before the Safavid victory there were Western diplomats and traders in Iran, and relations increased under the Safavids. The great Safavid Shah Abbas (1587–1629) encouraged international trade through building roads, caravansarais, and workshops to produce the luxury textiles and ceramics demanded in the West. Silk was the main export. Disruption by military tribes, the low level of agricultural production, and the gradual change of Western trade routes to the Far East from overland to overseas, however, contributed to economic decline, reflected in political decline, and to easy conquest by Afghans in 1722. Frequent wars with the Ottomans also took an economic toll.

An important, seldom studied aspect of premodern social history is the position of women. The Quran allows polygamy of up to four wives, provided there is equal treatment for all. It also permits easy divorce for the husband, and there are a few other unequal measures. On the other hand it provides for a woman to inherit property (half the amount granted a man). It does not legislate veiling, a practice that existed in the Byzantine and Sasanian Empires and spread from them to Muslim Arabs. Once veiling spread, two vague Quranic verses were interpreted to sanction veiling. Veiling and seclusion were apparently characteristic of the well-to-do urban classes and did not extend to the majority of women.

The position of Muslim women varied more by time and place than is generally realized, as reports from travelers and scholars regarding the early Safavid period indicate. Many sources show that Islamicized Turkish and Mongol women were much freer than the older settled populations. Their elite women were influential, and men and women danced together in the Bektashi order and elsewhere. More dramatic information comes from an Italian traveler at the time of Shah Isma'il, who writes: "The Persian ladies themselves follow in arms the same fortunes as their husbands, and fight like men, in the same way as those ancient Amazons who performed such feats of arms in their time." Another Italian description from the same period says that women wear costumes open at the breast, show their bodies, and are wanton. He appears not to be talking about prostitutes, whom he discusses separately regarding the taxes they pay the government. One more Italian description says that women "wear robes of silk, veils on their heads, and show their faces openly." There seems to be no evidence of the top-to-toe veiling found in late nineteenth-century urban Iran; and the evidence of Safavid miniatures suggests that women dressed colorfully and attractively, with head-coverings as partial and diaphanous as among Iranian tribal women today. By the late seventeenth century, however, Chardin says that women covered all but face, hands, and feet, were very closely guarded, and that upper-class women were idle.[7] Perhaps growing religious "orthodoxy" was tied to increased seclusion of women, as such seclusion has in various periods been considered Islamic.

It is rarely appreciated that the Safavid experience largely created the clear line of political demarcation and hostility between Twelver Shi'ism and Sunnism, even though doctrinal differences had long been recognized. Before the Safavids, as noted, while the Sevener Shi'is were clearly marked off from the Sunnis, who often considered them politically dangerous, the Twelvers for many centuries had mostly accommodated themselves politically to the Sunnis, and numerous religious movements combined Twelver and Sunni ideas.

The aggressive insistence of Isma'il and many of his followers on cursing the first three caliphs (who were regarded by Sunnis as, along with Ali, the holiest "rightly guided" caliphs); forcible conversions of Iranian Sunnis to Shi'ism; and persecutions of Ottoman Shi'is seen as a

Safavid fifth column resulted in a clear politico-religious split between Sunnis and Twelver Shi'is. From Safavid times through the nineteenth century each group considered itself to be the true Muslims, with the other group often seen as heretics and enemies, and Safavid shahs and Ottoman Sultans exchanged insults along these lines.[8]

Most pre-Safavid theological Shi'ism was not highly political, and tended to take the lack of any fully legitimate government in the absence of imams as a sign that existing governments, whether Sunni or Shi'i, could be obeyed. This official Shi'ism was centered in a few Arabic-speaking territories that did not border on the pre-sixteenth-century Ottoman Empire. In areas that did border on the empire or were part of it, as in northern Syria, western Anatolia, and bordering eastern Iran, religious movements classified as Twelver Shi'i because of their devotion to the twelve imams remind us more of some of the "extremist" sects earlier associated with Isma'ili (Sevener) Shi'ism. Incarnation of the divinity in leaders, egalitarianism, and warlike militancy against "heretical" regimes characterized these groups both before and during the rise of the Safavids. Safavid Shi'ism in power stressed the Shi'i law and theology brought in by jurists and theologians partly imported by the Safavid shahs, and also incorporated other elements favorable to the rulers' political position and social conservatism. Few of these elements were tied to the "extremist" religious ideas that had helped bring the Safavids to power. Among "extremist" elements not suppressed was a stress on the semidivine powers of the ruler himself, which in the case of Isma'il and his successor Tahmasp were often considered actually divine by the Safavids' followers. Divine claims were frequent in extremist Islamic movements, and had been voiced regarding several pre-Safavid religious rebels by groups in Anatolia, where the Safavids got their military start. The Safavids, as part of their Twelver ideology, also claimed descent from the Seventh Imam (meaning every preceding imam), which gave them impeccable Twelver credentials. Research has shown that the earliest writings about the Safavids put forth no such claim, but it was inserted later into existing and subsequent works in order, clearly, to shore up the Safavids' politico-religious claims. Western travelers noted the divine worship of their rulers by the Safavids' followers, particularly the fighting tribes.[9] Claims to divinity or incarnation are against the doctrines of Islamic orthodoxy, both Sunni and Twelver Shi'i, which stress the strict unity of God. As time went on and orthodox teachings were increasingly propagated, the divine claims of the Safavids were muted, but their claims to descent from an important imam continued to give them a religious aura not held by any subsequent Iranian dynasty.

The theology of pre-Safavid and Safavid Shi'ism has not been sufficiently studied to be summarized, but something may be said about the changing role of religious leaders, which bears upon later politico-religious developments. During and immediately after the Safavid rise there were high officials, largely from among the Safavids' original backers, who combined military, political, and religious functions in a way that recalled their origin in a militant sectarian movement that had no specific religious functionaries, and apparently no Shi'i texts to teach. Soon after taking power, however, the Safavid rulers entrusted theologians and jurists with various religious roles, while decreasing the religious duties of other high officials. In the early Safavid period the theologians and their followers and progeny were dependent on the financial and political largesse of the shahs, and they understandably did not give the shahs political or ideological trouble. This conciliatory position was easy for these ulama to maintain in periods when shahs did not flout Islamic law or treat them badly and when, as through the early seventeenth century, the shahs seem to have been mostly popular and to have contributed to the economic well-being of Iran.

Over time, however, the factors conducive to an alliance between court and ulama changed. Economic bases for ulama independence of the shahs grew; these were not all specifically Shi'i, but in the last few centuries they have operated more strongly in Iran than elsewhere. Throughout the Muslim world Muslims may make bequests of their property or money as *vaqf* (inalienable endowment). There are two general kinds of vaqf, sometimes called charitable or religious, and private. Charitable vaqf is given for institutions like schools, hospitals, mosques, and shrines, all of which are controlled and administered by ulama. All add to the wealth and power of what we may loosely call the "church," as well as providing posts for men with religious training. Private vaqf income usually goes to the donor's descendants (it is often used to avoid the strictly regulated inheritance shares laid down in the Quran), but even here a guardian from the ulama is required, and this guardian is paid from the vaqf income. As vaqf is, in theory, inalienable, it should have grown ever larger over the centuries; in fact it tended, even before modern changes, to be subject to confiscation. Under a long-lived dynasty like the Safavids that wished to stress its own piety and itself made vaqf contributions, the size of vaqf property and the number of ulama and religious students supported by it grew considerably. Such inalienable income gave the ulama a strong economic base from which some of its members could, if so inclined, bite the hand that fed them.

More specific to Shi'ism was the ulama's success down to the present in keeping direct control of certain religious taxes, the so-called *khums* (one-fifth) and *zakat* (alms), and not having them pass through the hands of the government. Although this has been little studied for Safavid times, it is known that later the ulama were able to use a combination of moral and minor physical pressure to collect, especially from the merchants and other well off bazaar traders and artisans, the khums. Most of this was supposed to go for welfare and charity, but as these include the support of poor students and sayyeds (men claiming descent from Mohammad) and payment of employees of welfare institutions, the taxes brought a significant net increase in the wealth and power of the religious classes.

With the increasing wealth of the Safavid ulama, the development of a growing ulama of local Iranian origin, and the creation of intellectual and material conditions for the ulama to be increasingly independent of the state, there also grew up a division between two kinds of ulama that, in general, has lasted. On the one hand there were government-appointed and -supported ulama who filled official religious posts, including the *imam jom'eh* or leader of the chief Friday prayer of each city, and various judicial figures. On the "nonofficial" side were those who fulfilled no governmental functions but taught, preached, and made judgments in ulama-run institutions and courts, receiving their income from vaqf revenues and the gifts of their followers. The most learned of the ulama, who had reached the highest level in their studies, became *mujtahids*, who were capable, if they attracted a following, of giving authoritative interpretations on questions of religious law. In Safavid times there were very few mujtahids, but there was gradually an "inflation of honors" so that first the number of mujtahids, and recently that of ayatollahs (originally the leading mujtahids but now encompassing many older mujtahids) expanded greatly over time. The most important function of a Shi'i mujtahid was to exert ijtihad to give new interpretations of law and doctrine in response to new questions. Although the Sunni ulama outside Iran in fact made some new interpretations, the latitude for Shi'i ulama to do this was greater. Like other differences between Sunnis and Twelver Shi'is, the power of the mujtahid to interpret doctrine is not a "purely" doctrinal one but has roots in the greater socioeconomic strength and independence of the Iranian ulama and also in the decentralization of power in Iran, owing to great difficulties of communication, sparse and scattered population, and the independent power of nomadic tribes.

In late Safavid times some mujtahids claimed that they had more right to rule than did the impious, wine-bibbing shahs. They did not yet say they should rule directly, an idea that came forth only with Ayatollah Khomeini, but that the shah should carry out their rulings when given and defend the nation militarily.[10] The political claims of the Iranian ulama developed further from the eighteenth century on.

Another feature of Safavid Shi'ism was the greater development of theology under the Safavids than under contemporary Sunni dynasties. This was largely due to the fact that the Safavids were the first rulers to patronize Twelver Shi'ism; there was a need to put Shi'i ideas into Persian in order to make them more accessible; and also to deal with new questions arising from the existence of a Twelver state. Along with the development of theology there was also a flowering of philosophy based on combinations of Greek philosophy, mysticism, and Shi'ism. In much of the Muslim world philosophy flourished in the tenth and eleventh centuries A.D., after which it was increasingly suppressed, but in the East, especially Iran, there was a virtually uninterrupted philosophical tradition. Muslim philosophy was based on Aristotelian and/or Platonic and Neoplatonic philosophy, which Muslim philosophers often tried to show as compatible with Islam and the Quran. When philosophy and the Quran seemed in conflict the Quran was interpreted "allegorically" to conform with the natural law themes of philosophy. Iran was the home of such philosophical giants as Avicenna and Nasir ad-Din Tusi, some of whose works have continued to be taught in religious schools down to the present. The Safavid period gave impetus to new efforts of Shi'i philosophers to reconcile Greek philosophy specifically with Shi'ism. Iranian philosophy of the past several centuries is sometimes called "theosophy" because it incorporates a more mystical and religious element than does the philosophy of such early giants as al-Farabi, Averroes, or Avicenna, but some recent scholars have overstated the religious and theosophical element of later figures and understated their natural law rationalism. Great Safavid philosophers like Mir Damad and Molla Sadra were attacked in their own times, and many of the orthodox considered Greek style philosophy dangerous and its practitioners, who were themselves ulama, as claimants to usurp the role of more conventional ulama. The philosophers represented a small intellectual elite, whereas the masses and bazaar classes generally followed the more traditional ulama, as they still do.

One reason, rarely noted, why Shi'is were more open to philosophical rationalism than Sunnis is that Shi'i theology was based on a system of thought closer to Greek philosophical and natural law concepts than was Sunni theology. In the early Abbasid period the Mu'tazilite theological school partly based on Greek ideas became predominant in Sunnism. Mu'tazilites put forth as their central idea the Unity and Justice of God. According to them justice ('*adl*) was a rational, comprehensible concept and God had to act in accordance with it. The implication that God was limited by natural law, along with other Mu'tazilite concepts, was rejected by more traditionalist Muslims, and another theological school, the Ash'arites, gradually won out among most Sunnis. The Ash'arite school rejected natural law, with some Ash'arites going so far as to say that God recreated the world each moment, so that there were no secondary causes, apparent causation being based on God's mercy to mankind. Twelver Shi'i theology, however, became predominantly Mu'tazilite, with a belief in natural law and earthly causation. In Ash'arite theory justice is, in general, what God chooses to do. Mu'tazilites sometimes say that God must follow the rules of justice; by implication whatever happens on earth that is unjust is the fault of men and women, not of God. Mu'tazilism, as the last point implies, also teaches free will. Although theology is less important in Islam than in Christianity, with teaching centering rather on law and on the Traditions of the Prophet and imams on which law is based, Shi'i theology as it trickled down through sermons and decrees may have had a political impact. The central concepts of justice and injustice or oppression ('*adl* and *zulm*), important to most believing Muslims, are of overwhelming importance to the Shi'is, and the idea that rulers who have abandoned '*adl* for zulm are following their own will, not God's, is natural to Shi'i thought.[11]

The last Safavid ruler, Shah Sultan Hosain, in the early eighteenth century enforced strict Shi'i orthodoxy; philosophers and Sufis were suppressed and orthodoxy enjoined. The internal decline of the Safavids made them easy prey to foreign invasion, however, in this case by Sunni tribal Afghans who sacked the capital, Isfahan, but ruled only from 1722 to 1730. The eighteenth century was to be one of decentralization, rule by tribal leaders, and economic decline. Significant developments, however, occurred in the religiopolitical field.

Religious developments in Iran now as before were tied to Iran's socioeconomic structure. Although Iran had been the seat of strong and prosperous states and empires in ancient times, agricultural decline and aridity apparently grew over centuries. Hence when Turkish nomadic tribes invaded Iran beginning in the eleventh century they did not, as had earlier nomadic invaders, settle or fit into interstices between settled areas, but rather, finding arid lands suitable for nomadism, spread that way of life. The spread of nomadism and decline of settled agriculture contributed to a kind of "tribal feudalism" in which tribal leaders provided the armies and were paid in rights to revenue collection. Real rule in many tribal, peasant, and even urban territories thus rested with tribal leaders and the central rulers had to rule indirectly, playing one urban or tribal faction off against another, and trying to keep on good terms with the ulama, whose ideological and economic power was growing. The strength of the Safavids depended in part on their encouragement and control of long-distance and foreign trade. With the development of overseas trade by Europeans and the decline of overland trade to Asia, however, Iran, aside from regions adjacent to the Persian Gulf, was increasingly bypassed. Eighteenth-century decentralization and tribal rule thus had some economic causes, and there seem to have been declines both in production and in international trade.

After the invasion of the Iranian and Shi'i capital of Isfahan by militant Sunni Afghans, the leaders of the Shi'i ulama moved to cities in Ottoman Iraq built around the tombs of the first imams—Najaf and Karbala. This area remained the center of Shi'i leadership from then until quite recently, and this gave the Shi'is a new advantage over the Sunni ulama in their growing independence of the government. Financially independent in Iraq, the leading Shi'i ulama were not subject to economic or political pressure from the Iranian government. (Some analogy exists to the premodern popes, who had their own territory and could not be intimidated by temporal rulers; as contrasted with the Orthodox Christian leaders of Constantinople and Moscow, who were subservient to rulers in these capitals.)

In the late eighteenth century the power of the ulama was further increased by the outcome of a struggle between two schools of Shi'i thought—schools whose conflict now sharpened and, for most believers, concluded. The losing school was the *akhbaris*, who believed that each Shi'i could rely on, and interpret, the Traditions (*akhbar*) of the Prophet and imams, and hence ulama were not needed to interpret doctrine. This school represented those who wished to lessen the ulama's role (even though it was expressed by some of the ulama), and hence was unlikely to win out. (Gobineau speaks of nineteenth-century akhbaris as bourgeois, which seems probable.)[12] The winning school of *mujtahidis* or *usulis* said that mujtahids were needed to interpret the foundations (*usul*) of the faith. The role of the mujtahid was defined by saying that each believer must choose one mujtahid to follow as a "source of imitation," and that ordinary believers below the rank of mujtahid were not, as the akhbaris said they were, competent to interpret the faith. One must always be guided by a living mujtahid, whose rulings take precedence over those of a mujtahid who has died. Mujtahids, unlike the imams, were not infallible. The mujtahids strove, via their knowledge, to know the infallible will of the Twelfth Imam, but they might fail on particular points. The need to follow the rulings of a living mujtahid, who was less fallible than any temporal ruler, gave a basis for power in the hands of the mujtahids that was far greater than that of the Sunni ulama. There was now a clear doctrinal basis for appeals to the ulama over the head of a ruler, and for claims by the leading mujtahids to make political decisions, provided they touched on Islamic principles, independently of temporal rulers. These powers were increasingly used from the early nineteenth century on.

Another important mid-eighteenth-century development was Nader Shah's rise to power within Iran and foreign conquests. In part because he conquered Sunni lands to the east and had many Sunnis in his armies Nader tried to deinstitutionalize Shi'ism in Iran, and he confiscated Shi'i vaqfs on a large scale to the economic gain of his regime. He wished to make of Shi'ism a fifth orthodox (Sunni) school of law, but this idea was rejected by both sides and scarcely outlived his death in mid-century. By the mid-nineteenth century Shi'i vaqfs had become as extensive as before.

Although Shi'ism had been spread with much coercion, by the eighteenth century it was deeply and widely embraced by nearly all native Persian speakers in Iran as well as a numerical majority of its ethnic minorities. Within the Safavid and modern borders only ethnic minorities bordering on Sunni conationals abroad—most Kurds in the west, the Turkomans in the north, the Baluchis in the southeast and a minority of the Arabs of the southwest—remained Sunni. In addition there remained more scattered religious minorities: Jews, Armenian and Nestorian Christians, Zoroastrians, and the gnostic Sabeans on the Iraqi border, as well as the semi-Shi'i Ahl-e Haqq ("Ali Ilahis") centered among the Kurds.

The eighteenth century also saw the development of a new, more philosophic school of Shi'ism, the Shaikhi school. As their main political importance appeared in the nineteenth-century Babi movement, discussion will be limited to their role in the formation of that movement, below. In general the eighteenth century, though a period of economic decline, civil war, and decentralization, saw the development of several important politico-religious trends.

In the above summary treatment, only a few highlights of Iranian pre-Islamic and Islamic history could be noted, and stress has been placed on those that tie together religious and social movements in a way that provides some background for recent developments. It should be realized, however, that Iran also has a long history of cultural, scientific, political, and economic developments having little connection with religion, which occupy the pages of many lengthy histories. In the arts Iran has a continuous history of excellence in both poetry and the visual arts, best known in the West through Persian miniatures and carpets and through a felicitous translation of a second-rank poet and first-rank scientist, Omar Khayyam. Iran was virtually the only area in the first wave of Arab conquests that kept its own language rather than adopting Arabic (although the new Persian was and is written in Arabic script and is full of Arabic vocabulary). With the rise of local dynasties in Iran in the ninth through eleventh centuries, owing only theoretical obedience to the Abbasid caliphate, poetry and prose began to flourish in the new Persian language and feelings of special Iranian identity were often expressed. In addition to literary figures, the trained Persian bureaucracy helped keep alive such a Persian linguistic and cultural identity even when Turkish-speaking tribes ruled Iran. Cultural and governmental forces thus preserved an Iranian identity during the pre-Safavid centuries when there was rarely a single state covering the territory of today's Iran.

The development of Shi'ism in Iran gave some focus to feelings of a separate local identity. Until the twentieth century the Shi'i component of this identity was more important than the Iranian one, although it was often unnecessary to distinguish the two. From 1501 until this century, Iranism and Shi'ism were for many people parts of a single blend.

2

Foundations of Nineteenth-Century Iran

In addition to the factors just discussed, other forces were at work in nineteenth-century Iran shaping a political and socio-economic situation that culminated in revolt and rebellion. During this period the economy and society were gradually transformed through interaction with the increasingly industrialized and imperialist West. Although earlier, via trade, the West had had an impact on Iran as on other Asian countries, the industrial revolution made the West a growing exporter of manufactured goods that could often be sold more cheaply than locally produced handicrafts and hence it undermined local handicraft production. This had partially disruptive socioeconomic effects. At the same time, Western demand for Asian raw materials grew, so that Asian countries increasingly became exporters of raw materials and importers of manufactures, to the detriment of many in the popular, artisan, and trading classes and to the benefit of some consumers, long-distance merchants, and landlords. These changes have not been studied in as much detail for Iran as they have for Egypt and India, but the trends were similar, if less dramatic owing to a lesser Western presence and trade.

Before entering into the vicissitudes of nineteenth-century Iranian politics we will discuss long-term forces at work in this period. Aside from the new strength of the Western politico-economic impact, most of the forces were related to those operating since about the eleventh century. At that time large-scale incursions of nomadic Turkish tribes associated with the invasion and rule of Iran by the Seljuq Turks strengthened the regional, semifeudal power of tribal and other military leaders and weakened central governments. Many nomadic tribes were almost autonomous, owing largely to their military power, and could obtain the products they did not produce themselves through trade with local villages and towns. They were difficult for a central government to control, especially in view of Iran's mountainous and arid terrain, lack of good communications, and dearth of navigable rivers. These factors contributed to considerable local autonomy even for non-nomadic groups in pre-twentieth-century Iran, and to frequent periods of decentralization, often under local tribal rulers, with only a few relatively centralized dynasties—the Seljuqs, Mongols, and Safavids. From the eleventh through the nineteenth centuries nomadic tribes essentially managed their own internal affairs, subject in centralized periods to tribute and pro forma confirmation of tribal leaders by rulers, and tribes often ruled over villagers or even townspeople who inhabited lands in their area.

Beyond this, the tribes constituted the best fighting forces in Iran—their mastery of horsemanship and of the latest weapons gave them a decisive advantage over townspeople, whom the shahs generally did not try to train militarily. The military advantage of the tribespeople probably increased in the eighteenth century, which may be one reason for eighteenth-century tribally based decentralization. In the Ottoman Empire, Iran, and elsewhere, the first introduction of firearms in the form of cannons strengthened the central government, which was the only force wealthy enough to afford cannons and a trained artillery. With the development of efficient handguns, however, small decentralized bands could make good use of them, especially if they owned horses and knew how to shoot from the saddle. Research in this area, and on the impact of trade with the West in the sixteenth through eighteenth centuries, is modifying the older view that the nineteenth-century impact of the West on the Middle East was sudden.[1]

Every important Iranian dynasty from the Buyids (945–1055) through the Qajars (1796–1925) was either tribal in origin or relied on tribal armies to take power. According to one estimate, nomadic tribes made up about half the Iranian population in the early nineteenth century and a quarter at the end of the century; if we make a very rough estimate that Iran's population doubled from about five million to ten million between 1800 and 1914, the absolute number of nomads remained about the same.[2] The impact of this large, semiautonomous, and militarily powerful group of tribes on Iranian life and politics has yet to be appreciated.

In periods of weak government or decentralization tribal or tribally based entities continue to assert their autonomy even today. Although there is no universally agreed-upon definition of what should be called a tribe, in general Iran's tribes identify themselves by distinctive words that translate as "tribe" or "tribal confederation" for their larger units and "clan" for a subunit, and they usually believe their tribes and clans to be related by family ties. Most Iranian tribes either practice, or once practiced, pastoral nomadism, which in Iran generally involves two main tribal migrations, from summer to winter quarters and back, dictated by the need for year-round pasture for their flocks. In addition, most tribes practice agriculture during the months of settlement. Tribal women, like most peasant women, are not veiled, and they usually do more physical labor than the men, including spinning, weaving, cooking, agriculture, and animal husbandry. There is considerable internal autonomy and decentralization among tribes, and the top leaders are needed mostly for war and for relations with the government and other outside groups. Among the important non-Persian ethnic groups in Iran having a partially or totally tribal nomadic background are: the Turkic speaking Turkomans (Sunni) in the north, Qashqa'is in Fars Province, and Shahsevans in Azerbaijan; the Kurds (mostly Sunni) in the west; the Lur speaking Bakhtiaris and Lurs between the Kurds and Qashqa'is; the Arabs in the southwest, the Baluchis (Sunni) in the southeast; and many other smaller tribes. Few tribespeople speak Persian as their first language and this intensifies the decentralizing potential of the tribes, as does the Sunnism of the Kurds, Baluchis, Turkomans, and a minority of Arabs who also have people of the same ethnic group adjacent to them across Iran's borders.[3] These four and the Shi'i Azerbaijani Turks have the most autonomist tendencies of all Iran's ethnic groups.

If tribal leaders with well-armed and devoted followers made up a major element of the Iranian ruling group, there were also other key, often overlapping, elements. Under the Qajars the strongest single ruling group was usually the court, headed by the shah and including legions of royal relatives, among whom the queen mother and favorite wife or wives were often very influential. Qajars were frequently named governors of provinces, including some royal women, whose appointments were, however, for the purpose of receiving revenue only. The central and regional treasurers (*mostaufis*) tended to be hereditary, using a private code writing and techniques that they kept in their families to perpetuate their monopoly. Nearly all offices in the rudimentary central and regional bureaucracy were bought (as they were in much of premodern Europe). As the government needed more money for Western arms and goods there developed a virtual yearly auction where governorships were usually given to the men who bid the most; tax collecting and other positions were also sold or subfarmed. This system, which had the advantage of giving the ruler or governor ready cash in advance, had the greater disadvantage for national prosperity of encouraging officials to overtax, since they were not sure they could hold their posts and hence were not concerned to leave the peasants enough to maintain fertility, investment, and productivity. There were exceptions to the yearly bidding, notably the governor generalship of the wealthy and strategic northwest province of Azerbaijan, which went to the crown prince, with real rule often under a minister; and some princes were governors elsewhere. Even in such areas taxes were increasingly used to extort as much as possible from the peasant majority.

A feature of the bureaucracy was the possibility of rising from humble origins within the royal household to a top position. Two major chief ministers of the long-ruling Naser ad-Din Shah (1848–96), Mirza Taqi Khan *Amir Kabir* and Mirza Hosain Khan *Moshir ad-Dauleh*, as well as the later longstanding chief minister Ali Asghar Khan *Amin as-Soltan* illustrate this;[4] the father of the first was a steward in the royal household, the grandfather of the second a bath attendant who rose in royal service, and the father of the latter a Georgian cup-bearer who rose in this service. (It is, however, wrong to draw conclusions about social mobility outside courtly circles from these examples. While Islam knows no aristocracy or other theoretical privileges based on birth, aside from the pensions and respect due to descendants of Mohammad, the sayyeds, not enough research has been done to say whether there was more social mobility in Iran than in other premodern societies.)

If aristocratic blood, in the Western sense, scarcely existed in Iran, where titles were usually purchased and were not automatically passed from father to son, landholding was of major importance in conferring status and power. It is not certain whether it was more frequent for already rich and powerful courtiers, tribal leaders, ulama, and merchants to add to their power and security by purchasing land, or alternatively for powerful landlords by virtue of their landed wealth to enter into positions of influence. Recent writing tends to favor the former idea, which makes land more an adjunct than an original source of power. Tribal leaders, courtiers, ulama, and merchants tried to control large amounts of land, and might purchase tax-farming rights for lands that they could sometimes convert into property rights, as private property in land grew in the nineteenth century. Despite poor statistics, sources suggest that in the nineteenth century large landownership increased and peasant ownership fell, and by the end of the century most land was held by noncultivating owners and farmed by sharecropping tenants. As the century progressed more merchants bought lands and they, along with some traditional landlords, began to meet Western demand by using their lands increasingly for export crops like cotton and opium, which spread in the course of the century. The spread of export crops meant periodic profits for some peasants, especially the relatively richer ones, but it generally increased stratification in the countryside as poor peasants could not make needed investments, while merchants and landlords could. It also put Iranians more at the mercy of fluctuations in the world market demand and in weather, as the spread of export crops meant a decline in subsistence crops which, in times of export problems, could not be compensated for by foreign earnings. The terrible famine of 1869–72 and later famines were partly due to the rapid spread in opium growing.[5] On the other hand, some peasants benefited from export crops and from cheap imports.

Islamic law, which called for inheritance of fixed shares of the property by each family member, led to some breakdown of family estates, but it was possible to keep estates together through the creation of a family vaqf, and sometimes through outright evasion of Islamic law. Officials who incurred the shahs' displeasure might have their property confiscated and sometimes lose their lives, and total or partial confiscations after an official's death were frequent. Thus there appears to have been much upward and downward mobility for a few at the centers of wealth and power (sometimes as far downward as the grave), while some families show continuity of wealth and public office, and far more show continuity in poverty and powerlessness. Wealthy merchant families sometimes moved into landholding and governmental circles. Regarding mobility, case studies covering the last two centuries suggest considerable continuity in occupations and even town leadership in provincial cities at least until the end of Qajar times, while Tehran saw more social mobility, a normal pattern for a capital city that grew with great rapidity and to which many of the most enterprising, ambitious, and even speculative persons from other towns were attracted.[6]

Governmental bureaucracy and functions were both very limited throughout the Qajar period, although they tended to increase some in the latter part of the dynasty. The chief purpose of the bureaucracy was to collect taxes, including customs duties, and the main use made of moneys collected (as of the money paid for the right to collect taxes) was to support the collectors and the provincial and central courts—especially the shah and his entourage in Tehran. Public works of an elementary kind, such as the building and repair of roads and caravan-serais (as had been done by some Safavid and other rulers), were seldom undertaken. Institutions considered governmental in the modern West, like schools, hospitals, and most law courts, were, as in most Islamic states, the responsibility of religious leaders, who collected religious gifts and taxes. Apart from rendering money, governors and other officials were responsible only for keeping order.

Surprisingly, only slight attention was given by the Qajar shahs to the creation of a modern military force that might protect them from external attack and internal revolt. Many Asian rulers had early seen the need of military self-strengthening to protect their countries' independence. Recognition of the need for modern armed forces had encouraged the early nineteenth-century modernization programs of such rulers as Egypt's Muhammad Ali and the Ottoman Empire's Selim III and Mahmud II. They found that modern armed forces required translation bureaus, Western education for some students, modern schools, and local armament factories. Although Iran had less commercial and other contact with the West both before and during the Qajar period than did Egypt and the Ottoman Empire, it remains surprising that Iran did not follow their lead even in the late nineteenth century. The only Qajar to appreciate the need of a modernized military was Crown Prince Abbas Mirza, governor general of Azerbaijan in the early nineteenth century. Abbas Mirza made use of the French and British instructors provided for by treaties to introduce a Western-style armed force in Azerbaijan which, following the terminology of Muhammad Ali and Selim, he called the *Nezam-e Jadid,* or "New Order" (meaning "New Army"). Like his non-Iranian predecessors he had trouble with ulama who claimed his innovation was un-Islamic, particularly in its use of Western-style uniforms, and like them he found complaisant ulama to justify such innovation as the means to protect the abode of Islam. Abbas Mirza also sent students abroad to study practical subjects, established good relations with Europeans, and encouraged good treatment for religious minorities.

Abbas Mirza died in 1833 before he could take the throne, and subsequently there were only sporadic attempts to bring in Western military instructors from various countries to train parts of the armed forces. Of these only the small, Russian-officered Cossack Brigade late in the century became a serious and disciplined force, but it was used chiefly for protecting the shah and his court. Otherwise the Iranian army was notable for its disorganization, for the sale of rank to men or boys with no military capability who pocketed their soldiers' salaries and then had to allow the men to make a living by following whatever trade they could, to the neglect of drill and training. Apart from the Cossack Brigade formed in 1879, the government could sometimes rely on tribal forces that were not part of the regular army, and in return it allowed them some freedom to loot and plunder. Lacking a strong army or police force, and lacking roads and railroads with which to reach the provinces, the central government had to rely upon indirect means of rule, such as dividing opposing forces, encouraging factional fights, offering bribes, sometimes as gifts or annuities, and holding in Tehran hostages ("guests") from powerful tribes and families.

More dangerous than powerful tribes and families to the power of the government was the great influence of the Shi'i ulama. Whereas the Safavid rulers, through their claim of descent from the imams and through their considerable control of many religious leaders, had been able to escape some of the most dangerous consequences of the growing socioeconomic power and ideological pretensions of the ulama, this was increasingly untrue of the Qajars. The Qajars could claim no religious descent or charisma, though they adopted the Iranian royal custom of calling themselves the "Shadow of God" on earth. Unlike the Safavids they had few important dependent ulama. They appointed the leader of the Friday prayer (imam jom'eh) for each city, as well as certain judges, but these men were outranked in the eyes of the populace by mujtahids not tied to the central government. As noted, the ulama hierarchy was economically self-sufficient through its direct collection of religious taxes and through vaqf donations, while the residence of the leading ulama in Ottoman Iraq continued through and beyond the Qajar period and helped reinforce ulama independence. If a leading mujtahid should speak out in favor of a different governmental policy or against the practices of a ruler, it was the mujtahid to whom his followers owed obedience.

The Shi'i shrine cities in Iraq had enough income, through endowments and donations, to support a large community of religious leaders, scholars, and students, who lived in independence of the Iranian government. Even within Iran various sources of revenue led to considerable wealth for the ulama, some of whom doubled as land-owners or merchants. The wealth was unevenly distributed, and there were poor and middling mollas as well as rich ones (the latter often having outside sources of income), but as a corporate group the ulama were well endowed, and this wealth promoted their power and independence. Many ulama and sayyeds associated with them also received governmental gifts and annuities, which, however, did not always assure their loyalty.

Many functions that in modern states are governmental were carried out in Qajar Iran, as in most traditional Muslim societies, by the ulama. These included all levels of education, most forms of judicial and legal activity, and social and charitable services. Iran was almost as late to introduce modern or secular education as military reform, and aside from the Dar al-Fonun of Tehran founded in mid-century by Mirza Taqi Khan *Amir Kabir* to train army officers and civil servants, Iranian education was in the hands of the ulama, and the government had nothing to say about curriculum or anything else. Teaching was traditional and Islamic, concentrating at lower levels on reading, writing, and memorization of the Quran (often without understanding its Arabic), and at higher levels on Arabic and the traditional Islamic sciences. In Iran, Muslim and even some ancient philosophy was taught far more than in Sunni schools to the west. Only near the end of the Qajar period were there a few attempts, largely private, to modernize schools. Some girls managed to get an education, either at school or at home, and a few reached the level of learning and accomplishment considered necessary to be a mujtahid, although these were not generally considered mujtahids, and most Shi'is held that being male was a necessary quality for a mujtahid. There was, and still is, however, a wide network of educated women mollas who cater to women's religious gatherings and ceremonies, giving readings and commentaries on the Quran and telling stories from the lives of the imams.[7]

Unlike education, the administration of justice was de facto divided between ulama-run sharia (Islamic law) courts and administrative courts using 'urf or "customary law," often arbitrary, presided over by the shah, governors, and their representatives. In general, the former dealt with family and personal status law, with wills, contracts, and other legal documents, and with breaches of Islamic law, whereas the latter concentrated on criminals and rebels against governmental authority. Throughout the Qajar period there was a trend on the part of the government, particularly when there were strong reforming chief ministers, to extend the power of governmental courts and legal prerogatives—a trend that was resisted by the ulama.

The ulama had strong ties with the bazaar classes (called in Persian *bazaaris*), including both the bazaar elite of merchants engaged in long-distance and international trade and the larger group of bazaar artisan-shopkeepers, organized into guilds. Ulama and bazaaris often belonged to the same families; much ulama income came from levies paid mainly by bazaaris; the guilds often celebrated religious or partly religious ceremonies for which the services of ulama were needed; and piety and religious observance were among the signs of bazaar standing or leadership. (Even today respectable bazaar shopkeepers and merchants are often addressed as "Hajji," whether or not the speaker knows if the addressee has made a pilgrimage justifying this form of address.) Entry into the ulama through study was an avenue of upward social mobility and entailed more respect than entry into Qajar service. Mosques and shrines were a major area of *bast* (refuge) for individuals and groups that feared governmental arrest or harassment. Although some of the ulama, especially those with government appointments, sided with the government, and some might cheat, extort, hoard, or take bribes, in general the ulama were seen as doing this less than government officials. The ulama could also sometimes be appealed to by the popular classes as well as the wealthy to represent grievances before the government. Several times in the Qajar period, and most notably in the Tobacco Protest of 1891–92 and the Constitutional Revolution of 1905–11, an important sector of the ulama helped lead popular movements against a government seen as complaisant to the encroachments of foreign imperialists.

The position of women in Qajar Iran has scarcely been studied, but a few generalizations may be broached on the basis of available material. One is that women's positions varied considerably, as was and is true in other Islamic societies, according to class and social status. In theory, Iran, like other Muslim societies, followed Quranic rules concerning women and the family, with some additions from later Muslim law including a few special to Twelver Shi'i law. The Quran gives men permission to marry up to four wives if they are treated equally (the same chapter of the Quran says that no matter how hard a man tries he will not be able to treat wives equally, which some Muslim modernists argue was meant to outlaw polygamy). The Quran provides for easy divorce for the man and restricted divorce rights for the woman, male guardianship of women and girls, and the evaluation of women's testimony at one half that of a man. Women's inheritance is also half that of a man, but this, plus the fact that a married woman continues to hold her own property, is more favorable to women than were most Western laws before this century. As noted, the various forms of veiling are not Quranic, although many Muslims interpret the Quran as enjoining the veil. Guardianship of children (after an age which varies by school of law but which is young for Shi'is) goes to the father in case of divorce.

In practice, there has been and is considerable variation in women's position. Polygamy has never been widespread, for both social and economic reasons, and in premodern periods it was characteristic mainly of the ruling elite, some of whom had harems and observed strict veiling and seclusion in part as a sign that they could afford numerous wives and servants—a form of "inconspicuous consumption." Even harems were rarely the dens of idleness and iniquity imagined by Westerners.[8] Social custom also restrained frequent divorce, as did the custom of the male bride-price (or dower), most of which was to be paid in case of divorce. Even though men might find ways to avoid its payment, the practice had some restraining effect, as did disapproval of divorce in some social groups and between the families who originally arranged the marriage. Another rare but possible protection was the insertion into the obligatory marriage contract of special provisions, such as that the husband could not take a second wife without the first wife's permission.

Important variations existed among different social groups and classes. In Iran and the Middle East nomadic tribeswomen do most of the tribe's physical labor, are unveiled, and are less segregated than traditional urban women; on the other hand, they tend not to inherit as the Quran says they should. The virtual universality of these nomadic practices in the Middle East and their congruity with the tribal-nomadic way of life, which does not permit women to be idle or segregated but also discourages releasing the family's limited property into the hands of the new family that the bride joins, suggests that such conditions go back in time. Peasant women also do hard physical work and reports from the nineteenth century indicate that they were mostly unveiled. Veiling has been mainly an urban (and hence minority) phenomenon. It is also wrong to take veiling as a sign of a complete lack of freedom or of useful activity. As in the West, running, or helping to run, a household was in every sense an important and productive activity, without which society could not function and children could not be reared. Women in various social groups also engaged in activities more universally considered "productive," such as spinning, and weaving textiles, including important market and export items like Kerman shawls and Persian carpets, for which Western demand began to boom in the 1870s. In tribal and village carpets and textiles most of the creativity in design and color had come from women down through the centuries. There were also professional women who served the needs of other women, like midwives, ambulant saleswomen who visited women at home, healers, and others, including the women mollas mentioned above.

Some women at the court had great power, especially queen mothers and favorite wives. The mother of the teen-aged Naser ad-Din Shah exercised great influence on him after he came to the throne in 1848, and later his favorite wife was also influential. (Her residence became the headquarters of a court-centered conspiracy that brought down the reforming but pro-British chief minister Mirza Hosain Khan *Moshir ad-Dauleh*). On less elite levels ordinary women were often prominent in bread riots and other urban movements, and this tradition was carried forward in their significant participation in the Tobacco Protest of 1891–92, the Constitutional Revolution of 1905–11, and especially the Revolution of 1978–79.

Even in the area of modesty and sexual behavior, all was not as it seemed either in law or in stereotypes. An early nineteenth-century treatise written by a woman or women of the educated upper class tells other women how to flirt, fool, or get around their husbands, and engage in other dubious pleasurable activities, while another treatise by a man constantly admonishes women not to mistreat their husbands in various ways—admonitions that would not be needed if women behaved according to theory. A mid-nineteenth-century Orientalist wrote that many women followed the precepts of the first book, around which there was a virtual women's cult.[9]

If Shi'ism was somewhat special in Islam in its institutionalization of female mollas, it was also special in another, more controversial feature—temporary marriage. In this form of marriage, early outlawed by Sunnis, the duration of the marriage is stated in the contract—anywhere from some minutes to ninety-nine years. As in all marriages, the husband gives a sum of money. The temporary wife or wives could be in addition to the four maximum regular wives. Temporary marriage flourished in Shi'i pilgrimage centers where mollas might be intermediaries; both Sunnis and Westerners often characterized the custom as "legalized prostitution." It has, however, other uses, and even when of short duration it has the advantage that the children are legitimate and the temporary wives, even when professionals, are not breaking any law and are less stigmatized than prostitutes. (It should be added that, contrary to the view of some apologists, straight prostitution has long existed in the Middle East and was not checked either by polygamy or by temporary marriage.)

Enough has been said to suggest the variability and the productivity of women's roles. As in other premodern and modern societies most women had fewer rights and less power than men of the same social group, who tended to dominate them, but their lives had more variation and possibilities for fulfillment than are acknowledged in the usual Western stereotypes about Muslim women.

As noted, religious minorities consisted mostly of recognized "People of the Book" (monotheists with a scripture)—Jews, Nestorian and Armenian Christians, Zoroastrians, and the small gnostic Sabean community near Iraq. The Jews and Armenians were concentrated in towns, and they, like the Sabeans, were often occupied with certain crafts, such as gold- and silverworking shunned by some religious Muslims, as well as moneylending at interest, which was forbidden to Muslims. Although these communities were recognized and had internal autonomy in many matters under their own religious laws, and although they were better treated than minorities in much of European history, they were often impoverished second-class citizens. Shi'i concepts of ritual purity made intermixture between them and Muslims more difficult than in many Sunni countries. During the nineteenth century, coreligionists of the Jews, Christians, and Zoroastrians abroad, including Christian missionaries, tried to improve the education and position of their Iranian coreligionists with some success. As in many third-world countries, however, the cultural ties of parts of these communities (and later of some Baha'is) to Westerners, who sometimes intervened on their behalf, opened them to usually unfounded accusations of being agents of Western imperialism. Twentieth-century governments of whatever stripe have all restated protection of recognized religions, although practice has not always equaled theory.

In the early nineteenth century vertical community ties between richer and poorer in tribe or clan; city guild, faction, or quarter; and religious community, including Sufi orders and the ulama corps, were often felt more strongly than were regional class ties between persons with similar relations to the mode of production. By the late Qajar period, however, the development of regional and national markets, improvements in communication and growing sociopolitical crises and grievances made nationwide groups like merchants, artisans, the new intellectuals, and even the leading ulama identify and communicate with each other on a national basis far more than they had before. Thus in late Qajar times we find nationwide mass movements with unprecedented coordination and some self-conscious regional and national social and class groupings.

A new factor in Qajar times was the growing power of a nonindigenous, untraditional group who profoundly affected society—foreigners, and, at long distance, the governments and economic groups they represented. Although Iranian towns had not nearly as many foreign nationals as did the cities of Egypt, the Levant, or Turkey, Iran was nearly as affected as they by the policies of foreign governments and some foreign businesses. Ever since the strategic involvement of France, Britain, and Russia with Iran during the Napoleonic Wars, Iran came to be affected particularly by the policies of Great Britain and Russia. In addition to European interest in Iranian trade, and later in concessions for European economic activity, Britain and Russia had very strong political and strategic interests in Iran. Britain was concerned to retain control of the Persian Gulf, to keep other powers out of it, and to safeguard southern and eastern Iran in order to help hold India. Russia, after taking Transcaucasian territory from Iran in two early nineteenth-century wars, tried to make northern Iran an area of overwhelming Russian influence, and also tried, as did Britain, to control the central government as much as possible There were at times "forward parties" in Russia who hoped to take more territory and push Russian influence to the point of being able to use, or even reach, the Gulf.

Neither Britain nor Russia wished to allow the other to take further territory in Iran, or to make Iran a protectorate, and this mutual desire to forestall control of Iran by the other party was the most important factor in maintaining Iran's formal independence. This independence was often *purely* formal, as Iran did not dare take a step that might seriously displease Britain or Russia unless it had very strong support from the other country. Even the support of one of the two might be insufficient if the other were displeased enough. Nineteenth-century diplomatic files are filled with accounts of discussions by Iranian leaders with British and Russian representatives trying to get them to approve policies that in a truly independent state would be a matter for internal decision. As most

Western scholars read the British but not the Russian or Persian archives, they get the impression that British intentions in Iran were significantly reformist and progressive, but a fuller acquaintance with Persian and Russian sources does not support this view. On the whole, the British favored those reforms that would facilitate their trade and the lives of foreigners and those tied to them; when genuinely reforming nationalists became strong, as during the constitutional revolution, and wished to limit foreign privileges in Iran, the British opposed them.

European governments pushed and promoted the commercial interests of their own nationals. Here again the difference between Britain and Russia is smaller than it is often said to be. It is true that the Russian government often offered subsidies and rebates to encourage exporters to Iran and elsewhere, and also promoted banking and railroad schemes in part in order to spread Russian political influence. The British, however, also considered railroad projects mainly from their own strategic viewpoint, and both governments eventually opposed and blocked all railroads, primarily for strategic reasons. The British government also played a large role in encouraging or discouraging investment in other economic schemes; discouraging the vast concession of Baron de Reuter in 1872 but then using Reuter's claims to block Russian railway concessions and officially aiding the compensation of Reuter in 1889 through the important concession for the Imperial Bank of Persia, with attached rights for mineral exploitation. In the late nineteenth and early twentieth century the British government was particularly active in helping its subjects to attain concessions, including the disastrous tobacco monopoly concession of 1890 and the very important D'Arcy oil concession of 1901. (All of this is discussed in more detail below.)

Foreigners were also favored by unequal treaties that freed them from internal customs duties, which Iranian traders still paid, and held customs duties at ports of entry to very low levels. Many factors blocked the development of modern industry and transport in Iran, despite some abortive attempts by ministers and Iranian businessmen in Qajar times. Difficulties of communication, low population, vast and hard to penetrate distances, decentralization, and a lack of modern education and training were among the indigenous factors limiting economic development, and to them were added the legal impossibility under unequal treaties of protecting infant industries or handicrafts, and the lack of interest of the Qajar government in improving industry, infrastructure, or agriculture. The jealously guarded and decentralizing power of tribes, ulama, and certain cities and regions was sometimes exercised against attempts at modernization. If one looks at the Middle East and North Africa as a whole it cannot be an accident that those areas where nomadic tribes, and often religious groups, had the greatest power were the last to centralize and industrialize—besides Iran, Morocco, Libya, Saudi Arabia, the rest of Arabia, Afghanistan, and Central Asia may be mentioned. Iran was in fact less controlled by nomadic tribes than many of these, and hence was able to centralize and begin industrialization before most of them.

Iran's dependence on Western economic forces; its political and military weakness; its government's search for Western advice and approval; and Russian and British protection of the Qajars against revolts made Iran a country with very limited independence. Iranian internal politics in the Qajar period are frequently shadow politics, with real politics often occurring not only, as in many countries, behind the scenes, but even beyond the seas.

3

Continuity and Change Under the Qajars: 1796–1890

Political and socioeconomic developments of the Qajar period may be understood against the above general background. Iran was reunified in the nineteenth century under the Qajar dynasty (1796–1925), which owed its long life, despite unpopularity, largely to repeated support from the two European powers most involved in Iran—Great Britain and Russia. The Qajars were preceded by the late eighteenth-century Zands, who ruled from the southern city of Shiraz and like the Qajars were of tribal origin. The Zands were one of Iran's few very popular dynasties. They protected trade, built bazaars, shrines, and caravanserais, and were personally benevolent. (Their popularity and their refusal to call themselves shahs, preferring to be called "deputies" either of the Safavids or, even better, of the people, made them the only rulers whose names were not taken off streets and monuments after the 1979 revolution.) The Zands came to power, like most dynasties, at the head of a tribal federation, and their chief rivals were the leaders of another such federation, the northern Qajars. A Qajar leader castrated in boyhood, Agha Mohammad Khan, was captured and kept under house arrest in Shiraz, but on the death of a Zand ruler he escaped and returned to lead his tribal forces in battle, taking over much of Iran by 1790. His cruelty, especially in plucking a reported twenty thousand eyes from men of Kerman, was long remembered. Assassinated in 1797, he was succeeded by a nephew, Fath Ali Shah, who ruled until 1834. Qajar reunification of Iran had at least the virtue of ending the civil and other wars and economic disruptions of the eighteenth century.

During the rule of Fath Ali Shah the first major nineteenth-century European incursions in Iran occurred, as a byproduct of the Napoleonic

Wars. Napoleon, along with the short-lived Russian emperor Paul, wished to invade India, which was also threatened by the Afghans. To forestall this the British sent Captain John Malcolm from India to sign an 1801 treaty with Iran, which promised British military equipment and technicians in return for Iranian support if Afghanistan or France moved toward Iran or India. Soon, however, there was a Russo-British rapprochement, and Iran, still looking for an alliance against Russia, which had taken Georgia from Iranian control, signed the Treaty of Finkenstein with France in 1807. In it France promised to help Iran regain Georgia and to supply Iran with military equipment and training, and Iran promised to declare war on Britain and aid France if it decided to invade India. The French sent a military mission under General Gardane, which began to train Iranian troops in modern methods and also to study Iran in preparation for a possible invasion of India. Again the timing of the treaty was bad for the Iranian government. In the same year, 1807, after Napoleon's European victories, he and Tsar Alexander signed the Peace of Tilsit. This reversal led to a new Anglo-Iranian alliance in 1809, followed by two further treaties by 1814 that together ended Iranian ties to France, and said Britain would give Iran financial and military aid if it were attacked by any European power.

The Qajars' interest in these treaties came largely from their desire to gain Georgia, over which they fought the first Russian War, 1804–13, where the defects of their troops, despite some attempts at modern training and armament, were demonstrated. By the 1813 Treaty of Gulistan, Russia gained important Caucasian territory and exclusive rights to have warships on the Caspian. The nineteenth century thus introduced Iran to the inscrutable ways of Occidentals, who might break treaties within less than a year of signing them, switch allies and enemies at their own whim, and hence behave in ways that Iranians versed in politics could only consider utterly irrational.

Wars with the West and high military expenditures brought economic drains. These began to be felt seriously in Fath Ali Shah's nineteenth-century wars against Russia and continued during later wars with the British and in attempts to arm and improve the Iranian military. When the burden on the state treasury was too great to be covered by revenues, it was traditional to give out tax-free rights to revenue collection on landed or other properties. Such grants were usually called *tuyuls*. The first war against Russia forced Fath Ali Shah to give out much state land and property as tuyuls in return for military aid. As often happened in Iran and elsewhere, such grants frequently tended to become hereditary, while remaining tax exempt, which meant that the rest of Iran had to pay higher taxes in order to produce the same income for central and local rulers.

Whereas the first Qajar, Agha Mohammad, had been able to keep the land tax (Iran's basic tax) to the reasonable level of 10 percent (an approximation given the absence of a good land survey, but considered a rough average), Fath Ali Shah, largely because of his military expenses, doubled this tax to about one-fifth of the harvest, near where it remained throughout most of the Qajar period.[1] Few official measures were taken in the Qajar period to increase agricultural productivity, which might improve peasant income and government revenue; most improvements were made by private individuals involved in export crops.

Aside from widespread nomadism, Iran's rural economy had other features that affected Iran's society and politics through the twentieth century. One was that aridity, which had increased through the centuries for reasons already discussed, limited the number of persons who could subsist in most of Iran. Iran's vast territory supported only five to ten million people in the nineteenth century. Most Iranians had to live and work in the countryside in order to produce enough surplus to feed urban populations. Widely scattered villages and peasant populations are less likely to get involved in rebellious and revolutionary movements than are the denser and more internally organized peasantries of the Far East. Most Iranian protest movements in the past two centuries have been urban-centered, with little peasant participation, except in the well-watered and populous northern regions, where the proximity and closer organization of peasants and the early introduction of capitalist relations in crops like rice and silk created "modern" class divisions and the potential for organizing peasants.[2]

In addition, Iran's aridity and relative lack of rivers suitable for damming have helped encourage an ancient capital- and labor-intensive form of underground irrigation channels, *qanats.* Skilled workmen built sloping underground canals, with periodic airholes to the surface, to convey water down from mountainous highlands until it is brought to the surface to be used by one or more villages. Aside from the technical ingenuity of this system, what must be noted is its fragility (true to some degree of most premodern artificial irrigation systems). Invaders or hostile rulers can starve out villages by ruining the system, and this makes villagers especially vulnerable to the powers that be. Also, unless villagers have enough surplus to hire skilled qanat diggers, payment is undertaken by a landlord, merchant, or bureaucrat, who in return for supplying water demands a larger share of the crop and may ultimately gain control of peasant land. With a rising demand for trade and export crops in the nineteenth century, it was persons with money to invest in irrigation, in new seeds, and in other improvements who appropriated a growing share of the agricultural surplus. Although some richer peasants were among those who improved their position, many peasants either fell in the socioeconomic scale or remained about the same. Those within and outside the village community with enough capital and knowledge to take advantage of new crops and markets profited, and large land-ownership, often of a more mercantile "modern" kind, increased.

The European presence in the Napoleonic period, and the first war with Russia, led Crown Prince Abbas Mirza, who ruled in Azerbaijan, to try Western military training of his forces and sending students abroad for training as means to improve the military against foreign threats. Abbas Mirza was much aided in his program by his chief minister, known like many notables by a title, Qa'em Maqam, a statesman, writer, and reformer of great ability. After the death of Abbas Mirza in 1833, Qa'em Maqam worked for the central government. Qa'em Maqam is known both in administrative and in literary history as the first person in modern times to try, mainly via example, to simplify the flowery and elaborate forms of Persian court prose. This reform was continued by several later figures, so that official Persian became, if not a model of simplicity and clarity, at least more broadly comprehensible than before, and literary Persian was in time simplified even more. (Premodern elaborate forms, as in many countries, helped rulers limit the comprehension of governmental writings to a small elite.)

The failure of Abbas Mirza's program of army modernization to expand was due not only to the lack of forceful, reforming Qajar leaders after him, but also to the opposition of decentralizing vested interests, which the center never felt strong enough to suppress. Many tribal and even urban leaders opposed a central army that might limit their role and autonomy; some ulama saw the Western instructors, drill, and especially uniforms of modern armies as infidel encroachments that might lead to greater Western incursions; and army officers and others who profited from the corruption of the old military system opposed reform. These obstacles existed through the Qajar period, and while a ruler might have taken a firmer position on army reform than did any Qajar shah, this would probably have entailed, as it finally did under Reza Shah (1925–41), bringing the tribes to heel, silencing the ulama opposition, and setting up a strong central bureaucracy. (Muhammad Ali's Egyptian army, for example, could only be built up when accompanied by a series of other drastic and centralizing reforms.)

Abbas Mirza's military forces had just been launched when they were faced with a challenge beyond their ability, and this too may have prejudiced people against them. The territorial provisions of the 1813 Treaty of Gulistan were unclear enough to create disputes between Iran and Russia. Negotiations did not settle the issues, and some Iranians began demanding revenge and the retaking of at least those territories they felt the Russians had occupied without treaty rights. Some preachers cited, probably mixing truth with exaggeration, mistreatment suffered by their coreligionists in Russian Caucasia. Influenced in part by leading and vocal ulama, some within the Iranian government encouraged the growing pressure for holy war (jihad) against Russia. Fath Ali Shah then proclaimed jihad, launching an attack on the Russians in 1826. The Iranian army, with only a minority of well-drilled and modernized forces, was decisively defeated. The Russo-Iranian Treaty of Turko-manchai in 1828 brought new gains for Russia. More territory was ceded to the Russians, who also were granted a cash indemnity for the cost of the war (a common policy of Western powers in the nineteenth century; lost wars were paid for not only in land but in "costs"). The extraterritorial and tariff concessions earlier partially granted to Russia were now fixed; Iran could demand no more than a 5 percent import tariff on Russian goods, and no internal duties could be levied on them. Also, Russian subjects and Iranians under their protection (in theory usually consular employees, but these provisions were abused by most powers to protect others) were exempt from Iranian law and to be tried by their own consular courts. Both extraterritoriality and the fixed low tariff later spread to other Western powers; the key treaty being that with Great Britain in 1841. As in other Asian countries where similar provisions came to apply, their main result was to open up the country to Western trade and businessmen, while refusing it protection of its own economic life or, often, of its own subjects.

Extraterritoriality appeared necessary to Western powers whose diplomats and private citizens hesitated to venture into countries whose laws appeared to them capricious, if not barbaric. The other side of the coin, however, was that consular courts were often ludicrously lenient, so that a major crime by a foreign national might go virtually unpunished. On the economic side, free trade was forced on Asia even before it was accepted in the nineteenth-century bastion of free trade, Great Britain. Free trade might benefit a Britain whose advanced industries produced cheaper goods than did those of the rest of the world, but in Asia, including Iran, forced low tariffs had a disruptive effect. Growing quantities of European manufactures that displaced Iranian crafts were freely imported, while the impossibility of protective tariffs under the treaties was one of several reasons why native industry could not develop. Many Iranian merchants were also hurt by the treaties. Unlike the Europeans, they were not exempt from internal tariffs and taxes. As early as the 1830s and continuing from then on, Iranian hand-manufacturers and merchants protested against the rising tide of European imports that were ruining their trades and requested the government to institute protections and prohibitions.[3] Under the unequal treaties, however, there was little the government could do, even had it been so inclined. Some Iranian merchants and enterprises tied to foreign trade benefited from the new situation, as did those consumers whose livelihoods were not undermined but who received cheaper imports.

If the economic effects of the Treaty of Turkomanchai's provisions took some time to make themselves felt, there were more immediate political effects. The two defeats by the Russians led to regional and tribal uprisings, and there is some evidence that the government deliberately helped to turn growing popular discontent against the Russians rather than itself. A Russian mission, headed by the well-known author Griboyedov, was sent to Iran in 1829, mainly to force the Iranian government to pay the Treaty of Turkomanchai indemnity. Generally, what ensued has been, as is frequent with such incidents, treated in the West as a matter of blind and unprovoked Iranian mob action stirred up by fanatical ulama. In fact, it appears that Griboyedov (married to an illustrious Georgian wife as anti-Iranian as he) and his party acted with foolhardy disregard for basic tenets of Iranian behavior and honor.

A report reached the Griboyedov mission that one or more Christian Georgian or Armenian women had been forcibly converted to Islam and brought into the harems of prominent Iranians. The Russian mission, against much that was sacred in Iran, forced their way into impregnable harems and took away such women to question them as to where they wished to live. Some women were allegedly held overnight. In the case of two Georgian women, married to an anti-Russian Iranian notable, the

Russians claimed that the women, who had converted to Islam and borne children, wished to leave Iran and return to territory now Russian. The rumor spread that they were being held involuntarily and forced to renounce Islam. The Tehran ulama tried first to influence Griboyedov, but then one of them issued a *fatwa* (religious decree) saying the rescue of Muslim women from unbelievers was lawful. The crowd that then went to the mission became uncontrollable. When Russian Cossacks shot a boy an attack by the Iranians followed, and Griboyedov and his whole mission, with one exception, were killed.[4] The episode was significant as the first important anti-foreign incident of religious inspiration, which embodied the resentment of many Iranians against their treatment by Western powers. (The incident was sometimes mentioned during the 1979–81 American Embassy hostage crisis as a precedent for Iranian violation of diplomatic immunity, but in fact, certain incidents in China form closer parallels to these events. In all of them, however, widespread antiforeign sentiment based on real grievances is involved.)

The Iranian ulama's power over the masses and ability to move in ways not thoroughly approved by the government had been shown both in ulama action for jihad, which helped precipitate the second Russo-Iranian war, and in the Griboyedov incident. The ulama also frequently sided with bazaaris in their complaints against the ruin of their trade owing to Western imports. On the other hand, before the mid-nineteenth century the ulama were rarely active in opposing government policies. The shahs of this period tried in general to treat the ulama well and show them respect, while the ulama, in turn, generally limited their political demands to questions they considered of immediate or over-whelming concern.

Further embroilment with a Western power, in this case Britain, was barely avoided in 1833 when Crown Prince Abbas Mirza, having recently put down tribal revolts in eastern Iran, was moving to take Herat. This city in western Afghanistan, with a large Persian-speaking Shi'i population, was then under Afghan rule but considered to be Iranian by Iranians. The British opposed having Iran control Herat and would have come to the aid of the Afghans, but conflict was avoided when Abbas Mirza died. His son and successor, Mohammad Mirza, was recalled by the central government and the war stopped.

The death of Abbas Mirza was a blow to the future of "reform from above" stressing the army, bureaucracy, and new education for both, which Abbas Mirza had launched in Azerbaijan on the model of Ottoman reforming sultans and Egypt's Muhammad Ali. Neither Fath Ali Shah nor his grandson Mohammad Shah made real attempts at modernization or centralization, and both governed in old ways, with the minimum of unavoidable adjustments. Fath Ali Shah was known more for his long beard, tiny waist, and huge harem than for any positive achievements. Because of his hundreds of progeny, an unflattering phrase, alliterative in Persian, became common: "Camels, lice, and princes are to be found everywhere."

Fath Ali Shah died soon after Abbas Mirza, in 1834. Peaceful accession of the crown prince, Mohammad Mirza, was assured thanks to diplomatic and military support displayed by the British, with the consent of the Russians. Subsequent peaceful accessions were similarly guaranteed by a show of support and force by these two powers, both of whom had an interest in keeping on the throne and immune from civil war a dynasty from which they had obtained major treaty concessions. Knowledge that the British and the Russians were behind the dynasty and would back each accession of a crown prince helped forestall revolts and rebellions against a dynasty that was widely considered incompetent and rapacious. Partly in return for their support, the British obtained in 1836 and 1841 treaties that gave them the privileges earlier conceded to the Russians. The British Treaty of 1841 included the famous "Most Favored Nation Clause," and with its subsequent extension to other countries' treaties it meant that all foreign powers were united to extend the treaty privileges of any of them, as new privileges were automatically extended to all.

During the reign of Mohammad Shah the strength of foreign powers, and especially Britain, grew, and it was in this period that the first petitions from bazaaris against Western competition were sent to the Shah. Important religious movements and revolts began in these years, possibly connected to dislocations in Iranian life brought on by foreign encroachments. One of these involved Iran's Isma'ili Shi'i community. In Iran there still existed a small group of Sevener or Isma'ili Shi'is, whose leaders were directly descended from the imams of the so-called Assassins, important in eleventh- to thirteenth-century Iran but then suppressed by the Mongol invaders. The Isma'ili community remained largely underground until the Safavids who, even though they belonged to a different Shi'i line, gave them permission to worship openly. The head of this Isma'ili community, who bore the hereditary title of Agha Khan, became involved in a provincial disagreement and, moved in part by personal ambition, launched a revolt in south-central Iran. He was defeated, and as a result he fled, along with many of his followers, to India, where there were many adherents of his branch of Isma'ili Shi'ism. The followers of the hereditary Agha Khans, based from the 1840s until today in India, believe them to be the descendants of the first imams, via the Egypt-centered Fatimid dynasty, followed by the Nizaris (Assassins). Hence they are considered living imams, the imams of the Sevener line never having disappeared like the Twelfth Imam of the Twelvers. Unknown to most, a small and often semisecret community of Seveners has continued to exist in Iran after the 1840s exile.[5]

Far more important for Iran from the mid-nineteenth century on was the messianic movement known as the Babis, an altered offshoot of which later spread both within and outside Iran as Baha'ism. The founder of Babism, Sayyed Ali Mohammad, later called the Bab ("gate" to the Twelfth Imam), was born in 1819 into a family of merchants in the southwestern city of Shiraz. Early choosing a religious vocation, he went to study with the most learned of the Shi'i ulama in the shrine cities of Najaf and Karbala in Ottoman Iraq. Here he became a follower of a movement within Shi'ism named the Shaikhi movement after its founder Shaikh Ahmad Ahsa'i (1754–1826). Shaikhi ideas included elements both more philosophical and more mystical than those of most orthodox Shi'is, but their most important special feature was a new "fourth pillar," which suggested that there is always a man in the world capable of interpreting the will of the hidden imam (and perhaps of communicating with him). After returning to Shiraz, in 1844 Sayyed Ali Mohammad proclaimed himself this door (Bab) to the hidden imam. Later, as his claims were rejected by most ulama and they began to treat him as a heretic, he sometimes announced he was the imam himself, returning as was predicted to institute perfection on earth. In Shiraz and later in Isfahan he preached against the corruption and venality of the ulama, and when civil authorities turned against him he attacked them also for their sins. The Bab had started with a small but devoted following, and this quickly grew; many at first came from the Shaikhi community, which had expanded in Iran since the late eighteenth century. On the other hand less radical Shaikhis now began, and continued, to insist that the "Bab" spoken of by Shaikh Ahmad Ahsa'i would not manifest himself openly, and that the concept was spiritual, rather than referring to an identifiable man.

It seems probable that the Babi movement, which developed into open socioreligious messianic revolt, can in part be understood as one of several mass religiopolitical messianic movements that appeared under the initial impact of the industrialized West in the third world. This impact tends to make third-world countries subject to new trade fluctuations, to undermine handicrafts, restructure agriculture to the detriment of some, and have other disruptive effects, at the same time as Western examples in law, religion, and custom may suggest new ideas on how to meet new problems. Among such messianic movements occurring after the early impact of the industrialized West are the Taiping Rebellion in China, the Ahmadiya and other groups in India and Pakistan, the Mahdist movement of the Sudan, and a variety of Christian and semi-Christian movements in Africa and Latin America. The new ideological content of most of these, as of the Babi movement, supports the idea that they are not simply "traditional" messianic revolts, but are in addition linked to new conditions brought by the Western presence.[6]

Once he lost hope of becoming the leader of a reformed Islam, the Bab not only denounced both secular and religious authorities, but announced a new scripture, the *Bayan*, which contained laws superseding many in the Quran. In his scripture and preachings the Bab spoke out for greater social justice, and his partially modern, perhaps "bourgeois," content is seen in such points as a high valuation of productive work, a denunciation of begging (not blameworthy in Islam, especially as it provides an occasion to give alms), a call for mild and humanitarian treatment of children and others, and the end to the prohibition of taking interest. He also called, if not exactly in modern economic terms, for guarantees for personal property, freedom of trade and profits, and the reduction of arbitrary taxes. He called notably for a higher position for women, who were to be educated and not to be beaten, and for limits on polygamy. The already educated but formerly secluded Babi poet and preacher, Qorrat al-Ain, was reported to have preached unveiled; most Babi women did not dare go that far at this early time.

Whether he claimed to be the gate to the Twelfth Imam or whether, as he sometimes later said, he was both a prophet and the imam himself returned to institute a reign of perfect justice throughout the world, the Bab aroused messianic sentiments among his followers. The differences of his scripture from the Quran he explained by a theory containing a progressive evolutionism rare in premodern thought. Muslims believe that there were prophets before Mohammad but that each brought an essentially identical revelation, from which some followers deviated and needed to be brought back to the true path by a new prophet. Mohammad, however, was the last of the prophets (even though Shi'is often seem to revere Ali and Hosain more, their messages are not considered to differ from Mohammad's). The Bab, however, said that each prophet brings a new message in accord with the growing maturity of humanity, and that each new message supersedes the last one. Hence the *Bayan* does not just interpret, but supersedes the Quran, while including the essence of its message. Past prophets are respected and their laws were needed during their own prophetic cycle, but those laws that are superseded are no longer valid. This doctrine was regarded with horror by pious Muslims and was seen as a dangerous heretical breakoff from Islam.

Political events now impinged on the Babi movement. Mohammad Shah died in 1848 and British and Russian protection served to assure the throne to the crown prince, the teen-aged Naser ad-Din, who was to reign for forty-eight years (1848–96). In Muslim countries interregna are often periods for disorder and revolt, as when there is no new king ruling from the capital many consider that no legal ruler exists. As crown princes took some weeks to travel from Tabriz to Tehran, interregna could be dangerous times for rulers and propitious ones for their opponents. The Babis tried to take advantage of this period to begin revolts, and they succeeded in establishing enclaves, first in a village in the Caspian province of Mazanderan and later in some cities. The Babi revolts were not well coordinated nationally, however, owing in part to lack of modern transportation and communication, and the government was able between 1848 and 1851 to suppress them cruelly, massacring many who had been offered safe conduct in return for surrender. The Bab himself was arrested even before the revolts began, and his civil and ulama opponents evidently decided that messianic feelings about him, considered a main factor in the revolts, could be dampened by his execution. Hence, he was taken to Tabriz, interrogated by the ulama about his religious beliefs, and sentenced to death by firing squad, in 1850. The first round of bullets sent up a cloud of smoke, which remarkably cleared to reveal no body, though the Bab was then found and executed, the first volley having merely cut his ropes.

After the suppression of the Babi revolts, during which one Babi conclave adopted a semicommunist doctrine, and the repression that followed, a small and desperate group of Babis tried to kill the shah in 1852. After this there were terrible tortures and executions of Babis, including the woman preacher-poet Qorrat al-Ain. The Babis who survived now had either to keep their beliefs hidden or to emigrate, concentrating first in Ottoman Baghdad. The successor as leader of the Babis, apparently chosen by the Bab, was called Sobh-e Azal. He was soon challenged by his more dynamic half-brother, Baha'ollah, who succeeded in attracting the great majority of the community. As part of the Bab's progressive theory of prophets, he had predicted that the future would bring a new prophet, "He whom God shall manifest," whose new scripture would supersede his own. In 1863 Baha'ollah declared himself to be this new prophet, and in his writings introduced a cosmopolitan, pacifist, liberal doctrine that largely replaced the Iranian radical messianism of the Bab.

The Baha'is proselytized outside Iran, but are also almost surely the largest non-Muslim religious minority in Iran, while the followers of the Sobh-e Azal, the Azalis, probably now number only a few thousand, nearly all Iranian. Neither group is officially counted as a religion either in Iran or in other Muslim countries. By Muslim law conversion is permitted to Islam or between non-Muslim religions but not *from* Islam, which is apostasy. Nonrecognition of the Baha'i religion is therefore not new and does not distinguish Iran from other Muslim countries; more significant is the question of how Baha'is and other minorities are treated in practice, which has shown some variation.

After 1863, the Azalis retained a strong radical and rebellious component, as well as a hatred for the Qajars that was stronger than their dislike of the Shi'i ulama, and so a number of Azalis were found among the precursors of, and participants in, the Constitutional Revolution of 1905–11. The pacifist Baha'is, on the other hand, eschewed direct political activity, although some of their acts had political implications, and declared their neutrality in the 1905–11 Revolution (which sometimes objectively meant support to the shahs). Many Baha'is received modern educations, and, like other minorities with Westernized educations and sometimes employment, were often suspected of representing Western interests, which added anti-Western feeling to the religious prejudices against them. As with other minorities, most Baha'is probably did nothing to draw hostility, but the acts or positions of only a few among a minority often suffice to add to hostile ideas about a whole religious minority. Besides having modern educations, Baha'is are often professionals or businessmen, and all this has made them frequent scapegoats.

The chief minister brought with him by Naser ad-Din Shah from Tabriz, Mirza Taqi Khan *Amir Kabir,* was heavily involved in the suppression of the Babis from 1848 to 1850. An extremely able man of humble birth in the royal household, Amir Kabir was the first person after Abbas Mirza to attempt modernization from above. As did most Iranian governmental and other reformers in Qajar times, Amir Kabir followed in part the example of the Ottoman Empire, to which he had traveled, although he was also impressed by what he had seen in Russia. He was primarily concerned, like reformers in other Asian countries, with military reform, beginning his attempt to reorganize the army on Western lines by strengthening the European-style education and training of troops. In order to strengthen the impoverished central treasury, he reduced the number of sinecures and took back many dubious tuyuls, replacing them with small pensions. He founded the first official gazette and the first higher school, the *Dar al-Fonun* in Tehran, which included both technical-scientific and military instruction. It was mainly taught by European teachers with the aid of local translators. For years this was the only modern higher school in Iran, as Naser ad-Din came to fear the upsetting effects of modern education and to discourage both its diffusion in Iran and travel abroad for study. (The effects of these and other policies by this long-lived ruler have scarcely been assessed. In general, Iran would have been better off if "modernization" could have been more gradual and indigenous before 1925 instead of being so much imposed from the top in a brief fifty-year period thereafter.) Under the Dar al-Fonun's auspices various Western books were first translated into Persian, the first Persian textbooks were published, and some government officials received their education.

The efforts of Amir Kabir to start modern industries were less successful. Although some factories were begun under his auspices, lack of governmental interest or preparation for factories, treaty preclusion of protective tariffs, and the lack of a prepared labor force, transport, and so forth aborted these enterprises. A few of his schemes for agriculture required less infrastructure and succeeded better.

Some courtiers, landlords, and ulama were threatened by Amir Kabir's reforms, which included measures that hit their economic and judicial powers. They might tolerate him until he achieved success against the Babi menace with his improved military, but once this threat was over many of them worked to get rid of him, aided by the queen mother and also by the imperious tone that Amir Kabir used with Naser ad-Din, perhaps not realizing that the boy had now grown up. A strong defamatory campaign to discredit Amir Kabir finally convinced the young shah that his chief minister was hungry for total power, so the shah dismissed him in 1851 and had him assassinated at his bath in Kashan the following year. Although Amir Kabir was in no way a populist or democrat, and though he lacked the diplomacy needed to keep the shah on his side and build up a reformist party, there seems little doubt that a measure of self-strengthening and centralization could have helped the future evolution of Iran. In most Asian countries self-strengthening from the top was an important prelude to more populist developments, but in Iran such self-strengthening began seriously only in the 1920s.

After the fall of Amir Kabir there was a resurgence of the forces that he had tried to limit in order to strengthen the center. These forces included the tribes and their leaders, landlords of various origins, courtiers, and the ulama. The actions of these groups against reform and reformist ministers, along with the informal guarantees of Iran's territory and of the dynasty given by Britain and Russia, inclined the Qajars to think that it might not be important to centralize and strengthen their military forces, especially as steps to do so called forth counterpressures and actions from vested interests.

The informal entente of Iran with the very powers that were exploiting her economically was not without difficulties, however. In 1856–57 the Iranian government once again tried to take Herat and was pushed back by the British army, and a British fleet also landed in the port of Bushehr, on the Persian Gulf. The British, already having trouble with their army in India, were willing to settle for the fairly mild Peace of Paris in 1857, in which Iran promised to renounce, and stay out of, Herat. After this peace British influence was predominant for a time at the Iranian court.

In the nineteenth century the results of contacts with the West appear to have been more negative than positive for Iran, and many traditional evils were reinforced rather than overcome. The costs of Iran's wars, including foreign arms and instructors, along with the import of new goods that added nothing to health, welfare, or education, whether they were sugar and tea for all classes or luxuries for the elite, meant a growing export of precious metals. Persian exports did not grow enough to pay for these new goods, or for imported manufactures like textiles and household goods. Also, the court itself imported arms and luxuries, and this brought increasing taxes. Although statistics are insufficient to prove whether the real income of the "average" Iranian rose or declined in the nineteenth century, and there are scholars who cite facts on either side, consular statistics and travelers' reports suggest that there were increased inequalities of income, and that the popular classes paid for the increased purchase of tea, sugar, tobacco and machine-made crockery and textiles with higher real prices for such vital items as meat, fruit, grain and bread, and vegetables. Iran became more dependent on Western goods and, in its agricultural exports, on world market fluctuations. These might briefly be helpful, as with the high-priced demand for cotton during the American Civil War, but they also made the country and its people more subject to unreliable markets than ever before. Land converted to export crops like cotton in the north or opium chiefly in the south could not suddenly be reconverted in time of lower demand or a bad harvest, and the conversion of land from food to opium, although usually profitable, contributed significantly to the terrible Iranian famine of 1869–72 and to later scarcities. Scholars who look at growing aggregate import and export figures tend to say that Iran was modernizing and growing more prosperous, while those who study areas of the peasant or urban economy in depth tend rather to find increasing stratification (which usually hurt the poor); growing income-distribution gaps; dangerous dependence on a few Western countries; and a lack of effective governmental steps to strengthen Iran's economy vis-à-vis the West.[7]

Lacking the base or determination to carry through essential centralizing reforms, the Qajars were also unwilling and possibly unable to carry through financial reforms that would have been a necessary concomitant of economic and political changes. Increasingly during the nineteenth century, governorships and subordinate positions were sold to the highest bidder at a kind of annual auction. This led many winners to try to get the most revenue from their lands in the shortest time, as they did not know whether they had any interest in the long-term productivity of the region, which would have required more moderate taxation; but they did want enough cash to win the next auction for a profitable territory. Many tribal leaders paid very little, but only promised to lead their forces in battle if the shah wished. Often the shahs had no way to enforce collection in distant tribal lands. City taxes were also very low, aside from the semivoluntary religious taxes paid by most bazaaris to the ulama, which did not go to the government. Peasants were taxed more heavily than any other part of the population; most of their taxes supported various levels of local or provincial tax collectors and little reached the central government.

Entry into the world market also caused numerous regional and local dislocations that were, on balance, more harmful than helpful to

Iranians. In the sixteenth through eighteenth centuries Iran had produced a significant quantity of silk, silk thread, soft Kerman goats' wool (a sort of cashmere), and textiles for export to Europe, and in the nineteenth century these exports declined. The British turned more to India for cashmere. One European firm, probably by design, imported diseased silkworm eggs to Iran in midcentury; silkworm disease spread rapidly, almost killing the export industry as well as the use of Iranian silk for Iranian textiles. Recovery was never complete.

Iran had an extensive textile production from the simplest to the fanciest cloths. Iranian handmade textiles, manufactured by men and women in home and workshop, were severely reduced by the import of cheaper factory-made textiles, chiefly from Britain and Russia. Although handweaving continues on a constantly diminishing scale, it has ceased to be a significant part of the Iranian economy. Many other crafts, particularly those providing housewares, were also increasingly hit by Western competition. The Iranian author of a *Geography of Isfahan* in the later nineteenth century laments how one craft after another had either disappeared or been decimated by Western competition to the detriment of Isfahan's economy,[8] and similar trends were noted elsewhere.

On the other hand, some goods benefited from Western demand. Among them were agricultural products like cotton, opium, and dried fruits and nuts. In addition, Kerman shawls made of handloomed Kerman wool with finely hand-embroidered "Paisley" (Perso-Indian) designs were temporarily popular in the West. More permanent was the popularity of Persian carpets, which, surprisingly, became a major item of Western demand only as late as about 1875. Both Western and Iranian (chiefly Tabrizi merchant) entrepreneurs were involved in their production and export. After the supply of old carpets dwindled, carpets came to be produced either in workshops or on a "putting out" system where dyed wool and often looms were supplied to weavers who worked at home by pattern for piecework rates. Such carpets were and are produced to Western tastes and specifications and often lack the live creativity characteristic of carpets produced for home or local use. Village and tribal carpets continued to be bought up, but even these were increasingly made according to Western demand. Carpet workers were chiefly women and children, usually working for very low wages in unhealthful conditions. Often they now contributed more than they had before to family income and hence raised this income, but at a heavy price. The introduction of early, non-colorfast aniline dyes in the 1870s further lowered quality. (It is wrong to think that the synthetic dyes used today, which do not run if properly used, are a main cause in lowered carpet quality, which, when it exists, is more due to other aspects of commercialization and mass production.)

Interaction with the West on unequal terms thus reduced large areas of economic activity and opened up or increased some others. Based on existing evidence it seems unlikely that the gains compensated for the losses—that carpets, for example, compensated for the decline in a great variety of crafts for internal and external consumption. While many imported consumer goods could be bought more cheaply than their local counterparts, this did not necessarily bring a better life to most Iranians. More sugar, tea, tobacco, and especially opium were consumed, which was detrimental to health, while prices of basic foodstuffs rose.[9]

Further impoverishing the central treasury was the auctioning of customs directorships, like many offices, region by region. Local directors competed to attract the most trade to their own point of entry by offering import duties below the official 5 percent (being accountable to no one since all they paid to the central government was their original bid), so that income from customs taxes was far lower than it should have been.

During the long period after 1857 that passed without wars, owing in part to Naser ad-Din's belief that the British would protect Iran's territorial integrity, military officers including those at the top were allowed increasingly to pocket the pay allotted to their troops, who were very badly trained and equipped and whose numbers were far below their official level. To live, troops had to practice a variety of full-time trades in town, and many did not even possess a rifle or uniform.

Iran's increasingly negative trade balance, deteriorating terms of trade, and the dramatic world fall in the price of silver, which made up Iran's currency, were further factors in Iran's growing economic problems. Some merchants, landlords, and officials were able to profit from new relations with the West by expanding their control of raw materials or crafts that were newly profitable, but this was not true of most Iranians. On the other hand, changes in Iran's economy and the development of merchants, entrepreneurs, and a few governmental people who could see the benefits of modernizing the economic, social, and legal system provided a base for ultimately effective opposition to the old regime, as did the discontents of the classes who suffered from the new conditions. The bazaar included both merchants who profited from new

outlets but resented Western competition, and other merchants and artisans who mainly suffered from this competition.

Beginning in the 1850s a new phase of Iran's relations with European
powers was characterized by the European drive to receive concessions
for particular economic activities. The first important concessions, for
telegraph lines, were granted to the British, who felt a need for rapid
telegraphic communication with India after the 1857 Mutiny and saw
Iran as the best overland link. This international line, begun in the late
1850s, was soon extended, by Iranian governmental desire, into internal
Iranian lines, so that the government could learn quickly what was hap-
pening in the provinces. (In 1891–92 and after, however, the telegraph
became an important weapon of revolt, keeping Iranian cities in touch
with each other and with the Shi'i shrine cities of Iraq.)

The most extensive concession ever granted by Iran, and perhaps by
any country, came in 1872 when the British subject Baron Julius de
Reuter, of news agency fame, received a concession granting exclusive
rights for railroad and streetcar construction, all mineral-extraction rights
except for a few already being exploited, all unexploited irrigation works,
a national bank, and all sorts of industrial and agricultural projects, in
return for a modest royalty and initial sum. Lord Curzon, himself a firm
economic and political imperialist, later called it the most complete and
extraordinary surrender of the entire industrial resources of a kingdom
into foreign hands that had probably ever been dreamed of.[10] The chief
Iranian promoter of the concession was the reformist prime minister
Mirza Hosain Khan. He profited personally from it, but probably also
thought that Naser ad-Din Shah and the Qajars were so weak and indecisive regarding economic activity that the only way to modernize, as he
thought important, and keep Iran from falling further under Russian
control was to have Englishmen lead in promoting transport, mining,
banking, industry, and agriculture.

Many modern Iranian reformers have been ambivalent toward the
West and Western governments, and in some periods, even within one
individual, there have been swings between a positive and a negative
reaction to the West. In Iran as in much of Asia the earliest reformers
tended to be pro-Western, and Mirza Hosain Khan fits this pattern. Such
reformers might have known that Western powers were exploiting their
country, but felt that the only way to become strong enough to resist
exploitation and Western control was to adopt modern Western methods
in many spheres, including education, the military, and the economy.

Mirza Hosain Khan, whose grandfather was a bath attendant who entered Qajar service, rose rapidly in the Qajar foreign service, holding posts in India, south Russia, and as ambassador to the Ottoman Empire. In all these posts he saw how much even relatively underdeveloped countries might gain by adopting Westernizing reforms, and he helped convince Naser ad-Din Shah to take the first trip abroad of any Qajar ruler, to Ottoman Turkey and Iraq. There he impressed on the shah the virtues of administrative and other reforms in improving the strength and prosperity of a country, and the shah was so impressed that he brought Mirza Hosain Khan back with him to try to introduce reforms in Iran, giving him various ministries. Mirza Hosain Khan made reform efforts especially in the army and judiciary, but like other reformers was opposed by vested interests and ulama. He helped bring on his own downfall by promoting the Reuter concession, which he saw as the most feasible way to economic modernization, but which others saw, with much justice, as a means of handing over Iran's resources to a British subject.[11]

On his first of three trips to Europe, in 1873, Naser ad-Din Shah found that the Russian government was hostile to the Reuter concession, and even the British government did not support Reuter, whose concession had not been their idea. Also, a coalition of Persians had formed against the concession during the shah's absence. The shah had wished to bring his wives on the European trip and they had gone as far as Russia, but affronting incidents such as stares, attempts to greet them, and so forth enabled advisers to convince the shah that offenses to royal ideas of honor might increase and that all women should be sent back to Tehran. The shah's favorite wife, Anis ad-Dauleh, was particularly angry at this, and blamed it on Mirza Hosain Khan, although he denied responsibility. The residence of Anis ad-Dauleh became, after her return, the center where opponents of Mirza Hosain Khan met. They were a mixed group of patriotic or anti-British officials, ulama, and others simply hurt by Mirza Hosain Khan's reforms. When the shah landed at the Caspian port of Anzali, the strength of this anti-Mirza Hosain Khan and anti-Reuter coalition was so strong that the shah felt compelled to dismiss Mirza Hosain Khan and to find a pretext to annul the Reuter concession. The latter was done via a concession provision stating that Reuter must start building his railroad by a certain date or forteit the £40,000 "caution money" he had paid. By blocking the necessary means for Reuter to start the railroad, the shah was able to declare the concession void, and he kept the money. Soon after, Russian concessionaires began to seek railroad concessions in Iran and only then did the British government step in to back Reuter, who had been pressing his claims. The British said that no railroad concession could be granted until Reuter's claims were met, and this was one of several factors that blocked railroad construction in Iran.[12]

Among the more felicitous changes launched by Mirza Hosain Khan were greater centralization of the judicial system and the introduction of a cabinet system of government with nine ministers, each with defined duties, which most ministers had not previously had. The shah's first European trip, under Mirza Hosain Khan's guidance, also encouraged some reforms, notably a modern postal system. In 1874 Amin ad-Dauleh, next to Mirza Hosain Khan the most important reformist minister of this period, was made minister of posts. Mirza Hosain Khan used Austrian advisers to help reorganize the army, and Amin ad-Dauleh used them to help modernize the postal system. In general, however, the shah was increasingly intimidated by defenders of the status quo—more so after the successful movement against Mirza Hosain Khan (who died mysteriously in 1881 after holding less exalted governmental posts). The long reign of Naser ad-Din Shah was characterized by far fewer self-strengthening measures or steps to promote economic and social development than were to be found in nineteenth-century Egypt, the Ottoman Empire, or Tunisia, and though this was partly due to the strength of decentralizing, traditional forces in Iran, it was also in part due to the character of the Qajar rulers. (The difference cannot be blamed on European pressures, which were at least as great elsewhere.)

Although the British government successfully used Reuter's unsettled claims to block not only Russian railway concessions but also some other concession seekers (Reuter's concession was so universal that most requests might be blocked on these grounds), there were nonetheless a few successful concession hunters. An important concession for fishing on the southern Caspian Sea bordering on Iran was granted to a Russian subject, who formed a company that retained a monopoly on Iranian caviar production until after World War I. Other concessions also went to Russian subjects, but the real concession fever recommenced only in 1888, when British policy toward concessions in Iran changed from lukewarm to strongly supportive. A special mission from the British conservative government under a new Minister to Iran, Sir Henry Drummond Wolff, was active in promoting economic concessions. Under pressure from Wolff the shah opened Iran's only navigable river, the Karun in the south, to international navigation. The Russians had pressured Iran not to grant transport concessions without their approval and protested this measure, which favored the British, but the Iranian government claimed that opening a river was not a concession. Wolff, along with Reuter's son, also reached an accord with the shah over Reuter's outstanding claims; the accord gave Reuter two important items from the first concession, the right to build a national bank (Iran had no modern banking system) and attached rights for mineral exploration and exploitation. Although the minerals included oil (also covered in the original Reuter concession), which some thought could be found in Iran, mineral exploration soon stopped and mineral rights reverted to the Iranian government. The bank, however, under the name of the Imperial Bank of Persia, opened, with its seat in Tehran and provincial branches, and with exclusive rights to issue bank notes or any negotiable paper. The Russians in return soon got rights to build roads in the north and to open their own bank, which they used largely for loans to important Persians.

In 1879 the shah, impressed by Russian cossacks while in Russia, founded the Iranian Cossack Brigade headed by Russian officers. These soon constituted a small, well-trained and disciplined force on which shahs could count, but at the same time it created one more means of diffusing Russian influence in Iran, and it could be used against Iranian movements that threatened the interests of the Russian government. This series of concessions, which returned only small sums to the government, although bribes to the shah and officials to promote them were quite large, meant that Iran in this period was falling even further under British and Russian control. The Imperial Bank of Persia's exclusive rights to issue notes were unpopular with Iranian merchants and money-lenders who had long issued their own notes of variable nature and circulation. There were several runs on the Imperial Bank's specie organized by Persian traditional bankers (with Russian backing, the British thought), and some of these came close to success. The Russian Bank with its governmental financing had fewer economic privileges than the British bank, but was useful to the Russians in enabling them to influence Iranian notables by making them loans on easy terms.[13] By the late nineteenth century, then, both the British and the Russians had heavy economic and political interests in Iran, amounting in some areas to real control.

4

Protest and Revolution: 1890–1914

The economic and political dislocations brought by the Western impact included the undermining of most Iranian handicrafts, the transformation of carpet weavers into laborers working for a pittance, the fall in prices of Iranian exports as compared to European imports, and a disastrous drop in the international price of silver, the basis of Iran's currency. These developments, along with the difficulty of being a trader independent of Europeans and the impossibility of setting up protected factories, led to growing economic discontents and resentment against European rivals. Even though some rural and urban groups benefited from trade with the West, they often had other grievances. Increasing Western political control of Iran was resented, and the numerous Iranian merchants and workers who traveled to India, Russian Transcaucasia, and Turkey could witness reforms and hear liberal or radical ideas suggesting ways that governments could change and could undertake self-strengthening policies of a kind that might better Iran's condition and free it from foreign control.

In the 1880s and after there were also a number of officials who advocated reform. Among ministers the most important was Amin ad-Dauleh, who held a variety of positions, chiefly minister of posts, and was generally considered a sincere reformer who disliked the corruption and foreign dominance he saw around him. Less forceful or powerful than men like Amir Kabir or Mirza Hosain Khan (with whom he had not got along), he could have only a small influence in the face of the power held by the long-standing chief minister, Amin as-Soltan. Mirza Malkom Khan, 1833–1908, a Western-educated Armenian Iranian expelled from Iran for forming a society modeled on Freemasonry, later became Iran's minister to Great Britain from 1873 to 1889, and concentrated his reform activities on promoting a modified Persian script and on writing reformist essays with very limited circulation.

In 1889 Naser ad-Din Shah took his third trip to Europe, which was heavily promoted by the British minister in Iran, Sir Henry Drummond Wolff, who hoped to further British financial interest in Iran, and largely succeeded. Among the concessions signed by the shah was one for a lottery in Iran promoted in part by Malkom Khan. After returning to Iran, the shah faced strong opposition to the lottery concession, coming partly from the religious element who noted that gambling was forbidden by the Quran. The shah canceled the concession and so informed Malkom Khan, who hastened to sell what he controlled of the concession for a good price before its cancellation became known. This and other actions resulted in Malkom's dismissal from his posts and the removal of all his titles. The somewhat tarnished but influential reformer now decided to undermine, or perhaps to blackmail, Iran's rulers by producing an oppositional and reformist newspaper, *Qanun* (Law), printed in London and smuggled into Iran. Preaching the virtues of a fixed legal system and the evils of arbitrary and corrupt government, *Qanun* concentrated its attacks on Amin as-Soltan. It was widely read among Iran's elite during its existence, until the death of Naser ad-Din Shah.[1] The only other free newspaper at this time, the older *Akhtar* put out by Iranians in Istanbul, was milder in its reformism, and hence less often forbidden entry into Iran. Within Iran there were only official journals. (The one freer paper launched with the encouragement of Mirza Hosain Khan in 1876, the bilingual *La Patrie*, lasted for only one issue, in which its French editor called for open and fearless criticism.)

Before 1890 most educated Westernizing reformists had been rather hostile to the ulama—as were reformist officials like Amir Kabir, Mirza Hosain Khan, Amin ad-Dauleh, and the Babi and Baha'i reformers. On the other hand, some ulama increasingly emerged as effective opponents of the alarming trend toward the sale of Iran's resources to foreigners. Moreover, the ulama's virtual inviolability and their ties to the guilds could make even secular reformers recognize them as useful allies in a struggle against foreign control. From 1890 through 1912 there was some reconciliation between secularists and ulama opposed to the regime's policies.

One architect of this historically unusual alliance between religious and radical elements was the internationally traveled Muslim reformer and pan-Islamist, Sayyed Jamal ad-Din "al-Afghani" (1839–97). Although he claimed Afghan birth and upbringing, probably in order to have more influence in the Sunni world than he could have had as an Iranian of Shi'i birth and education, Afghani was in fact born in Iran and had a Shi'i education in Iran and in the Shi'i shrine cities of Iraq. Educated in the rationalist philosophical tradition of Avicenna and later Iranian philosophers, who were far more taught in Iran than in the Sunni Near East, Afghani was also influenced by the philosophically oriented Shaikhi school of Shi'ism. In about 1857–58 he traveled to India, where he seems to have developed a lifelong hatred of British imperialism. After activities in Afghanistan and Istanbul and an influential stay in Egypt from 1871 to 1879, he continued his modernist and anti-imperialist writing, first in India and then in Paris, where he edited the anti-British and pan-Islamic Arabic newspaper, *al-'Urwa al-Wuthqa*.[2]

After activities in London, Afghani returned to the south Persian port city of Bushehr, whence he had left decades before for India. He apparently intended only to pick up books sent to him there from Egypt and to go to Russia to continue anti-British activities. The Iranian minister of press, E'temad as-Saltaneh, who had read *al-'Urwa al-Wuthqa*, talked the shah into inviting Afghani to Tehran. There he soon offended the shah, probably by violent anti-British proposals, but gathered a group of Iranian disciples. He apparently spoke to them of the need for uniting religious and nonreligious opposition to foreign encroachments. Forced by the shah to leave Iran in 1887, he spent two years in Russia and then rejoined the shah during the latter's third trip to Europe and received an invitation back to Iran. He first went to Russia, believing he had a mission from Amin as-Soltan to calm Russian hostility over concessions to the British, but in Iran Amin as-Soltan denied such a mission and refused to see him. In the summer of 1890 Afghani heard that the shah was planning to exile him and forestalled this by taking sanctuary in a shrine south of Tehran. He continued to gather disciples, to whom he explained such means of organized opposition as the secret society and the secretly posted and distributed leaflet. His contacts in Iran included his Tehran host, Amin az-Zarb, the wealthiest Persian merchant and master of the mint; Amin ad-Dauleh; some members of the ulama, notably the saintly, ascetic, and progressive Shaikh Hadi Najmabadi; and various reformers and ordinary people, like his devoted servant, Mirza Reza Kermani.

In January 1891, convinced that a leaflet attacking the regime for its concessions to foreigners emanated from Afghani, the shah sent soldiers who forcibly dragged him from his sanctuary and sent him on a forced march to the Iraqi border in midwinter. From Ottoman Iraq, and then from London, where he soon proceeded and joined Malkom Khan, Afghani continued to write and speak against the shah and his government, and he left behind disciples, some secretly organized, whom he had instructed in political action and agitation.

Discontent over the shah's concession policy came to a head after he conceded a monopoly over the production, sale, and export of all Iranian tobacco to a British subject, encouraged by Wolff, in March 1890. The concession was kept secret for a time but in late 1890 the Istanbul Persian newspaper *Akhtar* ran a series of articles severely criticizing it. The January 1891 leaflets that brought Afghani's expulsion attacked the tobacco concession among others, and new critical leaflets were issued by Afghani's followers in the spring. The tobacco concession elicited far more protest than any other because it dealt not with areas that were unexploited, or almost so, by Iranian businessmen, but rather with a product widely grown in Iran, and profiting many landholders, shopkeepers, and exporters.

Massive protests against the concession began in the spring of 1891, when the tobacco company's agents began to arrive and to post deadlines for the sale of all tobacco to the company. The first major protest came in Shiraz, and its religious leader was exiled to Iraq. There he conferred with Afghani, who now wrote a famous letter to the leader of the Shi'i ulama, Hajj Mirza Hasan Shirazi, asking him to denounce the shah and his sale of Iran to Europeans. Shirazi did not immediately take strong action but did write privately to the shah repeating many of the points that Afghani had made to him.

A revolutionary movement now broke out in Tabriz, where the government was forced to suspend the concession's operation, and mass ulama-led protests spread to Mashhad, Isfahan, Tehran, and elsewhere. In December 1891 the movement culminated in an amazingly successful nationwide boycott on the sale and use of tobacco, observed even by the shah's wives and by non-Muslims, which was based on an order either issued by or attributed to Shirazi, which he subsequently confirmed. The government tried to suppress only the company's internal monopoly, leaving it with an export monopoly, but this proved impossible. A mass demonstration in Tehran culminated in the shooting on an unarmed crowd, causing several deaths, and this was followed by even more massive protests. The government was forced to cancel the entire concession early in 1892. The affair left the Iranians with their first foreign debt—£500,000 borrowed from the British-owned Imperial Bank for exorbitant compensation to the company. The movement was the first successful mass protest in modern Iran, combining ulama, modernists, merchants, and ordinary townspeople in a coordinated move against government policy. The movement's coordination throughout Iran and with the mujtahids of Iraq was facilitated by the existence and extensive use of the telegraph. Although many of the ulama were now bought off by the government and some quiet years followed, the "religious-radical alliance" had shown its potential for changing the course of Iranian policy, and the government did not dare grant further economic concessions for several years. The basic alliance of bazaaris (especially merchants), ulama, and secular or modernist reformers continued to be important.[3]

The tobacco movement also encouraged the growth of Russian influence at the expense of the British. To preserve his position, Amin as-Soltan assured the Russians that he would henceforth favor them, and his later policies bore this out. The British policy in 1888–90 of encouraging economic concessions by the shah—which was favored by Prime Minister Lord Salisbury and the Foreign Office but pushed with special energy by the British envoy Wolff—had backfired. Russian counterconcessions and Russian support for the tobacco movement led to an increase in Russian, and not British, influence.

Ulama opposition to the shah temporarily receded and some ulama were quieted by being given increased pensions, but attacks on the government from abroad continued. From London Afghani contributed strong articles to Malkom's *Qanun* and published letters sent to the Shi'i ulama in Iraq and Iran calling on them to depose the shah. Late in 1892 Afghani went to Istanbul as a guest of Sultan Abdülhamid, who kept him from publishing more attacks on the shah but encouraged him to spread pan-Islamic propaganda among Iranians and other Shi'is, asking them to lend support to the Ottoman Sultan, who claimed to be the caliph (leader) of all Muslims. With this aim Afghani formed an Iranian and Shi'i pan-Islamic circle in Istanbul, two of whose prominent members were Azali Babis who had by now become radical freethinkers—Mirza Aqa Khan Kermani, a writer and an editor of the newspaper *Akhtar,* and his close friend the writer, translator, and teacher Shaikh Ahmad Ruhi, also from Kerman. The circle sent out numerous letters to the Shi'i ulama in Iran and elsewhere, bidding them to give allegiance to the sultan-caliph. The Iranian embassy complained of this activity, implicitly directed at weakening the authority of the shah (hence the participation of irreligious radicals). The sultan agreed to the extradition of Ruhi, Kermani, and a third Iranian. While the three were in prison in the eastern Turkish city Trabzon, however, Afghani intervened, and the sultan agreed not to extradite them.

The devoted Iranian servant and follower of Afghani, Mirza Reza Kermani, who had been imprisoned for years in Iran for antigovernmental activities, came to visit Afghani in Istanbul in 1895. There Afghani gave him the idea of killing the shah. After his return to Iran, Mirza Reza made his way to the shrine of Shahzadeh Abd al-Azim just when the shah was planning to visit it in preparation for celebrating the fiftieth lunar anniversary of his reign. Mirza Reza pretended to be a petitioner and suddenly shot the shah on May 1, 1896. The shah was whisked away from public view, and his corpse was propped up in a carriage while Amin as-Soltan pretended to carry on a conversation with him—this in order to avoid the disorders and rebellions that often accompanied a change in monarch. The Cossack Brigade was notified to cover Tehran, and disorder was forestalled.

Further anxiety concerned possible pretensions to the throne by two of the Shah's powerful sons. Zell as-Soltan, the shah's oldest son, who was excluded from succession owing to his mother's low birth, had a long history of political power and ambition. Feared and powerful as autocratic governor of a large group of southern provinces, he had built up a virtual private army of Western-trained soldiers that put most of the regular army to shame, and he had not hesitated to put down anyone he considered a threat. His ambition to take the throne in place of his weak and sickly half-brother, Crown Prince Mozaffar ad-Din, was well known. Concern was also felt about his younger brother, Kamran Mirza Nayeb as-Saltaneh, frequently army chief and/or governor of Tehran, who had the advantage of being on the scene in Tehran. The combination of Amin as-Soltan, the Cossacks, and the clearly expressed support of both Russians and British for the legitimate heir, however, brought expressions of loyalty to the legitimate heir by both brothers.

Naser ad-Din Shah was scarcely an illustrious ruler, but he was a relatively strong one, under whom there were few serious tribal disorders or local revolts. The disorders he faced were more directly political, and he or his advisers at least knew when it was necessary to bend or give in. Unlike his son he did not squander his treasury, and the loan to compensate the tobacco company remained his only foreign loan. His interest in reform was sporadic at best, and he sacrificed or crippled the power of his only two serious reforming chief ministers when faced by the opposition of vested interests. In his last years he lost all concern for reform—a supposed project for codifying laws after the 1889 European trip came to nothing. Instead, he concentrated on his lifelong interest in women and young boys (one of the latter was said to be a repulsive constant companion) and on acquiring as much money and treasure as possible. He left no legacy of a state machinery that might weather what he must have known was coming—the rule of a weak and sickly successor.[4]

Mozaffar ad-Din Shah's relatively mild nature was shown in his treatment of Mirza Reza Kermani, who was interrogated but not tortured before he was hanged. The Iranian government also demanded from the Ottomans the extradition of Afghani and of his three followers still jailed in Trabzon. Sultan Abdülhamid refused to return Afghani, claiming he was an Afghan and not subject to Iranian jurisdiction. The three unfortunate progressives in Trabzon, however, who had no connection with the shah's assassination, were extradited, and the cruel new crown prince, Mohammad Ali Mirza, had them summarily executed in Tabriz. Continued Iranian demands for Afghani's extradition (Mirza Reza having said that Afghani was the only other person involved in the assassination) stopped when he became ill with cancer and died in 1897. These deaths and the cessation of *Qanun* ended one phase of the important "religious-radical alliance."[5]

Mozaffar ad-Din Shah's weakness was combined with mildness, and he was for a time open to reformist ideas. He permitted renewed activity by a man who had set up a modern type of higher school on the Ottoman model in Tabriz, where it had met with religious hostility. Such schools were now opened for the first time in Tehran. The shah also dismissed the unpopular Amin as-Soltan and later appointed the liberal and reformist Amin ad-Dauleh to be chief minister in 1897–98. The shah, however, also paid off his father's harem extravagantly, and was constantly eager for money to meet the incessant demands of his own courtiers, many of whom had come with him from Tabriz and pressed him to make up for years of lean waiting. The shah's doctors advised trips to European spas, and he wanted money for this too. When Amin ad-Dauleh was unable to raise a new loan from the British, and when his reform attempts in law and education aroused the opposition of ulama and courtiers, he was dismissed and Amin as-Soltan returned as premier.

One of Amin ad-Dauleh's projects was to invite in Belgian administrators to reorganize the customs, which had been farmed out by region, resulting in customs farmers underbidding each other to attract trade and also in farmers collecting far more than they paid in. The Belgian experiment was extended under Amin as-Soltan, and the Belgians' leader, M. Naus, was made minister of customs. This resulted in increased efficiency and collections, but also in widespread complaints by Iranian merchants that they were discriminated against in favor of foreigners, particularly the Russians, with whom the Belgians had close relations. The exact validity of these charges is unclear, but it is clear that many Iranian merchants had to pay more than formerly and that they blamed this on the shah, the prime minister, and the foreigners. Naus's influence soon extended far beyond customs, and he became de facto minister of finance.

Largely to pay for the foreign trips recommended by the Shah's doctors, Amin as-Soltan floated two large loans from Russia in 1900 and 1902. The first loan required Iran to pay off British debts and not to incur any other debts without Russian consent, and the second included major economic concessions. The Russians also insisted on a new customs treaty, signed in 1902, which gave key Russian goods lower rates than the already low 5 percent ad valorem. The income gained from the loans and from customs reform went largely for three extravagantly expensive trips to Europe that the shah and his entourage took between 1900 and 1905. Within Iran both government financial and economic conditions deteriorated.

Discontent with the government was becoming organized again. Secret oppositional societies became active in Tehran and elsewhere, and distributed inflammatory antigovernmental leaflets, called *shabnamehs* (night letters) because of their night distribution. Some members were afterward discovered and arrested. A new coalition among some of the leading ulama, courtiers, bazaaris, and secular progressives began to focus on the dismissal of Amin as-Soltan, who was seen as responsible for the alarming growth of loans and concessions to the Russians that were leading to Russian control of Iran. Even the British, alarmed at the growth of Russian influence, gave some money and encouragement to leading members of the ulama in Tehran and in the shrine cities of Iraq to help arouse activity against the Russian tide. Although they failed to stop the 1902 loan from Russia, the opposition became menacing enough to help force the dismissal of Amin as-Soltan (now adorned with the higher title of Atabak) in 1903. A decree execrating the Atabak as an unbeliever, attributed to the leading Shi'i ulama of Iraq, was widely circulated, although doubts were cast on its authenticity.[6]

The shah now appointed a reactionary relative of his, the Ain ad-Dauleh, as premier, but popular protests continued against the Belgian customs officials and against high prices. Secret societies grew, and some helped educate their members by reading and disseminating critical literature about Iran written in Persian abroad. This literature formed the basis for the ideological development of many Iranians who had not traveled abroad or received a modern education. It included works by men of Persian Azerbaijani origin living in Russian Transcaucasia, such as Fath Ali Akhundzadeh. His anonymous *Kamal ad-Dauleh va Jalal ad-Dauleh,* a collection of fictitious epistles describing conditions in Iran, was bitterly critical. This series of Persian letters was imitated by Mirza Aqa Khan Kermani, who also wrote other books and articles critical of Iranian conditions. Also widely read were the educational works of Talebzadeh, an Azerbaijan emigre to Transcaucasia, and especially the *Travelbook of Ibrahim Beg* by Zain al-Abedin Maraghe'i, a book of fictitious travels in Iran that mercilessly exposed the evils of Iranian society. Less known, but not without influence, were other critical works, such as James Morier's *Hajji Baba of Isfahan* in a translation by Mirza Habib Esfahani, which added whole pages of additional and more contemporary criticism to the original, and the *True Dream* by the progressive preachers from Isfahan, Jamal ad-Din Esfahani and Malek al-Motakallemin. Such fiction reinforced the impression created by the reformist political writings of Malkom Khan and others, and by the newspapers published abroad and sent into Iran (with greater freedom under Mozaffar ad-Din than under Naser ad-Din), which were now joined by *Parvaresh* and *Sorayya* from Cairo and *Habl al-Matin* from Calcutta.[7] The only papers that could be legally distributed in Iran continued to be official or semiofficial ones.

Some Iranians now began to plan revolutionary action, and revolutionary sentiment was strengthened by the Russo-Japanese War of 1904–05 and the Russian Revolution of 1905. Iranians knew that Russia would intervene against any attempt to overthrow or undermine the Qajar government, but with the Russian government fully occupied first with war and then with revolution, it was a propitious time to move. Also, the strength shown by the supposedly backward Japanese against the dreaded Russians gave people courage, as did the shaking of such a potent autocracy as Russia by revolution. The sight of the only Asian constitutional power defeating the only major European nonconstitutional power not only showed formerly weak Asians overcoming the seemingly omnipotent West, but aroused much new interest in a constitution as a "secret of strength."

The Iranian constitutional revolution is usually dated from December 1905, when the governor of Tehran beat the feet of several sugar merchants for not lowering their raised sugar prices as ordered, which they insisted were beyond their control owing to high import prices. A large group of mollas and bazaaris then took sanctuary (bast) in the royal mosque of Tehran—whence they were dispersed by agents of Ain ad-Dauleh. A large crowd of ulama then decided, at the suggestion of the prominent liberal mujtahid, Sayyed Mohammad Tabataba'i, to retire to the shrine of Shahzadeh Abd al-Azim and formulate demands for the shah. The crucial demand was for a representative *adalatkhaneh* (house of justice) of which the meaning and composition were left unclear—perhaps in order to maintain the unity of modernizers and traditional ulama. The shah dismissed the unpopular governor of Tehran, and in January 1906 agreed to the adalatkhaneh, upon which the ulama returned to Tehran.

The shah and Ain ad-Dauleh showed no sign of fulfilling the promise, however, and acts of violence against the innocent continued in both Tehran and the provinces. Preaching against the government by the popular radical preachers Sayyed Jamal ad-Din Esfahani and Shaikh Mohammad Va'ez increased, and provided a potent means of mass political enlightenment in the absence of an open oppositional press. Sayyed Jamal was expelled from Tehran. Confronting a strong popular attempt to keep Shaikh Mohammad from being ousted, an officer killed a young sayyed. After this a great mass of mollas and some others left Tehran to take bast in the city of Qom, in July 1906. Even more bazaar merchants and tradesmen in numbers reaching twelve thousand to fourteen thousand took bast in the British legation, and Tehran business was at a standstill. Now the protesters demanded not only the dismissal of Ain ad-Dauleh but also establishment of a representative assembly or *majles*—an idea put forth by the advanced constitutionalists. Although not yet among the agreed-upon demands, a constitution, or *mashruteh,* began to be discussed by the advanced reformers.

At the end of July the shah dismissed Ain ad-Dauleh, and early in August he accepted the majles. The first majles was elected by a six-class division of electors that gave great representation to the guilds (mainly middle-class elements who often chose ulama representatives). Subsequent majleses elected by a one-class system were dominated by the landlords and rich. Early majleses had many elected ulama as deputies. Tehran, the most advanced city politically aside from Tabriz, had disproportionate representation.

The first majles opened in October 1906, as soon as the Tehran deputies were elected. A committee was assigned to write the Fundamental Law, which the shah delayed signing until he was mortally ill, in December 1906; a longer Supplementary Fundamental law was drafted in 1907 and signed by the new shah, Mohammad Ali, in October. These two documents, based largely on the Belgian constitution, formed the core of the first Iranian constitution until its replacement in 1979, although after 1912 the constitution was more often honored in the breach than the observance. The intent of the constitution was to set up a true constitutional monarchy in which majles approval was required on all important matters, including foreign loans and treaties, and in which ministers would be responsible to the majles. Equality before the law and personal rights and freedoms, subject to a few limits, were also guaranteed, despite the protests of some ulama that members of minority religions should not have equal status with those of the state religion, Islam.

The majles quickly showed its patriotism by refusing a new Russian loan and beginning plans instead for a national bank, which, however, ultimately foundered owing to lack of capital. Two conservative constitutional provisions, for a group of mujtahids to pass on the compatibility of laws with Islam and for a half-appointed upper house, were approved but not implemented.

The new freedoms of press and assembly caused a sudden flourishing of newspapers, which not only carried direct political news and comments, but also published some of the best new poetry and satire. Particularly noteworthy was the *Sur-e Esrafil* with its poems and the brilliant political and anticlerical satire of the young writer Dehkhoda. Revolutionary societies or *anjomans* were formed throughout Iran, some of them based on older guilds or fraternal groups that now became actively involved in politics. The word *anjoman* was also used for the town councils, usually elected, which now appeared for the first time in many cities with parliamentary encouragement.

In January 1907 the ineffectual Mozaffar ad-Din Shah died, and was succeeded by his cruel and autocratic son, Mohammad Ali Shah. Although the new Shah had to take an oath to support the constitution, he did not invite any majles members to his coronation, and he recalled as prime minister the Atabak, who had been traveling abroad since his dismissal in 1903. As the constitution was not categorical about who really appointed the prime minister, and the majles wished to avoid a direct clash with the new shah, they accepted the appointment despite hostile telegrams from anjomans and arguments in the majles. Conflicts over the Atabak's return and over the constitution occurred between the conservative party in the majles, led by the two prime mujtahid leaders of the revolution, Sayyed Mohammad Tabataba'i and the less principled Sayyed Abdollah Behbehani and by liberal officials; and the smaller democratic left, represented especially by the deputies from the city of Tabriz led by the brilliant young Sayyed Hasan Taqizadeh. Tabriz and its surrounding province of Azerbaijan made up the advanced body of the revolution; more modernized economically, heavily involved in international trade, and in contact through travel and emigration with the similarly Turkish-speaking areas of Istanbul and Russian Transcaucasia (where many thousands emigrated temporarily or permanently every year, and whence arms were imported), Tabriz was uniquely situated to play a vanguard role. Some Tabrizis and other Azerbaijanis even preached socialist ideas, learned in Caucasia, and formed a small Social Democratic party.

The Atabak did not fulfill the shah's hope that he would get rid of the majles, but rather tried to strike a compromise between the shah and courtiers on the one hand and the majles conservatives and moderates on the other. In so doing, he aroused the distrust of both the autocrats and the radicals. He was assassinated by a member of a radical group on August 31, 1907; but there is convincing evidence that the shah was also planning his assassination and may even have penetrated the assassin's group.[8] The shah hoped to use the assassination as an excuse to suppress the revolutionaries, but in fact it encouraged them and increased their strength and boldness.

On the same date, August 31, 1907, the Anglo-Russian Entente settling the two governments' differences in Tibet, Afghanistan, and Iran was signed. The growth of the German threat to Britain encouraged this treaty, which hurt Iranians who had counted on British help against Russian intervention. The treaty divided Iran into three spheres, with northern and central Iran, including Tehran and Isfahan, in the Russian sphere; southeast Iran in the British sphere; and an area in between (ironically including the area where oil was first found in 1908) in the neutral zone. The Iranians were neither consulted on the agreement nor informed of the terms when it was signed.

After an unsuccessful attempt on his life, the shah achieved, following one failed coup, a successful coup d'état with the help of the Russian-led Cossack Brigade in June 1908. The majles was closed and many popular nationalist leaders, especially those of more advanced views, were arrested and executed. The radical preachers Jamal ad-Din Esfahani (caught while trying to flee), Malek al-Motakallemin and the editor of *Sur-e Esrafil*, Mirza Jahangir Khan (the last two had Azali Babi ties), were among those killed. Taqizadeh along with some others found refuge in the British Legation, whence he went abroad for a time.

While the rest of the country bowed to royal control, the city of Tabriz which, exceptionally, had formed an armed and drilled popular guard, held out against royal forces. The leaders of this popular resistance were brave men of humble origin. One of them, Sattar Khan, had defied the royal order to put up white flags as a sign of surrender to the approaching royal forces, and had instead gone around with his men tearing down white flags, thus initiating the Tabriz resistance. With the help of his coleader, Baqer Khan, Sattar Kahn and their men held out for months against an effective siege by royalist troops. When food supplies became critical the Russians sent troops into Tabriz ostensibly to protect Europeans, but effectively they took over. Many of the popular forces, known alternatively as *Mojahedin* or *Feda'iyan,* both implying self-sacrificing fighters for the faith, left for the nearby Caspian province of Gilan, where they were joined by a local revolutionary armed force, and together they began a march on Tehran. Meanwhile the Bakhtiari tribe, which had grudges against the Qajars and had some leaders who were genuinely liberal and others who wanted to control the central government themselves, helped liberate Isfahan from royalist forces and began moving northward toward Tehran. The Bakhtiaris and the northern revolutionaries converged on Tehran in July 1909. The shah took refuge with the Russians and his minor son Ahmad was made shah with the moderate Oxford-educated Naser al-Molk as regent.

The second majles was elected under a new electoral law calling for a single class of voters, and was marked by differences between what were now considered parties—the Moderates, led by Behbehani, who was assassinated by a left extremist in 1910, and the new progressive and nationalist Democratic party led by men like Taqizadeh, who was unjustly forced to leave Iran after Behbehani's assassination, with which he was unconnected.

Iran's chief problem remained finances, with the related problem of reestablishing control over the provinces, many of which were more subject than ever to tribal disorders and robberies, and remitted little of their due taxes. Desiring a foreign treasurer general unconnected with the British or the Russians, the Iranians consulted the American government and brought in a young American expert, Morgan Shuster, to control and reform their finances. Shuster planned to set up a tax-collecting gendarmerie, and to head it he proposed an officer in the British Indian army, then with the British Legation in Tehran, Major Stokes, who agreed to resign his commission and position. The Russians protested that the Anglo-Russian agreement meant that they should control any such officials in the north and convinced the British to support their position. In November 1911 the Russians sent an ultimatum demanding the dismissal of Shuster and the agreement of Iran not to engage foreigners without British and Russian consent. The majles refused the ultimatum, but as Russian troops advanced toward Tehran, the more compliant Naser al-Molk and the "moderate" and heavily Bakhtiari cabinet forcibly dissolved the majles accepted the ultimatum, and dismissed Shuster in December 1911.[9]

These events marked the real end of the revolution, which may be considered a short-term failure, but which left an important legacy. In addition to the constitution itself, a series of financial reforms ending feudal grants and regularizing financial practices remained on the books, as did steps toward greater civil jurisdiction in the courts, and the majles as a guardian against certain foreign encroachments. Another important new feature of the period before and during the revolution was the entry of many women into the political arena. Although women had long participated in bread riots, they now put on political demonstrations, and there were women's anjomans and a women's newspaper.[10] This trend was to grow significantly after World War I. Finally, the ulama-bazaari-secular alliance had again showed its ability to arouse political action and change policy, even though the alliance was strained by internal differences.

Although the constitution was never abrogated, no new majles was elected until 1914, Russian troops continued to occupy the north,

anjomans were dissolved, press censorship restored, and power returned
to a conservative cabinet under the watchful control of Britain and especially Russia. Despite the constitution and political awakening that remained as positive achievements, many reverted to apathy and cynicism
when faced by the restoration of foreign and conservative controls.

In 1901 a British subject, William Knox D'Arcy, had been granted a
concession for oil in all Iran except the five northern provinces—Russian
reaction being forestalled by the ruse of presenting the (Persian) text of
the concession to the Russian legation at a time when the premier knew
that the Russians' translator was away. Although the first years' explorations were discouraging, oil was finally discovered in the southwest in
1908. The Anglo-Persian Oil Company was formed in 1909. In 1912 the
British navy converted from coal to oil, and in 1914 the British government bought a majority of shares in the company holding the concession. The British backed the virtually autonomous Shaikh Khaz'al, the
most powerful Arab leader of Khuzistan province, and also entered into
independent relations with the adjacent Bakhtiari tribal leaders.[11] British
troops were stationed in this neutral zone region, and the British exercised a control in the south comparable to that held by Russia in the
north. Given their decades of experience with the British and Russians, it
was no wonder that many Iranian nationalists and democrats turned to
the Germans for support during World War I.

5

War and Reza Shah: 1914–1941

1914–1921

World War I brought new problems and devastation to Iran. It promoted revolutionary and democratic sentiment and fueled the desire among many to reconstruct Iran as an independent country. New movements for social change came to a head in the postwar period.

When war began, the Iranian government declared neutrality, but Iran was strategically located and four powers used it as a battlefield. The Turks moved into Azerbaijan in the fall of 1914, after the Russians withdrew. The Germans played on Iranian anti-British and anti-Russian sentiments. The Kaiser was presented as a partisan of Islam, and Iranians were urged to respond to the Ottoman sultan's call for a Holy War on the Allies. British power spread when that of the Turks, Germans, and Russians declined.

Even before the war the British tried to negotiate with Russia for a new partition of Iran, with Britain to control the neutral zone where the oil was. When war came, England promised Russia postwar control of Istanbul and the Straits in return for British rule in most of Iran's neutral zone, and a secret treaty for this was signed in March 1915. Unlike the 1907 Treaty, this contained no reference to Iranian independence but said that, in the Russian sphere, Russia expected recognition of its "full liberty of action,"[1] and did not limit British activities in its zone.

The year 1915 saw the extension of fighting in Iran, with new hardships for the population. In the south the German agent Wassmuss, "The German Lawrence," organized a tribal revolt against the British, who were also active in the south. The Russians moved more forces into the north and forced the dissolution of the new third majles. Most of the majles nationalists were pro-German and anti-Russian, and they now formed a provisional government at Qom. The young Ahmad Shah continued to reign in Tehran, and so there were two governments, neither of which had much authority in a divided Iran. Later Allied advances forced the nationalist government to retreat to Kermanshah and then to flee Iran, but many of its members continued active in Istanbul and Berlin.

The Germans sent money to Iran and in 1915 invited Hasan Taqizadeh to Berlin to create a Persian committee to disseminate propaganda and possibly create a nationalist government. Taqizadeh's review *Kaveh*, 1916–22, was widely read in Iran. His coworkers included important writers like Mohammad Ali Jamalzadeh, son of Jamal ad-Din Esfahani, and Hosain Kazemzadeh, later editor of another nationalist paper, *Iranshahr*. The wartime issues of *Kaveh* were largely nationalist and pro-German, but also had cultural content.

In 1916 the Russians were dominant in the north and the British regained control in the south. That year the British formed a local force, the South Persia Rifles, under the command of Sir Percy Sykes. By late 1917 the British controlled the south.

Nineteen seventeen was a year of turmoil with battles throughout Iran. The power of Iranian nationalists at Qom and in central Iran ended when the Russians moved into the area. British and Russian troops occupied nearly all Iran by late 1917, although the British still fought Qashqa'i tribal forces into 1918. Foreign control was weakened, however, by events in Russia. The March Revolution aroused hopes that Russian troops would withdraw, but this occurred only in the fall, when Russian troops in Iran revolted and were recalled by the new Bolshevik government. This had a liberating effect on the north even though the British moved into some of the positions abandoned by the Russians.

The war had a devastating effect, as the country was a battlefield, on which many were killed, and farmlands were ruined by invading armies. Peasants were taken from the fields and forced to work on military projects. Irrigation works requiring careful upkeep were destroyed, and cultivated areas and livestock were reduced. In some Asian countries, like India and China, the war stimulated industrial and urban development, but in Iran it caused a fall in urban enterprise and population, even though some types of local trade and crafts were stimulated. Central authority declined, and local landowners and tribal chiefs reasserted their independence and rebuilt their power.

The war's disruption awakened many Iranians to the need for strong and independent government. Nationalists' influence grew and there were wartime uprisings. The most serious antigovernmental and nationalist movement was a revolt in the Caspian province of Gilan, from 1917 on. A local leader, Kuchek Khan, led a movement for more democratic and egalitarian rule. The partisans of this movement were known as *jangalis* (forest dwellers) because they operated in the wooded area of Gilan. By 1918 the jangalis controlled Gilan and parts of nearby provinces. In Azerbaijan a democratic movement also reached large proportions toward the end of the war. The movements were not separatist but hoped to spread their reforms to all Iran.

When the war was over, Iran faced heightened problems, among which were food scarcity, high prices, the revived power of tribal chiefs and landlords, and the diminished power of the central government. The British, whose troops occupied most of the country, spent money freely in Iran during the war to ensure the complaisance of tribal and governmental leaders and, by the war's end, had great influence over Iran's rulers.

Late in 1917, the Bolsheviks renounced Russia's unequal treaties, loans, and concessions. Revolution in Russia and the disorders caused by war gave impetus to revived social and nationalist movements, which challenged British supremacy. In 1918 trade unions were formed in Tehran and Tabriz, among postal, printing, and other workers, and there were some successful strikes. Reform movements were especially strong in Tehran, and in the northern provinces of Gilan, Mazanderan, and Azerbaijan.[2]

Adding to discontent was a severe famine in 1918–19, which may have killed as much as one-quarter of the population in the north.[3] The famine was related to wartime Western incursions, a reduced crop area and small harvest, food needs of foreign troops, and worsened distribution. Famine was aggravated by hoarding and speculation by landlords, dealers, and officials.

From 1918 to 1921 Britain moved to consolidate control over Iran. British subsidies to the government helped insure its complaisance. In the summer of 1918 the British made Kuchek Khan halt the advance of his forces and sign an agreement that limited his control to Gilan, letting

British troops control neighboring areas. Soon afterward an Iranian government, headed by Prime Minister Vosuq ad-Dauleh and subservient to
the British, was formed, and was kept alive by British subsidies. The
British government, particularly Foreign Secretary Curzon, wished to
formalize British control over Iran by a treaty that would amount to a
British protectorate. Iran was useful both for oil and against Russia,
and British control could make Iran part of a cordon sanitaire around
the Bolsheviks.

The Iranian government, hoping to gain popularity by backing a
nationalist cause, tried to attend the Versailles Peace Conference to receive restitution for Iran's wartime sufferings. Iran demanded reparations and territory taken by Russia in 1813 and 1828, but the conference
did not listen, saying Iran had not been a belligerent.

The Bolshevik government encouraged nationalists in Iran with a
note detailing the repudiation of tsarist privileges. All Russian concessions in Iran were renounced, except the Caspian fisheries concession,
which was left to further negotiation; capitulations were given up and
Iran's debts to Russia cancelled. The Russians proposed a friendship
treaty with Iran, but the pro-British government, which was negotiating a treaty with Britain, delayed this. The British sent new troops to
Iran, and Iranian complaisance was underwritten by large bribes to the
treaty's negotiators. Negotiations were secret, but the treaty was made
public after Premier Vosuq ad-Dauleh signed. By the Anglo-Persian
Treaty of 1919, the British would supply advisers for the Iranian government; British officers and arms would be sent to the army; a large British
loan would pay for the advisers and army; the British would develop
transportation and communications; and the tariff would be revised.[4]
The treaty was interpreted as a British protectorate ensuring administrative and economic control.

The United States and France were concerned that the treaty would
give a monopoly to British advisers and interests in Iran. The American
minister reported home essentially endorsing the "Persian patriots'"
view of the treaty as a protectorate.[5] In response to American queries
whether American advisers would be permitted in Iran, Curzon said that
if they met with British approval they could come, and the British tried
to keep four French law professors from coming to Iran.

The British acted as though the unratified treaty were in force, sending a mission to take over Iranian finances and also military and administrative advisers. Iranian reaction to the treaty became more hostile

through 1919. A nationalist movement with goals counter to the treaty grew. Iranian newspapers attacked the treaty and its signers, and demonstrations against it occurred in many areas. The government dealt with opposition by jailings and the banishment of opponents from Tehran. The government also tried to manipulate the majles elections.

Resistance to the treaty continued through 1920, and in some areas merged with a popular democratic movement. This movement grew especially in Azerbaijan, a region much affected by Western incursions and ideas. A Democratic party was formed there under Shaikh Mohammad Khiabani, a leader of the 1905–11 movement in Azerbaijan. By April 1920 it was strong enough to force the government's agents to quit Tabriz. The movement was reformist and also expressed newly awakened national sentiments of the Turkish-speaking Azerbaijanis, some of whom felt oppressed by the Persian central government. Khiabani formed an autonomous local government and renamed the province Azadistan (Azad=free). Reforms like price control were undertaken to counteract continued inflation. The success of the Azerbaijan movement encouraged similar forces elsewhere.

The British, however, continued to act as if the treaty were in force. They sent experts to reorganize the armed forces, got an option for a railroad from Iraq to Tehran, took much control over Iranian finances, and brought about a revision of the Iranian tariff. The tariff law of 1920 was favorable to British imports, letting them enter at lower rates, and, hence, providing less protection and revenue. The tariff was unfavorable to Russia. Russo-Iranian trade almost stopped; goods formerly imported from Russia were in short supply, while those exported there lost markets. Reliance on British trade made the trade balance more negative. The justification for British financial control—solving Iran's fiscal problems— did not materialize: inflation continued, and tax reform was not tried.

Inaction was dangerous, given Iran's increasingly rebellious mood. Growth in discontent and its more leftward orientation appeared in the consolidation and changes in Kuchek Khan's movement in Gilan. The movement had shrunk when British and White Russian forces occupied much of north Iran, but grew again in the winter of 1919–20. In the spring of 1920, Red Army troops landed at Anzali to chase out White Russian troops there, and this helped clear out forces hostile to the jangalis. Kuchek Khan got increasing leftist support and was encouraged by the Bolsheviks. In June 1920, Kuchek Khan's forces, in control of all Gilan, declared the establishment of an Iranian Soviet Socialist Republic, although the measures taken were more democratic-reformist than so-cialist. A Communist party was formed in the area, but Kuchek Khan and many other governmental leaders had disagreements with the Com-munists, who were following a radical line favored by Ahmad (Avedis) Soltanzadeh. The jangalis aimed at changing all Iran on the Gilan model and threatened the conservative central government. Lenin, however, followed a pragmatic line and in 1920 began secret negotiations for a Russian agreement with the Iranian government, which, once attained, implied giving up on imminent revolution.

Middle-class nationalists often did not sympathize with Kuchek Khan's movement, but it bolstered their desire to change the govern-ment. Conservative nationalists wanted to divert attention from internal problems and hoped that an anti-British display would reduce demands for social change. Radical and antiradical forces were thus united against the pro-British cabinet, and this brought the resignation of Vosuq ad-Dauleh in June 1920. A government formed under a moderate national-ist, Moshir ad-Dauleh, announced the suspension of the Anglo-Persian Treaty until British and Russian troops quit Iran and the majles could debate freely.

The British and their Iranian allies forced the resignation of Moshir ad-Dauleh in the fall, and the new prime minister, Sepahdar, was more complaisant to the British. He put British officers in command of the Cossacks and prepared to submit the treaty to the newly elected majles. The Sepahdar government was never able to put the treaty to the majles, however, owing to continued opposition.

The government suppressed the Azerbaijan movement through use of the Cossack Brigade. Khiabani was killed and reprisals taken. There were, however, outbreaks of violence in Azerbaijan in the next two years. The Kuchek Khan forces extended their control to the province of Mazanderan, but split internally. The left wanted confiscation and na-tionalization of land, which Kuchek Khan refused. After the Congress of the Peoples of the East in Soviet Baku in the fall of 1920, in which Iran got much attention, the Iranian Communist party adopted a more mod-erate program. Iran was seen as between feudalism and capitalism, and socialist measures were rejected; unity with bourgeois groups and win-ning of the peasants through land reform were stressed. Some of the jangali left, particularly those leading the army, rejected this approach, but the Communist party leadership began negotiations with Kuchek Khan to reestablish a united program.

Iran's government now turned to the United States for backing and aid. The United States was showing new interest in Iran and its oil; and, in August 1920, the State Department instructed its Tehran representative:

> It is assumed that . . . you have discreetly and orally conveyed to the Persian Foreign Office information to the effect that the Department believes that American companies will seek concessions in the northern provinces and that the Department hopes that American companies may obtain such concessions. . . . The Department has taken the position that the monopolization of the production of an essential raw material, such as petroleum, by means of exclusive concessions or other arrangements, is in effect contrary to the principle of equal treatment of the nationals of all foreign countries.[6]

Iran's government wanted American advisers for ministries, including Finances and War; and an American manager for an Iranian national bank, and oil and transport concessions to the United States.

In the face of hostility, the British became doubtful about their treaty, and the United States began to consider taking over some of England's former position. Late in 1920 the Iranians requested a loan from the United States. The American government did not respond immediately, but negotiations for advisers and concessions continued.

In 1920 and 1921 negotiations were also proceeding for a friendship treaty with Soviet Russia. A treaty was needed to formalize the Russian renunciation of concessions; to reestablish normal trade broken off during civil war in the Caucasus; and to define future relations between the two countries. Negotiations broke down when Iran insisted on the return of territory taken by Russia in the nineteenth century.

By early 1921, there had been no attempt at basic solutions to problems that had been aggravated by the war. The economic crisis had abated, owing to a revival in agriculture and the end of fighting. Problems of economic structure remained as before. A British observer noted that landlords had independent armies for rent collection, peasants were like serfs, and in the villages, "a parasitic group of underlings . . . were growing rich by robbing their master, and also by bleeding the poor farmer."[7] Only in Azerbaijan and Gilan were economic reforms like price control and rent reduction begun. There was, however, a new breadth and intensity of nationalist and reform movements. These movements could take much credit for keeping Iran from becoming a virtual British colony. By early 1921 the British ceased to press for their treaty, owing to strong Iranian opposition, backed by American and Russian official opinion.

The postwar social movement in Iran had a rather sporadic and regional character. The negative effects of the war help account for both the genesis and the limitations of this movement. The war did not stimulate urban development or national economic cohesion, but furthered regionalism and disunity. The popular movement was disunited, and did not have a national program that could challenge the government or exercise strong influence on national affairs. Western intervention also lessened the effectiveness of popular movements.

The immediate postwar period did, however, see intellectual developments that helped spread nationalist ideas. The second series of Taqizadeh's Berlin-based *Kaveh* included high-level research on Iran and expressed patriotic, secularist, and reformist themes. Taqizadeh's view in this period was that except in promoting the Persian language, Iran should totally follow Western models to progress and be independent. Among *Kaveh*'s topics were public education, equality for women, the need for a strong central government and to control the tribes, and advocacy of sports and more translations from Western languages. There were also other nationalist publications as well as publications by Communists and socialists.

1921–1925

Dissatisfaction with Iran's postwar governments, especially among nationalists, along with absence of any strong national party, made it possible for a small group of men to overthrow the Sepahdar government. Sayyed Zia ad-Din, known as a pro-British moderate, led the civilian side of this movement. More important was participation, along with his troops, of the self-made Cossack Brigade commander, Reza Khan. While there is no written evidence of British Foreign Office involvement in the coup, the commander of British military forces in Iran, General Ironside, backed Reza Khan's rise to power in the Cossack Brigade and encouraged him to undertake a coup. The Iranian gendarmerie, a quasi-military force begun in 1911, which during and after World War I sided with the Democrats and in some cases with the Communists, joined the movement.[8] Sayyed Zia became prime minister in a new government following the Cossacks' entry into Tehran in February 1921, with Reza Khan as war minister. Control over the modernized Cossack Brigade, was a power base for the new government, and particularly for Reza Khan. By 1921 the British saw a protectorate was impossible and favored a strong government that could suppress the jangalis and other threats from leftist or Russian-backed movements.

The accession of this government marks a turning point in Iranian history. The government showed a new independence of the West in many matters, and Western interference became more indirect. Reza Khan was primarily interested in building a strong centralized state, and his reform efforts were mainly measures for centralization and efficiency, including suppression of tribal and autonomist movements and strengthening the army and bureaucracy. The demands of the middle classes and some nationalists were partly met through centralization, the growth of trade and of the civil service, the rejection of open British control, and the expectation of further reforms once the strengthened army took control of the country.

Despite his moderate and pro-British background, Sayyed Zia issued a proclamation promising land reform, national independence, a plan for a modern, industrialized economy, and other social reforms. This program suggests the power of the reform movement, which influenced Sayyed Zia's words. Sayyed Zia also announced the annulment of the Anglo-Persian Treaty. He hastened to conclude the Russo-Iranian Treaty, signed on February 26, 1921, which led to the restoration of normal relations with Russia.

Articles I and II of the treaty contained Russia's renunciation of imperialist policies and all tsarist treaties with Iran. Article III recognized the Russo-Iranian border of 1881, which meant a small cession of territory acquired after 1881 by Russia. Article IV promised nonintervention by Russia in Iran's internal affairs. Articles V and VI, much discussed since, prohibited any armed organization in Iran or Russia whose aim was to "engage in acts of hostility" against the other, and allowed Russia to intervene against the troops of any power using Iran as a base of operations against Russia. Majles ratification of the treaty was delayed for a year, partly owing to these clauses, but ratification came soon after a statement by the Russians that "Articles V and VI are intended to apply only to cases in which preparations have been made for a considerable armed attack . . . by the partisans of the [tsarist] regime which has been overthrown or by its supporters."[9]

Further treaty articles renounced Russian loans, ceded to Iran all assets of the Russian Bank, Russian roads, telegraph and telephone lines, and all other concessions and property. Russia retained rights to the Caspian fisheries, and a new contract for them was later negotiated.

Extraterritoriality was renounced. The Iranians promised not to cede any former Russian concessions or property to a third party.[10]

Some economic recovery came with the resumption of more normal trade. Reza Khan concentrated on modernizing and strengthening the army, which increased his power. Personal ambition and policy disagreements led Reza Khan to force Sayyed Zia's resignation and make him flee Iran. A new cabinet was formed under Qavam as-Saltaneh, a powerful official with more liberal leanings than most of his class, but real power was increasingly in the hands of Reza Khan.

The first concern of the Qavam-Reza government was to put down movements that threatened the established order. Particularly urgent for them was Gilan. In May 1921, a government was established in Gilan including both Communists and the non-Communist forces of Kuchek Khan. There was discord over the extent of reforms, and by late 1921, Kuchek Khan turned against the left and expelled them from the government. Internal discord made it relatively easy for the Tehran government to march in and take over at the end of 1921; Kuchek Khan was not taken but froze to death.

Also in 1921 there was revolt among Kurds and others in Khorasan, in northeastern Iran (separate from the majority of Kurds in the West). Anti-foreign and anti-government feeling were high enough among the tribespeople and peasants to permit the temporary establishment of a new government in the area, based on a program of radical social reform. The government used its superior armed forces to put down this movement in the fall of 1921.In January 1922 came another revolt in Azerbaijan, led by the leftist gendarmerie officer, Major Lahuti, who was soon chased out and went to Soviet territory, where he continued to be an influential writer until his death in 1957.[11]

There were further popular outbreaks in late 1921 and early 1922, but then the postwar social movements in northern Iran were suppressed. They had suffered from geographical disunity and lack of a national program or party, owing to the backward economic and social state of Iran, its territorial disunity, and the absence of strong urban leadership groups. Many who favored change, including some Democrats, Socialists, and Communists, backed the Zia-Reza coup and Reza's early reforms. The postwar popular movements had helped prevent the retention of power by men who were open tools of the British. The new government, with its greater backing and growing army, which incorporated the Democrat-oriented gendarmerie, was more effective against protest movements than the older pro-British government had been. Middle- and upper-class nationalists were alienated from protest partly because of their fear of radicalism and regional separatism, and partly because most of them initially supported Reza Khan's government and program. Largely due to Reza Khan's growing and increasingly efficient armed forces, by the early 1920s all protest movements were put down and trade unions and opposition propaganda were increasingly suppressed.

The 1921–25 period saw the further development of nationalist ideas. Though journals were censored and sometimes closed, newspapers of varying orientations continued to publish. A few were still published abroad, notably *Iranshahr,* edited in Germany 1922–27 by Hosain Kazemzadeh Iranshahr and widely read in Iran. It developed further the program of Kaveh and advocated secular nationalism, including universal secular education, women's rights, and Persian-oriented centralization as against local languages. It voiced anti-clericalism, hostility to the Muslim Arab conquest of Iran, and glorification of pre-Islamic Iran—themes that became common among many Iranians for decades and were, minus their original democratic orientation, made into the official nationalism of the Pahlavi shahs.[12]

Reza Khan undertook the organization of the army on the British model and created the first sizable modern armed force Iran had seen. Tax collection and finances were centralized. The government also reopened negotiations for American advisers. The American government was interested in Iran but did not want to act counter to the British, who were seen as an antidote to Bolshevism.

In the summer of 1921 the Iranian government sent the diplomat Hosain Ala to Washington to discuss an oil concession and a program for American advisers. The Iranians requested technical advice, a loan, and investment for modernization to stop the threat of communism. The United States government was cautious about British interests but talks progressed. Standard Oil Company of New Jersey negotiated a concession for the oil of north Iran, excluded from the Anglo-Persian Oil Company (APOC) concession.

The Standard Oil concession was ratified by the majles in November 1921, but brought protests from Britain and Russia. The APOC objected to the breaking of its oil monopoly, the Russians said the concession violated the terms of the Russo-Iranian treaty, and some Iranians objected to American influence. The Standard concession forbade transfers of rights to other companies, but, to assuage the British, Standard agreed to share oil with APOC on a fifty-fifty basis, in return for compensation elsewhere. This violation of terms made the government heed objections to the concession, which was de facto nullified. In August 1922, negotiations began for a northern concession to the Sinclair Oil Company.

Negotiations for American advisers, particularly to reorganize finances, continued. When the State Department recommended Dr. A. C. Millspaugh, then in charge of oil affairs in the department, the British did not object.[13] They apparently felt that as Iran would not allow British advisers, Americans would be next best.

Millspaugh signed a contract with the Iranian government that gave him full control of the Iranian budget and financial administration. The Iranians would grant no concessions and make no financial decisions without Millspaugh's agreement. Several Americans accompanied Millspaugh's mission. His program centered on increasing taxes and the efficiency of collection and attracting more foreign capital investment. He used the army to insure tax collection. His main contribution to taxation was to introduce, with the approval of Reza Khan, indirect taxes whose collection was assured but which hit the poor. Millspaugh sponsored a tobacco tax, a match tax, and a government sugar and tea monopoly, all of which affected the lower classes the most.[14]

Regarding foreign investments, while Millspaugh and the Iranian government were eager to attract American capital, Great Britain, still the most influential power, was hostile to inroads by others. Negotiations with Sinclair reached fruition in 1923, but Russian and British opposition, as well as strained relations with the U.S. after an American vice-consul's death at the hands of a crowd in Tehran, caused Sinclair to drop the concession.[15] This left Iran without the loan attached to the concession. Iranians became disillusioned with the American financial mission, and there was much hostile press comment.

Millspaugh tried to prevent Russo-Iranian agreement on the Caspian fisheries and on tariffs, though his claims on these points went against the 1921 Russian-Iranian Treaty. No agreement on these issues was reached while Millspaugh was present, and Russo-Iranian trade suffered. Millspaugh's failures made him increasingly unpopular, and disagreements with Reza Shah led to Millspaugh's resignation in 1927.

The British, rebuffed in their attempt to control all Iran, continued to try in the south. They took four years to evacuate their troops there, and considered plans for an autonomous state, including Khuzistan, the main oil province. These plans centered on Shaikh Khaz'al, the powerful Arab tribal chief. The British negotiated with Khaz'al and promised support against the central government. At the end of 1923, Khaz'al formed a group aiming at an independent south Iranian federation and got some Bakhtiari and Luri groups to follow him. The government put down the Lurs, but Khaz'al and his allies declared independence. The central government was now too strong for the rebels, however, and Khaz'al was met by the army and forced to surrender in 1924. Soon after this, Reza Khan negotiated with the British, who saw it was in their interest to come to terms with the newly powerful regime. The British henceforth usually supported Reza Khan.

Reza had taken over real control of Iran and in 1923 became prime minister and persuaded the weak shah to leave for Europe. The nationalist cleric Hasan Modarres broke with him over his proposal for two years' compulsory military service, which was also opposed by other ulama fearful of Western influence in the army and by many landlords. Conservatives then controlled the majles, but in elections for a fifth majles Reza Khan got support from the radical Socialist and reformist Revival Parties, both led by ex-Democrats. Some in the Revival Party were important in Reza's subsequent governments, like the jurist Ali Akbar Davar, the military officer Abd al-Hosain Taimurtash, and Mohammad Ali Forughi, a future prime minister. All advocated a reforming strong central state. Most Socialists, despite their more leftist program, also supported Reza Khan. With such support and electoral manipulation Reza got a fifth majles in 1924 that endorsed an extensive reform program, including compulsory military service, the abolition of titles, the obligation of all to have birth certificates and family names, a bill devoting new taxes to a trans-Iranian railroad, a metric system, and the adoption of the Persian solar calendar dating from the hijra.

Before Reza completely centralized power several parties, including both Socialists and Communists on the left, were active, as were a variety of organizations, newspapers, and journals. The Socialist and Communist Parties set up the Central Council of Federated Trade Unions in 1921, which led several strikes. As was true of earlier leftist groups, Azerbaijanis and Armenians had the strongest representation.

In 1924, influenced by Atatürk in Turkey, Reza inspired a campaign for a republic. This was too radical for clerical and other conservatives, who inspired hostile demonstrations. Reza capitulated on the republic. To placate the ulama he encouraged a clerical campaign against the

Baha'is. Also in July, U.S. Consul Robert Imbrie was beaten to death in a clerically led incident in Tehran to which the regime was rumored to be tied.

After being sure the British would not react, Reza in 1925 moved to change the dynasty. After a politic pilgrimage to Najaf and winning over considerable clerical support, he took the name of Pahlavi, evoking a heroic ancient dynasty. He then had the majles depose the Qajars in October 1925. Only four deputies voted no—Modarres, Taqizadeh, the left nationalist Yahya Daulatabadi, and Mohammad Mosaddeq. A constituent assembly endorsed the dynastic change in December, only three Socialist deputies abstaining.[16]

Under Reza Shah, Western incursions became far more indirect than before. The new shah was faced with a country still requiring major changes to undertake significant modernization. A Western observer in 1926 noted Iran's backwardness as compared to most Asian countries and claimed that the position of Iran's women was lower than in almost any other Muslim country, adding, "There is a tremendous gulf between the women of Cairo and Constantinople and the women of Teheran, even those of the very highest position."[17] Backwardness also continued in agriculture, and the wartime fall in agricultural production was not completely overcome by 1925.

There was little economic development before 1925. The poor had a growing tax burden, while the rich evaded taxes. The only important economic development took place in the British-owned oil industry. Production shot up from the prewar low of 80,800 tons a year to 4,556,000 tons in 1926.[18] Iran had several complaints against the British, claiming manipulations that lowered royalties and a failure to train Iranians for skilled jobs. Aside from royalties and the employment of some Iranian workers, the oil industry had little effect on Iranian socioeconomic life. It was in an isolated area where the British supplied almost all the economic needs. Before 1925 Iran failed to make productive use of royalties. The oil industry was an enclave that had little effect on the rest of the Iranian economy beyond what was contributed by royalties, which continued to be low.

If industry and agriculture remained backward in the postwar period, so too did other sectors, like health and education. Foreigners, especially missionaries, ran the first modern hospitals and schools, and Iranian governments did little. Only a small minority of Iranians was educated.[19] Regarding women, a few advances were made before 1925, as several

schools, welfare organizations, and journals were begun. Women's activities often encountered clerical opposition and even physical attacks.
Mohtaram Eskandari, the wife of the Socialist leader Solaiman Eskandari
and head of a girls' school, set up the Patriotic Women's Society. It
campaigned for new laws, had literacy classes, published a journal, and
staged plays. The best-known woman leader of the period, Sadeqeh
Daulatabadi, sister of Yahya Daulatabadi, was an active educationist and
journalist. She had to leave Isfahan in 1921 when her journal was shut
down. She then went to Paris and got a pioneering university degree and
returned to be active in Iran in the Reza Shah period. Urban women were
heavily veiled in public and segregated from men. Few jobs were open to
women, though they were subject to the worst exploitation in carpet and
textile workshops. Pioneering women leaders who worked for women's
education, welfare, and rights were joined by male intellectuals and poets
who wrote for these causes. The resulting schools, orphanages, and organizations laid the foundations for later improvements in women's position.[20] Changes in women's status long affected mainly the middle and
upper classes, though some classes and orphanages also helped poor
women.

For all its relative backwardness, Iran in 1925 felt great pressure for
change. To exist as an independent nation, Iran needed a civil service,
army, and efficient tax system. The middle classes grew after the war, and
many of them wanted new outlets for their talents and capital. The
revival of foreign trade meant a growth of Iranian merchant capital,
while profits achieved by speculators and others in the war were also
potential sources of investment. Before 1925, there were bare beginnings
of industry, notably textile mills, mostly in Isfahan, but this was insufficient to meet the middle class and modernizers' desire for investment
and modernization. Pressure mounted for industrial tariff protection
and for modern transportation to develop a national market and insure central control over the provinces. Also, the government wished to
break down the tribal-nomadic way of life in order to end a threat to
state power. The strengthening of the army and of the central government, the suppression of rebellious tribes, and the first majles-approved
modernizing measures were launched by Reza Shah before he became
monarch and formed a basis for further modernization.

Reza Shah soon began a further impressive program of modernization, though without reforming the old agrarian structures. "Modernization from above" was seen by Reza Shah and those around him as the

way to make Iran a strong, self-respecting nation that could hold its own in the modern world.

1925–1941

Reza Shah's reign saw a number of major changes in Iran's economy and society, but despite a formal retention of the constitution and majles elections, decision making was increasingly monopolized by the shah. Political life under Reza Shah was extremely limited, owing to the Shah's despotic controls and suppression of opposition. The death of Eshqi was early attributed to Reza Shah. The clerical opposition leader Modarres was imprisoned in 1929 and killed nine years later. Mohammad Mosaddeq, a high-born Western-trained liberal nationalist intellectual who started his Iranian official career as a teen-ager, continued briefly to attack Reza Shah's programs in the majles. He was soon put out of office and retired to his estate, reemerging to prominence in World War II. Other high-level oppositionists either kept quiet or were, at least for a time, co-opted by the regime, as was the former democratic leader of the constitutional revolution, Taqizadeh, who became minister of finance and minister to England. Such nationalists, as well as many advocates of women's rights, found Reza Shah's nationalist, secular program attractive enough for them to subordinate their other aims to it, at least for a time.

More striking was the fate of some of Reza Shah's top advisers and aides. Abdol Hosain Taimurtash, a highly able adviser and negotiator on whom the shah depended heavily, died in prison after the oil negotiations of 1933, in which the shah suspected him of double dealing. Sardar As'ad Bakhtiari, whose national power dated back to the constitutional revolution, became a leading supporter of Reza Shah, but was arrested and murdered in prison. Lesser men suspected of disloyalty were similarly treated, although some old and new politicians continued to serve Reza Shah throughout his reign. The majles became a rubber stamp and the constitution was paid lip service only. Communist and socialist groups and propaganda were outlawed by a 1931 law against "collectivism." The most important arrests under this law occurred in 1937, when fifty-three men were arrested, forty-five of whom were sent to prison and came to form the nucleus of the later Tudeh Party. Effective censorship meant that only official nationalism stressing national homogeneity, anticlericalism, modernity, and strength, which were read into the pre-Islamic past, could flourish.

The years 1925 to 1941 saw the partial fulfillment of a far larger modernization program than had ever been attempted in Iran. If the emphasis below seems critical, this may be a counterweight to the more usual listing of impressive changes, which may easily be found in various publications.[21]

Between 1925 and 1930 foundations were laid for a program of modernization from above. The income from high taxes on sugar and tea was saved for use on a railway. In 1925 a uniform land tax, to be based on a new land survey, was established. A conscription law, with universal service, was enacted in 1926. Army reform and strengthening was a primary concern of Reza Shah, and military expenses were for a time the largest budget item. This meant that the armed forces were large and modern enough during Reza Shah's reign to maintain governmental authority. Civil service reform in 1926 established a bureaucracy with certain ostensible educational standards. Like the army, the bureaucracy grew prodigiously and was a force supporting the government. The civil service became the major outlet for educated young men, and there was pressure to create more jobs in it, to which the government often responded.

The growth of the army and the bureaucracy contributed to urbanization, and Tehran's population grew greatly. Nearly all civil service jobs were in the capital, owing to a policy of centralization, with all important decisions made in Tehran. The growth of Tehran created new jobs for most urban groups. The army and civil service were channels for the spread of new ideas, although censorship and government propaganda limited published ideas largely to official nationalism.

A series of legal reforms in 1925–40 progressively reduced the judicial role of the clergy and increasingly introduced a modern, nonclerical judiciary and a uniform, centrally controlled legal system. From 1925 to 1928 three new codes of law, partly based on French models although incorporating large parts of a codified sharia, were approved. A new Commercial Code in 1925 curtailed ulama influence in commercial matters and recognized joint-stock companies and other principles of modern Western commerce. In 1926 a Criminal Code was approved, and in 1928 a Civil Code. A 1929 law restricted religious courts to marriage and divorce matters. In 1939–40 sharia courts were abolished and European-model civil and penal codes adopted.[22] Some ulama objected, but they had little strength against the bureaucracy, the army, and the commercial middle class. The role of clerics in the judiciary was greatly reduced, as only those who could pass examinations covering the new laws and modern subjects were allowed roles in the courts.

Judicial reform, new taxes, internal security, and centralization permitted the establishment of a more modern economy. Also important was Reza Shah's declaration, in the spring of 1927, that Iran would take control of its tariff policy within a year and not be bound by tariffs negotiated under duress. He also announced that other "capitulations" favoring foreigners would be abolished. (This was more easily accepted by the West, given Iran's new legal codes, which were adopted partly to end the capitulations.) In 1928 new commercial treaties were signed with most Western nations, raising tariffs on many goods. Tariff policy was primarily based on revenue needs, and protective tariffs on goods that competed with existing or projected industries were not yet enacted.

If some reforms encouraged capitalism, others strengthened the position of landlords. Any village in the possession of one person for thirty years became his private property. This legalized expropriations that had occurred since the nineteenth century. In many areas there was still a division of ownership, with peasants and nomads having some traditional rights to the land they worked. Laws of 1928–29 requiring registration of property strengthened doubtful claims to land. The wealthy might register land to which peasants had titles, as the upper classes influenced the courts and government.[23] Land registration laws, as in many countries, were a modernizing step taken at the expense of the poor.

The 1928 Civil Code also strengthened landlords. Although the code shows French influence, it largely restated sharia principles, updated where modern exigencies required. The Civil Code recognized de facto ownership as proof of ownership, thus confirming usurpations, and the code was weighted toward landlords.[24] Generally tenants had to comply with the landlord's interpretation of an oral agreement. According to Ann Lambton: "It will . . . be clear that very little attention is paid by the Civil Code (or any other body of legislation) to the regulation of the relation of landlord and tenant. In general the scales are weighted in favour of the former, and little or no protection is afforded to the latter."[25] While agricultural machinery imports were exempt from tariffs, and industrial crops untaxed, few mechanized farms were inaugurated. The old system remained profitable, as labor was cheap.

The early years of Reza Shah's rule also saw a successful effort to disarm and settle the nomads, mainly in order to suppress power centers that might be a threat. Many tribes were forcibly settled by government troops. No alternative way of subsistence was provided, and most tribes had to continue their husbandry and agriculture on inadequate land. Ex-nomads could support far less livestock when they could not move from summer to winter grazing quarters, and livestock died from severe winters and lack of grain. Tribes were settled at the cost of impoverishing nomads, and decreasing livestock production. Many tribespeople awaited only the demise of Reza Shah to resume migrations. Tribal uprisings that protested this policy were cruelly suppressed.

The years 1925–1930 marked the beginning of educational reform. Earlier some Western technology, ideas, and languages had been taught in foreign missionary schools, private schools, and a few government schools. Although a public school program had been provided for after the constitutional revolution, internal troubles prevented its being carried out. In 1926 the majles voted that a small part of the land-tax receipts should go to a public elementary school system, and the amount increased over time. A uniform school curriculum on the French model and emphasizing academic training was adopted. In 1928 foreign and private schools were required to teach in Persian and follow the public school curriculum. Another 1928 law provided for sending Iranian students abroad each year. Exemption from military service was a strong motive for attending secondary and higher schools. Still, it was mostly the middle classes and the wealthy who went to school, and education was almost nonexistent in rural areas. Under Reza Shah an average of 4 percent of the budget went to education, while the military and security took a third of the national budget. Education was secular, and, like legal reform, it reduced the power of the ulama. Between 1928 and 1930 several laws and decrees enhanced the state's control over religious schools. The 1928 Law of Uniformity of Dress, which established Western dress for all men, said that theology students, to be exempt from Western dress and conscription, would have to take a government-run examination.[26] Many ulama, and especially their sons, entered the new professions and their schools under the Pahlavis, while religious schools came to have little appeal for the elite and to recruit largely from other classes.

An active movement for the emancipation and education of women, led by several courageous women campaigners, existed in Iran even before 1925.[27] Reza Shah's early modernization program relaxed somewhat the social restrictions on women, and encouraged the adoption of European dress and manners at home, although the government moved slowly in this matter in the 1920s. Modern dress was decreed for all Iranian men except clerics in 1929, but urban women continued to wear their traditional outer dress in public for several years more. For most urban women this consisted of the chador and a face veil, though some abandoned the face veil. The Civil Code retained most of the sharia provisions that affected women: divorce easy for men but difficult for women; guardianship of children by the man in case of separation; consent of the father for a daughter's marriage; and polygamy and temporary marriage. A husband could kill an adulterous wife and her lover with impunity and could keep a wife from a job "degrading" to him or her. The only reforms were a rise in the legal marriage age and a requirement that all marriages be registered in civil bureaus. On the other hand, the spread of male and female secular education and emphasis in a variety of men's and women's writings and activities on modern, rather than ulama-endorsed ideas, began to encourage new roles and attitudes regarding women.[28]

By 1930 the foundations for a program of economic modernization from above had been laid. Most important was centralization, accomplished via a growing bureaucracy and a strong army. In the Reza Shah period, the main public expenditure was on the armed forces, which took by far the largest share of the government budget. The army was used primarily to strengthen the government's authority within Iran. The classes who benefited from the changes included government employees, army officers, students, professionals, and merchants, while the poor did not benefit. Reza Shah terrorized or jailed potential opponents, and there was no chance for organized union activity or oppositional politics.

From about 1930 to his abdication in 1941, Reza Shah embarked on an ambitious modernization program, with government control over the economy. Many of his economic and other measures were modeled on the reforms of Atatürk in Turkey; often Reza Shah would inaugurate a reform a year or two after a nearly identical one had appeared in Turkey. Basic causes of reform were internal, however. The world economic depression increased Iran's economic problems, and there were several peasant and tribal risings in the early thirties. The depression, by lowering demand for Iran's products, threatened Iran's trade and production.

Partly to meet these threats, the government began a strong program of state-centered economic development.

Given the existing social and economic structure, the state was the logical initiator of development. Private capital was too undeveloped and too attracted to safe, quickly profitable fields like land and moneylending to be directed to industry, which often involves high initial investment, slow returns, and competition with Western goods. Purchasing power was too low and transport too undeveloped to ensure a large internal market. Even potential investors in modern enterprises were eager, as elsewhere, to have the government carry infrastructural costs and to guarantee their companies against losses.

In 1920 Iran had a very backward transportation system, with about two thousand miles of usable roads, designed more to facilitate Western penetration than to link Iran internally. Road construction, with the help of foreign firms, increased road mileage over ten times from the midtwenties to the late thirties. In 1920 it cost two hundred dollars a ton and took two months to take goods from southern ports to Tehran; by 1929 motor transport of goods was general, and the same trip took one or two weeks and cost fifty dollars a ton. Motor vehicles in Iran rose from about six hundred in 1928 to twenty-five thousand in 1942. Road construction was still extremely limited and underfunded, and the lack of roads in most areas remained an obstacle to development.[29]

Reza Shah was determined to build a railroad to connect north and south Iran, and funds for this were collected from 1925 on. In 1928 an agreement was signed with a German and American syndicate, but it was annulled in 1931, and in 1933 a new contract was signed with a Scandinavian consortium, which worked until the railroad was completed in 1938. Work and orders were divided among many countries, partly to avoid control by any one power. Railway construction created the first Iranian work force numbering in the tens of thousands outside the Anglo-Persian Oil Company.[30]

The North-South Trans-Iranian Railway was designed to help ensure the political, economic, and military control of the government and to provide an economic link between north and south, but its high cost, estimated between $150 million and $200 million for a single-track road, was a great drain on national wealth. Most came from those least able to afford it, through regressive taxes, and a national road system could have been cheaper and more useful. As one analyst concludes,

The evidence . . . suggests that the railroad brought few benefits, while taking from the taxpayers a great deal of resources that could have been more productively spent on roads, schools, industries, and the like. . . . The allied armies . . . certainly made much more use of the railroad than did the Iranian economy either before or after the war. It is sad to think that the nationalist Reza Shah may have inadvertently taxed Iranians heavily for the benefit of the Soviet and British armies.[31]

The government inaugurated an airline service, and expanded telegraph, telephone, and radio communications. Transport and communications were a major achievement of the Reza Shah regime, though road building was financed largely through a road tax levied on common consumer goods, the railroad by regressive sugar and tea taxes, and the money poured into the railroad could have been better spent elsewhere.

In industry as in transport, government encouragement and financing brought rapid growth. Forms used included government ownership, partial or total ownership by the shah or a bank, and private ownership, often with governmental guarantees or subsidies. In the 1920s, small, privately owned textile factories expanded, but real growth came only in the 1930s. Approximately thirty modern large factories owned by the government were built, plus another two hundred small factories, with both government and private owners.[32]

Nearly all cities had electric light and power plants by the late 1930s. Large sugar refineries, spinning mills, weaving mills, food and grain processing, and soap factories were built. The state Tobacco Monopoly operated a highly profitable plant in Tehran.[33] Industry was concentrated in textiles and agricultural processing, in which capital outlay was low and the savings from producing close to the market or source of supply were great.

Industry was guaranteed by government monopolies on some items, government licensing of industry to ensure against competition, and government financing and loans. To promote Iranian goods the government required civil servants to dress in Iranian-made clothes. There was, however, an inflationary rise in the Iranian price index in the late thirties, caused largely by the encouragement of high prices.[34] Reza Shah's industrialization rested more on the capture of existing or reduced markets than on the creation of expanding ones, which would have required higher incomes for the majority and increased, efficient production.

Regarding city workers, strikes and unions were outlawed, and low wages were the rule. A gesture toward factory regulation came in a 1936 law creating standards of construction, hygiene, and workmen's compensation, but there was no inspection. The law outlawed strikes and unions. Long hours with low wages remained the lot of workers, with women and children, especially in carpet workshops, the most exploited.

Government help and guaranteed high profits to semiofficial trade monopolies favored investment in commerce, rather than in the more essential industry, as commerce required less capital and promised quicker returns. In 1940 there were twice as many commercial as industrial corporations, and their total capital was twice as high. Management and control of enterprises was lodged in Tehran, with little local initiative or decentralization. Economic development centered in Tehran, which, by 1940, was the scene of 58.5 percent of all domestic capital investment.[35] Development of industry and other economic enterprises was a crucial step toward modernization and true independence, but it was often done in ways that led to inefficiency and corruption.

In the 1930s there was also extensive urban construction, especially the modernization of main streets and of downtown Tehran. In general, the middle and upper classes benefited most, whereas the more populous classes bore the major cost of the fine new buildings and streets. Finance in the 1930s was characterized by a large increase in government income, expenditure, and financial control. Banking came under national control with the provision for a National Bank in 1927. The role of the National Bank as Iran's leading financial institution was ensured in 1930 when the right to issue bank notes and other national banking privileges were withdrawn from the British Imperial Bank. All banking in Iran came under government control; the Agricultural and Industrial Bank was formed in 1933 and the Loan Bank in 1939. These banks provided a large share of the capital used for Iranian industry, trade, and transport. Their capital came from tax monies, while profits from the enterprises they helped went to private individuals, officials, or the government. Credit on reasonable terms went to the upper classes, while peasants, smaller bazaaris, and workers remained subject to usurious rates.

The Reza Shah regime avoided foreign debt by means of large increases in indirect taxes. Government expenditure, in terms of the pound sterling and not the deflated rial, rose tenfold from 1923/24 to 1941/42.[36] Oil royalties provided only about 10 percent of the budget, the rest coming mostly from indirect taxes. Rial income of the poorer classes in the 1928–40 period was approximately stationary. The government budget in rials, however, rose over elevenfold.[37]

By the late 1930s and early 1940s half of government income was
going to industry, transportation, and trade, while the ministry of war
was the third spender, after the ministries of transport and industry.[38] A
key to Iran's problems remained its agrarian structure, which encouraged low productivity, medieval methods, and investment in land and
usury. A 1934 study of agriculture showed the government strengthening the old system. Large landlords with several villages owned about
half the land, while 95 to 98 percent of the agricultural population was
reportedly landless. Sharecropping was prevalent on the vast majority of
land. Contracts were oral, unclear, and designed to keep tenants from
accumulating a surplus.[39]

In the more prosperous northern provinces of Gilan and Mazanderan, some peasants paid fixed rents. More prevalent throughout Iran
was renting by an intermediary with a short-term contract who sub-
contracted to peasants. Most state and vaqf land was rented like this. The
system hurt agriculture by encouraging high short-term profits and discouraging investment. The village headman (*kadkhoda*), who had once
represented in part the villagers' interests, was now a landlord appointee,
as was the man in charge of water distribution.

Tradition based the crop division on five factors—land, labor, water,
seed, and animals—with the provider of each to get one-fifth of the crop.
In practice the weight given to each factor varied. The peasant might get
from one-fifth to seven-eighths of the crop, depending on where he lived
and what he supplied. Many peasants were also subject to landlords'
dues and taxes, to state taxes, and to a share in the pay of village officials.
Peasant conditions were best in the northwest, but were bad elsewhere.
Peasants were often hungry, diseased, and malnourished. Although mi-
grating tribes were better off than peasants in health, food, and independence, settlement reduced them to the level of the peasant, which is one
reason it was resisted.

In the 1920s and 1930s there was no agrarian reform, although there
were a few technical improvements. The regime's policy strengthened
the position of large landowners. Unprofitable state lands were put on
the market in 1934, but on terms that only the rich, military officers,
or officials could afford. Through expropriation and forced sales, Reza
Shah made himself by far the biggest landlord in Iran.

The later 1930s saw little change. A law of November 1937 made
landlords responsible for proper cultivation of their estates on pain of

confiscation, but no regulations for enforcing this law were drawn up, owing to landlord opposition. In Sistan province state lands were to be sold to peasants in 1937, but landlords and officials used their power to take over the land.[40]

A few measures were taken to increase agricultural productivity. A 1937 law encouraged the improvement of badly cultivated lands or wastelands through agricultural loans. A few agricultural schools and experimental stations were founded, notably the Agricultural College at Karaj, near Tehran. In 1940, a Five-Year Plan for agriculture was launched. Its operation was interrupted by the war, but its success was always problematic.

The lack of measures to improve the lives of the poorer classes hindered fundamental economic change. Few landlords and merchants were moved to invest in modern enterprise when traditional exploitation of land and peasants continued to be profitable. Peasant labor was so cheap that landlords had little desire to encourage innovations. In the depression, prices for agricultural goods sold by peasants fell more than the prices of the manufactures they bought. Peasants got no protection against dispossession or rent increases.

Landlordism and declining rural standards were the weakest point of Reza Shah's modernization. If Iran were to develop large-scale industry an expanding national market was needed to provide purchasers for industrial goods. Instead, the consumer-goods market declined in the 1930s, except for luxury products. Agricultural productivity and peasant living standards could not be raised without reform.

Toward the tribes, Reza Shah continued a policy of military control without economic solutions. The government also tried to suppress autonomist sentiments among the Kurds and other tribal peoples and national minorities. Some tribes like the Lurs were decimated by governmental policies.

Foreign trade under Reza Shah shows both the problems and the achievements of Iran's new relations with the West. Iranian foreign trade surpassed its prewar level by the 1920s. Trade with Great Britain prospered, more than counterbalancing the fall in trade with Russia.[41] Iran could not sell its exports, or had to sell at ruinous prices, after the 1929 crash. There was a disastrous drop in the sterling value of the rial. The real value of trade in the early 1930s fell to less than one-third of the 1929 level. This fall was greater than the world average, despite efforts to encourage trade.[42] Given continued taxation on items of mass consumption, Iranians could buy fewer of them in the depression years.

The regime tried to overcome Iran's negative trade balance and to halt the rial's fall by a Monopoly of Foreign Trade Law of 1931. The government took control of imports and exports, with the aim of balancing them. Smuggling and evasion limited the monopoly's effectiveness, and it was soon relaxed, mainly in the interests of big merchants whose exports had been restricted. The law provided a favorable trade balance only in its first year, although the negative balance was reduced. Control of currency exchange was abandoned, largely under foreign pressure, and the rial dropped further.

The world economic crisis, characterized by a sharper drop in agricultural than industrial prices, hurt Iran. The price of manufactured goods from the West remained high, while the price of Iranian goods on the world market fell about in half. By 1932 the 1929 price level of imports had effectively doubled.[43] To maintain a more equal trade balance, Iran cut its imports, especially in mass-consumption articles, and consumption levels fell.

The government and large merchants formed several joint semiofficial trade monopolies, which had exclusive control of foreign trade in several items. These monopolies put many smaller merchants out of business. Monopoly profits were often government-protected and high. Guaranteed profits enabled the monopolies to withstand the uncertainties that undid small traders, and trade became increasingly controlled by large Tehran merchants. Protection of big traders, as of big landlords, limited the capital going into manufacturing.

Increasing the prices of necessities were customs duties, which averaged 30 percent in the early 1930s, and even more later.[44] Prices were further raised by guaranteed monopoly profits and by excise taxes. Recovery of the import and consumption of the basic items occurred in the late 1930s but was incomplete. In the late 1930s more industrial goods were imported as new industries were built, and arms imports grew. Imports of medium-priced and luxury goods increased but mass-consumption imports remained low. By the end of the decade, with Reza Shah's political and economic turn to Germany, Germany had become Iran's leading trade partner. Capital invested in commercial corporations by 1940 was greater than that in industrial, transport, and banking corporations combined.[45] On the positive side, there was a major increase in all modern sectors of the economy, whether industrial, commercial, or infrastructural, and in the new social institutions that accompanied this modernization.

Political and social life in the 1930s had many of the same features as the economy. Centralization was the rule in politics as in economic life. There was no elected self-government in villages, towns, districts, or provinces. Officials were appointed from and accountable to Tehran. In 1938, local administrative units were reorganized into a nationwide hierarchy, with divisions often cutting across traditional cultural and ethnic lines. Administrators and subjects might speak different languages and have different educations and values.

Education saw important advances. The government for the first time put a regular and increasing share of taxes into education, so that educational expenses rose from $100,000 in 1925 to $12–13 million 1940.[46] Still, less than 10 percent of the population received any elementary education, and, for secondary education, the figure was under one percent. In 1935 Tehran University was founded, giving Iran its first modern university, and it was opened to women. Students were also sent abroad by the government in increasing numbers. However, traditions of disdain for manual and technical work and the effects of overcentralization hurt education. Control over details of education remained in Tehran, and the course of study was formal and academic. It did, however, introduce modern sciences and other modern subjects, laying the basis for a continued modernization of society. Official nationalism propagated an emphasis on Iranian history and literature, with stress on the pre-Islamic empires and de-emphasis of Islam. All schools, including foreign ones, were made to teach in Persian. Foreign and missionary schools were put under increasing controls and finally expropriated in 1939–40. As the legal and educational positions open to those with religious educations declined, sons of the ulama tended increasingly to get secular educations and jobs. While the educational system developed under Reza Shah can be criticized for being overcentralized, elitist, and concentrating on governmental needs, it did expand Iran's first nationwide system of public education at all levels, which was crucial to the further development of education and society.

The government also sponsored the creation of, first, Boy Scouts and then Girl Scouts, and some modern initiatives in sports and the arts. Social welfare, including public health and hospitals, also registered some important advances under official auspices for the first time.

The partial emancipation of Iranian women was one of the most important changes occurring during the Reza Shah regime. A growing women's movement since the early twentieth century and the Westernization of middle- and upper-class life, as well as women's entrance into factory work, teaching, and nursing, helped relax traditional restrictions on women's lives. A gradual lessening of restrictions took place through the 1920s and 1930s. More problematic was Reza Shah's unique absolutist approach to changing women's dress which, following a trip to Turkey, he saw as a hallmark of national modernization. After preliminary steps in 1935, in 1936 women were ordered to unveil and dress in Western-style clothing. Some women saw this as the equivalent of going out naked and refused to leave their homes, as gendarmes sometimes tore chadors from women on the streets. According to Houchang Chehabi,

> The forced unveiling of Iranian women ... was, among all of Reza Shah's modernization policies, the one that contributed most to his unpopularity among ordinary Iranians. Between January 1936 and the monarch's abdication in 1941, police and gendarmerie used physical force to enforce the ban, thus violating the innermost private sphere of close to half the population. ...
>
> The practice of limited coeducation for prepubescent children in traditional maktabs was discontinued after girls were forced to go to school unveiled. ... While educational opportunities improved for women ... many girls in observant families were deprived of education, as their parents took them out of school. ... Reza Shah's efforts to give both women and men uniform dress codes in line with Western fashions ... while meant to unify the nation by eliminating visible class, status, and regional distinctions, in fact deepened another cleavage in Iranian society, i.e., that between westernizers ... and the rest of society, which resented the intrusion in their private lives.[47]

Women's education was encouraged by the regime, although over three times as many boys as girls continued to receive an education. There was a de facto decline in upper-class polygamy and in inequality in marriage and divorce in the modernized classes, and a rise in paid work for women. These trends affected primarily middle- and upper-class women, who did not obtain political rights or complete economic and social equality, though their advance in a decade was considerable. Women's organizations, also mainly middle and upper class, continued for a time to work, provided their aims were considered consonant with those of the regime. In 1935 the Shah promoted the creation of a Ladies'

Center, which was to participate in the unveiling and modernization campaign, and marked government control of the women's movement.

The Reza Shah period, for all its apparent independence of Western control, was affected by the Western powers, as is seen particularly in Reza Shah's economic program and foreign relations. Foreign investment grew at a rapid rate, notably in the oil fields, but also in transport and communications. In foreign policy, Reza Shah was friendly first to the British and later to the Germans. Compared to the Qajars, Reza Shah acted with significant independence of foreign powers.

The major western power in Iran continued to be Great Britain, whose capital investment in the oil fields during the 1930s overshadowed all Iranian investment in trade and industry. There were more workers employed in the oil fields than in all other industries combined.[48] There was a major dispute over the terms of the oil concession, but this did not end with any real loss to APOC. A series of accumulated postwar grievances caused Reza Shah to cancel the APOC concession in 1932. British threats and Reza Shah's fear of internal revolts were among the factors bringing Reza Shah to accept a revised concession in 1933, which did not significantly improve Iran's control or royalties. The concession's area was reduced but its termination was changed from 1961 to 1993, by which time most of the oil could be gone. Great Britain continued to reap huge profits and pay low royalties, to be the economic masters in Khuzistan, controlling retail trade as well as the oil industry, and greatly influencing southern politics.

Reza Shah chafed under British influence, and the British were unpopular with Iranian nationalists. This hostility, combined with a German drive for economic and political influence in Iran, led to a rise in Germany's position in the late 1930s. German firms had a large role in the Trans-Iranian Railroad. The Germans opened sea and air communication with Iran and provided most of the machinery and contractors in Iran's industrial, mining, and building program. Germany was the leading country in Iran's foreign trade from 1939 to 1941, controlling about half of it.

The Germans also advanced militarily and politically. Nazi ideology and agents were prominent, and the Germans declared Iran a pure Aryan country. Reza Shah was not averse to Nazi phrases and methods, which suited his dictatorial and nationalistic inclinations. On the eve of World War II, Iran housed German agents, and the government had economic and political commitments tying it to a pro-German policy.

Despite its limits, Reza Shah's modernization had important results. For the first time, a significant modern bourgeoisie was created, albeit with strong traditional features. Iranian capitalists used nepotism, bribery, government aid, and quick high profit, but many were also interested in industrialization, modernization, and greater economic independence. The middle class was augmented by several new groups: a growing bureaucracy, increasingly influenced by Western education and ideas; army officers, who became a privileged caste; doctors, lawyers, and teachers, imbued with Western ideas and methods; technical specialists, engineers, journalists and writers. As these groups developed in the cities, the service trades there also grew—the bazaars expanded and new retail stores were built to accommodate new needs. A rapid growth of the urban classes occurred under the Reza Shah regime. A new urban working class was a product of this period. Migration to, and modernization of, Tehran made it the center of working and middle classes, often at the expense of provincial cities. Economic structures were changed through a reinforcement of private property and of the position of landlords and merchants, along with an increase in the relative weight of more modern enterprises, transport, banking, and industry. A breakthrough had been made toward economic growth. Nevertheless, agriculture still employed the great majority of working Iranians. Traditional methods in agriculture left productivity extremely low. Nothing was done to improve the conditions of the peasantry, and the government's demands on peasants, in the form of taxes and military services, were greater than before. On the other hand, many rural boys got some education, national identity, and contact with the modern world through military service.

If new opportunities existed for entrance to the privileged classes and the numbers in these classes grew, these opportunities scarcely affected most of the population. Reza Shah's work for rapid modernization from above, along with his militantly secularist cultural and educational program, helped create the situation of "two cultures" in Iran, which became more acute in later decades. The upper and new middle classes became increasingly Westernized and scarcely understood the traditional or religious culture of most of their compatriots. The urban bazaar classes continued to follow the ulama, however politically cowed most of the ulama were in the Reza Shah period. These classes associated "the way things should be" more with Islam than with the West or with the new myth of pre-Islamic Iran, whose virtues were essentially Western. As summarized by Vanessa Martin,

> The presiding ethos of the new system was a militant form of secular nationalism, with a vision of Iran regaining the glories of its pre-Islamic past. . . . The eras of the Achaemanids and Sasanians were recalled as glorious examples of what Iran could still become. . . . A major step to the return to past glories was perceived to be secularism, and the division of religion and state. Reza Shah . . . was . . . determined to remove the influence of religion from politics and above all to undermine the political influence of the clerics. Iran did not, unlike Turkey, have a tradition of a powerful state and acquiescent Sunni ulama, so it was not possible even for Reza Shah to go as far as disestablishing Islam. . . . The emphasis on the pre-Islamic past was also intended to help forge a modern national identity, but to a population that was . . . [mainly] devout Shi'a, the vision meant little.[49]

The state took numerous measures to weaken the clergy, taking away most of their role in law and education, and even finally instituting state control over vaqf land. In the same period, however, the clergy kept their ties to large parts of the population and even began an internal reorganization. Ever since the major Shi'i ulama left Iraq after World War I and settled in Qom there was the basis for an Iran-based clerical institution which, while in retreat, continued to have considerable internal organization and influenced the popular and bazaar classes.

Iran's economic development and reform program produced some striking results: industry, transport, education, women's and the rights of religious minorities all grew. There was a reversal in official attitudes toward Zoroastrians—from being an impoverished minority, they became embodiments of the virtues of ancient Iran.

On balance, Reza Shah adopted a path of centralized control that might have been in part unavoidable for a government that wished to modernize a society with so many divisive centers of power. His rule saw significant modernization of Iran, laying impressive foundations in industry, transport, education, and other fields, but at the expense of several segments of the population. The often-forcible suppression of discussion and opposition and the neglect of the rural and tribal majority were not necessary concomitants of modernization and left Iran with problems and resentments that continued into the next decades. In cultural matters, the class-related division between those who identified

with a modern construction of Iranian nationalism and those who identified with tradition and Islam continued to be a problem in subsequent
decades. The Shah's increasingly autocratic ways and turning against
even trusted subordinates left him without major support by the end
of his reign, as was also to be true decades later of his more sophisticated son.

6

World War II and Mosaddeq: 1941–1953

World War II, 1941–1945

With World War II, Reza Shah and his development program came to a sudden end and new problems appeared. During the war the United States became a key influence, while Russian and British activity in Iran continued.

At the outbreak of war, in September 1939, German influence in Iran was paramount. German agents were active, and the shah's sympathy for the Germans was no secret. This sympathy caused concern once the Nazis invaded the Soviet Union in June 1941. After that the Germans wanted to use Iran as a base against the Soviet Union, and the Allies needed Iran as a supply route to the Soviets, which would be impeded by a German fifth column. The British and Russians sent a note to the Iranian government demanding the expulsion of the Germans. When Reza Shah procrastinated, on August 25 Russian and British troops entered Iran.[1]

Allied pressure forced the shah to abdicate in September 1941, and he was deported and died in 1944. Iran was once more divided into three zones by the British and Russians, although now the division was for war purposes. Soviet troops were in the north, British in the south, while Tehran and other important areas remained unoccupied. In January 1942, Great Britain, Iran, and the Soviet Union signed an alliance. The Allies guaranteed to help safeguard Iran's economy from negative effects of the war and to withdraw their troops within six months after the war's end.[2]

Reza Shah's abdication put the kingdom under his Swiss-educated son, Mohammad Reza (b. 1919), who was for years less brusque and

dictatorial than Reza Shah and did not imitate his policy of bypass-
ing constitutional government. With Allied encouragement, cabinet-led
government revived, the leadership coming mostly from politicians who
antedated Reza Shah. For the first two years of occupation, the majles
remained the same as before 1941, and hence was filled with Reza Shah's
appointees and conservatives.[3]

The occupation, the abdication of Reza Shah, and new economic and
social problems created by war meant growing instability and unrest.
Internal trade was disrupted by the use of the Trans-Iranian Railroad
mainly to send supplies to the USSR. The demands of Allied troops
contributed to an urban boom but also made inroads on supplies. As
prices for scarce staples rose, these were bought up by speculators,
which forced prices higher.[4] The Iranian government took little effective
regulatory action. Difficulties grew with a bad harvest in 1942, which
brought famine in many areas.

In 1942 the government asked for an American financial mission to
bring order into finances and the troubled economic situation. Dr. A. C.
Millspaugh was again called upon, and he writes that he was urged by the
State Department to accept: "I was informed . . . that the United States
after the war was to play a large role in that region with respect to oil,
commerce, and air transport, and that a big program was under way."[5]

The government's industrial and commercial activities remained inefficient, and the Persian government was seen by Millspaugh as more
corrupt than it had been twenty years before.[6] Bureaucratic capitalists
and landlords with business interests worked in the majles to continue
the government's policy of high subsidies to businesses and government-
sponsored monopolies. Inflation tended to demoralize civil servants on
low, fixed salaries, who had to take bribes to live. The government was
the instrument of the upper classes, and regressive tax and other policies
continued to hit the majority.

Although the government took few steps to meet wartime problems,
the political and social situation did change. In September 1941, the
survivors of fifty-three men who had been arrested in 1937 for communist activity were released from jail. They joined with others to form the
Tudeh ("masses") party in late 1941. In 1942 the party held its first
conference, electing a central committee and adopting a provisional program, which was at first moderate and liberal, but the party's initial
united-front character was undermined in part by its consistently pro-
Soviet line.[7] During the war the Tudeh grew and recruited some promi-

nent liberals. Its main center was the north, where it was favored by the Russians, who, like the British, were ready to use their position to support favored political movements. The North was also an economically advanced region and the locus of the large Azerbaijani and Kurdish minorities. The party was strong as well in the Isfahan textile area, in the oil fields, and in several cities.[8]

Inflation, scarcities, and dissatisfaction with the government led to a growth of oppositional organizations and protests in 1942 and 1943. From 1942, trade unions reappeared, and were able to operate openly. Most were Tudeh-led.[9] The revival of a free press led to a flowering of newspapers, which were often advocates of political and economic change. In Tehran in December 1942, there were bread riots, owing to the acute grain shortage, aggravated by hoarding and speculation.[10] War and Reza Shah's abdication gave a chance for tribes to reassert some independence and to rearm. The British, who followed their policy of backing southern tribes, found tribal leaders useful allies in protecting conservatism in the south.[11]

Various American advisers were called into Iran in 1942 and 1943. After the United States entered the war, American troops came to Iran to help transport war supplies across the Trans-Iranian Railroad. In the war years the American role in Iran became greater than ever before. A major American activity was the second Millspaugh mission. Millspaugh was engaged as administrator general of finances in November 1942, and in May 1943, his extensive control over Iranian finances and the economy was clarified by the so-called Full Powers Law. His purview included finances, banking, government industry, commerce, and emergency wartime controls. Americans were put in charge of all key economic departments.

Millspaugh's chief measure was to introduce a progressive income tax bill in 1943. This could have helped the government balance its budget and begin to equalize the tax burden, but it was largely vitiated through nonenforcement.[12] Some of Millspaugh's efforts were less constructive. He worked to improve grain collection and storing, but ended government subsidies, which had allowed some cheaper bread to be sold, thus increasing bread prices. Little was done to maintain government enterprises, as Millspaugh was concerned to rid the government of these and promote a free-enterprise policy. Millspaugh's efforts brought opposition from both conservatives and reformers, the former objecting to controls that interfered with their interests, and the latter to his failure to cope with high prices or industrial inefficiency. When Millspaugh tried to fire the head of the National Bank in late 1944, Iranian opposition grew. This opposition caused the mission to resign, with most of its program having had little effect.[13] Millspaugh attempted some important changes, but these could only have succeeded had he followed a consistent reform policy and brought Iranian reformers into the administration of this program.

In 1942 and 1943 the United States missions sent to advise the Iranian army and gendarmerie took substantial control of these forces.[14] Colonel H. Norman Schwarzkopf was put in charge of the Iranian gendarmerie, and he reorganized this internal security force along American lines. American influence in these two branches continued throughout the postwar period, and the contract for military and gendarmerie advisers was renewed several times.

The later war period did not see any solution to Iran's wartime economic problems. Allied troops spent large sums, which contributed to inflation. The disruption of supply was serious, and famine broke out in some areas. Speculation, hoarding, and black-market operations multiplied, often causing great suffering. The cost-of-living index issued by the Iranian National Bank rose from 100 in 1939 to 269 in 1942, 650 in 1943, and 757 in 1944.[15] In some parts of the country the rise was even greater.

The war brought new opportunities for profit to those in the middle and upper classes who dealt in goods or credit, but caused suffering to the popular classes and those on fixed incomes. The war also stimulated urbanization and created larger groups of merchants, professionals, and others occupied in urban services for the Allies. The working class also grew, as railroads, construction, and expansion of the oil fields and refinery led to new demand for workers. Journalists and writers also flourished, and discussion of a variety of political ideas became the order of the day.

The war's disruption of the economy appeared in state finance, which encompassed almost all the modern economic sector. In wartime, current expenditures absorbed most government outlays, leaving little for development activities. Most state enterprises operated at a loss during the war, and funds had to be poured in to meet this deficit. Foreign technicians were scarce and equipment hard to replace. This, along with self-seeking and inefficient management of many state enterprises, meant that plant and production declined. From 1930 to 1941 government expenses on economic projects had been 30 to 40 percent of total government outlays, but by 1945–46 this was down to 7 percent.[16] Revenue from income taxes rose a little after the Millspaugh mission, but not enough to meet needs. No new non-AIOC factories were established, although efforts were made to improve the output of some existing factories.[17]

From 1943 to 1945 political activity increased greatly, owing to economic and social disruption, new political freedom, and the encouragement of various political groups by the Allies. German agents were active among southern tribes, and reached an agreement with General F. Zahedi to lead a southern tribal revolt should German troops reach Iran's frontiers. The British arrested Zahedi and stopped most of this activity, however, and British influence with the southern tribes became paramount.

In 1943 several parties emerged, most of which had nationalist programs and a small middle-class and intellectual following. The British allowed Sayyed Zia ad-Din, the old exiled prime minister, to return. With British encouragement, he formed a party finally called the National Will party. This soon became the focus of right-wing politics and the main opponent of the Tudeh. The party advocated a return to old Islamic customs and the abolition of many of Reza Shah's reforms—making a largely traditional and religious appeal. Its main support came from ulama, merchants, landlords, and tribes.[18]

Elections to a new majles were held in 1943, resulting in a large conservative majority, partly because of dishonest elections. Sayyed Zia and his party were a key conservative influence. On the left were eight Tudeh deputies and about twenty-four sympathizers. Between the Tudeh and the right was a nationalist group led by deputy Mohammad Mosaddeq, a political leader known for his early opposition to Reza Shah and to foreign control.

Political struggles with international implications occurred even before the war's end. In the north, the Russians encouraged left-wing officials and kept out many non-Russian foreigners. The Russian presence encouraged demands by Azerbaijanis and Kurds for autonomy and the use of their own languages. The Tudeh and leftist trade unions also grew in other areas. In the south, the British encouraged conservatives: tribal leaders, landlords, and religious leaders. Tudeh headquarters in several southern cities were destroyed by agents of the National Will party. While the British and Russians concentrated on their own spheres, the

Americans had advisers to several key government departments and the military. Thus all the Allies tried to influence Iranian politics to their own advantage.

The interests of all three, although partly strategic, centered on Iranian oil. The Anglo-Iranian Oil Company (AIOC) expanded its facilities during the war. The British wished to preserve their concession intact and keep out competition in the face of growing Iranian nationalist feeling and interest by other powers. Two American oil companies and then the Soviet Union opened negotiations for oil concessions in Iran during the war. The majles, however, passed a law, authorized by Mosaddeq and directed primarily against a Soviet concession, making it a crime to enter into such negotiations with foreigners for oil concessions. Although the Soviet Union and the United States remained interested in oil they achieved nothing during the war.[19] The bill against new oil concessions was one indication of Iran's increasing belief that oil should be used for Iranian ends. Nationalists, seeing the profits coming from oil, along with a relative drop in the value of Iran's fixed royalties as the value of the pound sterling fell and the price of oil rose, wanted new concession terms to give them a better return.

The war period in Iran was one of ferment. It saw a growth of economic problems: inflation, famine, deterioration of the modern sector, and disruption of government finances. According to an American expert who was then in Iran, the war "widened the already yawning gulf between the staggering poverty of the long-suffering masses and the wealth of the privileged few."[20] There was also an increase in urbanization and new urban groups, at the same time as traditional ways of tribes and religious leaders reemerged. Acute economic and social problems led to a growth of political organizations. Competing groups and ideologies—religious, nationalist, and socialist—vied for the allegiance of Iranians as never before. And, to compound internal problems and rivalries, foreign powers showed a stronger interest in Iran, with concern to control her politics and her oil.

Postwar Socioeconomic Problems

After the war, Iran's social and economic problems intensified, as did social conflicts and foreign interference. The immediate postwar years were characterized by a series of dramatic events that surpassed in scope the movements after World War I. Wartime and postwar crisis conditions contributed to the appeal of movements aiming at a radical change in social and economic life. As after World War I, the strongest radical movements were in the north, where they were now encouraged by the Soviets.

The center of postwar leftist activity, Azerbaijan, was the province with the most radical traditions, and resentment against the central government was strong for many reasons. Azerbaijan paid more taxes than any other Iranian province without receiving commensurate benefits. The Azerbaijani Turki language was not taught or permitted for official business, and there was resentment against forced Persianization. Russian presence in the province encouraged leftist forces and discouraged the right, especially as many large landlords fled when the Russians came in.[21]

The Tudeh party was strong in Azerbaijan, but in mid-1945 it was replaced by a new united front party called the Democrat party, which included a larger coalition of groups and classes and stressed autonomist demands. (The Democrats were not simply the Tudeh with a new name, as is often said). The Democrats took over military posts, and a provincial assembly was elected in Azerbaijan in November 1945. Most of the seats were won by the Democrats, the rest going to those who collaborated with them. Many posts were held by veteran Communists, some of whom had spent time in the Soviet Union.[22] The new provincial government, headed by Prime Minister Ja'far Pishevari, declared for autonomy, but not independence of the central government. A large portion of tax receipts was to remain in the province, local administration was to be based on self-government and not Tehran appointment, and the Azerbaijani language was to be used in the schools, including a new university. A land reform program included the lowering of rents and the distribution of land belonging to the government or to landlords who had fled the province. The presence of Soviet troops had allowed the Democrats to take over Iranian army posts without intervention by government troops. Otherwise, the Soviets avoided obvious interference.[23]

Similar events occurred in Kurdish territory, some of which was Soviet occupied, and much of the rest close enough to be under Soviet influence. The Kurds are divided chiefly among Iran, Iraq, and Turkey, and have strong nationalist sentiments. They resented the centralizing policies of the government and wanted provincial autonomy. In December 1945, a Kurdish autonomous republic was set up and, although its leadership was non-Communist, it was supported by the Soviets.[24]

The Soviets kept the Iranian government from sending in troops to suppress the new governments. The central government asked Soviet troops to leave and, with American encouragement, placed a complaint before the United Nations Security Council regarding Russian interference in Iranian affairs when Soviet troops remained beyond the date they were to leave, six months after the war's end. The Security Council decided to leave this to be negotiated between Iran and the Soviet Union. Troop withdrawal was agreed upon at the end of March 1946, in negotiations between the Iranian premier, the clever Qavam as-Saltaneh, who had been prime minister before Reza Shah, and the Soviets. Qavam promised not to use force against the autonomous regimes and approved, subject to majles confirmation, a concession for a joint Soviet-Iranian oil concession in the north. Qavam probably knew that neither of these agreements was definitive. Soviet activity in the north apparently violated the Russo-Iranian Treaty of 1921, promising noninterference by the Soviets in the internal affairs of Iran, as well as the troop-withdrawal limit agreed on by the Allies in 1943.

In 1946 internal leftward pressures continued and Qavam had to take account of them. No immediate action was initiated against the Azerbaijan and Kurdistan autonomous governments. Rather, Qavam and Pishevari reached an accord in June 1946, granting most of the Azerbaijani demands, including the province's keeping 75 percent of the taxes collected there and using the provincial language.[25] The left was also powerful in the south, as was shown by a major Tudeh-supported general strike in the oil fields in July 1946, which took out tens of thousands of organized workers in oil and other AIOC enterprises. Qavam took into his cabinet three Tudeh ministers in August.

The continued growth of trade-union and popular movements, as well as of the Tudeh and of reformism, were reflected in new social measures passed by the Qavam government in 1946. Most important was a new labor law, which limited hours of factory work to forty-eight, with overtime to be voluntary and better paid. Children could not work over six hours a day, and no child under ten could work in a factory, which suggests the previous child-labor conditions. Women were to have twelve weeks' maternity leave with full pay. Unions were allowed, and labor-management factory councils were to be set up in all factories. A minimum wage was established, along with higher skilled minimums, based on subsistence costs for a family of four.[26] In 1946 the government also issued a decree that landlords should give 15 percent of their share of the crop to the peasants.

Subsequent right-wing resurgence negated much of these laws' effect (although minimum wages remained), but their very passage by a landlord-controlled government indicates the strength of demands for change. There was an attempt to enforce the labor law, although inspection provisions were inadequate. The growth and strength of trade unions in the war and postwar period helped ensure their position, and AIOC, the biggest employer, complied with factory-council and minimum-wage provisions, so as not to be accused of breaking the law. However, increasing numbers of AIOC jobs were contracted out to small firms that did not comply.[27] The law increasing the peasants' share was hardly enforced. A landowners' conference in 1947 attacked the decree, and there was no attempt to compel obedience.

The growth of Tudeh influence was disliked by many Iranians and by Britain. After the Tudeh-led general strike in the Khuzistan oil area, British troops were ordered to Basra, Iraq, near Iran's border, and a British-supported exile, the son of Shaikh Khaz'al, raided Khuzistan from Iraq. Several southern tribal leaders, often allied with the British, announced their opposition to the Tudeh cabinet members. In September 1946, a southern tribal revolt began under the leadership of the Qashqa'i, whose chief demand was the dismissal of the Tudeh ministers. The revolt was backed by ulama and landlords, and probably the British. On October 17, 1946, the Tudeh ministers were dismissed.

The new American Ambassador to Iran, George V. Allen, was a major supporter of an Iranian anti-Communist policy.[28] Since the withdrawal of Soviet troops the Russians had less influence in Iran than the United States, and only the Tudeh and its allies were effective instruments of a pro-Soviet policy. Soon after Allen's arrival, in November 1946, the Qavam government sent troops north to put down the Azerbaijani and Kurdish autonomy movements, which was done very brutally. Some leaders fled, some hid, but others were executed. In Kurdistan the leaders were shot, and numerous jailings also occurred in both areas. The economic and social problems of Azerbaijan and Kurdistan grew after the reestablishment of central government control, and there was a severe famine in Azerbaijan in the winter of 1949.[29]

Part of the 1946 agreement between Qavam and the Soviets had been a promise of a joint concession for northern oil. The Tudeh was vociferously in favor of this, as were some others, but Iranian deputies were wary that it might be a wedge for Soviet influence. The support given by Ambassador Allen for rejecting the concession is generally considered an important factor in the majles's rejection of it.

Soviet influence in Iran thus suffered a decline in 1947, although the Tudeh remained active, particularly among trade unions, students, and intellectuals. The United States assumed a position of major influence, strengthened by 1947 agreements to extend the American military and gendarmerie missions, to provide for the purchase of military equipment in the United States, and a 1948 military-aid program giving Iran sixty million dollars worth of military equipment. Colonel Schwarzkopf was considered particularly valuable in maintaining the power of the Iranian government. "Schwarzkopf was tireless in inspecting all those places where trouble was brewing. He helped in no small degree to ensure firm government control in Azerbaijan and the northern provinces."[30]

By the end of 1947 conservative rule seemed well established, but discontent was still strong. The problems created by the war and previous developments had not been met. The peasants in postwar years suffered extreme poverty. Peasant landownership was down to a bare minimum as landlords and speculators had bought up much of the remaining peasants' land in hard wartime conditions. Debts, rents, and taxes tended to increase, and peasants had to borrow for capital requirements and current expenses. High interest rates and low income made it hard for peasants to repay the principal on loans.[31] High interest rates not only impoverished peasants (and urban dwellers), but kept capital from productive ventures and directed it toward the profitable but often unproductive field of money-lending.

Many peasants borrowed from their own landlords, and some lost their land for inability to repay debts. According to an extensive survey of Iran done by an American advisory group, "The villages and, for all practical purposes, the peasants are the property of the landlords, most of whom live in the larger cities or even abroad."[32] The growth of large landholdings and the immense holdings by the royal family multiplied the kind of middleman operations described for the 1930s. Renters and subcontractors took ever more of the surplus.

Sharecropping remained the main form of tenancy. By now many tenants had nothing to offer but their labor and could expect little better than one-fifth of the crop, unless this was too small for bare subsistence. The family income realized under such rentals may be imagined: "Under normal conditions each farmer can produce about 200 bushels of grain per year. Since most farmers own nothing, they get only the labor fifth, which amounts to 40 bushels. This means that the average farmer must live and support his family on approximately $110 per year."[33]

Tenants could be evicted or their rents raised without compensation for improvements. Although tenants were rarely forced off the land when traditional labor-intensive means of cultivation were employed, they were with the growing use of agricultural machinery. Machinery benefited landlords, since far fewer laborers were required.[34] Many peasants still owed dues and services. The most onerous was free labor service, and in many areas regular "presents" to the landlord were still demanded.

Most Iranian taxes were indirect, hitting those least able to afford them. After 1941 indirect taxation increased and other economic conditions became more difficult. Government monopolies, which made large profits from sugar, tea, tobacco, and other items of mass consumption, continued to be the largest single source of government income in the postwar period, accounting for one-third of the government's revenue in 1948–49. Customs duties, which were also felt by peasants and workers as they covered such items as sugar, tea, and cloth, accounted for 27 percent of the government's income in the same years. Income taxes, despite increases, accounted for only 8 percent of the government's income.[35]

Besides taxes, the government had a monopoly on the purchase and sale of wheat, Iran's principal crop. The price the government paid was below the free-market price, and this disparity grew in the war and postwar years. By 1948 the government was buying grain for one-third of its free-market price. This not only hurt peasants but led to a decline in wheat production, forcing Iran to import wheat in the postwar years.[36] (Similar policies and results occurred in the 1970s.)

Wartime and postwar inflation increased the pressures upon peasants. Scarcity meant profits for middlemen but hunger and debt for the peasants. Not only did wheat fields go out of cultivation when wheat was needed, but the production of cotton, the second major crop in Iran, fell by 1948 to about 14 percent of its 1937 level.[37] War also made great inroads on Iran's livestock. The postwar period saw some recovery, but little of it was reflected in peasant living standards. Although there were various announcements of sale of some government land to the peasants, before 1962 there was scarcely any practical outcome.[38] The government was known to peasants mainly through agents who bought grain, collected taxes, and recruited for the army. Most of them were underpaid, and tried to make up for their salaries by taking what they could from the peasants. It is not surprising that the social and health conditions of the peasantry were among the worst in the world. Peasants used primitive tools and suffered from lack of water or good seeds. Technological improvements under postwar conditions of land tenure offered them little.

The agrarian structure incorporated medieval features—feudal dues, primitive methods, and strip farming—with an exploitation facilitated by the development of a national and international cash market and the strengthening of the central government. The situation was pushing many peasants toward bare subsistence, tenancy, and rising debt. Major improvements seemed impossible under the pre-1962 structure, as most peasants had no capital and no guarantee that the fruits of improvements would not go to the landlord. Profiting from the agrarian structure were landlords, middlemen, overseers, headmen, officials, and moneylenders. They enriched themselves in various ways; by buying peasant goods cheaply, by lending at high interest, by selling goods at high prices, and by collecting rents. Peasant poverty encouraged the development of a hierarchy that reduced agricultural productivity.

The second important rural group is the tribes. During and after the war many returned to nomadism, although some remained settled. The tribal peoples were no longer necessarily better off than the peasantry. The destruction of livestock during the Reza Shah period and the war hurt the tribespeople, although the khans and a few other privileged tribespeople often remained wealthy. Some tribes continued to be a politically unstable force, capable of rebelling with deadly effect. There were also conflicts between nomadic tribes and the peasants and landlords whose land they cross and whose agriculture they occasionally disrupt. Among the settled tribes, conditions are much the same as with peasants, if not worse, the khans owning villages and tribespeople being reduced to the status of landless tenants.[39]

The chief beneficiary of the exploitation of tribal peoples and peasants was the large landlord. The crown, which confiscated vast areas under the Reza Shah regime, continued to be the largest single landholder in Iran, but there were other landlords with hundreds of villages. The composition of the large-landlord group changed more radically after World War I than before, as Reza Shah confiscated vast properties, while rising groups of merchants, contractors, bureaucrats, and especially army officers increasingly bought up land. Thus, although old families, religious groups, and tribal khans continued to own much land, there was extensive ownership by new groups, which also include overseers and kadkhodas who enriched themselves enough to buy up holdings. In general the new landlords were reputed to be not more modern in their methods, but often to seek short-term profit at the expense of both land and peasant.[40]

Landlords were mostly city-dwelling absentees, concerned to profit with little investment. Landlords were heavily represented in the government, as the scarcely secret or honest election practices ensured their election to the majles, and officials and army officers continued to buy land. Various schemes for irrigation and technology, the destruction of insects and disease, and rural education, tried since the war under such auspices as the Near East Foundation, Point Four, and the Seven Year Plan, brought some improvements, notably in eradicating the scourge of malaria, but were limited by peasant poverty. Poor peasants and agricultural laborers increasingly migrated to cities, where they made up an impoverished and politically volatile subproletariat. A very high rate of postwar demographic growth, about 3 percent annually, required new avenues for employment in both village and city that were rarely provided.

The towns' social structure presented a more complex and variable picture than did the countryside. A fair idea of living standards in towns may be gained from available statistics. More important, an assessment can be made of the crisis in urban life that has helped make Iranian cities, particularly Tehran, the scene of many major disturbances since World War II. Urban economic problems cannot be separated from rural ones. Low village living standards held down the internal market, thus limiting the expansion of consumer-goods industries. Also, rural poverty made it easy to pay low wages to industrial workers, whose ranks could be filled from the mass of unemployed and semiemployed city poor who came to the towns to escape a hopeless rural existence. The agrarian situation also contributed to the shunning of industrial investment by those with capital in favor of investment in land, speculation, moneylending, and quickly profitable trading ventures. Agricultural poverty and backwardness continued to be a major obstacle to Iran's postwar modernization.

The shaky foundations of Reza Shah's modernization showed up in World War II, which also aggravated problems. Maintenance of Iranian industry virtually stopped, equipment deteriorated, production declined, and capital sought other outlets. Wartime and immediate postwar scarcities and high demand meant that industries could operate inefficiently and still make profits. After 1947, however, a new flood of relatively cheap European goods led to crisis for Iranian industry. At the same time, export markets for Iranian goods shrank.[41] The bazaar classes also suffered from a postwar decline in demand. While wartime demand had encouraged expansion of the major urban bazaars, bazaar producers suffered from the end of Allied purchases and the revival of Western imports.

Modernization and economic reform were undermined during and after the war. Inflation, which leveled off slightly from its 1944 peak, became a growing problem again after 1947. The government foreign-trade monopoly, which allowed some control over imports, became inoperative in postwar years, as Westerners assumed more control in Iran and opposed any limits on their countries' exports. Widespread corruption in the customs administration brought falsification of receipts and of import and export permits, and foreign trade was no longer regulated.[42]

The small scope of industry is shown by the fact that only fifty-three thousand were employed in Iranian enterprises in 1950, or less than one-half percent of the population. This contrasts with sixty-seven thousand employed in the efficient British-owned oil industry, and one hundred and thirty thousand (or more) in hand carpetmaking.[43] As Iranian industry used mostly antiquated and inefficient machinery, and was said to employ many more people than necessary, industry's small place in Iran's economy can be appreciated.

Transport facilities, despite the expansion of the Trans-Iranian Railroad by the Allies, suffered a severe setback in maintenance during the war. In 1949 the condition of railroads and seaports was judged to be "approaching a point where it may seriously cripple the entire economy of the country."[44] A sudden drop in railway traffic after the war meant a great economic loss for the railroads. The cost of transporting freight rose and was five times as high per ton-km. in postwar Iran as in the United States, despite the much lower wages on Iranian railways.[45] After 1950, with American aid, some improvements were made in transport, but it remained underdeveloped.

Other aspects of Iran's economic backwardness in the postwar decade are indicated by the fact that no Iranian city had a modern water system before the 1950s and that per capita consumption of electricity and cement were well below that in Egypt and Turkey, not to mention more developed nations.[46] There was little modernization or expansion of the Iranian educational system. The number of university students per one thousand population was far below that of Egypt, Turkey, and other Asian countries.

The social structure of postwar urban Iran was not static, and increasing urbanization together with the emergence of new urban social groups meant the development of social unrest in cities. The growth of cities was stimulated by the World War II demand for urban goods and services, the expansion of the professions, and the continued growth of the army, gendarmerie, and bureaucracy. The accumulation of capital by Iranians who profited from the war helped to create a new middle class. Some of them wished to invest in productive industry, and the privately owned sector of Iranian industry expanded after the war. The new middle class tended to favor reforms that would improve economic stability and government efficiency. Its members wanted also to limit the power of foreign capital in Iran, represented chiefly by the AIOC.[47] The bazaar middle classes and parts of the new middle classes were a nationalist bourgeoisie who were increasingly willing to fight for Iranian economic and political independence and reduced foreign competition and control in Iran's economy.

The growing intelligentsia was also a newly significant social group. Educated in Tehran or abroad, the young Iranian intellectuals had little outlet for their talents. The demand, as distinct from the need, for professionals and scholars in Iran was outstripped by the supply. There was intellectual unemployment, and both students and mature intellectuals tended to identify their troubles with those of the Iranian nation. Intellectuals and students were in the forefront of many social protest movements, and they often spoke out for Iranian independence and fundamental social reform. The only major employment outlet for Iranian intellectuals was the bureaucracy, whose lower ranks were a seedbed of discontent at the same time as its top levels were known for their stake in the old regime. Dislike of foreign interference was characteristic of the young government employee.[48]

The lower-middle-class groups, the artisans and shopkeepers of the bazaars, have been a major focal point of postwar social and nationalist discontent. This group profited from wartime demand, but later suffered from the postwar economic crisis. Although it was not a new social group, its outlook changed in postwar years. Its members saw their position threatened by the competition of foreign goods and services, by governments' favoring of the new middle and upper classes, and by economic conditions that reduced Iranians' purchasing power. These people tended to identify Iran's problems with the operations of foreign interests. They were tied to a revived religious class that took advantage of the end of anticlerical despotism to reassert Islamic views and practices and to regain some of their former sociopolitical status.

The industrial working class, though small, became increasingly important after World War II. The war and postwar period saw the formation of numerous trade unions, finally grouped into three federations. Most unions owed their inspiration and leadership to the Tudeh party, but some were affiliated to other, including governmental, parties, and some were formed by employers to counteract true unions. Workers became a major radical force in Iran. Economic crises directly affected their welfare, and they led agitation for social reform and the nationalization of the oil industry. There were several important strikes in the postwar period, the majority of which had political as well as economic repercussions. Most famous was the strike of oil workers in the Anglo-Iranian fields in 1951.[49] Postwar unemployment was large—in absolute terms larger than before—owing to the wartime growth of cities. The unemployed were an element leading to social instability, and supporting movements for change.

At the opposite end of the scale were those few but powerful persons with a stake in the social structure. These included the upper bureaucracy, those who profited from the peasants, and some traders who profited from the underdeveloped distribution system to buy cheap and sell dear. Some industrial shareholders, many army officers, and those in the middle class who profited from foreign industry and trade were also among the "satisfied" group. Economic conditions in the towns were better than in the countryside, although the income-distribution gap was also greater. In the late 1940s it was estimated that 60 percent of town dwellers lived in slum conditions.[50]

Another largely dissatisfied group were the ulama, who took advantage of Reza Shah's abdication to reassert their position in many spheres. Most urban women went back to chadors, though without face veils, but the ulama wanted more reassertion of Islamic law and many also opposed growing foreign influence and control. Although most of the leading ulama were not then political activists, the active anti-British Ayatollah Kashani had a growing influence. He had variable ties to the small terrorist fundamentalist group, the Feda'iyan-e Islam, founded around

1945. The discontents and demands voiced by such men were to have increasing importance.

The postwar crisis in Iran, and the demand for change from many parts of the population, led even the landlord-dominated majles and government to undertake economic development. American influence in Iran grew, and as the United States was largely responsible for stabilizing the postwar Iranian government, it was natural to turn to an American firm for development aid. On Iran's invitation, the American engineering firm Morrison-Knudson made a survey and suggested a development program in August 1947. They put heavy emphasis on agricultural technology and little on industry. Raw cotton and wool production were to increase, but no new plants were planned to process them. Some Iranians, who felt that Iran's role as supplier of raw materials to the West and buyer of expensive finished goods was to be perpetuated, criticized the report. An Iranian economist prepared a specific plan late in 1947. Transport and agriculture were the two chief beneficiaries of his plan, but industry was allotted almost three times as much money as by Morrison-Knudson.[51]

A Plan Commission was set up to draft a bill for what was called the Seven Year Plan. The Commission's report to the majles in August 1948 showed the pressure of circumstances which had pushed the government to the plan. The report began:

> It is not concealed from anybody that the economy of the country is passing these days through a critical phase which has resulted in the weakening of the productive power of the country, the decline of exports, necessitating the importation of primary living needs from abroad, lowering of the purchasing power of the rial, increase of the cost of living, poverty and unemployment.
>
> The extent of this crisis is such that individual means and power, private initiative and undertakings, and even sporadic measures of the Government agencies will not be able to overcome it.[52]

At the same time, Americans had a large role in the Plan. Max W. Thornburg, oil executive, consultant, and an adviser in Iran, was one of the most influential. In 1948 Thornburg secured the services of Overseas Consultants, Inc. (OCI), a United States oil-related consortium, for the Iranian Plan. OCI was to do a survey of Iran's needs and help administer the Plan. In February 1949, the Development Plan Act was passed. OCI published a large report based on a survey it had conducted, emphasizing technical improvements, particularly in agriculture and transport. The report ignored the potential benefits of land reform, which Thornburg specifically denied.[53]

Neither the government nor OCI envisioned reforms in the social structure or land-tenure system. Improvement in agriculture was to come purely by technical and educational means. OCI recommended major improvements in communications and transport. Regarding industry, OCI noted that plants were inefficient, overstaffed, overcentralized, and technically backward. Most of these ills were attributed to government ownership, which was seen as always inefficient. "Fundamentally the profit motive must be present if efficiency and quality of management and production are to be achieved," the report stated.[54] The government was told to get rid of industry, and some expansion of private light industry was recommended. (Although the faults of government ownership in Iran were real, this might have been the only way to mobilize capital.)

The Plan as approved by the majles and the government had modest aims, and the rate of governmental development expenditure was to be far below that of prewar years.[55] Even the limited aims set for the first year and a half were not met, however, and after the loss of oil exports in 1951 the Plan was in effect suspended. Even sooner, most government agencies tried to get a share of the Plan funds, so that little could be spent on Plan projects.[56]

The Plan's scant accomplishment during its first year brought criticism from the Iranian press. It was charged that old ruling groups had passed the Plan only to allay unrest, and that they had no intention of working for economic change. The United States and Britain were blamed for backing men who cared little for Iran's economic development. The Tudeh, although outlawed after a man of doubtful affiliation tried to assassinate the shah in 1949, still controlled newspapers that attacked the Plan and its foreign advisers.

In June 1950, OCI made a statement detailing the Plan's failures and the old, corrupt forces that had used it. The Plan administration was accused of having no serious intent of carrying through the Plan.[57] No projects were being systematically followed, while funds were spent on unplanned projects. Owing to disagreements, the contract between OCI and Iran was terminated in January 1951. The Iranian Plan director stated that the main dispute centered on Iran's desire to industrialize much faster than OCI recommended. It is often said that the cutting off of AIOC royalties finished the Plan, but its de facto demise was assured before oil nationalization.

Industrial rehabilitation was the only part of the Plan with significant results. Government plants were revamped and sold to private owners, so that the majority of Iranian factories became private. Production rose from its postwar nadir. Increased foreign competition and continued low consumption meant, however, that ambitious expansion plans were abandoned. Some textile factories had to close again. Industrial rehabilitation was limited and would probably have occurred without a plan.

The Seven Year Plan and later United States-supported planning efforts in Iran assumed that the very groups with the most to gain by keeping the existing social structure could bring economic reform and development. The assumption that development was possible and desirable without a basic change in social structure fundamentally weakened planning in Iran. The Plan did not even provide for a basic change in tax structure, which might have mobilized the savings of the rich and made the poor better able to purchase Iranian manufactures. The economic and social crisis that the Plan was to overcome deepened during the Plan period.[58] This crisis and the profound discontent it engendered provided one basis for the powerful nationalist movement that characterized the years of the oil dispute.

The Oil Crisis and Mosaddeq

To summarize the involved postwar oil crisis, one may note that the Iranians had many grievances against the AIOC, and feelings about them became increasingly inflamed after the war. The fixed royalties provided for in the 1933 agreement had suffered a relative decline, as prices and profits had increased over three times. The AIOC was paying out an ever smaller percentage of its growing income as royalties. This was particularly galling in light of more favorable oil agreements between American oil companies and other countries. Iran also objected to having no say in the company, not even the right to see its books; to paying high prices for Iranian oil; and to the small number of Iranians trained for skilled jobs. The total net profits of the AIOC from 1945 to 1950 after deducting high British taxes, royalties, and exaggerated depreciation figures were £250 million while royalties were £90 million. The AIOC paid much more in income taxes to the British government than it did in royalties to the Iranian government. In addition, the increase of nationalist and radical sentiment after the war inflamed Iranian resentment over the political and economic control exercised by the AIOC. The AIOC was seen as a major cause and channel for British influence and control over Iran.[59]

The Iranian government began negotiations with AIOC for a different concession in 1947. The AIOC finally offered a "supplemental agreement," which was far from meeting Iranian demands, but which Iran's conservative government agreed to accept in July 1949. The agreement was highly unpopular, however, and was not passed by the majles. Elections to a new majles in 1950 centered around oil, and the nationalist National Front coalition of groups and parties opposed to the supplemental agreement and to subservience to foreign interests and led by Mohammad Mosaddeq scored major gains. The new premier, General Ali Razmara, delayed trying to push through the oil agreement, as he saw that majles and popular sentiment were against it. His pro-agreement position, however, was generally regarded as responsible for his assassination in March 1951, by a religious nationalist of the extremist Feda'iyan-e Islam group. (This was a small group of young fundamentalists who assassinated men they regarded as enemies of Islam.)

Popular sentiment and demonstrations were so marked that the majles turned completely to a pro-Mosaddeq position. Nationalization of the oil industry was approved by the majles on the recommendation of a majles committee in March 1951, and soon thereafter Mosaddeq became premier, replacing the shah's choice, Hosain Ala. Mosaddeq headed a coalition of secular and religious nationalist parties, the National Front. Earlier in negotiations with the British, Iranian demands had been backed by the American ambassador, Henry Grady, and by other American officials, who did not want to see British oil companies achieve a competitive advantage over their own. Later, however, American officials became increasingly alarmed at the radical implications of Iranian actions. The illegal Tudeh party gained strength through the nationalization period, after a decline of influence in the late 1940s, and Tudeh-led strikes and demonstrations helped push Iran toward anti-British and anti-American policies. The refusal of AIOC to meet the 50–50 profit-division pattern seen in new American oil agreements until it was too late, and its obstinacy on other issues, moved many moderates to favor nationalization, as did pressures from street demonstrations and threats of assassination.

The British early referred the dispute to the International Court at The Hague. The Court ruled it had no jurisdiction, implying that the matter came under Iranian law, and that Iran had the right to nationalize (compensation was always promised by Iran). In both Britain and the United States, however, Mosaddeq was pictured increasingly but inaccurately as a dangerous fanatic, likely to deliver Iran to the Soviets. In fact he was an anti-imperialist nationalist who intended to keep Iran from being controlled by any foreign country or company.

After nationalization Mosaddeq and his followers apparently expected to find the United States a neutral party that would make loans to, and purchase oil from, Iran. In fact, however, after some failed attempts by the Truman administration at mediation, the United States was increasingly hostile to nationalization, and American oil companies joined an unofficial but effective worldwide major-oil-companies' boycott of Iranian oil, sparked by the AIOC after nationalization was declared. The AIOC enforced the boycott with gunboats, saying the oil belonged to them, as it was stolen. The National Iranian Oil Company, set up to handle the AIOC fields and refinery and other oil in Iran, was able to produce some oil, but was not allowed to sell it during the nationalization period, except for a few late sales to Italian and Japanese "blockade busters." Thus, oil revenue was cut off from Iran, while the government continued to keep Iranian Oil Company employees on its payroll, in order to keep them from losing their income. Numerous attempts to negotiate, in which the United States often participated, came to nothing as AIOC, and even a later compromise World Bank plan, would have kept control and most profits in foreign hands.[61]

The new government was thus faced with economic problems even greater than those that had plagued Iran in the preceding crisis-ridden postwar years. To make matters worse, the British placed major restrictions on Iranian trade and on the convertibility of Iranian sterling balances in England. To counteract financial troubles, the Mosaddeq government introduced trade controls to encourage exports and discourage imports. Mosaddeq also hoped to get a sizable loan from the United States, which had previously been informally promised. He traveled to the United States in the fall of 1951 and tried to convince the Truman government that a loan was urgently needed if the left were not to gain power in Iran. The government refused a loan, however, on the grounds that Iran should settle the oil question before expecting aid. American hostility to Iran on oil nationalization, and American backing of the

British position, produced animosity in Iran towards the United States, whose aims had generally been thought different from Great Britain's. Later Iranian loan requests from the United States were similarly rebuffed, although some military and Point Four aid continued.

In the years of oil nationalization, the social and economic crisis in Iran intensified, and popular unrest, organized into different movements, increased. The oil issue was to a degree used by some Iranian leaders to divert attention from social problems, and there was little basic reform in the early Mosaddeq period. On the other hand, pressure for reform continued to mount, and the government and majles had increasingly to heed the demands of the people; in the latter part of Mosaddeq's rule more social reform measures were introduced. The reform aspect of the government might have continued to increase had it lasted longer.

The general line of the Tudeh in this period was to tie in popular nationalist demands and slogans with arguments suggesting that Iran would be better off if it would sever its ties with the West and rely on Soviet trade and good will. Pressure from both leftist and nationalist opinion was strong enough to encourage reforming economic and social measures. In the summer of 1952 Mosaddeq signed a decree saying that all landlords must give up 20 percent of their share of crop; 10 percent was to go to the peasant and 10 percent to newly created rural banks that would help the peasants with credit. To collect the unpaid back taxes of the rich, commissions were created throughout Iran that were entitled to jail, and confiscate the property of, those in arrears.[62]

Although Mosaddeq was very popular in Iran, the shah and his foreign advisers wanted him out, as did the AIOC and the British, under first Labour and then Conservative (Churchill) rule. In mid-1952 the shah dismissed Mosaddeq and appointed Qavam as-Saltaneh as prime minister. Mass demonstrations and sentiment for Mosaddeq were so great, however, that Mosaddeq soon returned to office with new plenary powers. It was widely believed in Iran that the United States was behind the attempt to replace Mosaddeq with Qavam.[63] Mosaddeq's charisma and lifelong courage and honesty made him vastly popular with most Iranians.

The restoration of Mosaddeq was a sign of new strength and determination by the nationalist coalition, and the signal for some serious reforms. In 1952 came efforts to enforce tax collection and reduce the landlord's share of the crop. Several irrigation dam projects were launched, and also a rural development program, along with the United States

Technical Cooperation Administration, which carried on agricultural education and pest control. Import limitations and government planning resulted in the first substantial postwar expansion of industry. Output of refined sugar, textiles, and minerals rose. The government began four large textile mills, several dry-fruit processing plants, a cement factory, and sugar refining plants. Measures to encourage exports actually produced a growing favorable trade balance in 1952 and 1953.[64]

The loss of oil revenue, decline in oil-related employment, and deterioration of economic relations with the United States and Britain continued to strain the Iranian economy, however. Lowered imports and scarcities contributed to inflation. There was still no basic agrarian reform nor enough taxes on the rich, which might raise living standards and capital for economic expansion. Iran suffered both from direct discrimination by Western governments and from a continued trend for prices on imported manufactures to rise while international prices of Iran's exports fell. Iran's terms of trade (the relation between export and import prices), which had already deteriorated in the 1930s, fell further. Taking 1948 as 100, they went to 90 in 1949 and to 69 by 1952.[65]

The United States continued to support the AIOC call for a world-wide boycott on Iranian oil. A letter from Max Thornburg to Clare Boothe Luce, United States ambassador to Italy, in May 1953, which spoke of his response to an Italian desire to import Iranian oil, gives some idea of how Americans helped enforce the boycott:

> My own comments on oil import request are summarized as follows: ...
> 1) While Italian companies are inhibited from selling oil without a government license, no such bar exists in the U.S. where there are thousands of independent oil companies, and which is a net importer of oil. Nevertheless, they have not chosen to buy Persian oil. This fact should throw some light on the American attitude.
> 2) For Italy to clear this oil and take additional cargoes would definitely indicate that it had taken the side of the oil "nationalizers", despite the hazard this represents to American Foreign investments and vital oil supply sources. This of course is Italy's right. It is only the prudence of the course that is in question.
> 3) The American people made generous contributions to Italy's rehabilitation after the war, and might regard this proposed act as ungracious.
> 4) Major oil companies, British and American, would be likely to resent it strongly—and remember it. The Caltex-Aramco group alone spends around $13 million a year in Italy for supplies which are sent all over the

world . . . in addition to using Italian crews, and Italian families (in Arabia about 1000 plus families). At a guess this might be multiplied by 5 or 6 to include all major oil companies. The total volume of trade the Italian Embassy representative in London mentioned at stake in Persia was $20 million a year. Italy could scarcely expect to keep both.[66]

In 1953 the struggles in Iran reached new proportions, with the government allowing the Tudeh party, whose popularity was increasing owing to the continued economic and social crisis, the growth of anti-Western sentiment, and the Tudeh's partial support for Mosaddeq, to operate more openly. The religious revival forces of the leader of the majles ulama, Ayatollah Kashani, who had a long record of opposition to Western, and particularly British, incursions in Iran, also became stronger. Oil negotiations were stalled. The British and Americans involved were unwilling to allow Iranians really to control their own oil, while the Mosaddeq government would not settle for less.

In late February 1953, General Fazlollah Zahedi, a former collaborator with Nazi Germany, was arrested for plotting with foreigners to overthrow the government. In March there were serious conflicts between Mosaddeq and the shah in which Mosaddeq emerged victorious after large popular demonstrations in his favor. The government released Zahedi as a conciliatory gesture, but there continued to be apparent military and foreign-inspired plots against the government.

In the first half of 1953, relations became increasingly embittered between Iran and the United States government. In January Mosaddeq wrote to President Dwight Eisenhower saying that the United States had supported the British in the AIOC controversy, had withheld aid from Iran, and had helped the British enforce an economic blockade. After a letter from Mosaddeq requesting economic aid, Eisenhower responded in June that the American people felt: "it would not be fair to the American taxpayers for the United States Government to extend any considerable amount of economic aid to Iran so long as Iran could have access to funds derived from the sale of its oil and oil products if a reasonable agreement were reached. . . . Similarly, many American citizens would be deeply opposed to the purchase by the United States Government of Iranian oil in the absence of an oil settlement."[67]

Although many Iranians knew from the first that the United States Central Intelligence Agency (CIA) was involved in the overthrow of Mosaddeq in August 1953, only gradually did details of these events become available in the Western world. The idea of overthrow became stronger in British and American official and oil circles over time. It gained some impetus from the replacement of the British Labour government by the Conservatives and, in early 1953, the replacement of the Truman government, which had refused to join schemes for Mosaddeq's overthrow, by the Eisenhower administration, with John Foster Dulles as secretary of state. Specific plans for Mosaddeq's overthrow clearly originated with British Intelligence, but were modified by the CIA. According to various sources including Kermit Roosevelt, he simplified the British plan and helped get it accepted by the very willing Dulles brothers (Allen, head of the CIA, and John Foster); by other high-ranking officials, and, via John Foster Dulles, by President Eisenhower. Roosevelt then traveled to Iran to put it into effect via Iranian contacts developed through American and British sources.

The period was relatively propitious, as there had been important defections from Mosaddeq, including some leftist leaders and groups in the National Front, and especially Ayatollah Kashani and some of his religious nationalist followers. Most of Mosaddeq's support, including the rest of the ulama deputies, remained, however, despite discontent over economic problems. A major cause of dispute between Mosaddeq and the shah had been Mosaddeq's attempt to get control of the army, which was still mostly loyal to the shah and influenced by its American advisers. Mosaddeq failed in this, although there were some Mosaddeq supporters at the top of the army, which remained a crucial weak link in Mosaddeq's control of the situation. During his premiership Mosaddeq had worked to limit the shah's powers as intended by the 1906–07 constitution, but although he succeeded in other spheres, he did not in the military.

The Anglo-American overthrow plan (in which the British could not participate on the scene as British officials had been expelled from Iran) involved telling the shah of the plan and its foreign backing and getting him to dismiss Mosaddeq as premier and appoint his own favorite, General Zahedi. The orders for dismissal and appointment were delayed, and Zahedi's forces delayed action a day further, allowing Mosaddeq to learn of the plot, apparently via the Tudeh, and to mobilize and abort the planned coup. As had been agreed in case of failure, the shah and queen flew in their plane from the Caspian to Baghdad, but when the Iranian ambassador there, a Mosaddeq man, moved against them, they went to Rome.[68]

There was now major antiroyalist rioting, and two CIA-financed Iranian agents-provacateurs hired a large crowd on August 17 to shout

Tudeh slogans and overturn statues of the Pahlavi Shahs. Pressed by the U.S. ambassador, the Mosaddeq government ordered the rioting suppressed by the army and police, which it was. This largely caused the crucial split between the two most powerful forces that could have united against a foreign-inspired overthrow of Mosaddeq—the Tudeh party and the Mosaddeq coalition. It brought the police and army effectively into the streets and helped to keep the Tudeh from defending Mosaddeq on August 19.[69]

On August 19, 1953, a crowd led by the strongmen (in a literal sense) of the bazaar in south Tehran and including religious leaders began to move northward, and were joined by military forces. Both Kashani and especially the leading Tehran Ayatollah, Behbehani, actively supported the coup. Roosevelt states that the crowd was inspired by his Iranian agents, and he had also received the cooperation of key men in the military. He speaks of the expenditure of less than $100,000 by the CIA, although Loy Henderson and others have said millions were spent, and there may have been British expenses.[70] Partly because of its recent bad experiences with Mosaddeq the Tudeh did little or nothing to call out its masses of followers to defend Mosaddeq, a policy for which it later engaged in strong self-criticism. Between the crowd and the army the Mosaddeq regime had no chance, and although the premier escaped he soon gave himself up. He was later tried by a military court, defended himself brilliantly, and escaped the death penalty asked by the prosecution, being sentenced to three years in jail, followed by house arrest in his village. His foreign minister, Hosain Fatemi, was killed, however, and there were massive arrests, jailings, and executions in subsequent years.[71] There is no doubt that the original coup was CIA-planned on the basis of British and American proposals, although Roosevelt took the initiative himself the second time. The coup could not have succeeded without significant internal disaffection or indifference, but without outside aid it would not have occurred.

The 1953 coup, which culminated a year later in an oil agreement leaving effective control of oil production and marketing and 50 percent of the profits in the hands of the world oil cartel companies, had an understandably traumatic effect on Iranian public opinion, which has continued down to the present, with varying intensity at different times. Although most Iranians understood almost from the start that both the British and Americans were involved, by most the Americans were and are especially blamed. Not only were the Americans more directly involved, but Iranians expected little more of the British, especially since their oil company was in question, whereas America had raised high hopes among some Iranians in the past. In the early stages of the oil dispute, men like Ambassador Henry Grady and Max Thornburg had expressed support for Iran's stand against AIOC's proposed terms, partly because they were unfair in comparison to those that the United States had to give elsewhere, and both they and Truman and Secretary of State Dean Acheson had aroused some hope that the United States might be a counterweight to the British. Iranian reaction to the progressive American betrayal of these hopes, accompanied by American media attacks on Mosaddeq as a virtual madman whose "support" for the Tudeh party and obstinacy over oil were supposedly driving Iran into the Soviet sphere, was rather parallel to the Iranian reaction to the Anglo-Soviet 1907 entente dividing Iran into spheres of influence. In both cases a power that had been seen by nationalists, on the basis of some experience, as a possible counterweight to a more dangerous foreign power ended up by combining with that dangerous power and undermining a popular nationalist movement. After 1907 it took a few years for the Iranian constitutional revolution to be overthrown by Russian pressure and troops, combined with British acquiescence and troops in the south. In 1953 the joint overthrow by two powers of a major Iranian nationalist movement was quicker, but the pattern was similar. In both cases the foreign power formerly favored by Iranian nationalists was especially blamed, as it was seen as a betrayer and not just an old enemy. Although both nationalists and leftists were long discouraged and persecuted, they did not forget or give up hope.

Mosaddeq's defense of Iran's independence, his defiance of AIOC, his charisma, and his overthrow with American and British support helped make him an enduring national hero. Oppositionists of the most varying views—Marxists, leftists, liberals, and rightists, both secular and religious—invoked his name and example, cherished his picture, and found appropriate quotations from him to support their views. These groups and Mosaddeq were united in their continued desire to lessen foreign control and influence and increase Iran's independence. As the post-1978 years showed even more than did 1951–53, reducing foreign control, necessary though this is, neither solves all important problems nor preserves the unity of coalitions that lack clear constructive programs and embrace a range of ultimately incompatible elements.

7

Royal Dictatorship:
1953–1977

General Character of the Period

The overthrow of the nationalist Mosaddeq regime in
August 1953 by an American- and British-supported coup changed
postwar Iran's situation in several basic ways, most of which remained
important for the quarter century of ensuing dictatorial rule. First, the
United States, which had had in the early postwar period an uneasy
partnership with Britain in influencing Iran—the British monopolizing
oil while the United States dominated in military and governmental advice and support—now became the dominant foreign power in Iran. This
was reflected in the United States taking a 40 percent share in the oil
consortium in 1954—the same large minority percentage as was held by
the AIOC, now redubbed British Petroleum (BP). It was also reflected
in America's ever-growing lion's share of military supplies and advisers
and in civilian and governmental programs, as well as in various forms of
investment by the United States government and companies that now
entered Iran in greater numbers.

Second, as a result of United States involvement in Mosaddeq's overthrow and continuing American support for the shah, however dictatorial he might become and however many persons were jailed and
tortured, earlier hopes that the United States might help in supporting a
more democratic government in Iran declined. There remained some
Iranians, however, who thought Americans were being fooled by the
British or by the shah and would pressure their government to change its
behavior if it only knew the truth. Older National Front leaders fol-

lowed this line, but from 1961 on, the successors of the National Front concentrated increasingly on opposing the shah.[1]

Third, the shah himself, who had earlier struck outsiders as an uncertain young man who had grown up fearing his harsh father, was increasingly prepared to engage in repressive and dictatorial acts, however much they might be covered over by superficially democratic or Western forms. Not only age and experience explain this change. During World War II the Allies had pressured the shah to adopt more liberal and democratic forms than had his father, but after the Mosaddeq threat to the interests of the world oil cartel, dominated by American and British companies, Western governments and corporations felt safer with a centralized government under a pro-Western ruler who would not again allow into power a regime that might threaten economic and political relations with the West. While many in the United States and Britain spoke mainly of a Communist threat, in which they may have believed, the source of most of their outrage in 1951–1953, as with Nasser's 1956 nationalization of the Suez Canal, was a non-Communist nationalist government taking over, in defiance of the West, economic and strategic resources important to the West. Occasional Western pressures to mitigate his dictatorship, as in the early 1960s, were finessed by the shah, who probably knew where the real priorities of American governmental and business interests lay. Such pressures were in any case rare. In the widely read American press between 1953 and 1973 there is very little basic criticism of the Shah or of United States policy in Iran; the shah was overwhelmingly presented as a progressive, modernizing ruler whose problems lay in a backward population and some Iranian fanatics. Only after the shah pioneered in the OPEC oil-price rise in late 1973 did part of the American press and a few officials begin to note some of his faults. Some, usually secret, official documents were more critical and realistic, but they rarely resulted in action.

Fourth, beginning in the 1950s and increasingly in the next two decades, the shah showed a growing interest in modernizing Iran's economy and society and in making the country Western in character and militarily strong. In this he followed his father's precedent, but whereas Reza Shah, with fewer economic resources and much lower oil income, had minimized economic dependence on the West in his modernization program, Mohammad Reza greatly increased it. This was partly owing to an emphasis, common in the Third World but here carried to extremes, on big showy projects, supersophisticated and expensive weapons, and fancy consumer goods, all of which put Iran in a position of long-term dependence on Western countries, especially the United States, and which were profitable to American companies. ("Dependence" here is a relative concept, unconnected with Dependency Theory, which understates the possibility of independent action by the Third World.)

Fifth, under the dictatorial regime that developed after 1953 there were increasingly only two ways to deal with opposition, whether religious, nationalist, or Marxist. One was repression, including jailing, torture, and killing (the latter two especially in the 1970s). The other was co-optation of oppositionists, used especially in the 1960s and 1970s. Oppositional students and other ex-opponents were brought into the ever-widening network of governmental jobs on the understanding that they would not talk or act out of turn. The increase in good governmental jobs, salaries, and perquisites as oil income grew made this an effective strategy for a time, but did not bring about real loyalty to the shah. Participation in decision making was not broadened and freedom of expression actually declined over time.

Sixth, after the Mosaddeq experience the shah decided he wanted an effective internal security service and set up the large organization known by the acronym SAVAK in 1957. Aid to SAVAK from the American CIA and the Israeli Mossad assured some efficiency, but added to feelings against the countries that helped train SAVAK. One part of SAVAK was involved in the jailings, beatings, and tortures that became notorious in the years before the revolution, but there were also suave, educated operatives in coats and ties who persuaded people of the dangers of speaking or acting out of turn. In addition, the shah maintained other intelligence services, partly to check on each other.[2] Numerous intelligence agents infiltrated opposition groups, and many informants, as in American and other intelligence services, worked part time for SAVAK. With jail, torture, or even death as the possible stakes, it is not surprising that even underground or exile oppositional groups were decimated and suspicious or that within Iran people were increasingly hesitant to discuss politics at all.

Seventh, as the shah (with some variation in different periods) built up his autocratic powers and associated opposition with disloyalty or treason, his retinue hesitated to confront him with uncomfortable facts. Without anyone to contradict him, he may have really believed the picture he presented in his words and books of himself as an enlightened ruler leading his people to a better life in a strong, independent Iran, opposed only by "black and red reactionaries" (religious fanatics and Communists). It is not credible that he did not know of the tortures he often denied, and he cannot have believed all he said, but did believe his beneficent picture of himself, underestimated Iran's problems, and overestimated his ability to solve them.

Eighth, the suppression or co-optation of much of the opposition over the years, including both its leftist and its more liberal or moderate elements, along with the growing gap between the masses and elite, made it increasingly likely that eventual effective opposition would come from those who could appeal to the traditional disaffected masses more than from Westernized liberals or leftists. Western values did not trickle down to the popular classes any more than did significant benefits from the modernization program. Ultimately the vast majority of Iranians became more anti-Western, more anti-shah, and more open to oppositionists who stood against the shah, the West, and Western ideas.

1954–1960

After the overthrow of Mosaddeq, the shah and those around him were determined to ally with the West and try to develop the Iranian economy along Western lines. The Mosaddeq experience of boycott and the refusal of foreign aid made the new regime believe that economic development depended on settling the oil dispute, which had been an implicit condition of American and British backing of the coup. Development was also seen as dependent on loans and direct aid from the United States.

From the time of his restoration, the shah was determined never to allow a Mosaddeq type of situation to recur. This meant emulating Reza Shah in ignoring the main thrust of the 1906–07 constitution, which had foreseen government by a cabinet responsible to a freely elected majles and had reserved few powers for the shah. It also defended freedom of speech and the press, with minor exceptions. Elections to the eighteenth majles early in 1954 were firmly controlled and candidates were chosen by the regime so that it, like subsequent majleses, was subservient to the shah. In 1955 the shah dismissed Prime Minister Zahedi, whom the Americans had seen as Iran's real strongman, and the shah became Iran's single ruler.

In the face of arrests and persecution, most opposition groups went underground, especially the Tudeh party, which was the most persecuted and most of whose leaders had to flee Iran. Iranian security forces uncovered a network of Tudeh or pro-Tudeh officers in the army, whose extent they may have exaggerated but whose existence was real. There were many executions and a widespread purge of the armed forces, and new legislation against oppositional organizations was passed by the majles.

The United States, particularly after the shock its government and business interests had received from the Mosaddeq years, was prepared to give extensive financial aid and advice to a regime that they knew to be strongly anti-Communist; which was making the right noises about economic development, social progress, and reform; and which seemed eager to take American advice regarding the use of United States aid. Also, the United States and Iran anticipated a new oil agreement pleasing to both regimes and to American oil companies, whose payments could provide some extra development funds. Immediately after Mosaddeq's overthrow the new government received a $45 million emergency loan from the United States. In December 1953, diplomatic relations with Britain, broken off during the Mosaddeq period, were restored.

A miscalculation by Mosaddeq and his backers had been that Britain and the West would face a shortage of oil if the large Iranian oil production were cut off. In fact, fields in Iraq and Kuwait, largely controlled by the AIOC, soon made up for this production, thus depriving Mosaddeq of his only real weapon (his attempt to scare the United States with a potential Communist takeover was counterproductive). Now, however, an opposite problem existed of reintegrating Iranian oil into a world system that was producing enough without it. Given world control of production and prices by the cartel of major oil companies, "the seven sisters," this turned out not to be difficult, especially since all seven companies were dealt in on Iranian oil and hence were not hurt if their production elsewhere was lowered. Discussions between AIOC (renamed British Petroleum) and other major cartel companies, and the United States government's renunciation of antitrust barriers to American companies' participating in an Iran consortium, paved the way for an agreement. In April an international consortium was established and began negotiations with the Iranian government. The consortium included: BP, 40 percent; Royal Dutch Shell, 14 percent; Compagnie Française des Pétroles, 6 percent; 8 percent each to Standard Oil of

New Jersey, Standard Oil of California, Gulf Oil Corporation, Texas Oil Company, and Socony-Mobil. The five United States majors later gave up one percent each of their share to a group of American "independents," who thus held a 5 percent share together.

The consortium reached agreement with the Iranian government in August 1954; it passed the majles with little opposition, and came into force in October 1954. The agreement was essentially for 50–50 profit sharing, which was common in the Middle East, with nationalization retained only in theory. In order to claim nationalization, the new forty-year concession took the form of a lease of most of the 1933 concession area. The concession was operated for the consortium by two companies for exploration and producing and one for refining. Nonessential housing and service functions were to be handled by the National Iranian Oil Company. All major decisions, such as production levels and the sale price of oil, remained in the hands of the consortium and its constituents, and the agreement was in essence similar to those in operation in nearby countries. A secret consortium accord that in effect limited production and income became known to Iran only in the 1970s. Soon Iranian oil began to regain its share in world markets and new income began to accrue to the government.

Iran was again able to embark on the now fashionable road of economic planning. Abolhasan Ebtehaj, governor of the National Bank (Bank Melli) and a widely respected economist and administrator, was appointed head of the Plan Organization (PO) in September 1954, and a second Seven Year Plan was scheduled to start in 1955. The final expenditure figure for this plan was $1.16 billion. At first all oil revenues were to go to the PO, but owing largely to characteristic corruption and mismanagement an increasing proportion of oil revenues was diverted to general expenses, and the proportion going to the PO fell to 55 percent. This plus inflation necessitated cutting down on several projects and having recourse to foreign loans. Of proposed Plan expenditures about 26 percent was allocated to agriculture, 33 percent to communication and transport, 15 percent to industry, and 26 percent to social services.[3]

In this and later plans large amounts of money, materials, and labor were devoted to building large dams for irrigation and power generation. Most dams have been poorly planned and wastefully expensive; more seriously, the stress has been overwhelmingly on the dams themselves, which are showy and spectacular, and on power generation. Often the subordinate local irrigation systems, without which the dams serve no agricultural purpose, were not built for years, if ever, nor have the areas been adequately studied to see if the planned types of irrigation and field allotment are suitable to the regions. Dams formed a part of the later agribusiness disasters in the province of Khuzistan. Planners, the shah, and many foreign advisers preferred large, impressive projects to those that would increase the output of the intensive labor of peasants, no- mads, and small-scale workers. In addition to inexperience, corruption, and sometimes bad foreign advice, Iranian plans suffered from jealousies between ministries and government departments that wanted the PO to give them the money and let them implement projects. The PO, on the other hand, wished to have ministries act under its instructions on de- velopment projects. This unresolved and continuing dispute, punctuated by currying of favor with the top by the involved parties, was one cause of Ebtehaj's forced resignation as head of the PO in 1959 and his replace- ment by more pliable and less competent directors in the next few years. Ebtehaj also disagreed with economically irrational royal interference with the plan.

The influx of foriegn exchange after 1954, chiefly from oil revenue but also from loans and aid, helped finance PO development projects, which progressed, however skewed they often were. The foreign-exchange in- flux also encouraged private investment, and investment and GNP both grew. Increased corruption and the lack of control of imports or credit led to serious inflation, while the impossibility of real trade-union orga- nization, or effective strikes or collective bargaining helped keep wages down, thus widening the disparity between rich and poor. Price rises were concentrated on necessities like grain, which particularly hit the poor. With no control on imports or on the export of currency there was a bad fall in foreign exchange reserves, which helped precipitate a finan- cial crisis in the autumn of 1960.

Before the early 1960s the regime was apparently deluded by the rise in GNP, the efficiency of the army and security forces in suppressing opposition, and by American economic and military support, into think- ing that no major structural reforms were needed. The shah may have thought that enough other landlords would follow his example of selling land relatively cheaply to peasants so that no government-enforced land reform would be needed. The shah's case was, however, very special. His father had acquired, mostly by dubious means, about two thousand villages, and after Reza Shah's abdication there was a clamor for the return of these lands to their former owners. When this appeared almost impossible the shah turned over the land to the majles for disposition, but later took it back and inaugurated his own sale of these lands to cultivating peasants. It was not widely known that the money realized from these sales remained under the shah's control or that about a third of the land was given to wealthy favorites and members of the royal family.[4] (Mosaddeq's opposition to the shah's distribution program was not based on opposition to land reform but on his conviction that these lands did not really belong to the shah, and that any reform program should be initiated by the government.) The shah's example was not followed, and the majles and senate (an upper house half appointed by the shah included in the constitution but instituted only in 1949), representing mostly big landlords, blocked land-reform legislation.

By 1960 the shah and his American advisers were convinced some kind of land reform was needed and a bill was drafted for the division of large estates. Opposition by big landlords, represented in the legislature, and also by important ulama, led by the top "source of imitation" (*marja'-e taqlid*), Ayatollah Borujerdi at Qom, brought the amendment of this bill so that by the time it passed, in May 1960, it was so full of exceptions as to be virtually meaningless. Borujerdi's declaration against it helped make it a dead letter.[5]

Among the signs of the shah's pro-Western orientation was Iran's joining the Baghdad Pact in October 1955, along with the other "Northern Tier" countries, Iraq, Turkey, and Pakistan, and also Great Britain. The United States stayed behind the scenes and joined several of its committees but was not formally a member. The pact was considered a hostile alliance both by Nasser's Egypt and by the Soviets, who began to beam hostile broadcasts in Persian into Iran. National Front sympathizers opposed the pact as a means of increasing Anglo-American control of Iran.

In 1958 three new oil agreements ratified by the majles and covering areas outside consortium territory paved the way for more control by Iran over its oil. The first was with the Italian governmental AGIP company, and the other two with private American and Canadian independents; all of them provided for an essentially 75–25 percent profit-sharing deal in Iran's favor, with the foreign companies to bear most of the exploration costs. NIOC also carried out some explorations on its own. The vast majority of production continued to come from fields under consortium control, however, as AIOC had been careful in 1933 to retain all the promising areas in its concession.

In response to pressures for more democracy the shah introduced a two-party system with the hope of making elections appear more real, and also of giving himself leverage against the dominant party should he need it. The governmental Melliyun (Nationalist) party was headed by Prime Minister Manuchehr Eqbal, and the "opposition" Mardom (People's) party was led by Asadollah Alam, one of the shah's oldest confidants and a large landlord. There were no real differences between the two, and both parties were creatures of the shah.

1960–1963

In early 1960, with the approach of elections, problems such as serious inflation, growing corruption, and signs that the economic boom of the late 1950s was about to burst brought to the surface a real opposition outside the two official parties. When campaigning began in June 1960, opposition became strong and vocal. It included a number of prominent personalities, among whom was Dr. Ali Amini, a descendant of the late-nineteenth-century liberal minister Amin ad-Dauleh. Minister of finance during the consortium negotiations and later ambassador to Washington, a post from which he was dismissed, he became a critic of Eqbal and, by implication, of the shah. Although he was, then and later, widely associated by Iranians with the United States, he was considered to represent a liberal wing of American policy makers, like John Kennedy, who did not want to rely on the shah's dictatorship and wished to institute some serious reforms. At the same time National Front leaders began to speak out for free elections and against the government.

The formation of a second party and some official statements implying that the 1960 elections would be free also encouraged various oppositional groups and individuals. Prime Minister Eqbal, however, announced that no pro-Mosaddeq or Tudeh candidates could be elected, and he appeared determined also to exclude independents of Amini's stripe. Eqbal, probably with the shah's connivance, apparently arranged a pact between the two official parties by which each would get a certain number of majles seats, with a majority for his Melliyun party.

As the election results began to come in and evidence of vote fraud grew, open discontent mounted sharply. By late August 1960, the shah decided to dissociate himself from the obvious vote rigging and from Eqbal's growing unpopularity. The shah therefore voiced displeasure with the conduct of the elections and "advised" elected deputies to resign, to pave the way for new elections. With this expression of no confidence from the ruler, Eqbal and his cabinet had to resign. The shah named as prime minister Ja'far Sharif-Emami (who was called to this post again in the 1978 crisis). The elected deputies resigned, with reluctance.

The new government appointed a committee to draft rules for the conduct of elections, which were announced for January 1961. But popular discontent began to be expressed on other matters. Sharif-Emami had to admit Iran's bad financial condition and its low foreign-exchange reserves. A stabilization program was announced that sounded serious, but which was regarded skeptically by those who knew the Iranian elite's skill in circumventing rules. Under this program many import duties were increased in order to discourage nonessential imports; the Central Bank (Bank Markazi) was given powers to limit domestic credit; and strong restrictions were placed on buying foreign exchange. Inflation had been triggered largely by too much credit, little control on foreign currency, purchases of too many nonessential imports, and too little productive investment. But those affected by controls often had enough influence to evade them. Many in the middle and popular classes had been seriously hurt by inflation and saw it as one means by which those with power or influence became enriched at their expense. Hence discontent grew.

The new elections were again considered dishonest, although they were not as flagrantly so as the previous ones. Several independents were elected, including even one National Front leader, Allahyar Saleh of Kashan, despite the strong pressure against National Front candidatures, and official exclusion of such a candidate in Isfahan.

Notwithstanding these difficulties the shah evidently felt reassured by the birth of his first son and heir in late 1960. The shah's first marriage to Princess Fawzia, sister of King Faruq of Egypt, in 1939 had produced one daughter, Shahnaz, but in Iran as in many countries women were not allowed to inherit the throne. Fawzia apparently left the shah. His second wife, Sorayya Esfandiari, with a Bakhtiari father and a German mother, bore no children and the shah divorced her in 1958. His third wife, Farah Diba, he married in early 1960 and she later had two sons and two daughters. She also gained power and influence in cultural and social welfare matters, which did not interest the shah particularly, and acquired her own circle of patronage and influence. Although growing

opposition to the shah encompassed many of his blood relatives, especially his powerful twin sister, Princess Ashraf, and her progeny, Farah
was not generally implicated in the corruption and repressive actions of
the court. It was, however, noted that in traditional style the (queen's)
Diba family was widely represented in the leadership of cultural and
social welfare institutions. In the case of the queen's cousin Reza Qotbi,
the young head of National Iranian Radio Television since its foundation
in the mid-1960s, the appointment was justified by ability and intelligence, shown in choice of staff and in patronage of innovative theatre
and musical groups and film projects unconnected with radio or television (although radio and television were media for government propaganda). Not all the queen's relatives had such justification for their influence, however, and even less did many of the shah's.

To return to the crisis of the early 1960s: the 1961 majles was faced by
major problems. The National Front, seeing the growth of popular opposition and the disarray of court and government, denounced the recently completed elections, with much justification, as fraudulent, and
demanded the dissolution of the majles and a new round of truly free
elections. The majles, seeing that it had to identify to some extent with
the growing opposition, became the scene of numerous denunciations of
corruption in the PO, NIOC, and other government departments. More
seriously, strikes were threatened, and Tehran's schoolteachers, led by a
member of Tehran's independent opposition, Mohammad Derakhshesh,
went on strike and demonstrated before the majles for higher pay. During the demonstration two teachers were killed by the police. This was
the breaking point, and there were rumors of a military coup backed by
the shah or, alternatively, of serious royal concessions. The shah apparently considered bringing National Front members into the government
and had a long interview with Allahyar Saleh. They were unable to reach
agreement, and the next day the shah sent for Ali Amini, the ablest
member of the independent opposition, asking him to form a government. Amini apparently made two conditions, both granted by the shah:
that Parliament be dissolved, and that the shah give him an unequivocal
statement of support.

Amini succeeded Sharif-Emami in April 1961, at a time when it was
widely believed that the survival of the government depended on its
ability quickly to implement major social and administrative reforms.
Amini, despite, and in some cases because of, his American ties, was for a
time in a relatively strong position with various sectors of the popula-

tion. His voiced opposition to the governments of Eqbal and Sharif-Emami gave him some credibility with National Front and other oppositional groups, except for the underground or exiled Tudeh party. It was known that, unlike other prime ministers, he had imposed terms on the shah, and this added to his prestige. The dissolution of the majles at first also pleased the National Front and other oppositionists, who expected new elections soon; when it was seen that Amini expected to rule by decree without a majles, however, much of this support dissipated. Some National Front militants also distrusted Amini because of his part in negotiating the consortium agreement and his ties to the United States.

Amini settled the teachers' strike by awarding the teachers a pay raise and making their leader, Derakhshesh, minister of education. More dramatic was his appointment of Hasan Arsanjani, a lawyer with a radical background, as minister of agriculture. Amini had two ex-ministers arrested for corruption and promised a vigorous anticorruption drive. He needed the shah's support in view of potential opposition from the army and, in the case of land reform, from landlords and some ulama, and the shah needed Amini in order to recoup some power and popularity, but he did not want Amini to become strong or popular enough to undermine a return to his one-man rule.

Amini felt that strong government and reform were possible only with a lengthy, and technically unconstitutional, period of rule without elections or a majles. He and the shah agreed to undertake this and to rule by decree. The unconstitutional failure to call for new elections within a month of the dissolution of the majles led to demonstrations headed by the National Front. In July 1961, a demonstration resulted in the arrest of several National Front leaders and strong restrictions of National Front political activities, which had been open for only about a year. In November a royal decree allowing the government to legislate by decree without a majles brought on further pro-election agitation both from the National Front and from groups opposed to anticipated land reforms. In January 1962 came both the first major land-reform decree and a major riot by Tehran University students, brutally suppressed by the police and army. The students used National Front slogans, but other groups may also have been involved. The government chose to blame "right-wing elements" and arrested several rightist personalities. One man who had been stirring up trouble was the dismissed director of SAVAK, General Taimur Bakhtiar, who saw himself as a potential prime minister if Amini were forced to resign because of disturbances. Amini persuaded the shah to exile Bakhtiar, who went on to plot against the regime until he was finally killed by the shah's order in a "hunting accident" in Iraq. Partly to broaden the base of popular support, from late January 1962, the Amini government devoted itself seriously to implementing the land-reform decree (which, to retain some semblance of constitutionality, was presented as an "amendment" to the toothless 1960 law, but in fact was a wholly new law).

In its relations with the United States, the Amini government was in a relatively strong position. Whereas in the cold-war atmosphere of the mid-1950s the United States government was concerned mainly that Iran be anti-Communist, anti-Soviet, and have a large military force, there were by now some moves toward United States detente with the Soviet Union and war was not considered imminent. It was increasingly seen in the United States, especially during the Kennedy administration in 1961–63, that it might be important to American strategic and economic interests in the area to have an Iranian government with a broader internal base, greater efficiency and popularity, and less corruption than existed in the 1950s. From the unconditional support of the shah, provided he stayed firmly on the American side of the Cold War, United States policy shifted somewhat during the Kennedy years. The shah was asked to deal with corruption and inefficiency, and United States loans and grants decreased. Amini was, as was recognized in Iran, welcomed by the United States, whose officials urged the shah to support him and his reform program. A stress on certain reforms abroad by the Kennedy administration led to some of these changes. The shah was unhappy with American reform pressures, especially as they threatened his one-man rule, but felt he had to make some concessions. Amini had the immediate problem of improving the financial situation. The existing stabilization program had not accomplished a great deal. In its fifteen months in office the Amini government moved toward improving Iran's foreign-exchange position via drastic cuts in nonessential imports and restrictions on foreign travel and purchases of foreign currency by Iranians. But serious problems came in April 1962 when Amini and his new finance minister, Dr. Jamshid Amuzegar, tried to get all ministries to reduce their budgets. The shah refused to reduce the army budget, and so in July Amini resigned, giving as his reason the inadequacy of American aid. Clearly the shah would allow powerful and partially independent ministers to exist only so long as the alternative appeared even more dangerous to his own power. Now Asadollah Alam, the shah's old friend, became prime minister.

Amini never had the cooperation of the National Front forces, who mistrusted him for having accepted the Finance Ministry and the ambassadorship to America from the shah, and they opposed his decision to rule unconstitutionally without a Parliament rather than holding the free elections that they demanded, which would surely have resulted in major National Front and oppositional gains.

Prime Minister Alam met with National Front leaders, who asked for free elections and other freedoms, which were refused. In December 1962 the National Front created a new unified central council and began open attacks on the shah. Most of the central council and many other National Front leaders were arrested soon thereafter, and the shah simultaneously tried to create a reformist image by adding other reforms to the land reform of 1962. To demonstrate his own and his regime's popularity he called early in 1963 for a national plebiscite on a combined six-point reform program including (1) land reform; (2) sale of government-owned factories to finance land reform; (3) a new election law including woman suffrage; (4) the nationalization of forests; (5) a national literacy corps, mainly for rural teaching; and (6) a plan to give workers a share of industrial profits. The vote, which was boycotted by the National Front on the grounds that such programs should be referred to a freely elected majles, was held in January 1963, and, like most such referendums, was overwhelmingly favorable. (Later other reform points were added to these. The program was called the White Revolution, and later by a phrase best translated as "The Revolution of the Shah and the People," but nearly always referred to in the regime's publications as "The Shah-People Revolution"—perhaps awkward style was less important than putting the word "shah" *first*.) The most important of the reforms in practice—land reform and the sale of factories to private industry—helped move landlord capital into industry and other urban projects and to lay the base for a state-dominated capitalism in city and countryside. Land reform also undercut landlord political power to the benefit of the central government.[6]

Although one constituent wing of the National Front, soon to develop into the Freedom Movement, included both lay and clerical religious leaders, notably engineer Mehdi Bazargan and Ayatollah Mahmud Taleqani (who became prominent revolutionary leaders in 1978–79), in general the National Front now had little connection with the large ulama-led opposition movement that developed especially in 1963.

In the Mosaddeq period and subsequently some leading ulama had at first been pro-Mosaddeq but had then backed off from opposition to the shah's regime and had become relatively pro-shah because they had feared the rise in secularist and Communist power under Mosaddeq. Also, Ayatollah Borujerdi of Qom, who became the sole marja'-e taqlid (source of imitation) until his death in 1961, was not unfriendly to the shah and his only important antiregime fatwa came in opposition to the land-reform proposal of 1960. Pressure by prominent ulama may have helped reshape this land reform into innocuousness. Since Borujerdi's death there has not been a single, universally recognized marja'-e taqlid, but several men emerged as leading ayatollahs: among them Mohammad Hadi Milani in Mashhad; Kazem Shariatmadari, an Azerbaijani residing in Qom; and later Ruhollah Khomeini, also living in Qom, who first came to prominence in 1963, because of his oppositional activities. The economic and political crisis that had increased open opposition to the autocratic regime and to its subservience to Western powers affected religious leaders and their followers as it did other groups. The shah's regime labeled the religious opposition as a purely reactionary and largely selfish response to reform, particularly land reform and the woman suffrage included in the new electoral bill. Others have responded that Khomeini and Shariatmadari did not oppose land reform and that woman suffrage was not an important issue, given Iran's rigged elections; rather the crucial issues for Khomeini and others were dictatorship, subservience to the United States, and good relations with Israel.[7] It seems there is some truth and some exaggeration on both sides of the argument; although the latter points apparently were stressed by Khomeini, he and his colleagues also attacked the electoral law, in part but not exclusively for its woman-suffrage provision (he and his associates did not in later years oppose woman suffrage), and some religious leaders, although probably not Khomeini, also opposed land reform.[8] As on many questions in many periods, it is wrong to characterize the outlook of the ulama leadership at this time either as purely "reactionary," as did the regime and most of the foreign press, or as "progressive," as did some Iranian students abroad. Those opposed to dictatorship and to Iranian dependence on the United States may say that the ulama-led forces played a positive role in weakening both of these in 1963 and since, but this does not mean that the ulama were partisans or even nonopponents of many reforms that might help the majority of the population. In the event, land reform turned out to be not very helpful, but had Arsanjani's original plan been carried out it could have been so, and ulama arguments against it in 1962–63 were not based on an economic analysis of how the regime and vested interests would manipulate it in the future. Later, however, Khomeini did criticize the faults in practice of land reform.

Ayatollah Khomeini (see chapter 8) had written a work attacking Reza Shah and highly critical of monarchy as early as 1944, but in the late 1950s he was closely associated with Ayatollah Borujerdi at Qom and politically rather quietist.[9] He did not moderate his views, however, and in early 1963 began to preach against the shah in the chief, Faiziyeh, *madrasa* (religious school) of Qom. In March 1963, on the anniversary of the martyrdom of the Sixth Imam, Ja'far as-Sadeq, the madrasa was attacked by paratroopers and SAVAK, a number of students were killed, and Khomeini was arrested. Released after a short detention, Khomeini resumed his denunciations of the government and its policies. He attacked United States control of Iran and denounced America as an enemy of Islam, partly because of its support of Israel. Interestingly, even in a violent attack on the shah delivered on June 3, he, like most of his colleagues, at this time presented himself as a defender of the (monarchical) constitution: "the constitution has been bought with the blood of our fathers, and we will not permit it to be violated."[10] The next day, on the anniversary of the martyrdom of Imam Hosain, Khomeini was arrested before dawn. When the news became known in Tehran processions of mourning for Hosain turned into demonstrations. Demonstrations spread the next day to the university and to Shiraz, Kashan, and Mashhad. Despite heavy deployments of troops on Friday, June 7, the uprising continued, with one pamphlet calling for Holy War against the regime. The demonstrations were finally suppressed after several days, with loss of life in the hundreds or more.

Although the National Front wing that had religious and bazaar ties participated in the later days of rioting, the National Front had not expected riots and there was not prior collaboration with Khomeini. After the 1963 riots there was to be more cooperation between religious and nationalist opponents of the shah both within Iran and among students and exiles abroad. As was the case in 1977–78, discontent was sparked in part by a few years of painful economic crisis and inflation following several boom years that had helped the rich much more than the poor or the petty bourgeoisie. As in 1977–78 the shah responded to the crisis and to discontent by partial reforms, which were far from meeting the demands of opposition groups and encouraged them to voice their demands more openly. The crisis of 1960–63 was less serious than that of 1977–79, however, and the shah was able to restore his autocratic power by beefing up his security forces, shooting demonstrators, arresting large numbers in the religious and nationalist opposition, and putting forth a program of reform that for a time appeared to have substance. Partly owing to governmental controls and new policies encouraging industry, and partly for cyclical reasons, immediate economic problems were overcome and Iran soon entered a new phase of rapid growth that made many forget that a whole range of basic problems remained untouched and new ones had appeared.

The religious opposition movement continued after June 1963. Khomeini was released from arrest in August 1963 and SAVAK issues a statement saying agreement had been reached with him and the other leading oppositional ayatollahs that they would stop interfering in politics. But Khomeini asked his followers to boycott the parliamentary elections of October 1963, and was again arrested and held until May 1964. At that time SAVAK announced another understanding with him but he denounced this. In October 1964 the majles passed, with an unusual number of negative votes and speeches, a bill to grant diplomatic immunity to American military personnel and advisers. Shortly afterwards the majles agreed to a $200 million loan from the United States for the purchase of military equipment. Both the connection between the two bills and the capitulatory nature of the first were publicly and strongly denounced by Khomeini, who saw them as signs of bondage to the United States. After Khomeini's attack was circulated as a pamphlet, he was exiled to Turkey by the government in 1964, whence he went to Iraq in 1965. There he taught and spoke, with many of his words eventually brought into Iran as writings or cassettes, until his exile, probably under Iranian pressure, from Iraq to France in 1978.

Reform, Boom, and Bust: 1963–1977

The socioeconomic policies of the consolidated autocratic regime in the later 1960s and early to mid-1970s appeared to many, especially outside Iran, as a great success story, and in support of this contention they could point to large increases in Iran's GNP, impressive industrial, agricultural, and infrastructural projects, and a number of social welfare activities. On the other hand, many opponents of the regime proclaimed that all the reforms were fraudulent, that growth benefited mainly the rich, and that there were no structural changes. In fact, the social and economic changes and projects undertaken by the shah's regime in this period may be seen as contributing to a capitalist type of agriculture and of industrial growth, with a natural emphasis on state capitalism, given the autocratic nature of the regime and its monopoly control of the ever-growing oil income.[11] For purposes of brief analytic treatment the years 1962–77 may be seen as a unit in this building up of a predominant state capitalism, undermining of semifeudal forms of landownership seen as a bar both to development and to central government control of the countryside, and encouragement and subsidy to private capitalists. (Some authors, reacting against simplistic equations of Iran and other countries, reject terms like "capitalist"; in fact *every* area is unique but one needs general terms to indicate comparable structures.) Instead of proceeding year by year or five-year plan by plan in discussing the basic features of the economy, it seems more enlightening, within the short compass of this chapter, to deal with developments in key economic sectors over the whole period after 1962 and to stress analytic conclusions rather than details that may be found elsewhere.[12]

Land reform, which was legislated early in 1962, was the earliest phase of new economic policies and of an agricultural program which, by 1977, was clearly going in directions very different from those envisaged by the original architect of land reform, Agriculture Minister Hasan Arsanjani. The first phase of land reform, passed in 1962 and implemented over several years, sold to peasants, on the basis of (usually low) tax evaluations by their landlords, villages held by landlords with over one village. The landlord was allowed to keep one village or, and this was often the option chosen, the "equivalent" of one village by holding, say, the best of the traditional one-sixth divisions of the village in each of six villages. The latter option not only gave the landlord more and better land, but gave him some say in the running of six villages instead of one. Within Iranian villages some sharecroppers had cultivating rights which assured them of a certain share of the crop, and one family might own more than one such right, or might, if they owned oxen or parts of an underground water channel, hold a right without actually being cultivators. On the other hand, about 40 percent of the cultivating villagers were laborers paid in cash, kind, or both according to hours of work done and without cultivating rights. Those who drafted the reform may have been unaware of the number of laborers without cultivating rights who would be left out of reform, but, on the other hand, the shah had spoken out in favor of small landlords, whom he did not wish to buy out and who he said were more productive than large ones. Although population growth limited the number of viable beneficiaries, a more equitable division would have been possible with a more radical taking over of land and equalization of landholding, with cooperative farming where appropriate, than the shah's regime wished to carry out.[13] Hence the reform, like most capitalist land reforms, was unequal even in its relatively progressive first phase supervised by Arsanjani, and even on the level of villagers in the same village; some got more, some got less, and some got nothing.

A widely praised feature of the Iranian land reform was Arsanjani's pragmatic solution to the lack of cadastral surveys for most villages, which would have made very slow any reform based, as in most countries, on acreage limits for landlords. By making the top limit the traditional village unit, the expensive and time-consuming problem of surveying was avoided. As in many countries, some landlords found ways to evade the top limit. Since land reform had been mooted for some years before 1962, and particularly since the government's abortive attempt in 1960, landlords had a chance to make partly fictitious sales or gifts to relatives or friends in order to lessen their legal holdings in return for real control or compensation. Moreover, the bill, with some economic reason, excluded orchards, pastures, plantations, and mechanized farms. It was easy to convert much of one's land to one of these. Although in some areas land-reform officials, who in the first period tended to be young and enthusiastic, tried to disallow any such changes made after passage of the law, this was often not done. In the end, despite many previous reliable estimates that well over half of Iran's land belonged to large landlords with over one village, the best estimate is that something like 9 percent of Iran's peasants got land in this first phase.[14] This is not an insignificant figure, especially as peasants affected by the first phase, unlike those in later phases, usually got whole farming units, i.e., an amount of land equivalent to that which had previously supported their families, and their payments to the government were generally lower than their former rent in kind. By law all peasants receiving land had to join a credit cooperative, and many such cooperatives were formed. These cooperatives were supposed to provide for the credit needs of peasants who formerly resorted to landlords and usurers (who might be peddlers or traders who theoretically charged no interest but instead overcharged for their goods). Studies have shown that the cooperatives were grossly undercapitalized and could not provide enough low-interest loans to those who needed them, so that usury continued at almost the same rate as before, and richer peasants who could borrow more from the cooperatives often re-lent money at high rates to poorer villagers. Also, there were no adequate controls to ensure that loans were used for productive purposes, as they were supposed to be, while the provision that only landowning peasants could be members and receive loans discriminated, amongst others, against credit-worthy village craftspeople, particularly female carpet weavers.

Despite these problems the early record of those who got full shares in the first stage of reform was rather good. Many peasants began to invest in new equipment, including deep wells with motor pumps. There has never been any adequate agricultural education or extension service in Iran, however, and the assumption has been that problems can be solved by a combination of tinkering with property rights and agricultural units and using modern and often expensive equipment from the West without testing its appropriateness to Iran. The traditional means of irrigating much of Iran has been the underground water channel, or qanat, which gets its water from the mountains. It involves a great amount of skilled labor but allows for a democratic division of water and does no ecological harm. The deep wells and pumps, however, after working well for a few years, were found often to lower the water table significantly and some areas that were once cultivable no longer are. Modified qanat construction might be a better approach.

Related problems have arisen, or will arise, in some areas from the use of tractors for plowing (their import has been favored and subsidized by the government). Large amounts of thin topsoil are plowed up in this fashion and in some cases deposited into streams and rivers, which then flood more often and may even change their course. The whole relationship between pasture and farmland has similarly been upset for the worse by new technology. Although American and other Western companies and governments are to blame for overselling such technology, the Iranian regime and many Iranian specialists who should know better were caught up in the idea that what is modern and Western is good. They should rather have studied the difficult problems of an arid country with few remaining forests and thin topsoil, and tried to meet Iran's specific conditions, which may involve modifications of traditional methods rather than straight borrowing from the West. Little has been done even with such a proven reliable method as reforestation; the old regime preferred buying tractors to planting trees. Western agricultural machinery was given preferential treatment over Iranian equipment, and little research went into improving existing methods.

In short, even for the favored peasants of the first phase of reform not enough was done to make available to them appropriate means to increase production for most of them to become significantly more prosperous. As government price controls increasingly favored city dwellers, considered politically volatile, and in effect subsidized foreign grain growers by paying them, but not Iranians, world market prices, peasants became a disfavored class, although there were exceptions. As for the laborers who got no land in villages affected by the first reform phase, they were less likely to be hired by cultivating peasants than by the old landlords, and most of them joined in the swelling migration to the cities, which reportedly reached over 8 percent of the population per year in 1972–73, although this was well above the average 1956–76 rate.[15]

In the spring of 1963 Arsanjani was forced to resign as minister of agriculture, largely because the shah never allowed another man to become too popular and pose a potential threat to his autocracy, and Arsanjani was clearly popular among Iran's peasants. Arsanjani wanted to transfer as much landlord land as possible to the peasants and promoted slogans and expectations of this kind. After his departure, subsequent phases of land reform were far more conservative than the first, and little was done to supplement the first phase, as Arsanjani and many peasants wished, with adequately capitalized multipurpose cooperatives or extension programs with new seeds and other aids to improving peasant output.

The second phase of reform, after its revision under conservative pressure, amounted more to a regularization of the existing system than redistribution of wealth. This stage was to cover, in theory, all remaining villages not in the excluded categories, except for vaqf villages, which were put on ninety-nine-year leases. The landlord owning one village or less was given a series of five choices, among them cash rentals, division of the land based on the former crop division, and sale to the peasant (which very few landlords chose). In a later phase, applied in 1969, all peasants were to get land through installment purchase, but since this generally meant only a percentage of the land they cultivated equal to the percentage of the crop they received under the old system, the majority of Iran's peasants did not get enough land for subsistence and had to find additional farming or other work. In the majority of Iran's villages covered by the second and third phases there were thus far fewer peasants who could make a living than in phase-one villages, and migration to cities by both laborers and poor peasants grew. Migration was also accelerated by population growth. Villages were also hit by the problems of inadequate loan funds, no extension services, and manipulation of prices by the government, which favored the towns and foreigners and disfavored the countryside.

Most government economic and technical aid and encouragement from the late 1960s on went into a small number of large agricultural units, while the small and middle peasant, to say nothing of the impoverished agricultural laborer, were increasingly starved of government help and discouraged from managing their own affairs on a comprehensive cooperative basis. The government bias toward big units was shown within a few years of agrarian reform especially in two policies, embodied in two major programs. One was the law for the creation of farm corporations. In these units one or (usually) more villages were combined into a corporation, with peasants "persuaded" to turn over their recently received lands to the corporation, in return for which they got one or more shares, according to how much land they gave in. Wages were based on a combination of land and labor, but since farm corporations use modern machinery not all shareholders could be employed, and former farm laborers could hardly ever be employed. These groups contributed to the massive migration to overcrowded cities. Farm corporations were run by government specialists sent from Tehran, and required large expenditure for machinery, and for salaries, housing, and other buildings for the nonfarmers. Farm corporation directors often claimed that their enterprises were profitable, but their basis of calculation did not include the government's initial and overhead expenses, and the claim of profitability was not credible. It is clear that, in the early phases at least, peasants generally disliked the farm corporations, although there are no known studies of their attitudes years after joining. It would be surprising, however, if a peasant would put in as much productive effort into a farm corporation as he would on his own farm. About one hundred farm corporations were created by 1978. After the revolution they were often dismantled, suggesting both their unpopularity and unprofitability.

The other form of large production that was favored, at least until 1977, was huge agribusiness, partly owned and operated by multinational corporations. These farms of five thousand to twenty-five thousand hectares were generally built below new dams, especially in Khuzistan. Despite their supposed concentration on "new" land, they too cleared off many small peasants, and those who did not become agricultural laborers joined the rural exodus. Agribusinesses generally farmed only a small part of the land they held, and their relative contribution to the Iranian economy was seen as dangerously small by Iranian experts. Before 1978 some of the largest agribusinesses, especially in Khuzistan, were taken over by the government in part because of poor performance. Both agribusinesses and farm corporations have been proven to be far less productive than middle peasants.[16] This is largely because they have involved huge expenses in preparing the ground for irrigation and heavy machinery in a land of low-cost labor suited to cheaper home-manufactured implements. They appear to have been favored both by foreign farm equipment manufacturers and by Iranian special interests who skimmed off large sums, which they invested in more profitable ventures. They often concentrated on unproven export crops and hence lowered Iran's food production and contributed to a growing dependence on food imports.

Government policy also favored private mechanized farming. Toward the reformed villages, however, the government did little in terms of economic or technical aid, or aid in forming multipurpose cooperative societies. In some spheres there was progress in a minority of villages, as in the military-service literacy corps, supplemented to a small degree by health and development corps. In the more direct problems of production, however, the government did little. Few of the technical benefits of the "green revolution" were diffused; there were scarcely any efforts to pool resources for machinery; and extension services and technical education remained extremely inadequate. Most cooperatives remained purely credit societies, instead of giving the aid in marketing and production that a multipurpose society could give. Restrictive cooperative loan policies described above favored a growing disparity of income within the village, also favored by the digging of deep wells, which often monopolize water that once was more democratically divided from underground channels. The well-owner can sell a precious resource.

In favoring mechanized extensive farming and disfavoring the small and medium peasant, despite the latter's proven higher productivity per person within Iran itself, the Iranian government adopted a policy that might have been economically rational in a country with large cultivable territory and a shortage of labor. In Iran, however, the present cultivable surface is too small for a heavily underemployed rural labor force, and to push ahead with large mechanized farms rather than more intensive techniques operated by peasants with a personal stake in their own lands was counterproductive. The production record of agribusiness was miserable; farm corporations contributed less than would the same amount of government capital and effort spread over reformed villages, and increases in agricultural production were low. Although official statistics on the annual rise in agricultural production state that it was about 4 percent a year, this figure is almost universally considered unreliable and based on the need to mask the shocking reality that agricultural production rose more slowly than population. A more reasonable estimate is that agricultural production rose about 2–2.5 percent a year, population 3 percent, and consumption of agricultural products about 12 percent. With rising mechanization, the unemployment or very low income of agricultural laborers, and the rise in rural population, there was a rapid stream of rural migrants into the cities, especially Tehran—cities without the housing, amenities, or even jobs to cope with them. The agrarian situation plus a growth in food consumption meant a rapid rise in agricultural imports, which would create a major problem when oil income began to run out. The government also reduced sheep production, forcing ever more imports of meat and wool. Despite the huge migration to towns rural population grew slightly, owing to natural increase,[17] but migration was concentrated among men of working age, leaving agriculture further weakened.

If the government favored the big over the small in both city and countryside, it also favored the cities—already wealthier and more powerful—over the countryside. This was shown particularly in price controls on basic food products, which for a time kept down the vocal discontent of the volatile urban masses. These controls were often based on fixed low prices paid to producers for certain agricultural products—prices that further depressed agricultural incomes relative to urban ones.

Similar problems were felt by tribal-pastoral peoples. Although it was probably tribal khans who instigated a revolt related to land reform among the Qashqa'i and Boir Ahmadi of Fars province in 1963, ordinary tribespeople also suffered from the government's agricultural policies. First, townspeople and wealthy farmers were more likely to take advantage of loopholes in the land-reform law to lay claim to disputed tribal land than were tribespeople who had less influence with the authorities. Second, the nationalization of pasture, one of the points added to the White Revolution, took away tribal control of pastureland and made tribes increasingly subject to governmental whims, policies, and gendarmes. Agricultural and other projects spread at the expense of pasture, and tribespeople were less and less able to support themselves by a primarily pastoral existence. In the 1970s especially the government became increasingly convinced, partly persuaded by American businessmen, that instead of relying on the nomads' sheep for much of Iran's meat the government should underwrite the creation of large meat, poultry, and dairy farms, with expensive imported equipment, cattle and feed. Like other large agricultural projects these were both costly and unproductive, besides the fact that Iranians prefer fresh sheep and lamb to the beef and imported frozen meat that the government's policies toward pastoralists increasingly forced on them. Mohammad Reza Shah, like his father, in fact pursued a policy of settling the nomads—not by force of arms but by depriving them of their livelihood so that they had increasingly to become agriculturalists or enter the subproletariat of the urban slums.[18] As in the case of peasant farming, the regime felt that nomadism was not modern whereas big American-style animal farms were; and wealthy Iranians and Americans profited from the latter. In both cases a way of life in which ordinary people had learned to make maximum use of marginal resources, and which could survive with tested modifications, was increasingly sacrificed to a wholesale use of inappropriate modern Western imports. (Since 1979 some nomads have moved back into lands taken from them, and the last chapter in this old struggle has yet to be written.) Although in both agriculture and industry large mechanized enterprises made up a minority of total units, the important point is that investment and efforts were heavily concentrated on such units while small producers were disfavored. Land reform may never have had primarily economic goals; a major aim was to cut landlord power and bring peasants and nomads under direct government control, and this was accomplished.

The industrial sphere has been somewhat more connected to Iran's Five Year Plans than have major agricultural changes (land reform, in particular, was not suggested in the plan that covered the period in which it was launched). The defects of the first Seven Year Plan have been noted above. Later plans have become increasingly sophisticated in technique and personnel and increasingly comprehensive in coverage, although a running battle between the "independent" Plan and Budget Organization and the ministries that were supposed to carry out its projects but preferred to control their own, was a continual cause of delays and immobilization. In the late 1950s an Economic Bureau was set up for the Plan Organization assisted by a group of Western advisers under the auspices of Harvard University. The only general evaluation published by a member of this bureau is almost totally negative about planning in Iran, and notes that the main economic advances experienced by Iran in the past half century have occurred not through planning but because of nationalism—such as the increasing control over oil, tariffs, and relations with foreigners.[19] It is thus best to be wary on the subject of planning in Iran. The regime indeed followed a general economic strategy, which was much influenced by increasingly large oil revenues. It is likely, however, that much of this strategy might have been followed without the mechanism of a Plan Organization, although the latter had some effect and played the ideological role of indicating that the government was thinking ahead for the benefit of the whole country, and using the most modern mechanisms to ensure rapid economic and social progress. Often the dictates of the shah in fact determined economic policies.

Governmental strategy toward the economy since the 1960s included rapid development of import substitution industries, especially large enterprises that used much modern and labor-saving technology. Despite a few showy "crackdowns," mainly on retailers or vulnerable targets, extremely large profits were encouraged for both domestic and foreign companies, while less was done for those on the bottom rungs of the economic scale. The above policy was justified by some according to the theory that in early stages of development, income distribution must worsen, and that those at the top of the scale should be favored since they save and invest more than those at the bottom. The rival theory that, at least in the stage Iran had reached, much greater equality of incomes is needed for self-sustaining development if a mass consumer market where people could buy back what they produced were to be achieved, was rarely stated. The regime's race for greater size, military strength, and modernity, with its concomitants of unemployment, waste, corruption, and poverty, affected both agriculture and industry. In both spheres heavy inputs of foreign capital, personnel, and imports were favored by official policies. The shah in the 1970s voiced the expectation that Iran would become one of the world's five top powers in the twentieth century: such a fantasy encouraged heavy collaboration with multinational corporations and short shrift for the everyday needs of most Iranians. The essential mechanisms of the above economic strategy are fairly simple, although not well known to nonspecialists. Oil income was one factor in a generally regressive tax structure, encouraging the government not to enforce its mild income tax and not to institute other progressive taxes. The government could essentially do without tax income and did not try seriously to use taxation either as one means for more just income distribution or to prepare Iranian tax collectors and citizens for the day not long hence when oil will start to run out.

More seriously, the impetus given by oil to the dramatic economic boom experienced by Iran from 1963 until the late 1970s, with per capita GNP rising from about $200 to $1,000 in real terms, and with one of the highest growth rates in recent history for a sizable country, did not lessen the income disparity between the rich and the poor, but the contrary. Gains were concentrated at the upper levels, owing largely to government policies.

In industry, government policies, at least since the 1960s, favored both the private production of relatively expensive consumer durables with a large foreign component and a concentrated market in Tehran, and also the concentration of economic enterprises in or near Tehran. This helped both Iranian and foreign investors, who by law were free to repatriate their profits. (Foreign direct investment outside oil was, however, not very large; foreign sales and personnel were far more important.) Because of its oil income, the government could renounce industrial taxes to favor certain industries or itself build industries or infrastructure that favored large industries; and the government was able on the basis of oil income to pay higher salaries to the higher administrative echelons, thus enabling them to purchase consumer durables.

The relevant government policies included preferential high tariffs, prohibition of certain imports, very low rates for bank loans to large industries, tax holidays, licensing of only a few industries in each field, and preferential treatment for foreign capital. High tariffs and prohibitions may have been needed in some cases at an initial stage in order to launch an industry, but tariffs were seldom lowered, so that there was little incentive to operate efficiently or to direct capital toward those branches of production using local inputs. An unneeded variety of automobiles were assembled and partially produced, while many goods that could be made for popular use in small plants were either imported or handmade in insufficient quantities. Lowered tariffs could rationalize production by reducing the production of complex goods requiring many imported elements and encouraging production of simpler, more popular goods, which should need less tariff production as their manufacture is relatively less expensive. Capital-goods production could also have been encouraged by new tariff policies.

Credit policies were designed to favor large enterprises and the rich Iranians and foreigners who owned and ran them. In general, subsidized rates considerably below the market price of money were available only to large enterprises, whereas small shopowners and craftspeople were starved even for unsubsidized bank credit, since their plants did not provide sufficient collateral for loans. They were generally not eligible for normal bank rates of about 12 percent, but had to borrow in the bazaar at 25 to 100 percent. More employment and less income inequality could have come from an opposite loan policy, with higher commercial rates charged to the big industrialists and subsidized rates to the small owners. (Difficulties in getting bank loans were probably one factor in mass attacks on banks in 1978, although other factors were more often mentioned.)

Tax holidays of various kinds were given to encourage foreign investors, or investors in certain regions. Although this policy was publicized as a way to decentralize industry out of the Tehran region, by offering tax inducements to factories built at least 120 km. from Tehran, it was found that the concentration of industry in the Central province where Tehran is located increased after the policy was enunciated, with a ring of industries built about 120 km. from Tehran.

Although legally a company did not need a license in order to operate, any sizable company did need one to import, export, or deal with the government. Government licenses were given out only to a few companies in each field, their main theoretical rationale being to keep a field from getting so overcrowded that plants overproduced and could not operate to capacity. The need to get and keep a license, like many other government rules, required that top persons in a company spend much time in Tehran cultivating one or more leading people in order to insure the receipt of a license or other needed favors. Regarding licenses and other matters, credible stories circulate of the highest-ranking Iranians (including Princess Ashraf and her son Shahram) who took 10 percent or more of a new company's stock gratis in return for insuring the delivery of a license. Such practices, along with other industrial practices listed above, and other forms of corruption, significantly increased the sale price of Iranian goods, thus limiting their domestic and ultimately needed foreign market. They also further skewed income distribution. Corruption, which mushroomed with the growth of oil income, is in part one more mechanism that pushes wealth up and out. It also made the culpable more subject to royal control. Besides the shah's growing fortune, in the 1970s corruption in the court, royal family, and the elite was so massive as to add significantly to the opposition. Many foreign firms were also involved in payoffs to individuals.

As to foreign capital, although foreigners could legally own only a minority share in Iranian industries, they were subject to few other restrictions and could repatriate profits freely. Brochures for foreign investors proclaimed that profits on capital of 30 percent were normal in Iran. Economists who know the country often spoke of 50 percent, and profits in trade and industry of 100 to 200 percent were not unknown. Hence the "traditional" Middle Eastern reluctance to invest in "unprofitable" industry gave way to an industrial boom concentrating on the assembly of consumer goods and aimed largely at a restricted, relatively wealthy market. Such a boom carried within it major problems.

Foreign investment in Iran was much smaller than was the import of foreign goods, and foreign corporations encouraged the shah's mania for the ultramodern and sophisticated. In armaments the shah bought billions of dollars worth of the latest weapons, often while they were still on the drawing board. Imported high technology computers and other instruments were fed primitive statistics and controlled semiautomatic factories. Iran became a huge market for American grain, some of which was used to feed the imported American cattle and poultry that were supplementing and replacing the nomads' sheep. Sophisticated foreign equipment demanded foreign technicians and workers, who in the 1970s streamed in by the tens of thousands. Americans and Europeans were concentrated in the high technical posts, Far Easterners often held skilled labor positions, and Afghans came in for unskilled jobs, often depressing wage rates. The skilled foreigners, to the contrary, got higher salaries than Iranians—sometimes several times higher—and this, plus their behavior and their pushing up the price of scarce housing, helped make them objects of resentment.

It is within the context of industrial policies favoring large profits by a few capital-intensive industries that the occasional campaigns against "profiteers," or in favor of shareholding by factory workers, which were given more publicity than the above policies, should be evaluated. Such measures were either scapegoating or palliatives in face of rising profits, income inequalities, high inflation, corruption, and a failure to meet government promises of greater economic and social equity. Along with certain other policies they were designed to allay the discontent of the class that evinced, through fairly frequent, illegal, and unreported strikes, its continued discontent—the factory workers. Partly through government favoring of workers in large factories by shareholding and other measures, which were, however, less dramatic than their announcements would make it seem, and partly through rising wages for qualified workers, workers in large factories and in certain trades became a relatively favored group in the mid-1970s. One cannot, however, take reports regarding groups of workers whose wages, say, tripled in a few years, as typical of the popular classes en masse. As for the jailed or exiled "profiteers," they were more often disfavored bazaar merchants or members of minorities than rich modern Muslim businessmen.

All this does not mean that the government's industrial policies produced only negative results. The rate of industrial growth was one of the highest in the world, and rose further with the impact of huge oil revenues since 1974. What was questionable was the continuation of preferential policies toward Western-style industries; the disfavoring of small crafts and industries, which contribute to production, to employment, and to greater income equality; the favoring of foreign investments and the kind of production requiring a huge foreign presence; and the underwriting of heavy consumer durables. These contributed to the overcentralization of the national market in Tehran, and to the development of a kind of demand which meant that "import substitution" led to a rise in imports of food, capital goods, and many consumer goods. Thus, many of the problems often noted by Iran's own planners—such as overcentralization in Tehran and a few large cities, too many automobiles and luxury imports, too much dependence on foreigners, and above all the growing income-distribution disparity—were fed by the government's own policies.[20]

With what has been said, it is not surprising that income gaps widened in the 1960s and 1970s. Although no good income survey exists, there are family expenditure surveys, and on the basis of these Iranian and foreign economists have made studies with similar conclusions. Briefly, since the 1960s, income inequalities in Iran, which were already great on a world scale, increased, and this increase was particularly dramatic after 1974, when oil income shot up after the great price rise. The size and increase in Iran's distribution gap are notable whether the top decile or two are compared with the bottom decile or two, or whether one takes the Gini coefficient, which measures deviation from the norm all along a normal distribution scale. In addition, an important Iranian study shows increases in income inequality in all major dimensions: between the top and the bottom, between the cities and the countryside, within the cities, and within the countryside.[21] All this occurred despite a repeatedly expressed government determination to reduce income inequality. However, as noted, overall it was primarily the rich who were subsidized by oil and other governmental money, and the poor much less.

This does not mean that most of the poor literally got poorer. Given the huge increase in GNP per capita, the rich could get much richer and many of the poor get somewhat richer. The poorer classes started from such a low income level, however, that even doubling or tripling their effective income would not bring them to anything like European working-class standards. Also, they saw the conspicuous consumption of the elite all around them, and this gave rise to increasingly vocal discontent. The consumption patterns encouraged by this distribution along with dizzy oil-based growth after 1973 created a host of national problems: constantly increasing spending on imports; orientation of the economy toward dependence on foreigners; the huge population flow into overcrowded cities; and a lack of urban low-cost housing and sky-rocketing housing prices, exacerbated by the growing presence of foreigners whose high wages added to rising prices and scarcities, particularly in housing. More equitable income distribution could both be aided by and contribute to a policy of economic decentralization and dispersion of the population, and could create a market for goods with greater Iranian inputs. A policy favoring peasants and small producers could boost production, add to employment, and encourage population dispersion, especially if crafts and small industries were developed in or near villages. Only diversified investment including towns and villages can humanely meet the needs of Iran's rapidly growing population. Big industries are needed, but so are small ones.

The oil component of Iran's economy became increasingly important over time. Even before the OPEC quadrupling of oil prices led by the shah in late 1973, oil provided a steadily rising income as production went up, and also an increasing percentage of plan funds, rising finally to 88 percent of these. In the late 1960s and early 1970s Iran was able to renegotiate the terms of its agreement with the consortium so that Iran took some control of production levels and pricing, leaving a guaranteed supply to the consortium companies for marketing. Although this involved a partial return to nationalization, it did not hurt the consortium companies; to the contrary, they have profited immensely from every OPEC price rise.

The 1973 Arab-Israeli War led to an Arab oil boycott on Western suppliers of Israel and an effective doubling of oil prices. At the OPEC meetings late in 1973 the shah pushed successfully for a redoubling of prices, arguing with some justice that oil prices had been kept low while prices on all other commodities had risen. Later there were grandiose statements by the shah that Iran would soon become one of the world's five great powers with average incomes equal to the best. The shah seemed not to realize that huge sums could not simply be thrown into the Iranian economy without serious results in terms of inflation, shortages, and overheating the economy. In early 1974 he presided over an official conference where, in the face of ineffective opposition from some planners, he vastly expanded the expenditures programmed for the current Five Year Plan.[22]

Ironically, the shah was in part undone by his OPEC triumph and its consequences within Iran. The processes described above—stress on big industry and agriculture with the resultant overrapid migration and shortages in housing and other goods and services—increased to crisis proportions. In cities shortages of food items, power blackouts, traffic jams, overcrowding, and pollution made life increasingly difficult, and loud arguments and physical fights in the streets were one sign of the strain.

The shah's virtual mania for buying large amounts of up-to-date and sophisticated military equipment from abroad had free rein from 1972, when the Nixon administration underwrote the shah as the policeman of the Gulf, and agreed to sell him whatever nonnuclear arms he wished. Western governments and corporations, with the United States in the lead, were happy to sell, with little consideration on either side of possible negative consequences. Western eagerness to sell billions of dollars of military equipment to Iran each year was reinforced by the economic drain on the West caused by the OPEC price rise; arms purchases seemed a fine way to recycle petrodollars. After the British pullout from the Gulf, the British and American governments were happy to see Iran become the gendarme of the area, fighting leftist-led rebels in Oman's

Dhofar province and threatening other potential disturbers of the status quo. The British provided Iran with more Chieftain tanks than they had in their own armed forces, and the United States let the Shah be the first to buy a series of sophisticated fighter planes, often before they were in production or their reliability had been proved. Iran also began to construct a sophisticated American-designed electronic intelligence network called IBEX for American surveillance of the Soviet Union. Along with all this equipment, as well as numerous less sophisticated items like Bell helicopters, went a large number of expensive foreign technical advisers and instructors and their families, who contributed to inflation and whose behavior often caused justified indignation among Iranians.

American military suppliers like Grumman, Lockheed, and Westinghouse took over key positions in the economy. Many potentially productive Iranians, including a high percentage of the technically trained, were increasingly concentrated in the armed forces and in building projects for army and naval bases and for facilities to transport and house military equipment. New housing starts, and particularly the use of cement, were at times outlawed or rendered impossible because of the heavy demands on cement and other building materials for sheltering military equipment. Thus the growing housing shortage and rise in home prices was tied to military spending, and foreigners' and foreign contractors' willingness to pay high rents added to the problem. The stress on big and complex projects increased, and as there had never been any adequate program of technical education there were not enough Iranians for skilled and technical jobs, much less scientific or managerial ones. Hence the importation of foreigners grew, further contributing to overcrowding, shortages, inflation, and anti-American feeling.

Inflation and other economic problems contributed to the appointment of Jamshid Amuzegar as prime minister in mid-1977. He immediately launched a deflationary program, which brought a sudden growth in unemployment, especially among the unskilled and semiskilled, and this, coming after rising expectations, helped create a classic prerevolutionary situation. The combination of inflation, shortages, and large and evident income-distribution inequities probably contributed more to growing discontent than did the standard factor cited in the West of "too rapid modernization." It was mainly *how* modernization was carried out, and the results of these policies, that were important.[23] Cultural uprooting was also important in the late 1970s, when Westernization was challenged by radical new interpretations of Shi'ism, associated particularly with Ali Shariati (see ch. 8).

While some of the American press and even some government officials began to criticize the shah after he pioneered the OPEC price rise, major United States business interests became more closely tied to, and even dependent on, the shah's regime than ever. This was especially true of three key sectors of American business: armaments, oil, and banking. Producers of high technology, grain and agricultural equipment, and consumer goods also had large sales in Iran. Iran's huge advance orders were more than once responsible for bailing out an American arms manufacturer, some of whom spent vast sums, often illegally, lobbying Iran for business.[24]

The several American oil companies who together marketed 40 percent of the large consortium sales of Iran, the world's second largest oil exporter, profited increasingly from Iran and from high oil prices. Finally, several American banks received and helped invest huge amounts of Iranian money, both from the Iranian government and from funds sent abroad by the shah, the royal family, other rich Iranians, as well as the Pahlavi Foundation, which was an effective charitable front for many profitable royal investments. American banks also owned percentages of Iran's banks and held shares in Iranian businesses. Given these and other Western business interests in Iran and the Anglo-American desire to use Iran strategically in the Gulf, against Russia, and against possible trouble with bordering radical movements in Muslim countries, it is no surprise that United States representatives in Iran predominantly went along with the shah's reported desire that they not contact the opposition, and with his rosy assessment that the opposition consisted of small and unimportant groups of Marxists and religious fanatics. Although the United States under Carter may have influenced the shah some concerning human-rights violations, neither the United States government nor major American business interests wanted to see a fundamental change in Iran's orientation in the direction of nonalignment, reduction of arms and other deals profitable to Americans, or the building up of a more independent, self-sufficient economy. American government and business interests thus preferred the shah to any truly popular alternative, which would have had to reduce American economic and political influence, and might alter Iran's pro-American foreign policy. The only reforms favored by the United States were ones that would not change Iran's pro-American oil, strategic, and economic policies.

To add a brief word about major political developments since 1963 which, until 1977, had none of the drama or importance of the early 1950s or the early 1960s: as the Melliyun party of Eqbal was discredited by the electoral fiascoes of the early 1960s, a new party called Iran Novin (New Iran), was encouraged by the shah. Some of its leaders reputedly had Freemasonic ties, which Iranians often associate with the British. The first prime minister from this party, Hasan Ali Mansur, like Amini and Alam from an old, rich landholding family, ruled only from March 1964 to January 1965, when he was fatally shot by a religious terrorist. There was also an attempt on the shah's life in 1965. Another Iran Novin leader, Amir Abbas Hoveyda, was appointed prime minister in 1965 and held the post for an extraordinary twelve and a half years, owing to the lack of economic and political crises in this period, the apparent success of the government's economic and social policies, and Hoveyda's ability to carry out the shah's wishes without appearing as a threat to the shah's power. In March 1975, the shah announced that the legal parties would be merged into a new single Rastakhiz (resurgence) party headed by Hoveyda. Membership was required of most government and university employees, as well as many others. (At the same time the shah's first autobiography, called in English *Mission for My Country,* was withdrawn from circulation and a new edition minus the passage saying that only Communist and fascist countries used one-party regimes was later issued.) The Rastakhiz party was allowed to have two wings, but each was headed by a loyal pretender to succeed Hoveyda. Instead of mobilizing most Iranians for the regime, the Rastakhiz added significantly to discontent.

The economic and social development of the 1960s and 1970s, of which a critical assessment is given above, was not without positive features, and an early minister of the economy of this period as well as various figures in the PO's high quality staff and in some other departments are generally credited with a number of useful projects and policies. Some industrial, infrastructural, educational, and social welfare achievements were net gains for Iran. Although his low opinion of women as expressed to the journalist Oriana Fallaci is well known, the shah was apparently convinced that it was economically beneficial and would contribute to his modern image to have more women educated and in the labor force. Just as organizations like trade unions and chambers of commerce could exist only under official control, but nonetheless managed to express some of the needs of their members, so independent women's organizations were merged into a single Iranian Women's Organization under the patronage of Princess Ashraf.

Owing partly to pressure from this organization a Family Protection Law was passed in 1967 (repealed and passed in stronger form in 1975). The law introduced a number of important reforms into marriage, divorce, and family law, which until then had been rather strictly based on the sharia and the Quran. To try to make the new legislation Islamically legitimate, a feature of Shi'i (and some Sunni) law was utilized whereby special provisions can be inserted into the required marriage contracts, such as one saying that a husband cannot take a second wife without the first wife's consent. Reform provisions were henceforth to be inserted into all Muslim marriage contracts. According to the new law men could no longer unilaterally divorce their wives, but all divorce cases had to go to court and grounds for divorce by husband or wife were similar. Guardianship of children, which in Islamic law goes to the husband after an age that varies by school of law but in Shi'ism is young, was now to be awarded by the courts according to the merits of the case. No man could take an additional wife or wives without the permission of the previous one(s), and if he did so this was grounds for divorce. While opponents of the shah are right to say that this law was neither totally egalitarian nor universally applied, especially among the popular classes, this is true of such reform legislation everywhere, and is not a good argument against such legislation as one important step toward changing the unequal treatment of the sexes. Even the real problem of lengthy and complex court procedures could have been met by further reform. Unluckily for women's rights, this cause and the Family Protection Law became associated with an increasing unpopular regime and with Western-style mores disliked by religious traditionalists.[25]

Such displays as the shah's coronation and especially the huge celebration in 1971 of a mythical 2,500th anniversary of the Persian monarchy (which had not existed between A.D. 640 and A.D. 1501) showed up the discrepancy between the seemingly unlimited wealth the shah could throw around and the poverty, however slightly mitigated, of most of his subjects. It was hard for many to give the shah credit for any achievements when so much more could have been done with his oil billions (ca. $20 billion a year after the price rise), and when there was little freedom of speech or press and opposition was so ruthlessly suppressed, particularly after the rise of guerrilla groups in the 1960s and 1970s. The effective suppression of the Tudeh after 1953–54 and of the National Front after 1963 as well as the exile or jailing of Khomeini and other oppositional figures helped change the character of the opposition. In part it became more than ever concentrated abroad, particularly among the tens of thousands of Iranians studying in the West, many of whom belonged to various leftist groups, while an increasing number combined leftism or Third Worldism with their interpretation of Islam. The increasing circulation by cassette and leaflet of the talks and writings of Ayatollah Khomeini in exile in Iraq encouraged the religious oppositional trend both outside and within Iran.

With the improvement of relations between Iran and the Eastern European countries in the 1960s and later with China, both the pro-Soviet reformism of one wing of the exiled Tudeh party and the pro-Chinese position of the other wing seemed increasingly unattractive to antishah radicals inside and outside Iran. Beginning in the late 1960s there was a rise in small urban guerrilla groups who carried out a number of assassinations, hitting a few American military personnel and advisers. These groups came to coalesce primarily into two important ones: the Marxist Feda'iyan-e Khalq and the Islamic leftist Mojahedin-e Khalq, both of which became, toward the end of the 1978–79 revolution, large and open revolutionary groups. Guerrilla activities contributed something to the increase in political repression, jailing, tortures, and executions from the late 1960s on; many of those executed were tied to these groups. On the other hand, they also suggested to many oppositionists that it was still possible to act against the regime despite its formidable repressive machinery.[26] At the same time religious and bazaar opposition to the regime continued to be expressed indirectly in sermons, meetings, and ceremonies. The bazaar economy was hurt by the regime's favoring of big, ultramodern enterprises and of foreigners and disfavoring of bazaaris, who bore the brunt of attacks on "profiteers." Given the economic dependence of the ulama on bazaaris and the political influence of each of the two groups on the other, governmental attacks on both helped create a strong oppositional coalition.

By 1977 an economic recession, inflation, urban overcrowding, government policies that hurt the bazaar classes, glaring income gaps, and conspicuous Western-style consumption by the elite and the lack of political freedom or participation were all widely felt and belied the numerous official predictions that the "Great Civilization" was just around the corner. The effective suppression of secular oppositionists, whether from the National Front or Tudeh, left room for the religious opposition, whose sermons, processions, and plays with themes like the martyrdom of Iman Hosain by tyrants were understood to refer to contemporary tyranny, but could not be suppressed.[27] In addition the association of the shah's regime with Western culture, commodities, and vices brought on a traditionalist reaction even among many former Westernizers, which often took an Islamic form.

Clockwise from top left: Sattar Khan, leader of the Tabriz freedom-fighters; Mirza Jahangir Khan, editor of *Sur-e Esrafil;* Sayyed Jamal ad-Din Esfahani and Malek al-Motakallemin, leading popular preachers. All but Sattar Khan were killed following Mohammad Ali Shah's 1908 coup.

Clockwise from top left: Shahsevan tribeswoman of Azerbaijan, 1975; Baluchi, near the Afghan border, 1973; Kurd at a town market, 1974; Arab family, Ahwaz, Khuzistan, 1974.

Qashqa'i tribespeople on autumn migration, 1977.

Qashqa'i factory worker, Marvdasht, 1977.

Family weaving at home, Kerman, 1974.

Carpet workshop, Ardebil, Azerbaijan, 1974.

Blackface clown of the popular theater, Shiraz, 1977.

Ta'ziyeh (passion play) on the death of Ali, Taleqan valley, 1979.

Dr. Ali Shariati (d. 1977), leading ideologist of progressive Iran.

Ayatollah Mahmud Taleqani (d. 1979), a socially conscious cleric.

Left to right: Abolhasan Bani Sadr, Mehdi Bazargan, and Ayatollah Khomeini, early 1979 (photo provided by Yann Richard).

Ayatollah Kazem Shariatmadari, moderate constitutionalist from Azerbaijan.

Women's section, prayer meeting at the University of Tehran, 1979.

Men's section, Mehdi Bazargan (at right) and Sadeq Ghotbzadeh (second from left) in front row.

Silk reeling factory, Gilan, 1974.

Oil workers, Abadan, 1974.

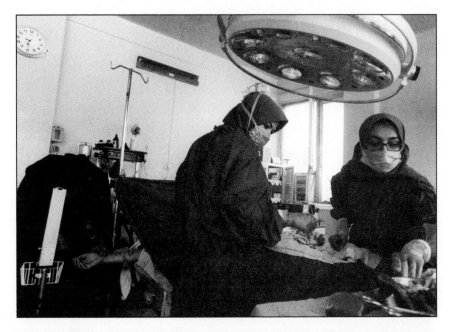

Women physicians in operating room.

Couple in contemporary Tehran.

8

Modern Iranian Political Thought

Intellectual and Literary Trends to 1960

Before coming to contemporary Shi'i thought it will be useful to discuss briefly literary and intellectual trends that formed part of the background for more recent writers and thinkers. (Premodern religious trends—majoritarian and dissident—were discussed in chapter 1 and will be given relatively minor attention here.)

The "two-cultures" phenomenon in Iran (that is, different cultures for the elite and the masses) is largely a phenomenon of the Pahlavi period, before which there was a gradation but no sharp break between elite and popular cultures. This can be seen in such elementary spheres as dress, homes, styles of furnishing, means of locomotion, and mosque attendance. It also appears in literary forms; "folk culture," which in the nineteenth century and before cut across classes, has increasingly been relegated to the popular classes. Such folk culture includes the folktale, a widespread genre now most important to the popular classes, especially in the countryside.

Better known to outsiders is the "passion play," or *ta'ziyeh*, in reality a series of plays centering around the martyrdom of the imams, especially of Imam Hosain, whose small forces were slaughtered in Iraq by the army of the Umayyad caliph Yazid. In the first ten days of the holy month of Moharram, a series of these plays are performed, today mostly in rural and popular class areas (though in the nineteenth century they were also patronized by Qajar shahs and notables). A variety of personal and political feelings are expressed by the audience—comprising men, women, and children—in the course of such plays. For example, spectators, especially women, who see innocent children die in the play as they do in reality can find an outlet for their grief; while many, particularly during periods of political discontent, find in the ta'ziyeh stories of Imams Hosain and Ali a paradigm of just struggle against unrighteous tyrants, a theme often given explicit political resonance. The themes of the martyrdom of Ali, Hosain, and other imams are reiterated in less elaborate ways in other forms of popular religious culture, notably by the *rauzeh-khan* who tells these stories with the aid of a few pictures and props. This can be a woman molla at women's gatherings, and props may include puppet shows.[1] Sermons in mosques can also be political.

There is a gradual gradation between the "religious" ta'ziyeh and the "secular" humorous folk play. Some plays have both elements. The predominant form of secular folk theatre does, however, differ from most ta'ziyehs in its choice of secular subjects, and its comic, rather than reverent, view of its characters. Like the ta'ziyeh the folk theatre in the pre-Pahlavi period was a multiclass phenomenon, with middle-class urban families as well as peasant villages hiring theatre troupes for special occasions such as weddings. The folk theatre, like that in much of the world, is characterized by stock characters, notably the black- or white-face clown who can defy social convention with impunity. Like many folk theatres it is also openly or subtly obscene and in other ways too represents the "World turned upside down"; the respectably pompous merchant bested by his wife and/or a poor youth; the hypocritical molla unmasked, and so forth.[2] In this theatre as in ta'ziyeh women's parts are taken by men, but the audience includes men, women, and children. There is also a lesser known form of popular theatre found in women's theatre games, performed by groups of women in their homes. As in public folk theatre the world is turned upside down, and the follies and weaknesses of the dominant group (men) are revealed—whether it be hypocrisy, impotence, or whatever. The women in these plays, much like the poor in the others, often succeed in outwitting their husbands or other male oppressors.[3] Like the ta'ziyehs the popular theatre may have very different effects in different periods; in politically quiet periods they may just provide an outlet for feelings against sexual, political, and personal repression; as crises approach, however, people's attention turns increasingly to the evils of such injustices and the need to combat them, and the plays and rauzeh-khanis increasingly become a political medium for expressing such ideas, and the character traits stressed in their heroes change accordingly.

Reza Shah banned ta'ziyeh performances, which were allowed a limited comeback under Mohammad Reza under whom, however, limits were put on folk theatre by demanding (nonexistent) licenses, scripts (for improvised comedy), and so forth. But the major assault on such theatre, as in much of the world, came from Western-style film, radio, and TV, which helped limit popular theatre increasingly to villages and small towns.

Beyond popular literature there were also other manifestations of the multiclass nature of pre-Pahlavi culture, even though some cultural forms were limited to the secular and religious elites respectively. Among the multiclass cultural forms that have declined visibly even in the past twenty years is knowledge and recital of the best classical poetry, including poets like Hafez and Sa'di, by unlettered men and women in both city and countryside. Western visitors knowing Persian frequently remarked on such long recitations with amazement. Related were coffeehouse poets who generally gave dramatic recitations from the *Shah-nameh* (*Book of Kings*), the Persian national epic composed by the poet Firdausi; these continued to exist, but in smaller numbers. (It should be noted that Persian has one of the world's outstanding poetic traditions, often of great difficulty and subtlety, so that the phenomenon described is the equivalent of English peasant men and women being able to recite very lengthy passages of Shakespeare, Milton, and John Donne.) This phenomenon, perhaps because of modern schools and distractions, has declined notably, and Iran's poets have become mainly the property of (one part of) the propertied. Folk poetry, rarely written, continues to exist, but it too has a reduced role.

Even "mystical" Sufi orders, which brought members together for special religious practices outside the usual ulama-mosque network, were both more important and more of a channel for interclass cultural communication in the past than they have been since the cultural and religious changes of the Pahlavi era.

In view of the changes that have occurred in Iran since 1978, it is well to remember that both folk and high literature had strong anticlerical features; in folktales and popular plays the molla or *akhund* (the same as *molla* but more often pejorative) is most often showed negatively—as money-loving, hypocritical, and so forth—and hypocritical ulama are also found in written belles lettres more often than good ones.

As suggested in chapter 1, reformist thought did not begin in Iran after interaction with the West; rather Islamic Iran has always had important reformists and dissidents in such fields as philosophy, poetry, religion, and politics.[4] What is new about the nineteenth century is that Iran's weaknesses vis-à-vis the advanced West became clear to many, and that interaction with the West hastened and altered the nature of socio-economic change, producing both new problems and new possibilities of development. The main concern of many Iranian leaders and thinkers came to be catching up with the West. Although they differed somewhat regarding which elements of Western civilization must be adopted in order to do this, nearly all believed that much must be borrowed.

The earliest reformers were practical political leaders, a breed that has continued. The main ones have been mentioned: Abbas Mirza, crown prince and governor of Azerbaijan in the early nineteenth century, brought in Western advisers, sent students abroad, and got local ulama to validate his acts. His minister Qa'em Maqam contributed to the process of early Westernization and to the reform of writing style. Under Naser ad-Din Shah (1848–96), not a consistent reformist, there were two reforming prime ministers: Mirza Taqi Khan *Amir Kabir* and Mirza Hosain Khan *Moshir ad-Dauleh* (whose reforms are discussed in chapter 3). After Naser ad-Din's death, another reformer, Amin ad-Dauleh, became prime minister and attempted tax and other reforms. All these men were hindered, pushed from office and sometimes to their death by vested interests at court and among the ulama. There were many who gained in wealth and power from the old decentralized governmental system, which encouraged local power and corruption, and Iran was not economically as ripe for centralization as were countries with a greater Western impact and trade like Egypt, Turkey, or Tunisia. Also, Great Britain and Russia preferred the weak Qajar government, from whom they had favorable treaties, to the strong one desired by reformers and nationalists.

There also developed in the later nineteenth century unofficial, or predominantly unofficial, reformers, known primarily for their writings. They built on Iranian reformist traditions, including philosophy, Shaikhism, and Babism, more than has usually been realized, so that it is wrong to see them as pure and uncritical Westernizers, as some recent Iranian critics have done. Naturally, in view of the poverty, corruption, mismanagement, and lethargy seen in many aspects of Iranian life, most of them sought Western-style solutions to many of Iran's problems. This they did in somewhat different ways, which can only be outlined very briefly.

The first important such intellectual was Mirza Malkom Khan, discussed in chapters 3 and 4. It seems clear that he was the most complete Westernizer of the reformers in this period, having spent most of his life in the West and having only a nominal commitment to Islam. Before his dismissal from government service in 1889, he kept his Westernism somewhat disguised, and in reformist essays distributed in manuscript generally limited himself to calling for a rationalization of government departments, spending, and so forth. In the newspaper he formed after being dismissed from the government, *Qanun* (London, 1890–96), however, he called for the rule of a rational codified law, and at one point called for a constitution. He also attacked the long-lived prime minister, Amin as-Soltan, and did not spare the shah. His newspaper was smuggled into Iran, and along with the earlier moderately oppositional paper *Akhtar* from Istanbul, and the later *Parvaresh* and *Sorayya* from Cairo and *Habl al-Matin* from Calcutta, formed one of the bases for a reformist, and eventually revolutionary and constitutional group in Iran.

The story of most late-nineteenth-century reformist and revolutionary writers suggests the importance of residence abroad and foreign influence on Iranian enlighteners of this period. Although it is true that those who spent their whole lives in Iran had little opportunity to circulate reformist writings, but might consign their views to later-published diaries (as in the case of the minister Amin ad-Dauleh), foreign travel and experience did change the views of many. This travel was not always in the West. There were Iranian merchant communities in Russian Transcaucasia, in Istanbul, and in India, all of which areas were more modernized than Iran, and Iranian reformers were very often tied to merchants, both within and outside Iran. Sometimes they themselves were merchants, as in the case of the author of what may be called Iran's first novel, *The Travelbook of Ibrahim Beg* (vol. 1, ca. 1900).

Merchants were a particularly dissatisfied class in the late nineteenth and early twentieth centuries; they felt increasing competition from Western merchants, who they firmly believed were favored by Persian customs being under the control of a Belgian team. Although some profited from Western trade, they were subject to disabilities that Westerners were not, and capitulatory trade treaties helped make impossible the manufacturing ventures that some of them tried and others would have liked to. Thus numerous Iranian merchants at home and abroad supported reformers who called for an end to favors to the West, the rule of law, and the like.

A number of oppositionists with religious training and even functions can now be shown to have been secret secularists (or at least opponents of the leading ulama), who used a religious guise in order effectively to arouse large masses of people. A pioneer in this technique was Sayyed Jamal ad-Din "al-Afghani," whose brief biography was given in chapter 4. Until the early 1880s Afghani had more of a reputation for heterodoxy than religiosity, but after then, sensing a new pro-Islamic mood in the Muslim world, he began to speak more and more of Islam and pan-Islam, the unity of all Muslim countries, preferably under the leadership of the sultan-caliph of the Ottoman Empire, against an encroaching West. Although the term "pan-Islam" and the basic idea of it as a mass movement seem to have been coined earlier by the Turkish Young Ottomans, particularly Namik Kemal, Jamal ad-Din was more responsible than anyone for spreading the idea. This pan-Islamic movement, which involved some Iranian ulama and others and continued into the 1920s, has some significant points of comparison with the recent "Islamic Revival." Both may be seen more as political than spiritual reactions against Western imperialism and control in Muslim lands: in the 1880s following Russian, British, and French conquests, and today following frustrations about internal weaknesses, Western strength, and Israel, seen as a Western colonial enclave. Both tend to idealize Islam by going "back to the sources," particularly the Quran, and reinterpreting them. With Jamal ad-Din and his followers, who lived in largely traditional societies, this reinterpretation had a modernist and reformist bent: Western-style law and science, sometimes constitutions, and other reforms were found in the Quran. Today, however, the movement in Iran is only in part reformist; it is carried out more by ulama than by independent intellectuals and stresses the literal following of many Quranic rules. This greater conservatism after a century may most briefly be explained by saying that Jamal ad-Din and his Iranian followers were reacting against a traditional, scarcely reformed governmental and religious structure and naturally thought that Iran's problems might be solved by interpreting Islam in ways to bring it closer to the more successful, stronger, and better functioning West. Khomeini and his followers, however, reacted to a situation where Iran was felt to be a junior partner or puppet of the West, particularly of the United States, and in which cultural and economic Westernization of a certain type was occurring at breakneck speed with little regard for human consequences. When no traditional or Islamic government had existed for a long time and the formal power of the ulama had been curbed, it was easy to imagine that a return to an idealized Islam, so far past that no one remembered it, could solve Iran's problems: hence, in brief, the more "traditional" nature of thought and action in 1978–80 than in 1905–11.

Afghani's appeals to unity around Islam to fend off the West had a multiclass appeal, as do many nationalist and Third Worldist ideas, which see the Third World as uniformly exploited by an imperialist West, without drawing real class distinctions. Afghani was invited to Tehran in 1886 by the quite conservative minister of press, and stayed at the home of Iran's leading merchant, Amin az-Zarb, who was close to the prime minister and no radical. His son, like other unradical merchants, was very important in the constitutional revolution. Afghani scared the shah by his anti-British talk, and had to go to Russia, though he returned briefly later. Although Afghani is now known for fighting despotism, in fact his main target was the British, and his record on despots is ambiguous; he tried frequently to get into the counsels of rulers, succeeding with one in Afghanistan, but only tenuously in Egypt, Iran, and Turkey. He attacked the shah only after his expulsion from Iran in 1891. Although there is one recorded Egyptian talk in the 1870s where Afghani supports a constitution, none of his major writings or talks thereafter supports this or any other clear institutional brake on despotism. He was rather an apostle of self-strengthening against the West, whether by kings or not, and most of the reforms he advocated had this goal. His use of religious language and of lines from the Quran as more effective than secular arguments was vindicated in the alliance of ulama, merchants, and intellectuals that led the successful tobacco protest in 1890–91, although it is wrong to see him as the sole architect of this natural alliance.

After 1890, even formerly anticlerical writers like Malkom Khan and some radicals at Istanbul began to emulate Afghani's tactics. There is not space here to document the fact that Afghani's own Islam, which appears to have come from Iranian deist-philosophical traditions with a heavy Shaikhi influence, was very different from orthodox Islam, but that has been done elsewhere.[5] Clearly he was successful in his tactic, which was traditional in Shi'ism and in Islamic philosophy, of appealing in different ways to an unorthodox "elite" and the orthodox "mass." His name is venerated among both religious and irreligious in Iran today, and republication of his writings in Iran with new introductions was one means used by the oppositional but still "orthodox" religious forces to promote their ideas in the 1950s and 1960s. (The word "orthodox" is not quite accurate for Islam, which has no church doctrine; it refers to beliefs and practices followed by most of the ulama and population.)

The Iranians abroad with whom Afghani was closest had little claim to Islam, much less orthodoxy; nonetheless after 1891 they went along with Afghani's pan-Islamic program. Afghani and Malkom worked together in London in 1891, with Afghani contributing to *Qanun,* which now began to adopt a pro-ulama line. In 1892 Afghani accepted an invitation from the Ottoman Sultan Abdülhamid to go to Istanbul, where he remained largely under a kind of glorified house arrest until his death in 1897 from cancer. There he worked with a group of Iranians and Shi'is to write to Shi'i ulama suggesting they follow the (Sunni) Ottoman sultan-caliph. This would of course weaken the shah, whom Afghani now hated. Among the group were men in no way Muslim, even though they wrote their appeals and other antishah works in the most orthodox terms; specifically the writers Shaikh Ahmad Ruhi and Mirza Aqa Khan Kermani, who had been Babis of the orginal, Azali line, but by now appear to have been atheists. (Ruhi is photographed in one book leaning on a tablet that says "There is nothing but nature.") Kermani, a prolific writer, was also one of the first representatives of a trend that grew in importance among twentieth-century intellectuals: rejection of Islam and the Arabs for having ruined Iran, and a glorification of pre-Islamic Iran. This he began to do before meeting Afghani and adopting his pan-Islamic tactics.

Although Kermani now worked with Afghani, the nationalist trend rejecting Islam was quite a different line of thought: both trends have continued to today. Both can be said to represent kinds of nationalism (or, in the case of pan-Islam, a "proto-nationalism" that fed later individual nationalisms). Both had the typical nationalist feature of glorifying a period in the distant past when one's own people were stronger, more successful, occupied more territory, and had more scientific, artistic, and cultural achievements. Afghani (at least after circa 1881—before that he often spoke in Egyptian, Indian, etc., nationalist terms) and those in the Islamist line to the present identify this past with the early age of Islam, and blame decline on influences (usually foreign) corrupting or undermining true Islam, as it is interpreted by a given ideological school. This line of thought sometimes advocates unity among all Muslims, although even in Abdülhamid's time few imagined real political unity could be achieved. There are various ideas of federation and cooperation, and uncooperative Muslim leaders can be denounced as being not truly Islamic.

Kermani, influenced by the Iranian-born north Azerbaijani thinker, Mirza Fath Ali Akhundzadeh, saw the ideal past very differently, in the period of the great pre-Islamic Persian Empires that appeared populous, prosperous, and strong. Islam and the "inferior" Arabs were seen as destroying this greatness. Kermani even denounced all the great Persian classical poetry, except for the warlike and pro-Persian *Shah-nameh,* for inculcating passivity and corruption. Both the *Shah-nameh* and popular literature and attitudes do reflect considerable past anti-Arab ("lizard-eater") and even antiorthodox feelings, sometimes also expressed in poetry, art, and so forth. The radical anti-Arab and anti-Islamic ideas of Kermani were expanded by a number of twentieth-century writers and intellectuals—notably two of the greatest, the writer Sadeq Hedayat and the wide-ranging intellectual Ahmad Kasravi (see below). Both pan-Islam and its apparent opposite, anti-Islamic nationalism, are multiclass (some would say bourgeois) phenomena; both have been used by intellectuals and rulers with different emphases for their own ends. The Pahlavi shahs picked up pre-Islamic Iranian nationalism, cut off the radical elements that were central to its chief intellectual advocates (especially the communist religion and revolt of the fifth-century-A.D. heretic Mazdak), and made it a foundation of anticlerical monarchism. This use of it was possibly no more forced than the other, as the two great pre-Islamic empires were strong monarchies; on the other hand popular elements could be found in pre-Islamic religions like Mazdakism, Manichaeism, and Zoroastrianism, as could evidence that women and agriculturalists enjoyed higher respect in some pre-Islamic periods than in the nineteenth century. The main appeal of an idealized distant past, however, whether Islamic or pre-Islamic, was and is that a great variety of values may be read into it, while the evils of the present can be ascribed to deviation from the true Iranian or true Islamic essence. In a period when all society was at least formally Islamic, it was natural for many thinkers to blame Iran's problems on Islam and the Arabs, and to see in a nationalist interpretation of the distant Iranian past virtues that were often modern or Western ones. As Iran became more modern and Westernized, the evils of indiscriminate Westernization became more obvious, and Islamic ways for many receded into the background, it was natural for many after 1960 to blame evils on Western ways and to turn for salvation to an idealized Islamic past. Ironically, many in both trends, especially the Iranist one, were really Westernizers, understandably unwilling to admit wholesale borrowing from the West.

Before 1960, most recognized Iranian intellectuals with a following outside traditional religious circles were to a high degree Westernizers. The desire for rationalized law, rule, and economics was expressed both in the emigré newspapers published before the Constitutional Revolution of 1905–11 and the great majority of papers published in Iran during that revolution, of which *Sur-e Esrafil* with its brilliant prose satire by the writer Dehkhoda and *Iran-e Nau* led by the outstanding socialist Caucasian Rasulzadeh may be singled out. In addition to news, these numerous newspapers were full of new poetry and satires that spoke out against corrupt and hypocritical officials and ulama, and also took as a main theme criticism of the veiling, seclusion, and enforced ignorance of women. Before and during the revolution longer prose forms with themes similarly critical of Iranian mores and looking, at least implicitly, to Western models for improvement, played a role in enlightening Iranians. These, like the newspapers, were often read aloud and discussed to groups. The most famous such early twentieth-century work was Zain al-Abedin Maraghe'i's *Travelbook of Ibrahim Beg*, exposing a myriad of Iranian evils. There were also the improved translation of James Morier's *Hajji Baba of Esfahan* by Mirza Habib Esfahani, which was more savage and political about Iran's faults than the original, and the works by men of Iranian origin living in Russian Transcaucasia, notably Akhundzadeh and Talebzadeh.[6] The victory of Japan in the Russo-Japanese War aroused interest in Japan's secret of rapid self-strengthening, which many saw in the fact that Japan had a constitution and Russia did not; hence there was a spate of writings on Japan, some of which stressed for the first time the virtues of constitutions.

As to the ulama in the constitutional revolution, there were varying degrees of support for a constitution and of awareness of its implications. Among the popular preachers there were a number in the tradition of Afghani—men brought up with a religious education and filling, more than Afghani, religious functions, notably preaching, but who were not themselves believers in any usual sense. These included most notably two preacher friends from Isfahan—Malek al-Motakallemin and Sayyed Jamal ad-Din Esfahani, the former the father of the historian of the constitutional revolution, Mehdi Malekzadeh, and the latter the father of Iran's first great modern short-story writer, Mohammad Ali Jamalzadeh. Malek al-Motakallemin was long an Azali Babi, although by the time he became a preacher in the revolution he appears to have lost even this belief, while Sayyed Jamal ad-Din Esfahani was described by his son as a freethinker.[7] They both recognized the appeal of Islam to the masses and bazaaris, however. Before the Revolution they helped, with the participation of Isfahan businessmen, to set up and publicize an "Islamic company" that would boycott foreign cloth and goods and promote local products. In Tehran, the two became major preachers of the revolutionary and constitutional cause, explaining it in familiar Muslim terms emphasizing such Islamic concepts, particularly central in Shi'ism, as Justice and Oppression. Mohammad Ali Shah considered them among the most dangerous of his enemies and had them both killed in 1908, as he did the editor of *Sur-e Esrafil,* Mirza Jahangir Khan, also of Babi background.[8]

Among the more powerful ulama there was a variety of views, but the most prominent ulama of Iraq and many prominent ones in Iran remained proconstitutional throughout the revolution, although there were defections as the social revolutionary and even "anti-Islamic" potential of the constitution became clearer. The two main ulama constitutional leaders within Iran were very different types: Sayyed Mohammad Tabataba'i, who appears to have had genuinely liberal proclivities and considerable contact with other liberals, believed that a constitution would be the best way to limit the power of uncontrolled autocrats who were selling Iran to the Western powers. The more wily and powerful Sayyed Abdollah Behbehani had a long record of pro-British activity; he had been almost alone in refusing to back the anti-British tobacco movement, had taken personal presents and money from the British to organize movements against the Russians, and had helped arrange the use of the British Legation for the bast of 1906. To a degree his early participation in the revolution may be seen as part of his pro-British policy with an aim of advancing himself as he weakened the Qajars. He also wished to keep the constitutional movement conservative, while not openly turning against it. The third main leader of the Tehran ulama, Shaikh Fazlollah Nuri, did turn against the movement once it became clear that the constitution was not going to reinstate the sharia, but bring in many Western-style institutions and laws. The constitution and its form reflected more the ideas of Westernizing secularists, backed financially especially by merchants, than the ulama, although, as noted, provisions were inserted to protect ulama power. However, in 1909, a defense of the constitution was written by a younger mujtahid, Na'ini, that was endorsed by leading Iraqi ulama.[9] It does not appear to have been very influential when it was written, however; its real fame and importance came with its republication with an introduction by Ayatollah Taleqani in 1955, as part of the struggle against Pahlavi despotism, a struggle that until almost the end based itself largely on the idea of true application of the 1906–07 constitution.

The revolution saw writings and activities reflecting a wide range of political tendencies that went on to have an important future in Iranian politics. Quite early in the constitutional revolution, a Social Democratic party was founded in Tabriz. It was influenced by Iranian returnees and immigrants from the Russian Caucasus. In the second constitutional period, from 1909, this was mostly merged into the well-organized, nationwide Democratic party, whose program included land reform and other major social reforms. The Democrats dominated the World War I pro-German nationalist government that was forced from Iran in 1915, whence some of its members went to Istanbul and some to Berlin—both anti-Allied capitals. In Berlin the Democrat leader Sayyed Hasan Taqizadeh edited two series of the important newspaper *Kaveh* (named after a legendary blacksmith who liberated Iran). The first series, published during the war, aimed largely at getting Iranians to support the Central Powers against Britain and Russia, while the second was the main organ of the new Iranian nationalist culture. In addition to supporting new young writers like Mohammad Ali Jamalzadeh, it contained striking editorial features by Taqizadeh, in one of which he said that Iran must become wholly Western in every way if it were to progress; this is perhaps the high point of the Westernist view of nationalism, which Taqizadeh himself later modified.

The Constitutional Revolution also saw the beginnings of socialist writings by Caucasian immigrants like Rasulzadeh and Haidar Khan Amu Oghlu (the latter responsible for a few assassinations during the revolution and later a prominent Communist in the Gilan Jangalis). Iran was also involved in the Communist Congress of the Peoples of the East, 1920, and socialist and Communist writings and activities developed after World War I. These were, however, outlawed under Reza Shah and during most of his son's rule, so that this line of thought was far less expressed in writing especially within Iran than it would otherwise have been; like the Democrats the socialists and Communists were Westernizers. Already in the 1940s and 1950s there were socialist offshoots from the Tudeh, and in the 1960s and 1970s the number of socialist and Marxist movements, especially abroad, multiplied, and all expressed their positions in writing.

As was the case in Tsarist Russia and other autocratic countries, thinkers who wished to publish within Iran their criticisms of government and society usually had to do it indirectly, especially via poetry, fiction, and literary criticism, which involve ambiguity and are hard to pin down, rather than through directly critical essays, whose publication in most periods of modern Iranian history was not permitted. Such essays can be found in the relatively freer periods, like 1906–11, 1918–21, and 1941–53, and to a degree 1978–80, but most of the time it is the poet and author, not the editorial writer, who is the chief social critic. (This did not prevent the poet Eshqi from being killed by Reza Shah or numerous writers from being jailed, and often tortured, under his son.)

Literature is particularly well suited to criticize social customs the author considers unjust or outworn, and such social criticism is rife in modern Iranian literature from the *Travelbook of Ibrahim Beg* to the present. Significantly, one of the strongest points of attack by both male and female authors, in both prose and poetry, is the position of women, although authors of different periods and views differ somewhat on proposed solutions. In the poetry of the Constitutional Revolution and after there are strong attacks on the veiling that cripples women's activity, on the lack of education that cuts down women's contribution to society and harms their children's education, on their mistreatment by ignorant husbands, and on other aspects of their subordination. In the same first decades of the twentieth century, a number of women from upper-class and upper-middle-class backgrounds worked with some success to set up girls' schools and orphanages. By writers and activists alike, Reza Shah's opening of schools and universities to girls and his unveiling of women were welcomed as in part an outcome of their struggles. In the Pahlavi period there were a number of excellent women writers and essayists, as well as important women in other fields. Among the poets the two most outstanding were, under Reza Shah, Parvin E'tesami, a brilliant poet in the classical style; and, under Mohammad Reza, Forugh Farrokhzad, who lived the kind of free and varied life usually reserved for men, and dared write about her sexual feelings and activities in her poetry, shocking some of her contemporaries. The life and writings of Forugh may properly be classified as "feminist" (without any hostile implication to men).[10] Unfortunately, both these highly talented poets died very young.

It should be noted that before Shariati no significant recent writers complained about the too rapid Westernization of Iranian women. Although miniskirts, tight jeans, and makeup may offend some, attacks on them in recent decades turned out, predictably, to be a prelude to partly successful attempts since 1979 to return all women to restrictive clothing and to aspects of strict Muslim law.

Another area of literary attack going back to the first modern Iranian prose is the intellectuals' view of unpleasant aspects of Iranian mores as seen by Iranians themselves: hypocrisy, pretentiousness, unreliability, untruths, venality, and opportunism. These themes are stressed in the pre-1906 books discussed above and in revolutionary satires. They are also found in the groundbreaking collection of realistic short stories published by Jamalzadeh in 1921, *Yeki bud yeki nabud,* in which, among other things, the verbal pretensions of both the old-style ulama, with their incomprehensible Arabized talk, and the young European returnee, who fills his Persian with French, are mocked.

Sadeq Hedayat, generally considered the greatest modern Iranian prose writer, wrote in a variety of styles, optimistic and pessimistic, realistic and mystical-paranoid, which can be tied both to Iran's political state and his own fragile mental state. His more realistic and satirical works appeared between 1941 and 1947, when there seemed to be hope for democracy, and when he, like many other writers, was close to the Tudeh party. A number of short stories about rural and urban common people present with sympathy their hard life, their courage, and their subjection to irrational customs and superstitions. His masterpiece in the realistic-satirical genre is the novel *Hajji Agha,* an exposition of political, financial, personal, and religious hypocrisy in which Hedayat presents in the person of his title character many of the main faults that have kept Iran from progressing soundly.[11] Although Hedayat's surrealistic and drug-influenced *The Blind Owl* was translated much sooner into English and other languages, *Hajji Agha* is more important, or at least more comprehensible, as social criticism.

The two English-language Iran-centered novels of F. Esfandiari, *Day of Sacrifice* and *The Identity Card,* reflect this Iranian self-criticism. The former vividly portrays the father-son tensions characteristic of many Iranians, as well as an attempted political assassination; the latter shows the unending labyrinthine bureaucracy that keeps an Iranian from returning to America, where he lives, because he does not have an Iranian identity card. In all these prose works, the situations are socially important because they are seen by the authors and readers as typical of the situation in Iran.

Although a large number of authors in the 1941–53 period, including such famous ones as Sadeq Hedayat and Jalal Al-e Ahmad, had close ties to the Tudeh party, the one great author firmly associated with the party and its predecessors is Bozorg Alavi, who for over twenty-five years lived and taught in East Berlin, having been educated in Germany at the time when many Iranian nationalists were there. Alavi was one of the circle of "53" whose Marxist discussion group was arrested by the Reza Shah regime and sent to jail until Reza Shah's forced abdication. He, like the others in the group, became one of the founders of the Tudeh. Close to Hedayat and some other leftist authors, he considerably influenced literature and literary criticism. One of his well-known Persian works tells the story of the "53" and other novels and stories deal with social themes, including women. From Germany he wrote especially nonfiction about Iran and its modern literature. Unlike Jamalzadeh, who spent most of his life outside Iran but continued to write stories set there, he preferred more analytical writing in later years.[12]

Space does not permit extensive discussion of many writers of recent decades. Among the well known are the Azerbaijani Samad Behrangi, whose early death under mysterious circumstances was widely blamed on SAVAK, as were deaths of men discussed in the next section, Al-e Ahmad and Shariati (the heart attacks of the latter two are, however, attested by persons close to them). Behrangi was especially known for his adaptation of Azerbaijani folktales, most of which were censored, but one of which, *The Little Black Fish,* was widely read and published despite its symbolic progressive implications. Another progressive author persecuted by the shah's regime was the playwright Gholam Hosain Sa'edi, best known in the West for his story *The Cow* in its film version directed by the new wave film director, Daryush Mehrjui. Better known in the West for his English writings is Reza Baraheni, who in his essays reprinted in *The Crowned Cannibals* castigates not only the monarchical system but also male supremacy and other evils of Iranian culture. Like the majority of well-known Iranian writers since the late nineteenth century, these three and many of their contemporaries were *both* anti-regime and *secularist.* Again like most writers, they were leftists of different persuasions.[13] Only recently did religious publications come to outnumber secular ones and were there more than a few modern writers who stressed religion. On the other hand the authors mentioned above were read chiefly by a minority of the modernized elite, while religious preachings were heard by the popular classes.

Outside the belletristic category was the highly influential scholar, jurist, and essayist Ahmad Kasravi, who developed the trend of an anti-Shi'i Iranian nationalism. In his writings he coined numerous new terms from Persian roots, avoiding words of Arab origin, and openly criticized most Iranian religions. He developed a considerable following, became a natural target for the polemics of the religious, and was assassinated by a member of the Feda'iyan-e Islam in open court in 1946.[14]

The activities of the Feda'iyan-e Islam can serve as a reminder that there was also a continuous, albeit changing, tradition of Islamic thought and activity throughout the nineteenth and twentieth centuries that has perhaps not received the attention it deserves. The great nineteenth century Muslim philosopher Sabzavari developed further the tradition of original Shi'i philosophic thought, teaching, and writing represented in the Safavid period by such major thinkers as Molla Sadra and Mir Damad. The developing tradition of Shi'i thought, influenced both by philosophy and by Sufism, was represented in the twentieth century by such thinkers as Jalal ad-Din Ashtiyani and Allameh Tabataba'i, and reflections of this tradition may be found in recent ulama activists, including Ayatollah Khomeini, himself well versed in Muslim philosophy.

More directly political thought among practicing Muslims was also important. The Islamic defense of constitutionalism written by Na'ini has been mentioned, and other mujtahids wrote briefer and less comprehensive statements along the same lines. Under the Pahlavis, however, many ulama and other religiously oriented thinkers became less concerned with the constitution, which proved to be a feeble defense against autocracy, and more worried about the diminution in ulama positions and prerogatives on the one hand and the complaints of the ulama and their constituents against Pahlavi autocracy on the other. There was also growing concern about increasing deviations from what were seen as Islamic norms and about subservience to Western ways and Western powers. Such concerns could not be published under Reza Shah's censorship, but they were voiced in the early 1940s by Ruhollah Khomeini, who, as noted below, attacked Reza Shah's autocracy and the secularist influence of men like Kasravi. A less erudite attack in the 1940s and 1950s came from the Feda'iyan-e Islam, a group of young men of popular origin who published a fundamentalist program calling for a return to pure Islamic ways and laws and an end to Western influence, and who also assassinated their chief enemies. The most politically influential of the ulama in the early 1950s was Ayatollah Kashani, known especially for his anti-imperialist and particularly anti-British speeches and activities, and at times allied with the Feda'iyan-e Islam. At first cooperating with Mohammad Mosaddeq in the oil nationalization crisis, he later broke with him and backed his overthrow. The later 1950s were primarily a quietest period for the ulama, led by the conservative Ayatollah Borujerdi, but new trends began in the 1960s.

As was suggested above, most modern Iranian literature, especially until about 1960, has been anticlerical insofar as it touches the subject. Even Al-e Ahmad's attempts to rediscover religion in the 1960s resulted mainly in his anticlerical attack on hypocrisy witnessed during his pilgrimage. Shariati was also far more opposed to the average cleric than is often admitted.[15] The poems and writings mentioned above that defend the rights of women often attack ignorant mollas; so too do many satires from preconstitutional times on down, and many realistic writings. Further, the great majority of Iranian writing to which any significant attention has been given by lay readers (only a small sample of which could be noted here) has been explicitly Westernist and modernist, again at least until 1960, and in many cases much later. The evils depicted are, explicitly or implicitly, seen more as owing to Iranian customs and traditions than to Western imperialism and encroachments, and the solutions, if they are suggested at all, are seen as coming from Iranians finding ways to change their customs and traditions. It may be surmised that had literary publication been uncensored, more would have been said about the responsibility of the government in bringing or perpetuating certain evils, and along with this would have gone recognition of the government's considerable dependence on Western states, especially the United States.

It is almost impossible to imagine, however, that an honest writer would devote himself to showing how Iranian internal conditions must be changed, and how these changes were held back by powerful and hypocritical lay and clerical leaders if what the writer *really* meant was the opposite; namely, give more power to clerical leaders and put the entire blame for all evils on the court and foreigners, and then problems would be solved. If that had been the intended message, there would have been prudent ways in which it could be implied, just as Al-e Ahmad and Shariati found ways to put forth not exactly that message but still one that put much or most of the blame for Iran's problems on blind imitation of the West.

Twentieth-century Iran also saw a number of directly political thinkers and writers, whose works have been read mainly by their own followers, and who have rarely been the subject of scholarly analysis. Like
the writers discussed so far, political writers have been primarily secularist until quite recently. Socialist and Communist writings go back as far
as the Constitutional Revolution of 1905–11 and in their main line of the
post-World War I Communist party and the post-World War II Tudeh
party they tend to follow closely the Soviet line, although with variations
and internal struggles as to how it should be interpreted. Leftist guerillas
from the late 1960s on rejected the Tudeh line of sharing power peacefully in favor of armed struggle to overturn the system, although there
were and are numerous tactical differences within and between guerilla
groups.

Mosaddeq-style nationalism, directed mainly at freeing Iran from
great-power control, has continued to inspire Iranians of varied political
tendencies, including the bourgeois National Front, socialists of various
shades (like those in 1979's National Democratic Front led by Mosaddeq's grandson, Hedayatollah Matin-Daftari), and some of the more
secularist members of the early post-1979 regime. This varied following
suggests both the broad appeal of Mosaddeq's nationalism and anti-
imperialism and the fact that the rest of his program was not specific or
detailed enough to disqualify Mosaddeq as a source of inspiration for
any of the above groups. A leader of one of the groups in Mosaddeq's
coalition, Khalil Maleki, is regarded by some as Iran's most original and
astute socialist thinker, who successfully adapted his ideas to the special
conditions of Iran, although those belonging to other parties might con-
test this view.[16]

We thus arrive at the perhaps startling conclusion that the main lines
of Iran's literature and political thought in the past century have been
radically different from the culture most visible after 1979, and even
quite different from the complex, and *not* proclerical emphasis of the
"anti-Westernists" Al-e Ahmad and Shariati. To understand the rapid
changes in culture after 1961 we must remember the concurrent inten-
sification of a Westernizing despotism, closely tied to dependence on the
West, and especially the United States. We must also remember the overrapid rural-urban migrations, increased income disparities, socioeconomic problems, and *anomie* that lead people to go back to familiar
traditional moorings and to associate Westernization with suffering and

dictatorship. The religious and secular popular culture discussed at the beginning of this chapter persisted, in modified form, for the majority. For the mass of people traditional and religious cultural forms were supplemented by Western films and TV, not by Sadeq Hedayat. Hence the ta'ziyeh, the rauzeh-khani, the mosque sermon, and the religious club, plus the folktale and folk theatre formed the words and literature that expressed most closely the world view of the popular classes. It was to the educated strata of the urban (or newly urban) bazaar classes and youth that Shariati first appealed. It was he, more than all the poets and writers who made such brave attempts to employ the simple language of the masses in order to change their consciousness, who most touched their sensitive nerve. Once dependence on the West was associated with Western culture, and Western culture with moral decay, it was natural to seek Iran's salvation not in the Westernization pushed by the shah's regime but in a return to an idealized indigenous Islam.

Contemporary Shi'i Thought

After the 1960s, new trends of thought questioned the governmental image of progress and Western rationalism. Jalal Al-e Ahmad inspired a theory of alienation among new intellectuals, and the question of identity was later raised by a variety of writers. Some themes found among Iranian thinkers are similar to those in contemporary Arab thought.[17] Muslim ideologists prefer arguments taken from the Quran or Islamic Traditions—a preference found both among popular preachers and sophisticated intellectuals. When something is demonstrated with Islamic arguments it is more easily accepted. When Abolhasan Bani Sadr demonstrates with Quranic citations that property belongs only to God, and hence that Iran should nationalize enterprises that could enslave people, his demonstration is more effective for Muslims than are arguments taken from *Das Kapital.* The weakness of Shi'i ideologies is that of all apologists—namely, they try to show that their religion has provided in advance the key to all difficulties. A theme held in common with many Arab ideologists (for example, Anouar 'Abd al-Malek)[18] is Islam as the basis of anti-imperialist action. From a knowledge of the profound popular influence of Islamic slogans, and from a belief that Islam has a revolutionary aspect, Muslim ideologists associate Islam with struggles against colonialism and great-power domination. Here it is possible to present only a few trends, all with Shi'i overtones, but it should not be forgotten that various secular trends also continued to exist in Iran.

Iranian Identity in the Face of Westernization

The increasing cultural Westernization of the Pahlavis was resented by the popular classes, by the bazaaris, and by the ulama, whose prestige and positions were attacked. Westernized habits were associated with Western politico-economic domination, and anti-Westernism and anti-regime ideas turned increasingly to the masses' Shi'i outlook. In the 1960s thinkers began to discuss defense against Westernization and returning to Iran's cultural identity. For this they denounced "Westoxication" (*Gharbzadegi*).[19] This reaction can be understood in the context of the anti-imperialist struggle of Mosaddeq, and of rapid Westernization after the 1953 coup d'état.

Jalal Al-e Ahmad was, in the 1960s, the intellectual leader of a new generation of Iranian thinkers. Born in 1923 into a clerical family in the Taleqan Valley near Qazvin, he witnessed his father's ruin after the laicizing reforms of Reza Shah. The father did not accept state control over his work as a notary, a post formerly reserved for ulama. Al-e Ahmad had to quit his family and work to pay for his studies. At twenty he became a Communist, in the years when occupied Iran was undergoing great social crises. Ahmad Kasravi's influence on him was very strong.[20] He quit the Tudeh party after the Azerbaijan events in reaction against Stalinism, and joined nationalist and socialist movements while teaching, translating, and writing stories with social themes. He was also an essayist, ethnologist, and critic. In the 1960s he became the conscience of many intellectuals, and wrote a classic essay against Iran's "Westoxication."

When the ulama became leaders of the opposition he returned to an interest in Islam and went on pilgrimage to Mecca in 1964. Until his death in September 1969 he defended Islam against the policy of Westernization at any price championed by the regime, although his conversion was more political than religious.[21] Al-e Ahmad found cultural roots and ties to the Iranian people in Islam. This feeling is found in a new way in Ali Shariati. After Al-e Ahmad died, Shariati took up the part of his work that was devoted to giving an Islamic response to the modern world.[22]

Two books by Al-e Ahmad will be discussed: *On the Loyalty and*

Betrayal of the Intellectuals, a work of historical sociology where the author judges the attitude of educated Iranians by their services to the Iranian nation; and *Westoxication,*[23] a violent pamphlet directed against a terrible malady that alienates Iranians from their identity and bewitches them with the West.

Al-e Ahmad's viewpoint on Shi'ism was both critical and positive. The Shi'ism imposed by the Safavids crushed the independent spirit of the ulama and encouraged the religiosity of martyrs (the vanquished). The popularity of the Twelfth Imam arises from his being the hope and refuge of believers against the insurmountable inequities of this world. Islam, weakened by divisions between Sunnis and Shi'is, by mystical groups, and by Babism-Bahaism, was vulnerable to imperialism. Iranians succumbed to the image of "progress" and played the game of the West. Al-e Ahmad attacks nineteenth-century Westernizers like Mirza Aqa Khan Kermani, Malkom Khan, and Talebzadeh, and defends the anticonstitutional Shaikh Fazlollah Nuri for upholding the integrity of Iran and Islam in the face of the invading West.[24]

This does not mean that Al-e Ahmad was reactionary. His struggle was for the identity of the Shi'i Iranian. What he asked of Islam, at the moment (ca. 1963) when it again became the symbol of a national struggle against monarchy, was to raise politics to its just position. The ulama should cease their interminable ratiocinations over details and externals and consider real problems. Then Islam might again be a liberator as it was for the seventh-century Iranians.

Al-e Ahmad's revolt, in part by its exaggerated tone, aroused the conscience of many Iranians. The Pahlavi regime had confronted differently the problems posed by the social and cultural transformation of Iran, spreading an official nationalist ideology. To soften cultural resistance, institutions patronized by the queen and honoring Iranian traditions were created. Some intellectuals found in them an aseptic place to express themselves and to write reports that were put aside. In these institutions no one could discuss religion or politics.

The paradoxical evolution of Al-e Ahmad from socialism to a political Islam was reflected in splits among intellectuals. Some, like the sociologist Ehsan Naraghi, remained secular while allowing Islam a role in national identity.[25] Others sought an alternative to Westoxication in a deeper study of Islamic philosophy. Those closest to Al-e Ahmad's path chose political opposition.

Ulama in the Political Struggle

While some ulama intellectuals avoided politics and produced philo-sophical and theological works, others increasingly took public polit-ical positions. The most important among the politicized ulama, Aya-tollah Ruhollah Musavi Khomeini, became a political figure of the first rank after the events of 1963, which put him in prison and then in exile, and especially in the revolution of 1978–79. Only his tenacious character and his critical thought could have led one to believe before the 1960s that this theologian would become anything but a high-ranking aya-tollah.

He was born in September 1902 in Khomein (between Isfahan and Arak) into a religious family; his grandfather had traded in Kashmir (whence the accusation by Mohammad Reza Shah that he was an Indian paid by the British). His father was killed by a landlord before he was five months old, and he was raised by his mother. From his elder brother he acquired a basic education. In 1919 he went to Soltanabad (Arak), where he became the disciple of Ayatollah Abdol Karim Ha'eri Yazdi, and two years later followed him to Qom. In 1927, after finishing the lower degrees of the theological course, he continued studying under Ha'eri, and on Ha'eri's death in 1936, Khomeini became a respected mujtahid. In 1930 he married the daughter of a rich Tehran ayatollah, Mirza Mohammad Saqafi, who saw a bright future for this "village molla." Khomeini had two sons, both of whom became ayatollahs—Mostafa, killed perhaps by SAVAK in 1977 at Najaf, and Ahmad, who always accompanied his father—and three daughters.

In 1944 Khomeini first published criticisms of the Pahlavi regime: in an open letter to the ulama he asked them to unite against the immorality of public life, and especially to react against "a certain adventurer from Tabriz who is unjustly attacking your creed." He was certainly referring to the anticlerical intellectual, Ahmad Kasravi.[26] In a 1944 book, *Secrets Exposed*, Khomeini attacks *Secrets of a Thousand Years* by Kasravi's disciple A. A. Hakamizadeh. Khomeini explains that he is answering a writer (unnamed) who has betrayed his country by attacking the ulama. "We must realize that writings that attack religious leaders help to de-stroy the country and its independence."[27] *Secrets Exposed* consists of six parts: (1) Divine Unity (*tauhid*); (2) The Imamate; (3) The Role of the Ulama; (4) Government; (5) Law; and (6) Traditions (*hadith*). Each time,

Khomeini cites a passage of the refuted writers, answers it, and gives his own doctrine.

When appropriate, he unsparingly attacks Reza Shah, seen as the enemy of religion. The idea of an Islamic government, dominated by mujtahids, is developed. He criticizes both the constituent assembly of 1925, which was forced at bayonet-point to install the new Reza Shah and the majles, which is used only to impose European laws and is unsuited to Iran. Only a sovereign elected by pious mujtahids, knowing divine commands and exercising justice without being prisoner to the pressures and ambitions of this world, can govern Iran with equity. The monarchy (*saltanat*) may even be suppressed, as "apart from the royalty of God, all royalty is against the interests of the people and oppressive; apart from the law of God, all laws are nul and absurd. A government of Islamic law, controlled by religious jurists (*faqihs*) will be superior to all the iniquitous governments of the world."[28] On the other hand, other passages seem to accept limited monarchy.

One scholar says that Khomeini in the 1950s had a "quietist period" in which he gave lessons and became a leading disciple and confidant of the chief (and conservative) ayatollah, Borujerdi (d. 1961).[29] Around 1960 the course in ethics given by Khomeini in the Faiziyeh Madraseh in Qom attracted more and more students. The teacher abandoned the traditional *minbar* of the mosque and spoke seated on the ground in a corner of the room, fascinating his audience by his criticism of the government's policies. He eventually became one of the successors of Borujerdi to the function of marja'-e taqlid (source of imitation), although some other ayatollahs were, in 1961–63, considered more important than he.

In 1962 Khomeini began direct combat against the Pahlavi regime. His exile from 1964 through 1978 after his 1963–64 battles with the regime did not stop Khomeini from continuing his struggles against the shah, imperialism, and Zionism via declarations and tape cassettes diffused, after he went to Najaf in 1965, by Iranian pilgrims to the holy cities in Iraq. In 1971, at the time of the royalist celebrations in Persepolis, he called upon the ulama to denounce political terror and the waste of Iran's resources. His refusal of all compromise with the regime constituted a revolution by contrast with many in the religious opposition who called only for constitutional reforms.

At this time was published from student notes the book *Islamic Government*, which puts forth three main ideas:

1. Monarchy is radically condemned. The Prophet, he says, asked the Byzantine emperor and the Sasanid Shah to abandon their illegitimate power. By means of war Islam was able to achieve a reign of justice. In Hosain's battle to keep Islam from degenerating into monarchy, he died a martyr. "Islam knows neither monarchy nor dynastic succession."[30]

2. Islam gives, in the Quran and Tradition (*sunna*), "all the laws and principles needed by man for his happiness and perfection."[31] These laws are just; they protect the oppressed and hungry against iniquitous rule. "The legislative power in Islam is limited to God alone."[32] That is why, in Islamic government, instead of having a "legislative assembly" one should have an assembly to apply Islamic law. In order to apply the law and preserve it from deformations, society needed the Prophet and the Imams. They are the only ones to know the law perfectly and to possess in full the virtue of justice ('adalat). After them it is the Muslim jurists (*faqih*, pl. *foqaha*) who should govern. "Authority must come officially from the jurists."[33]

3. Islam is in danger, corrupted by perverse doctrines—materialism, Christianity, Zionism—encouraged in Iran by the imperialist powers. The ulama must purify Islam, and publicize the political and economic aspects of the Quranic message. Islam must be made known, especially among those with university educations.[34] Among the ulama, there are many SAVAK agents and court mollas. Their turbans must be torn off and the religious milieu purified; only those who are soldiers of God should keep their religious dress, serving Islamic government. We must cut all ties to the administration of the demonic (*taghuti*) regime of the shah.

In another text, *The Great Holy War*, Khomeini addresses the ulama of the *hauzeh* (theological colleges) and exhorts them to correct their conduct in order to be examples to society. They are an avant-garde of the "Party of God" (hezbollah).[35]

Ayatollah Khomeini is not the sole marja'-e taqlid, and the uncontested leadership he achieved in the revolution did not eclipse the political thought of others. Among the best known ayatollahs playing different roles in the revolution and its ideology were Ayatollah Shariatmadari in Qom, who was very influential in his home province of Azerbaijan and in Khorasan, and Ayatollah Taleqani of Tehran, especially influential in liberal and progressive circles.

A moderate constitutionalist before and after the revolution, Shariatmadari became a leader of many who could not follow Khomeini. Born in 1905 in Tabriz, he studied first there and at nineteen went to Qom, where Shaikh Abdol Karim Ha'eri Yazdi had revived Qom's theological studies. He was a co-disciple with Khomeini, and became a mujtahid. About 1935 he reached Najaf and continued higher studies there. He then taught for about fifteen years in Tabriz and experienced Pishevari's pro-Soviet autonomist Azerbaijan in 1946. Invited by Ayatollah Borujerdi to teach in Qom, he stayed there, while keeping his ties with Azerbaijan. During the 1962–63 risings Shariatmadari played a major role, and it is generally agreed that he, supported by other ulama, saved the life of Khomeini when he was threatened by the regime.

The Islamic revolution brought out the traditionalism of Shariatmadari's positions: without breaking with Khomeini, he kept his distance. At the beginning of the revolution he supported popular protests against the brutal oppression of the shah and at first demanded, as did most others, the strict application of the 1906–07 constitution, which foresaw a veto power on legislation by a committee of five mujtahids. He thus indicated that, unlike Khomeini, he was not against a constitutional monarchy with mujtahids participating in power. After the revolution, renouncing official posts, he gathered around him various currents— liberal, moderate, and conservative: bazaar traders unhappy with the recession, and Azerbaijani regionalists. The mainly Azerbaijani Muslim Republican People's party used his name, but he was too prudent to voice support, and even acquiesced in its self-dissolution after the December 1979 struggles in Tabriz. In this he was faithful to his principle that the ulama must abstain from direct intervention in politics.

Although he never published a book systematically presenting his religious and political thought, Shariatmadari expressed his ideas through interviews. He said that an Islamic government does not a priori exclude monarchy, though the injustices of the Pahlavi regime and its subservience to the West removed its legitimacy. Shariatmadari reproaches most Muslim revolutionaries with taking the means (constitution, revolution) for the end. Speaking of some "Islamic revolutionaries," he asks if it is right to admire Che Guevara more than Imam Hasan. He defends himself against the accusation of reformism: the criterion of political action is not Marxism or socialism, it is Islam, and we can say that if on certain questions the Prophet was revolutionary, on others (the fight against slavery, against usury, etc.) he was "reformist."

With his subtle, seductive personality and the patience with which he agrees to answer all questions, Shariatmadari contrasts with Khomeini.

We will not detail the power struggles of these two leaders, whose positions are often divergent. Where Khomeini, an innovator, crystallizes all religion around political positions, Shariatmadari, a very learned theologian, concentrates on maintaining traditional Shi'i positions. Some have said that their quarrels are superficial, masking a corporate solidarity, with divergences allowing all Iranians to follow a leading theologian. But perhaps Shariatmadari's rallying of conservatives and moderates represents the schism between a high clergy for whom the revolution, while allowing them to gain prestige and power, can be a social threat, and a lower clergy with populist tendencies around Khomeini. The former group has recourse to the integrity of theological dogma as an arm to defend its shaky power. Reportedly, several top ayatollahs are in disagreement with Khomeini and closer to Shariatmadari, who was pressured into silence in 1980, and was reported in early 1981 to be under house arrest.

Another prominent ayatollah in the Islamic political movement, Mahmud Taleqani (d. September 1979), was very popular, while remaining less powerful than Khomeini. He had been, since the 1950s, one of the leading ideologists of the religious opposition to the Shah. He entered personally into political combat, and was jailed or kept in internal exile for many years. Born in 1910 in the valley of Taleqan, Mahmud Taleqani pursued theological studies at Qom. He began to teach in 1938 at the Sepahsalar theological school in Tehran, and was jailed for six months in 1939 for his opposition to the religious policies of Reza Shah. He struggled for Mosaddeq together with Mehdi Bazargan and Yadollah Sahabi. After the coup d'état of 1953 he was arrested for having hidden at his home Navvab Safavi, the leader of the Feda'iyan-e Islam. He was imprisoned several times in the 1960s, notably for having demanded the application of the constitution and for having struggled along with Bazargan and Sahabi in the Freedom Movement of Iran. In 1971 he was exiled to the Southeast. In mid-1977 he was arrested for having supported the leftist Muslim guerillas, the Mojahedin, and was only freed by popular pressure at the beginning of November 1978.

Taleqani played a prominent role in the 1978–79 Revolution, serving as a link between lay groups like the National Front and religious ones. He served similarly in several crises of the new regime, and led, by designation of Ayatollah Khomeini, the Friday prayers on the campus of Tehran University that began in Ramadan, 1979. Quite isolated among the ulama, he was nonetheless the most popular of them, winning by far the highest number of votes in the 1979 elections to the constituent assembly. Years of strain contributed to his ill health and he died of a heart attack on September 10, 1979.

Ayatollah Taleqani appeared as one of the most liberal and progressive among the Iranian ulama; Sunni minorities approached him with their requests, as did also leftist groups, as they knew that Taleqani would welcome them and remember their common struggles against the shah and SAVAK. Possibly his long stays in jail with the nonreligious opposition helped him understand them. In the last months of his life, until one final statement, he ceased his former public statements differing from Khomeini's policies.[36]

Among the works of Taleqani were commentaries on the Quran and the *Nahj al-Balagha* (a collection of sayings, sermons, and letters of Ali). Taleqani presents his doctrine in a plain style, within the limits of traditional doctrines.[37] His more original work treats socioeconomic problems. In 1955 he edited, with introduction and notes, a 1909 political treatise by Ayatollah Na'ini. In his introduction, taking up Na'ini's arguments, Taleqani says religion has always been a threat to dictators who, concentrating all power, make idols of themselves. Divine unity, *tauhid,* in struggling against this idolatry, liberates men from slavery and submits them only to God, who is absolute truth, justice, and wisdom. Government of men belongs (1) to God; (2) to divine law; (3) to the Prophets and Imams, whose thought and spiritual force are entirely at the service of divine law and who claim no monarchical title; and (4) to the just ulama and believers. Men's efforts to govern themselves like the Constitutional Revolution, democracy, and socialism, can be steps toward tauhid if people see that the aim is beyond them. People must continue the effort to better the regime and fight against dictatorship, in the sense of Na'ini's book.[38]

In his *Islam and Property, in Comparison to the Economic Systems of the West,* Taleqani developed his capacity for analysis. This is a response to contemporary problems presented in an historical context.[39] Taleqani discusses successively:

1. The evolution of property since the origins of humanity; the division of labor, exchange, money, laws, and the ideal community; the first economic theories, and the industrial revolution.

2. The appearance of workers' power: here he examines Marxism, class struggle, extreme forms of capitalism, the dictatorship of the proletariat, and classless society. He criticizes Marxism as naive, for thinking

inequalities can be suppressed by giving special privileges to workers' rule and by suppressing metaphysics. He explains such excesses in the context of struggles against capitalism.

3. The economy in the light of faith: Eschatology gives Islamic doctrine a transhistoric view of the economy; the legislator must both take account of spiritual aims and detach himself from his class conditioning. Human laws (*'urf*) are fragmentary, limited by history, and subject to change. They are easily diverted by a tyrannic power; are influenced by passions; and must be applied by coercion. Only Islam is the perfect legislator—it encourages reason to follow the path of God instead of misleading it; frees man from the slavery of human customs; teaches all to distinguish good from evil; and makes of a man controlled by passions a controller of himself. Because of these qualities, Islamic law (*fiqh*) is not accessible to all; only mujtahids can decide its application.

4. The economic bases of Islam and the roots of its precepts: God is the absolute owner of the goods confided to us; this is opposed to capitalism, for which property is absolutely free; and to socialism, which suppresses individual property. These two excesses permit the enslavement of man. The author applies this principle to analyzing the system of landownership and vaqf; in Islam, before Westerners came, feudalism (*tuyuldari*) never implanted itself durably. In Islam landownership is never absolute, and land reverts to the one who puts it under cultivation.

5. Money and the economic problems tied to it: Interest (*riba*) has created capitalism. Islam forbids hoarding but encourages commerce, which brings the distribution of riches. Utilizing a socialist slogan, Taleqani declares: One should take from everyone according to his abilities, and give to him according to his needs.

6. The specific features of the Islamic economy: Taleqani insists on the freedom of economic activity, of the production and distribution of goods. Natural resources belong to those who render them productive. But there are limits, whose control is assured by the state (especially mineral resources).

7. Class differences, privileges, and their origin: Class privileges are not necessarily tied to money: for example, in the military classes. Islam, while recognizing differences among men, refuses the privileges engendered by monarchical regimes. Taleqani gives a history and criticism of the French Declaration of the Rights of Man, which is hypocritically advocated by the very people who constantly violate it. Inviolability of the principle of property opens the door to all the abuses of capitalism.

Notable is the passage where Taleqani, aware of the harm a priestly class can do in some societies, affirms that no such thing exists in Islam, where the ulama have no privileges and must, as in the early days, sit at the same level as others in assemblies. However, as noted, only mujtahids can interpret Muslim law correctly. A mujtahid is recognized by his justice and his faculty of interpreting, but he, even more than others, is subject to the same law.[40] Taleqani was one of several thinkers who had written in favor of decentralizing the function of marja'-e taqlid and proposed the creation of a doctrinal council that would convene the most esteemed ulama of the different regions.[41]

Taleqani remained limited by his theological formation; his contact with the West and modern ideological systems was indirect, and he does not deal with certain important questions concerning the economy: taxes, nationalizations, the banking system, and so forth. However, his appeal to Islamic morality has progressive aspects and includes an appreciation of social problems. This helps explain his popularity among leftist Muslim groups, like the Mojahedin-e Khalq.

Other ayatollahs have expressed, in books and in the press, diverse positions on democracy and political problems, and there is a large and powerful conservative group whose writings repel any progressive or reformist tendencies and combat both communism and laicism.

Lay Shi'i Politico-Religious Thinkers

The most original Islamic thinkers are those who, not having had the training of traditional ulama, have had educational contact with the West, which allows them to voice clearly, and with a new vocabulary, a critique of what they oppose, and to define a new Islamic ideology. Here are discussed three of them: Mehdi Bazargan, Ali Shariati, and Abolhasan Bani Sadr.

Bazargan addresses chiefly middle classes, merchants, and lower civil servants, while Shariati and Bani Sadr became the ideologues of young revolutionary intellectuals. All three say Islam is not against progress and that it has an answer to materialist ideologies in its positive approach to modern science and technology—points that traditional theologians cannot demonstrate.

Mehdi Bazargan was one of the most important politico-religious leaders of the revolution. From the 1950s to the revolution he presented a modern image of Islam. He criticized traditionalists immersed in a theoretical theology focused on minor points of faith. He also utilized his reputation as an engineer and professor to show that Islam was in accord with scientific and technical progress. Islam, he said, is a pragmatic doctrine, adapted to the modern world. Bazargan tried to answer secular ideologies on their own ground.[42]

Born in 1905 into a family of Tabriz bazaar merchants, Bazargan completed his education at the Ecole Centrale in Paris.[43] Returning to Iran in 1936, he worked at the National Bank, and then taught thermodynamics at Tehran University. After World War II he became a close collaborator of Mosaddeq, who named him in 1951 to head the oil-nationalization committee. After the fall of Mosaddeq, Bazargan joined the secret resistance movement. In 1961 with Taleqani and Yadollah Sahabi he founded the Freedom Movement of Iran, which was later proscribed and brought all three prison terms. Prison did not silence Bazargan. An indefatigable speaker, he also wrote treatises presenting Islam in modern form, with a new vocabulary and examples taken from contemporary culture and technology.

A frequent theme in Bazargan's writings is a refusal to separate the spiritual and the temporal. This separation, a feature of Western Christian culture, is found in decadent Muslim society, whose theologians and philosophers turn aside from this world, which they leave to base men, while they deal only in words.[44] For Bazargan there is no frontier between religion and politics. Religion must control and inspire politics, and not the contrary. He critizes the shah's trinity of "God-Shah-Country," in which "Shah" occupied the central place.[45] Religion must set the aims and principles of politics; the means are a human problem.

Bazargan's attitude toward the West is mixed admiration and disgust. He sees the West as the example of technical and scientific civilization, and also of social and political principles in which faith does not enter, such as democracy, the rights of man, and humanism. Europeans do not despise religion, unlike the Westernized Iranian bourgeoisie. But Bazargan severely criticizes Christianity as unable to give believers directives for practical, social, and political life. Westerners have to turn for guidance to philosophic-political doctrines made into idols, like socialism, Marxism, and so on, which Islam does not need, as it is a complete religion.[46]

In politics, Bazargan is more concerned by the problem of justice than by concrete social struggles. In a small book on labor, one looks in vain for references to workers' problems or social legislation.[47] Bazargan's influence and his popularity among the Muslim petty bourgeoisie

are due to his courageous political activity with Mosaddeq and his opposition to the shah. A prudent reformer, he sees Islam as in accord with
democracy, reason, and science.[48] If he criticizes Islam's fossilized and
often compromised theologians, he does not question Shi'ism. To meet
injustices and tyranny while avoiding social conflict and communism, he
asked the Shi'i ulama to take more interest in temporal affairs, and found
welfare, cultural, economic, and political institutions to lessen social
inequalities. If this had been done, he said in 1962, a truly egalitarian Islamic government could exist "without recourse to revolution or
bloodshed."[49] Thus, the man who became the Islamic Republic's first
prime minister in February 1979 is a modern and liberal Muslim, but
seems to underestimate the immense social problems which agitate Iran.

Ali Shariati did the most to prepare Iranian youth for revolutionary
upheaval. Events made this Muslim sociologist, shortly after his 1977
death, the ideologist of the revolt. In the opposition demonstrations, his
portrait was carried beside that of Ayatollah Khomeini.

Ali Shariati was born in 1933 in Mazinan, a village near the desert, in
Khorasan in northeast Iran. His father, Mohammad Taqi Shariati, was a
well-known preacher. Shortly after Ali's birth, his family moved to
Mashhad, the capital of Khorasan and center of Iranian Shi'i pilgrimage;
there he received his secondary education. At seventeen he entered normal school and two years later became a teacher. He began to write and
translate works on Shi'ism and became involved in the pro-Mosaddeq
opposition.

At twenty-three he entered the Faculty of Letters at Mashhad. He
wrote articles published by local journals. He also married a student
companion and served his first prison term. In 1959, he received a bache-
lor's degree, and, as one of the top students, had the right to a scholarship
abroad. He was not allowed to leave for a year, and then went to Paris,
where he was a sympathizer of the Algerian liberation movement. He
studied religious history and sociology, although his thesis, contrary to
what is often said, was not in these fields but in Persian philology. Among
those whose influence he notes were Louis Massignon, for whom he had
a deep admiration and with whom he studied Fatima, daughter of
Mohammad and wife of Ali; Frantz Fanon, whose *Wretched of the Earth*
he translated; and Jean-Paul Sartre. In 1964 he returned to Iran with a
doctorate. At the frontier he was arrested and held for several months.[50]

In 1965 he first taught in a large Khorasan village, then in a Mashhad
high school. He soon became assistant at the University of Mashhad,

where the content and success of his courses led to his dismissal. He then went to Tehran where his reputation as a lecturer spread quickly. He was frequently invited to talk, especially at the Hosainiyeh Ershad, a progressive Muslim institution created in 1969. His lectures were recorded and diffused by mimeograph. Late in 1973 the Hosainiyeh Ershad was closed by the regime. Shariati hid, but his father was imprisoned as a hostage. After a few months, Shariati gave himself up and was held for eighteen more months in solitary confinement. Upon release he returned to Mazinan under virtual house arrest. In the spring of 1977 he decided to leave Iran, which was made possible by the relative liberalization of the regime. However, the authorities at the last minute refused his wife authorization to join him, and when he came to the airport in London he found only two of his three daughters. He died shortly afterward on June 19, 1977.

There is as yet no complete bibliography of Shariati, and as many of his works were short mimeographed lectures, or transcriptions from cassettes, while others appeared under pseudonyms or in obscure reviews, it is hard to establish one. Since 1977 these short texts have been reproduced, sometimes brought together and sold openly.[51] Shariati often added notes to his texts, but the oral style remains evident except in a few rare works like the autobiography *Desert (Kavir)*, composed in lovely poetic language. The titles of his lectures suggest his major themes: "Ali, the Superman of History," "Man, Islam, and the Doctrines of the West," "Eqbal, Architect of the Renewal of Islamic Thought," "Community (*umma*) and Imamate," "The Sura *Rum:* A Message to Responsible Intellectuals," "Shi'ism, the Perfect Party," and so on. His works are being reedited and regrouped by the revived Hosainiyeh Ershad.

The style and the context of Shariati's lectures did not encourage literary or scientifically argued works. He was above all a great orator who profited from the short time he knew he had to hammer into the conscience of his audience certain key ideas. Their arrangement was less important than the need to say as much as possible without losing his audience's attention.

Shariati wished to be a politico-religious thinker in the context of the Third World liberation struggles. He felt acutely the problems of colonialism and neocolonialism and attacked especially cultural colonization, which alienates people from their roots. Iran is especially exposed to this danger: Al-e Ahmad had denounced fifteen years before this Iranian malady in his *Westoxication,* long forbidden by the censor.

Shariati believed that the undermining of national culture had politico-economic consequences. Western ideologies paralyzed the indigenous reactions of Muslim peoples. Neither capitalist liberalism, which causes and profits from this illness, nor Marxist or socialist doctrines, which have lost their dynamism and envisage an antihumanist and antireligious levelling, can provide a way out. Shariati saw in Islamic humanism the sole ideology that could save Iran and all oppressed peoples. Islam should be followed, not in the degraded form found in contemporary Muslim societies, but in the form of Mohammad's ideal society, which the Umayyads had plunged into decadence and tyranny.

Faith gives the individual his determination to struggle and the group its cement. For Shariati atheistic societies are sad and unattractive, as material satisfactions are deceptive. A religious and somewhat mystic spirit, Shariati refers constantly to the early Shi'i heroes, to whom he devoted many lectures: Ali, Hosain, Abu Zarr Ghefari, Horr, and others. He sees two Shi'i principles as the motors of liberation: (1) The imamate, a systematization of "leadership," the spiritual and political domination of a leader over a people who accept him willingly. The community (*umma;* from the same Arabic root as "imam") is not, as in Christianity, united by the mystic presence (of Christ) but is united by its movement, around its leader. (2) Justice, which has been elevated by Shi'ism to the rank of a theological principle: God must be just, and the human community cannot accept a tyrannical law that killed the imams and plunged Islam into decadence.

In a group of lectures gathered in one volume, Shariati presented a strong distinction between "Alid Shi'ism" (from Ali, the first Imam) and "Safavid Shi'ism." Alid Shi'ism represents original Islam and is a movement of progress and revolution, with no division between intellectuals and the people—Islam in its progressive and dynamic phase. The Safavids, in making Shi'ism the state religion, degraded it into an institution, making it a means of political enslavement and turning it from its original aim—the search for justice and sacred duties. "Safavid Shi'ism" opposed Iranians to Ottomans; it mixed ethnocentrism and supernationalism with Shi'ism. Aberrant forms of worship were, says Shariati, borrowed from Christianity in Safavid times, like the theatrical plays on the martyrdom of Hosain (ta'ziyeh), which he says are copied from Christian "mysteries."

Shariati's Safavid Shi'ism is also Pahlavi Shi'ism, and today's "Safavid" ulama are those who play games of power. They renounce their role as awakeners, content themselves with futile debates, and make of Shi'ism a religion of the vanquished (the Moharram mournings), turning believers toward exterior forms and not toward a movement. They claim that in the absence of the Twelfth Imam any government is acceptable, thus becoming accomplices of Islam's atrophy and the separation of religion and power.

At the end of the book Shariati gives a table between the two Shi'isms, based on their main concepts, which we summarize:[52]

Alid Shi'ism	Safavid Shi'ism
vesayat	
The Prophet's recommendation, by divine order, to designate his family the most capable and meritorious on the basis of knowledge and purity.	The principle of a government, at first designated, then hereditary, perpetuated on the basis of race and kinship.
imamate	
Pure, honest, revolutionary conduct of the people and the correct foundation of society in terms of conscience, the expansion and independence of people's judgment. The coming of "superior men" incarnating the religious ideal to be taken as models.	Belief in twelve pure, saintly, extraordinary names; supermen like angels; little gods next to the great God; the only recourse for intercession and obtaining grace.
'esmat	
Belief in the purity of those spiritually and socially responsible. Negation of government by traitors, and dishonest clerics attached to the caliphate.	An exceptional quality of hidden beings not of the earthly human species, who cannot be in error; only the "Sinless Fourteen" (Mohammad, Fatima, and the twelve imams) had it. This belief makes infamous government natural, accepts dishonest theologians as they are not among the Sinless Fourteen.
velayat	
Offering one's friendship to Ali and following his path, in his manner, under his guidance.	Love of Ali alone; feeling oneself totally irresponsible.

taqlid

A logical, scientific, natural, and necessary relationship between nonspecialists and specialist theologians, for practice and juridical problems that demand specialization.

Blind obedience to the ulama, from whom one accepts absolutely, without reserve or logic, belief and orders. Quasi-adoration of the ulama.

'adl

God is just; the world is based on justice and consequently society must also be based on it.

A problem concerning the attributes of God and the afterlife (Last Judgment). In this world justice is to be left to Shah Abbas (to monarchies) according to the principle "render to God what is God's and to Caesar what is Caesar's."

ghaibat

Responsibility of men to decide their destiny, faith, and spiritual and social life, taking guidance from conscientious, responsible, pure men representing the leadership of the Imam.

Total irresponsibility; the uselessness of all action under the pretext of the Imam's absence—he is the only model to whom one is responsible.

entezar

Spiritual, moral, and doctrinal preparation for reform, revolution, and change. Firm belief in the fall of tyranny, the victory of justice, and the advent of the exploited classes to world revolution.

Spiritual, moral, and doctrinal submission to the present situation; justification of corruption, and seeing the divine decree in everything. Negation of responsibility, fear of reforms, and condemnation in advance of all movements.

By systematizing the concept of Alid Shi'ism, Shariati attained a double result; he detached himself from the petrified official Islam rejected by idealistic youth, and he brought a new and combative meaning to Shi'i concepts. Even prayer in this renovated Islam took on a political meaning, tied to action. This insurrectional meaning of common prayer was particularly developed in the 1978–79 Revolution. Refusing the fanaticism of Safavid Shi'ism, Shariati advocated an accord between Shi'is and Sunnis, as before the Umayyad schism.

Shariati also devoted several lectures to the role of women, published as *Fatima is Fatima.* He criticized the Western model, seen as fabricating women-objects and utilizing sexuality without marital ties for commercial ends. The West, in claiming to "liberate" women in its colonies, is really only trying to affirm its power by breaking up the unity of the Muslim family. Shariati favors women's participation in public life and severely attacks traditional principles of women's seclusion. But, he says, liberation and egalitarianism are words that risk going against nature. Westernization, which made these words a slogan, offers only an individualism in which women must choose between sacrificing their femininity in the hard professional struggle, or overdeveloping femininity in useless roles. The decadence of Muslim society and its contempt for women demand a reevaluation of woman's role, a search for a new model. Shariati uses the example of Fatima, daughter of Mohammad and wife of Ali, who shared her father's trials, and also those of Ali and of her sons, Imams Hasan and Hosain. She was the center of a family of fighters. She took on responsibilities and became socially engaged, equally to men but in a different way.[53] The "separate but equal" doctrine of Shariati regarding women has become popular with many Muslims.

The really political thought of Shariati is not very developed in published texts, even though everything leads to it. His stress on the community following the imamate suggests that Shariati, while making implacable criticisms of totalitarianism, dreamed of an Islamic totalitarianism, the only one he saw as respecting completely the individual, not enslaving him to anyone but God, and not reducing his autonomy to that of an economic producer. Islam is, besides, he says, the only basis for an ideology of permanent progress and revolution—halting any attempt at a return to tyrannical powers and any degradation of political relationships.

Shariati sees Western democracy as rotten, because the power of money and not electors dominates politics. It is also rotten in principle, as universal suffrage, while claiming to create equality, in fact ensures the crushing of the progressive minority by the conservative majority. In "The Community and the Imamate" he defines the "directed" democracy he advocates:

> It is the government of a group which, on the basis of a revolutionary progressive program that aims at changing individuals—their view of the world, their language, their social relations, and their level of living—and also at changing social forms in order to perfect them, has, with the above aims, an ideology, a well-defined doctrine, and a precise plan. Its aim is not that everyone by his vote or his acquiescence should be its partisan, but it is to make a society reach the level where, on the basis of

this doctrine, it begins to move toward this most elevated goal and to realize its revolutionary objectives. If there are people who do not believe in this path, and whose conduct leads to a stagnation or corruption of society, and if there are some who abuse with their own power, with their own money, this liberty, and if there are social formations and traditions, which keep men in this stagnation, we must suppress these traditions, condemn these ways of thinking, and save society from its own fossilized molds, by any means possible.[54]

The immense appeal that Shariati had for students and young Muslims is partly to be explained by the originality of his position. Coming from a modest religious background he acquired, through his studies in France, knowledge of modern ideologies, including liberalism, capitalism, Marxism, and existentialism, without ceasing to be a believer. Speaking a language accessible to Iranians who had only recently come to modern studies and who wished to understand, in order to refute, the ideologies of Western aggressors, he became celebrated by meeting their needs. He became famous at the time when Iran experienced a great expansion in higher education and when new social groups, without ideological preparation, were confronted by new cultural problems—accelerated urbanization, Westernization, industrialization, spectacular speculation and corruption, and many other phenomena tied to Iran's dependence on the West. Demographic growth affected most the less Westernized, poorer classes, who were the most religious. His ties to Islam made Shariati, who was well equipped to respond to other ideologies, the rampart against the undermining of traditional values. Islam, the religion of the Algerian National Liberation Front, of the Palestinians, was the religion of anti-imperialist combat. Feeling stifled by the West, Iranians rediscovered an identity.

Iran's new intellectuals had earlier seen Islam as something disconnected from the modern world's needs. Islam had even a negative role, turning attention to the hereafter, underpinning the regime by its silence, and presenting the defeatist side of religious combat, as it encouraged Muslims to cry for poor Hosain, who died miserably. Young Iranian Muslim intellectuals found in Shariati a revolutionary Iranian Shi'i response. No more the crying Hosain of the ta'ziyeh, but Hosain fighting and dying for a just cause.

Although Shariati's books were forbidden they circulated secretly, especially among Iranian students abroad. Among religious traditionalists a strong opposition to Shariati and the Hosainiyeh Ershad developed. The theologians' prestige was being defied by someone who had not studied theology who accused those who had of distorting religion for their own profit and contested the good faith of religious authorities' resistance to the monarchy. Their struggles were backward looking and defended their corporate interests and former privileges, whereas Shariati's struggle was radically revolutionary. Of the ulama's critiques of Shariati none, to our knowledge, was more than a polemic, usually with unfounded accusations (being an agent of Sunnism, of Wahhabism, or of Communism), with nothing constructive. Among the accusations of the great mujtahids against Shariati was that he wished to have an Islam without ulama and hence, by dividing Muslims on this point, to play the game of the anti-Muslim regime. Ayatollah Khomeini attacked the Mojahedin-e Khalq, heavily inspired by Shariati, on similar grounds, saying that one cannot be a Muslim if one does not recognize the power of the ulama.[55]

From the summer of 1977 on, however, Shariati's books were sold everywhere, by the hundreds of thousands. In front of Tehran University, bookstores are full of them, and sidewalk vendors have made a living by selling practically nothing else. The same is true in quarters near the Tehran bazaar, of provincial towns (even those without bookstores), and in the religious towns of Qom and Mashhad. Shortly after his death Shariati became a mythical figure of militant Islam. In the third volume of posthumous homages published in 1978 are found the names of many celebrated oppositionist intellectuals.[56]

It is too soon to predict what will be Shariati's lasting influence. Here we will not try to judge his still incomplete publications, nor to evaluate a person whose courage and spiritual qualities demand respect. We will limit ourselves to a few remarks: Despite the importance Shariati gave in his lectures to a critique of Western society and his insistence on saving a humanism threatened by decadent Christianity and materialism (both capitalist and Communist), his knowledge of the West was schematic. Understandably, he did not expand before his audience his portrait of the Christian mystic Massignon, or expatiate on the democratic ideals of many Western countries, but some of his polemics indicate that Shariati was not interested enough in the systems he combatted to study them closely.

Shariati also neglects the history of Iran; he admits that in his studies he disliked history, perhaps because of the use made of it. He refers very little to it; what interests him is an ideal original Islam, not its historic compromises. Hence, his analysis of the relations of Shi'ism with the government since Safavid times lacks references to accessible texts and documents. The Iranian ulama's major role in the Constitutional Revolution of 1905–11 is not discussed, except to criticize the use of *mashrutiyat* for "constitution." We have found just one page on the role the ulama should have in politics:

> But at the time of the (Imam's) Occultation, as there was no prophet and the Imam was absent, the mission of the prophets and imams fell upon the people themselves, and it is the people themselves who should learn Islam, put in practice the fundamental ideas of Islam, form Islamic society, and guide the people. Muslims must defend Islam, its power and unity, against Jews, Christians, and other enemies, carry on holy war, make the effort of interpretation [ijtihad], and oblige one group among them to specialize in the theoretical knowledge of Islam, the deducing of Islamic laws, and the resolution of the problems of society and the events of the time. They should confide to this group social and ideological leadership as well as responsibility for people's destiny. This group can decide the best, most honorable, most conscientious, most enlightened, and purest person for their guidance. And they can elect from among themselves someone in place of the Imam—which is the place of the Prophet of Islam! And they would invest him. In the execution of his heavy responsibilities—which are those of the Imamate—the people feel a permanent and direct responsibility and build the government of wisdom, of engaged wisdom, as Plato wished.... That is to say that the one who was chosen by God in the period before the Occultation (i.e., the Prophet and the Imams), during the Occultation is chosen by the people.[57]

Shariati thus takes the traditional theory of ijtihad, mixing it with democratic principles, but makes no historical or theological analysis, so that it is hard to know his precise position. This lack of precision does not keep young Iranian intellectuals and others from rallying to Shariati. All find in his energetic thought an Iranian response to their problems as Iranian intellectuals. Shariati helps them to set off to conquer the modern world without renouncing their Muslim identity.

Abolhasan Bani Sadr is one of the more original political ideologists and theoreticians of the Iranian Islamic movement. After having been close to Ayatollah Khomeini at Neauphle-le-Château, he became a rising figure in the new regime, and in November 1979 became acting foreign minister. In January 1980 he was elected first president of the Islamic Republic. His works are less popular than those of Shariati; they are also clearer. He analyzes problems and uses economic arguments.

Born in 1933–34 into a family of Ayatollahs originating in Hamadan, Bani Sadr studied at the university first theology and then sociology. In this period he met the French Marxist sociologist Paul Vieille, whose collaborator he became. Bani Sadr was already a known opponent of the shah's regime and participated in meetings organized by the National Front and by political groups at Tehran University, when he was forced into exile to France, where he pursued studies in economics and sociology. Much influenced by the 1968 student movement, he became a leader of students abroad opposed to the shah's regime. From 1972 he was in direct contact with Ayatollah Khomeini in Najaf.

In Bani Sadr's works may be distinguished economic articles (some in French) from more doctrinal texts. Both are directed to struggle: they denounce economic policies seen as delivering Iran to the control of imperialism, and also construct an ideology to mobilize Iran's vital forces. Several texts are instruments of political struggle: *Iran's Situation and the Role of Modarres* begins a study of contemporary history stressing the role of religion in the struggle against the Pahlavis. *The Hypocrites from Our Viewpoint* unites texts about the Mojahedin-e Khalq and the strategy of revolutionary combat after the 1975 split between Marxists and Muslims in the Mojahedin. Bani Sadr affirmed his attachment to Ayatollah Khomeini and refuted attacks made against Mehdi Bazargan based on truncated and misleading citations. *The Cult of Personality* is a treatise on ethics with a Quranic base, a critique of man's ambition and desire for power which, especially in economics and politics, are the main causes of oppression.[58]

Bani Sadr made himself a theorist of Islamic government in three other books: *The Economics of Unity (Tauhid)* is an attempt to construct a political theory dominated by the Quranic principle, "There is no god but God"; and hence there must not be economic domination of man by man. Islam returns to the principle that only God has the absolute right to property, a right delegated by the Prophet and the Imams to those in the community who deserve it, thanks to their labor. Before being a relationship between man and man, labor is a relationship of man to God.[59]

In a 1971–72 work, republished as *Manifesto of the Islamic Republic,* Bani Sadr sketches an Islamic political anthropology. The first part is a critique of the Pahlavi regime for putting Iran under the political, military, and economic domination of the West, and hence causing Iranians to lose identity and creativity and become consumers. The second part proposes solutions. In foreign policy one must ensure Iran's independence and reaffirm Mosaddeq's "principle of negative equilibrium." In domestic policy there must be true Islamic government, reviving the real structures of power, like mosques; suppressing harmful conflict between state and religion; and building a state without constraints. In economics Bani Sadr wishes to bring internal production and consumption back into balance. He thinks ending dependence on imperialists will bring a better distribution of wealth, greater justice, an end to the flight of intellectuals, and reduction in bureaucracy. Finally, the socioeconomic causes of alienation having ended, Iranians will no longer be in a passive dependent relation to world centers of decision. There will no longer be a schism between state and people, and a new Islamic society can be created. "Everyone is responsible for all; everyone is imam and guide of all"; such is the unity (tauhid) of society that religion has as its message.[60]

Finally, *The Fundamental Principles of Islamic Government* is a theoretical work concerning tomorrow's society, in the style of the great European nineteenth-century ideologues. The method used by the author is to analyze his subject according to categories identical to the five principles of Shi'ism. The first, divine unity, is a dynamic unification and a negation of polytheist trends (no one can be God's representative, or claim any participation in God's unity). This fundamental principle is the foundation of the other four. Because of this unity, one may condemn all human formations that oppress and divide people. "The principle of unity involves the negation of every sort of economic, political, ideological, or other bastion in which power can be concentrated."[61] The believer must try to achieve unity everywhere so that society will be in the image of the community desired by God. Devotions are a training to fight for this ideal: common prayer, fasting, pilgrimage (a sort of annual congress), and holy war (against evil impulses within) prepare one to combat oppression by making the everyday a constant rejection of all that is not God.

Thus, one must not adore any leader, neither Stalin, nor Hitler, not de Gaulle, nor Mosaddeq, nor Khomeini, as the cult of men leads to enslavement and totalitarianism. With Bani Sadr this principle goes very far, as all power coming from men is condemned, even if it tries to justify itself by religion. Bani Sadr reacts against the idea of God as an arbitrary and absolute will—an idea that theology developed in the decadent period of the caliphate, and which allowed the imposition of illegitimate and irreligious governmental authority. All false human authorities, who divide men, must be overthrown. Society must not be divided into classes, into dominant and dominated; and excessive property is a negation of God. Economic resources must be controlled so they do not lead to concentrations of power, depriving most people of their capacity to produce. Slavery, meaning massive workers' migrations from poor to rich countries, must be abolished. In Islamic government, only work justifies ownership of the product of labor, which excludes capitalism. The economy belongs to everyone, not to one class. Luxury must be eliminated, as it means poverty for the majority.

To Marxists, who say that religion obstructs class consciousness by transforming into prayer the revolt of the exploited, Bani Sadr says that differences between men come from God and should not be denied. They can be kept from engendering classes by putting special talents at the service of society. Bani Sadr criticizes ideologies which, after having brought people to power, are used as instruments of domination. Any belief used for domination is an opiate of the people:

> But would not Islam become an opiate if one made of it an instrument of the system? Since Islam is a religion that rests on universal laws and one nature, and which envisages liberation from the traps of these perpetual realities, it is not possible for it to become the opiate of the masses, unless one makes of it a scourge, as the present regime (1975) has institutionalized it and made it a scourge.
>
> Hence, in an Islamic government, belief must not be an instrument of government, but the government must be an instrument of Islamic belief. And this necessitates guarantees that it be the belief that governs.[62]

Islam was established on the basis of universal laws and human nature. The end does not justify the means.

The goal of Islamic government, to Bani Sadr, is not only to stop a person or group from monopolizing power; it is to suppress centralized power and the state as a form of oppression. Nationalism is a pretext to divide and oppress peoples; offensive armies should be abolished. Only a defensive army should be created, and should be organically based in society. Holy war is in reality a permanent revolution, in which there is no "model for imitation" (marja'-e taqlid); everyone must discover himself the cause for which he is fighting.

Two tendencies seem to dominate the writings of Bani Sadr; on the one hand a certain anarchist tendency, which pushes him toward rejecting any domination of man by man under any pretext, and toward rendering possible the installation of what he calls "organized spontaneity;"

on the other hand a tendency to make (in his Persian more than his French writings) all analyses, even in the social or economic domain, enter the traditional theological categories of Shi'ism. These two features give Bani Sadr's thought a contradictory quality, but it is also thanks to these tendencies that he attracts numerous partisans, who are trying to reconcile a desire for liberty with the rigors of Islamic law.

Conclusion

Critical analyses of recent Shi'i political thought have been made elsewhere, and here only a few general remarks will be offered.[63] First, the above survey of Iranian political thought since the late nineteenth century suggests the frequent reappearance of certain similar themes, often found in both religious and secular thinkers. One of the most important is anti-imperialism, accompanied by a determination to free Iran from Western economic and cultural dominance. This took a reformed Islamic form with Sayyed Jamal ad-Din, a more secular form with Mosaddeq and his main followers, and again a religious form in recent years. The Islamic nature of recent reactions even by many non-clerical leaders may in part be explained by the association of Western dominance with Western "cultural colonization," and of Pahlavi rule with secularism. Islam appeared, to those who rejected both liberalism and Marxism, as the natural ideological base from which to fight the West and the Pahlavis, especially as Islam was believed by, and familiar to, the great mass of Iranians. As with modernist and political adaptations of religion elsewhere, this utilization of Islam has involved new interpretations of old texts and practices, interpretations sometimes attacked by the more traditional and orthodox. It has also involved indiscriminate attacks on the West as a monolithic evil.

A more serious difficulty is that most modern Shi'i political thinkers have assumed that solutions to Iran's problems are essentially simple. They have tended to think that freeing Iran from foreign control and influence and setting up new and fairly simple political and economic institutions, for which they find an Islamic base, will solve Iran's problems, but this has not turned out to be the case. In essence, the new Islamic thought became a potent weapon in making a revolution, but had far less success in building up new institutions. The various books and pamphlets on Islamic politics and economics written in the past twenty years do not, even had they been followed in detail, provide an adequate basis for setting up a polity that could meet the widely recognized needs for social justice, mass participation in political and economic life, rights for minorities and women, a truly functioning economy, and so forth.

Intolerance by some leaders of ideas labeled "un-Islamic" or "counterrevolutionary" has narrowed the range of permissible discourse. By 2003 it was clear, however, that the dominance of thought couched in Islamic terms was not as durable a phenomenon as it once appeared, and that Iran's long traditions of religious dissidence and skepticism, rationalist philosophy, and even secularism and anticlericalism had once again come to the fore. Whichever tradition is dominant in the foreseeable future, it is to be hoped that Iranians have learned that the "two cultures" split, which separates the religious from the secular and the masses from the elite, does not benefit Iran, and that each of the two culture groups may strive to understand, learn from, and see the needs and contributions of the other.

9

The Revolution

Secular and Guerilla Opposition Forces

The continuing growth of malaise and discontent among most sections of the Iranian population as despotism and repression increased in the 1970s, promised political and economic decentralization failed to materialize, and economic difficulties grew in 1976 and 1977, despite huge oil income, led to an outbreak of opposition beginning in 1977. The appearance of open opposition to the shah would likely have occurred soon in any case, but its form and timing were to some degree a consequence of the human-rights policy enunciated by President Carter, inaugurated in January 1977, which implied that countries guilty of basic human-rights violations might be deprived of American arms or aid. The influence of the human-rights policy was not due to any significant American pressures, however, but to the belief by both the shah and the opposition that the United States might act for human rights. This belief helped give some Iranians the courage to circulate open letters and petitions in the hope that they might be heeded and would surely not be as severely repressed as before. United States diplomats and policy makers, however, refused significantly to pressure the shah on human rights. The human-rights questions occasionally discussed with the shah were arrests and torture, not liberalization or civil rights, and no threats of reduced support were made. The sporadic mention by official Americans of human rights helped make the shah waver in his confidence regarding American backing and hence in his response to the opposition, but this was more a sign of his mentality than of any actual threat. The liberal opposition was in part encouraged to activity by Carter's words, even though they were backed by few deeds.

There may have been additional reasons, rarely mentioned, for the shah to tolerate criticisms in 1977 that he would not have allowed earlier. Among them was that he knew he was ill with cancer, and that the throne might pass to his minor son, with regency going to Queen Farah, according to a provision he had initiated. In the fall of 1977, as on some previous and later occasions, there was a period during which pictures of the shah's activities were noticeably absent from TV and the newspapers (presumably because of illness; when he did reappear he looked bad). Instead, one saw frequent pictures of the queen engaging in a series of public-minded activities throughout Iran. At the time of the queen's birthday, photos of the queen alone (without the father-son members of the universal trinity) were for the first time plastered all over Iran's cities; and, extraordinarily, they were severe, unglamorous photos, suggesting a woman of determination who could rule. It seems logical to attribute some easing of dictatorship and of ironclad restraints on open opposition in 1977 to the shah's recognition that his designated successors would not be able to start off their rule with his type of strong hand, but would have to enlist some cooperation from various elements of the population, including an increasingly vocal opposition. As the crisis progressed, some of the shah's weakness may have been due to his cancer and medication,[1] which either included strong tranquilizers or had the same effect. Also, reforms in the judiciary and in reducing torture may have been as much due to pressures from world opinion, particularly Amnesty International and the International Commission of Jurists, which began before the Carter administration, as to any United States action.

Interviews and statements do indicate, however, that professionals and intellectuals were determined to utilize the American human-rights policy to wedge an opening by publishing their grievances, hoping to widen the crack in order to change government policies. In the spring and summer of 1977 several petitions and open letters were circulated. The fact that these letters came from non-"extremist" types—neither the militants of the religious opposition nor those on the left—should not be exaggerated, as it sometimes is, to imply that the "moderates" started the revolution and the "extremists" took it over. Radical petitions from either religious or Marxist elements could only circulate in greater secrecy, but this does not mean that these groups were inactive in 1977; and, on the other hand, the moderates were relatively too weak among the masses to keep leadership of the opposition.

Among the major 1977 letters were: a two-page open letter to the shah in June signed by leaders of the revived National Front—men whose association with the Front dated back to Mosaddeq: Karim Sanjabi, Shapour Bakhtiar, and Daryush Foruhar. The letter criticized the failure of the shah's reforms and particularly the disregard for human rights, enshrined in both the Iranian constitution and the Universal Declaration of Human Rights. It attacked shortages, inflation, and the squandering of oil, and called for fulfillment of the constitution, release of political prisoners, freedom of the press, and free elections. The letter circulated widely, and was especially influential among the new middle classes, whose reformist constitutionalist trends it voiced. Shortly after this letter another was sent to Prime Minister Hoveyda signed by forty well-known writers and professors demanding an end to censorship, free meetings, and recognition for the Writers' Guild, which had been suppressed some years before.

In the same period a group of lawyers began a series of protests; in May they had protested rushed changes in the judicial system, and in July, 64 lawyers demanded an end to special courts and strict observance of law without constant encroachment by the executive upon the judiciary. After a further letter protesting the judicial system in September, 143 lawyers issued a manifesto in October stating their intention of forming a Jurists Association, which was to monitor observance of human rights. Finally, a series of poetry readings with political content at the Irano-German Institute in Tehran in October attracted unprecedented crowds and became virtual antiregime demonstrations.[2]

One influence of the Carter human-rights program was probably in encouraging intellectuals to send and circulate (although they could not publish) their protests, which in the past would probably have involved jail sentences. Now they brought no immediate punishment, and although such direct criticisms were not published in the press or elsewhere, they did circulate from hand to hand and abroad. At the same time as these intellectuals' protests circulated, pressure from foreign human-rights groups like Amnesty International and the International Commission of Jurists, and from Iranian guerilla, religious, and other opposition groups kept up, while economic and social problems became increasingly acute. The shah thus made some gestures toward public opinion; in April 1977 for the first time a trial on antiregime charges was open to the public, the International Red Cross was permitted to inspect twenty prisons, torture was significantly reduced, and new laws, which were only partially improvements, were promulgated regarding military tribunals (before which political prisoners were tried). The writings of Ali Shariati, newly freed from censorship, now achieved vast sale.

In the face of growing public discontent and economic problems the shah removed Prime Minister Hoveyda in July 1977, but made him minister of court. The new prime minister, Jamshid Amuzegar, was a technocrat with high governmental experience as minister of interior; in economics and oil; and as leader of the official Rastakhiz party; his appointment indicated no basic change in political policy but at best a hope that a man with a better economic background could help solve Iran's growing economic problems. In fact, his attempts to cool off inflation and the overheated economy without reducing the huge sacrosanct military budget resulted in mass unemployment and other problems. Construction jobs in particular, which began falling in 1976, tumbled further and discontents increased.

In November 1977, the shah visited Washington, where he faced large hostile demonstrations; these were shown on Iranian television and made a great impression. Carter returned the visit, along with high praise of the shah, in December. It seems likely that, as the Iranian opposition believed, in return for Iran's moderating its stand on oil prices, the United States guaranteed continued arms supplies, diplomatic support, and a downplaying of the human-rights issue. In December Iran backed Saudi Arabia's oil-price-freeze policy, while American officials from then on played down human rights in Iran more than before.[3] From the end of 1977 on, also, there were numerous incidents of "mysterious" beatings and bombings of opposition leaders and protesters, generally attributed to the regime via SAVAK.

Once the door was opened to protest, however, it was not to be shut. There had already been far more protest in the years since the 1963–64 crackdown than a reading of the world press would lead one to suppose. Workers' strikes were quite frequent, even though opposed by officially supervised trade unions and confronted by threats of force. Much of the regime's policy of favoring workers in large factories and industries with higher wages and bonuses was based on fear of a labor movement, even though a nationwide movement did not materialize, owing to strict SAVAK surveillance.

At least as great a political threat were students, both at home and abroad. Most students were too young and idealistic to have been co-opted by the regime, and they had many grievances. Within their lecture halls they could sense the strain between those technical or politically harmless new ideas they were permitted access to and the many others their teachers could not voice nor their booksellers sell. (Books in Persian by Marxists and Iranian oppositionists were forbidden sale, even in the few cases when they were published, and there remained from Reza Shah's days a law against any advocacy of "collectivism" or "socialism.") Some teachers were dismissed and others were warned or suspended. This aroused opposition from students. With rapidly expanding universities and a large influx of poorly educated secondary students, many from rural areas, academic and economic frustrations also grew. Also, the great majority of university applicants failed to get in, and those who did were often dissatisfied with academic, housing, and educational conditions, as well as political ones. Hence there were frequent major student protests and strikes over the years, particularly in the main cities, and many campuses remained closed for months at a time. Although for years student protests tended to be concentrated in campus areas, once the national protest movement broadened in 1977–78, students had the habits, inclination, and experience that helped make them important participants in the revolutionary movement. A variety of political persuasions were represented on campuses, most notably Marxist groups and religious leftists. There was a trend among some women students in the 1970s to return to the chador or to adopt a new costume, with a large headscarf covering hair and forehead, a knee-length smock, and loose trousers, all in plain neutral colors, a costume that has become a kind of uniform for the women of the Mojahedin-e Khalq. Some students who wore the new costume or the chador were genuinely religious; others wished to stress their protest against the regime.

In the 1970s probably over one hundred thousand Iranian students were abroad at a time, and many of them opposed the Iranian government. The strongest oppositional group was the Confederation of Iranian Students, which grew out of earlier varied Iranian student groups abroad but coalesced in 1960 with considerable leftist and Tudeh party influence. Tudeh popularity among students dropped with the growing rapprochement between the Soviet Union, Eastern Europe, and Iran in the later 1960s (the Soviets built Iran's first steelmill and provided small arms, and in the same period economic relations with Eastern Europe developed). As Soviet policy toward Iran became conciliatory, the pro-Soviet Tudeh party lost much of its appeal to Iranian leftist opposition-ists, including students. Some turned to a pro-Chinese group that split off from the main Tudeh party, although this group lost much of its credibility as the Chinese too, in the 1970s after the shah recognized the People's Republic, drew up trade and diplomatic agreements with Iran. As time went on the Confederation of Iranian Students became in-creasingly radicalized and included numerous admirers of the small guerilla groups operating in Iran, the most important of which were the Marxist Fedaiyan-e Khalq and the Islamic leftist Mojahedin-e Khalq.

In the 1970s Muslim students' associations, sometimes entirely Ira-nian and sometimes from different Muslim countries, also became as important abroad as they were in Iran. Some, as in France, had ties with groups using the name of the National Front and venerated both Mosad-deq and Khomeini. Islamically oriented lay leaders of the 1978–79 Revo-lution were often involved in, or leaders of, such movements, including notably Abolhasan Bani Sadr, Ibrahim Yazdi, and Sadeq Ghotbzadeh. Through their propaganda, Iranian student groups abroad were among the first to awaken some in the West to the activities of the shah and SAVAK and to help enlist Western support and pressure against human-rights violations. Although some ex-student oppositionists at home and abroad were bought off by official offers of good jobs, and others were scared off from returning by penalties for belonging to the Confedera-tion and other activities abroad, still others continued their oppositional work before and during the Revolution both in Iran and abroad.

More important than their small numbers and few pre-1978 successes would indicate were the guerilla groups in Iran, recently studied by E. Abrahamian.[4] According to him, guerilla tactics were an outgrowth of the regime's bloody suppression of the 1963 riots, which made many think that open protests were sure to be violently suppressed. Militant students formed small secret groups, which translated and studied works by Mao, Guevara, and Fanon and discussed guerilla tactics. Three of these groups merged in 1970–71 under a name usually shortened as the Feda'iyan-e Khalq, whose best known theorist Bizhan Jazani was killed in prison in 1975; Hamid Ashraf, the leader who longest eluded the police, was killed in Tehran in 1976. Critical of Maoists and especially the pro-Soviet Tudeh, they hoped to create nuclei of armed struggle on the then popular model of Che Guevara and Regis Debray. They planned to spend a year in the mountains and forests of the Caspian province of Gilan, well situated for guerilla warfare and having a post–World War I history of such struggle. Two of their sympathizers were arrested, however, and the rest feared their plans might be revealed under torture. Hence they hastened Iran's first major guerilla operation in February 1971, attacking a gendarmerie post in Siahkal village and killing three gendarmes. Failing to find their two colleagues, they escaped into the Gilan mountains.

The shah reacted strongly, sending his brother to head a large well-equipped force which, after a manhunt that left several soldiers and thirty guerillas dead, captured eleven Feda'iyan. Ten were shot and the other died of torture. Despite the military failure, the Feda'iyan and other oppositionists looked to this day, which showed it was possible to shake the regime, as the beginning of a successful antishah movement. In the following weeks the government confirmed the importance of the Siahkal incident by arresting oppositionists, spreading anti-left propaganda, and outlawing the Confederation of Iranian Students abroad. Armed robberies, assassinations, and bombings followed, but by late 1976 some Feda'iyan thought that losses from such tactics outweighed gains, given the heavy toll in lives and the lack of mass struggles triggered by their acts, and this minority turned toward the Tudeh party. Both factions kept their weapons, and were able to use these, along with their training and experience, during the Revolution.

The other guerilla group, whose name is shortened to Mojahedin-e Khalq, also originated in the 1960s, but while the Feda'iyan came mostly from the Tudeh party and from Marxists in the National Front, the Mojahedin came mostly from the religious wing of that Front, particularly the Freedom Movement led since 1961 by Mehdi Bazargan and Ayatollah Mahmud Taleqani. The Freedom Movement was intended as a link between Shi'ism and modern ideas, but the government's brutality in 1963 caused some of its younger and more militant activists to leave the Movement and form a secret discussion group. The leaders of this group changed the Freedom Movement leaders' liberal interpretations of Shi'ism, deciding that true Shi'ism opposed not only despotism but also capitalism, imperialism, and conservative clericalism. As summarized by Abrahamian, one Mojahedin ideologist, Reza'i, argued that the realm of unity (or monotheistic order—*Nezame-e Tauhid*) the Prophet sought was a commonwealth fully united by virtue of being "classless" and striving for the common good as well as by the fact that it worships only one God:

Reza'i further argued that the banner of revolt raised by the Shi'i Imams, especially 'Ali, Hassan, and Hussein, was aimed against feudal landlords and exploiting merchant capitalists as well as against usurping Caliphs who betrayed the *Nezam-i Towhid.* For Reza'i and the *Mujahidin* it was the duty of all Muslims to continue this struggle to create a 'classless society' and destroy all forms of capitalism, despotism, and imperialism. The *Mujahidin* summed up their attitude towards religion in these words: "After years of extensive study into Islamic history and Shi'i ideology, our organization has reached the firm conclusion that Islam, especially Shi'ism, will play a major role in inspiring the masses to join the revolution. It will do so because Shi'ism, particularly Hussein's historic act of resistance, has both a revolutionary message and a special place in our popular culture."[5]

Given these ideas, it was natural for the Mojahedin to be on good terms with Ali Shariati; although many of their theories preceded Shariati's public lectures and writings, it seems likely that each helped inspire the other. A series of individual acts of violence from 1971 on resulted in heavy Mojahedin losses via arrests and executions; as with the Feda'iyan, the Mojahedin did not see such individual acts as their ultimate goal but as the only means toward revolution in a period of extreme repression. Most Mojahedin were children of bazaaris or ulama, and came mainly from the physical sciences. The Feda'iyan, largely from modern middle-class backgrounds, included more women than the Mojahedin, drew from the arts and social-science faculties, and included a number of industrial workers.

Some Mojahedin began to study Marxism, and in 1975 a majority of leaders still free in Tehran voted to declare the organization Marxist-Leninist. The transformation is suggested in a letter by Mojtaba Taleqani, son of Ayatollah Taleqani, to his father: "to organize the working class, we must reject Islam, for religion refuses to accept the main dynamic force of history—that of the class struggle. Of course, Islam can play a progressive role, especially in mobilizing the intelligentsia against imperialism. But it is only Marxism that provides a scientific analysis of society and looks toward the exploited classes for liberation."[6] This change caused a major split; most provincial members refused to change ideology, accusing their rivals of murdering one of their leaders and betraying two to the police. The Mojahedin split into two groups, and both continued violent action, but by early 1976, like the Feda'iyan, they had such heavy losses that they switched more to propaganda; the

Muslim Mojahedin mainly among students and the Marxist ones among workers. Thus, when revolutionary activities began in late 1977 there were two Mojahedin—Marxist and Muslim; and two Feda'iyan—pro-Tudeh and activist. All had organizations, weapons, underground publications, and revolutionary ideologies, equipping them for important roles in a revolutionary movement. Some had ties to the Palestinian resistance, particularly its left constituents, and this facilitated the entry of weapons from abroad after mid-1978.

Although several guerilla actions aroused horror among many—particularly assassinations of Iranian and American military and intelligence figures—there were peaceable Iranian oppositionists who argued that, given the atmosphere of repression, only such acts could indicate the vulnerability of the regime and keep alive hope for its eventual overthrow. It seems likely that the increase in jailings, torture, repression, and censorship in the 1970s was tied to the guerillas' activities, although repression was already strong previously.

The "Religious Opposition" and the Revolution

As suggested above, parts of various opposition groups—the predominantly middle-class and elderly remnants of the National Front, students inside and outside Iran, the workers, and the guerillas—had ties to the growing number of oppositionists who voiced their views in Islamic terms, here called the "religious opposition." The religious opposition can best be understood in terms of its own two major groups, even though they overlap the above groups; first, those with a traditional religious education and functions, and second, those with Western or Western-style educations who united modern and traditional ideas under an Islamic rubric. Many of these persons and particularly their ideas were discussed at some length in chapter 8—notably Ayatollahs Khomeini, Shariatmadari, and Taleqani among the first, and Bazargan, Shariati, and Bani Sadr among the second group, but here they will be related to the background and events of the Revolution.

A major grievance of the trained ulama against the Pahlavi regime was its continual whittling away at ulama power and influence, accompanied by the growing power of Western infidels and their ways. Reza Shah instituted examinations to qualify for wearing a turban and hence being one of the ulama; secularized the legal and educational systems, thus depriving many ulama of jobs; unveiled women; instituted university coeducation, and took other steps that weakened the ulama and their ideological hegemony. Mohammad Reza Shah moved further in the same directions, by trying to tame religion by setting up schools of theology in state universities, including the University of Tehran; by putting new controls on pilgrimages abroad; and by setting up a "religion corps" to parallel the literacy corps for the villages and teach an officially approved version of religion. Although no respecter of women, the shah came to see, partly under the pressure of the homogenized Women's Organization, that the encouragement of women in the labor force could help in Iran's economic growth. The Iranian Women's Organization, whose director Mahnaz Afkhami was made the Third World's first minister for women's affairs, headed a group that helped train women to read and to acquire other skills that might enable them to work for a living and to defend their legal rights, especially under the Family Protection Law of 1967/75. Both this law and the slowly spreading practice of coeducation were opposed in teaching and writing by Ayatollah Khomeini and some Islamic fundamentalists, as were more obviously disturbing signs of Western-influenced "decadence," such as sexy films, dances, and music; forms of women's dress that not only went against old veiling norms but were often tight or revealing; open drinking and gambling (both against Muslim law); and others. Westernization seemed inextricably tied to a decline in Islamic practices, quite aside from its economic ill effects.

There were several individual events from the mid-1970s that further aroused the ulama and their followers. One was the shah's scheme to redevelop the area around the holy shrine of the Imam Reza at Mashhad, which, like many shrines, was surrounded by a dense bazaar area that helped unify the bazaaris and the ulama. The plan was carried through and razed all buildings around the shrine, creating instead a green space and a broad traffic circle. It was so unpopular that bulldozers and construction equipment were often bombed or sabotaged, but it created something more attractive to "modern" taste. It dispersed Mashhad's bazaaris but further kindled their resentments. A related scheme for the Tehran bazaar, to cut through it with broad boulevards, which would, as in Mashhad, have dispersed potentially dangerous bazaaris, aroused so much opposition that it was not carried through. A drastic 1977 cut in government subsidies to the ulama for various purposes, carried out when Amuzegar was prime minister, also increased ulama discontent.[7]

Various attempts to create a monarchist ideology-mythology were also unpopular, both with the ulama and with other elements in the opposition. Although Iranian kings and rulers have had more of an ideological base than some recent works stressing ulama ideology would suggest, Iranian rulers since the rise of Islam did not go nearly as far as the Pahlavis in their attempts to glorify the monarchy—attempts that devalued Islam and were bound to arouse ulama. Reza Shah's identification with pre-Islamic kings was carried further by his son, who at a vastly wasteful 1971 celebration at Persepolis tried to give the world and Iranians the false impression that Iran had an uninterrupted twenty-five-hundred-year monarchical tradition (in fact there were a variety of titles for rulers—of areas that did not correspond to modern Iran—between the Muslim conquest and 1501, and again between 1722 and 1796). From abroad Ayatollah Khomeini denounced the celebration and monarchy itself.[8] The imposition of a new calendar dating from the pre-Islamic monarch Cyrus the Great instead of from Mohammad's *hijra* convinced many that the shah was out to uproot Islam. Growing government control and exploitation of rural and urban vaqfs were also of importance. The imprisonment of revered religious leaders, and their foreign or internal exile in the cases of Ayatollahs Khomeini and Taleqani, further aroused their colleagues and followers. It was also felt that the shah's downgrading of Islam was accompanied by his favoring of both foreigners and non-Muslim Iranians. In the case of the Baha'is, considered apostates from Islam by pious Muslims, this was a point that sometimes took on exaggerated proportions, while the words of some ulama occasionally went from anti-Zionism to anti-Semitism. A minority of Baha'is, Christians, and Jews had well-paying jobs and/or ties to foreigners or to the court; the importance of this was often exaggerated and so, like similar minorities elsewhere, these non-Muslims were sometimes resented. Officially the ulama and their partisans spoke and speak of protecting the recognized minorities. Resentment was also felt against reputed Freemasonic connections of some in the government and at court, as many considered Freemasonry anti-Islamic and pro-British.

The ending of Iraq-Iran cold and hot hostilities by treaty in 1975 resulted in a resumption of Iranian pilgrimages to Iraq in 1976, and an increasing number of tapes and writings reached Iran from Ayatollah Khomeini in Iraq. His uncompromising line gave courage to oppositional ulama within Iran, and much mosque preaching became increasingly hostile to the shah. Some within Iran, like Ayatollah Kazem Shariatmadari, took a more moderate line, but nonetheless eventually began to call for the full restoration of the 1906–07 constitution (meaning free elections, a government responsible to the majles, a weak shah, and a committee of mujtahids to veto bills not deemed in accord with Muslim law). The death of Khomeini's son Mostafa in Iraq in October 1977, assumed to be the work of SAVAK, added to the opposition.

In January 1978, the regime demonstrated the degree to which it miscalculated the strength of the religious opposition in taking one of its fatal missteps. Reportedly at the instigation of the shah, an article was published in the leading semiofficial newspaper, *Ettela'at,* violently attacking and slandering Khomeini. The article emanated from Information Minister Daryush Homayun (one of several former oppositionist students abroad who rose high in the shah's regime). The two-column article was entitled "Iran and Red and Black Colonization" and signed with a pseudonym. After generalities on the White Revolution and "black reaction" (of the ulama), the article attacked a religious leader chosen to direct the movement: "an adventurer, without faith, and tied to the centers of colonialism . . . a man with a dubious past, tied to the more superficial and reactionary colonialists." This man was Ruhollah Khomeini, better known as "the Indian Sayyed." Although his ties to India had never been brought to light, it was clear that he had contacts with the British. In his youth he wrote love poems signed *Hindi* (the Indian). The article ended by saying that Khomeini was opposed to the shah's reforms, and suggested that he received large sums from the English (via an Arab) to continue his fight against the shah.

The promotion of such calumnies showed the concern of the regime to discredit Khomeini, but events proved it to be a bad miscalculation. The following day theological students in Qom staged a massive protest and sit-in, which was broken up by security forces. This brought on a violent confrontation; at least seventy were killed in two days, making this the bloodiest incident since 1963.

The newspaper attack on Khomeini and the Qom incident may be seen as a key point—January 1978—in which much of the initiative in the protest movement swung from the secular forces, with their letters, petitions, organizations, and political poetry readings, to the religiously led opposition. Even if the authorities had had the sense not to calumniate Khomeini, the religiously led movement would probably have developed as the leading oppositional force. The religious opposition, especially if one adds those who admired Shariati and the Mojahedin, appealed to far larger numbers than did the secular liberals, and in any mass protest it is virtually certain that these people would ultimately have been decisive and would have turned to the leaders they trusted most. The government had been largely successful over many years in suppressing secular protests and had left a clearer field for the less manageable religious opposition.

The ulama and bazaar leadership, sensing their new power and the grievances of their constituency, helped in 1978 to organize massive memorial demonstrations for those killed in previous incidents, taking place at traditional forty-day religious intervals. Here was a brilliant example of political use of Shi'i traditions; the government would risk truly massive demonstrations if it outlawed traditional mourning gatherings occurring at the proper and traditional intervals: such a prohibition would have been unheard of, even under the shah. In addition, the forty-day interval gave an excellent hiatus to regroup forces, spread the word orally, bring people together almost automatically without the need to argue about date and place, and to utilize spontaneous or ritual emotion to intensify opposition to the regime. At one of the first demonstrations, in Tabriz in February, many banks, shops, and cinemas were attacked and destroyed, and the cry, "Death to the shah," was first heard. These and other such acts of destruction continued in later protests. Human life was spared, even of those considered enemies, and except for rare incidents involving a very few persons at the high point of late revolutionary fervor, even American lives were inviolable. Banks, shops, and cinemas were considered symbols of dependence on the West and infidels (banks had a significant percentage of foreign capital, and cinemas showed mostly foreign, often sexy, films).

Among the followers both of Khomeini and of Shariati (whose ideas were rarely distinguished by the masses in 1978–79) were the bazaaris, meaning not only those who had shops in the bazaar but also those who carried on retail and export trade and manufacture of a traditional rather than a modern type. Bazaaris are not a class in the Marxist sense, as they have different relations to the means of production; the journeyman artisan or worker in a small bazaar factory is in a different position from a banker or moneylender, who may be quite wealthy; nonetheless the expression "bazaari" has meaning in its involvement with petty trade, production, and banking of a largely traditional or only slightly modernized nature, as well as its centering on bazaar areas and traditional Islamic culture. These people are sometimes called "petty bourgeois," but this term seems inadequate, as some are rich wholesalers and bankers and some are workers. Most of them are united in their resistance to dependence on the West and the spread of Western ways. Although Western goods are widely sold in the bazaars, the growth of supermarkets, department stores, large banks, and goods like machine-made carpeting that compete with Persian rugs added to Western control of Iran's economy and reduced the role of the bazaar. Governmental favoring of non-bazaar trade and industry and various plans of "modernization" or dispersal of the bazaar, of which two have been discussed, were partly designed to weaken the bazaar's politico-economic cohesion and were seen as a threat. Among those who live much in the old way in the traditional economy, Western mores are often viewed with horror, and the "traditionalist" bazaar attitude along with the close family, financial, and cultural ties of the bazaar with the ulama, help explain the bazaar-ulama alliance that has been responsible for so much revolutionary activity in Iran since 1891. Religious taxes and gifts to the ulama for religious, educational, charitable, and political purposes come from bazaaris, account for a high percentage of ulama influence, and help cement the political ties between bazaar and mosque. In addition, bazaaris often held weekly "religious" meetings in homes, which provided an ideal network for discussing political problems and tactics. The extent and propinquity of small, open bazaar shops make the bazaar an easy area for rapid communication and organization.

Some in the modern economy who had recently moved from the bazaar were also attracted particularly by Shariati's blend of Islam with modern ideas. Despite the modernization of Iran, the bazaar remained a focal point of major political opposition movements from 1891 through 1979. This was partly due to the ease of organizing craft and religious circles that in time of crisis took on an increasingly political aspect. In addition, bazaaris have been closely tied to the ulama who, as noted, have given ideological leadership to many important oppositional movements. Most bazaaris are free of ties to the government, which might have made them hesitate (as did many in the modern middle class, often in governmental or quasi-governmental jobs) to join a really revolutionary movement. Although one tends to think of bazaaris as a group in decline, this is probably true only in a relative sense; the new middle class with Westernized educations and positions may have grown faster than they, but with the massive immigration from the countryside there was more need than ever before for petty retailers, bazaar wholesalers, and bazaar moneylenders and bankers, so that their numbers are considerable and have grown along with cities. According to Robert Graham, citing reliable estimates: "Despite the modernisation of the economy, the Bazaar still controls over two-thirds of domestic wholesale trade and accounts for at least 30 per cent of all imports . . . At the same time through its control of the carpet trade and other export items like nuts and dried fruits, the Bazaar has access to foreign exchange which has not been channelled through the official system. . . . One unofficial estimate puts Bazaari lending in 1976 at 15 per cent of private sector credit."[9]

Over the years the Pahlavis tried to reduce bazaar power by building new streets, shops, schools, and institutions away from it; by imposing grid patterns on bazaar streets, by controlling distribution, and by campaigns against "profiteers," chiefly bazaaris rather than the really rich, and by restricting cheap credit to bazaaris. Although a major shift in economic power to the modern sector occurred, bazaaris were neither cowed nor reduced in numbers.

One incident in the new militant bazaar-ulama alliance was a fight to keep Iran's most ubiquitous private bank, the Bank Saderat, considered by some to be the bazaaris' friend, from falling under the control of a Baha'i, Yazdani, who had acquired a 26 percent share in it. Working with ulama, bazaar merchants organized a campaign of withdrawals from the bank and Yazdani was forced to sell out. Bazaaris also helped to support families of victims of 1978's struggles, and provided financial support for the antiregime strikes that began in May 1978 among university students and teachers and in the fall spread to the workers and civil servants.

Another group important in the victory of the revolution was the subproletariat, often recent immigrants to town. These people lived in slums and shantytowns with few amenities; often left their families behind in the village; and suffered increasingly from the growing shortage of unskilled construction and other jobs from 1976 onward, combined with a rise in prices. Uprooted literally and culturally, and closer physically and culturally to the bazaar than to the modernized parts of town, they easily believed that drastic action should be taken to see that the oil billions they knew were streaming into Iran did something for them.

The key role of such rootless young males was first seen in the important Tabriz riot of February 1978, which began in commemoration of those killed in Qom in January but soon turned into a strong protest against the shah. The Azerbaijani police reportedly refused to act, and outside troops were called in, and began to shoot. A riot developed, led by youths, who attacked the banks, the headquarters of the shah's

Rastakhiz party, cinemas, and liquor stores. Some Azerbaijani autonomist feeling and belief (based on facts) that the area was neglected by the
center fed the movement. Radical students from Tabriz University also
joined. According to some reports about one hundred people were killed
and over six hundred arrested. This protest-to-riot pattern was to be
repeated later in Iran's main cities. Although villagers living far from
cities could not participate in such riots, many villagers who commuted
to urban jobs did participate.[10]

Another important group of participants in the Iranian revolution,
whose participation varied some by class and ideology but exceeded
anything hitherto seen in Iran, were women. In the student movement
within and outside Iran women had always played a role of some importance although, as in the West, most dominant leaders were men. Women
were important among the guerillas even before 1977, and a number
were jailed or died in shootouts. Since women's organizations had been
homogenized into the official Iranian Women's Organization, women
strongly opposed to the regime tended to shun such organizations and
indeed generally avoided wholly feminist causes, which they mostly saw
as divisive at a time when the main aim was to overthrow the shah and his
regime. As in many revolutionary movements, many politically conscious women assumed that their participation in struggle and the victory of their cause would give to women what they desired. It should
also be realized that many women did not consciously feel oppressed as
women, and showed no interest in women's causes. Therefore, the
moves of the shah's regime to modernize women's dress, education, and
work patterns, which in any case mainly affected middle- and upper-
class women, were not necessarily approved or even felt by the majority
of Iran's women, while the entry of women into factory work or commercial carpetmaking added to their burden of labor. Women's participation in politics during and after the revolution was multiclass and
gave many women a new sense of pride at their ability to organize, take
action in the public sphere, and sometimes risk their lives.

In the cultural climate of the 1970s, those opposed to the shah's regime
increasingly saw as bad everything the regime said was good. Thus, as
noted, we find the ironic phenomenon of some women university students from the mid-1970s on readopting Muslim modes of dress as a
means of stressing their identity with Islam, seen as morally and politically superior to the ways of the regime, and/or of stressing their

political opposition to the regime, whether or not they were believers. Even before the Revolution many tricky and important issues of principle regarding women were raised when Muslim and non-Muslim students tried to unite against the regime; on more than one occasion Muslim students demonstrated for sexually segregated dining halls and classes, and some women students were pressured into wearing the chador, while, on the other hand, university instructors or authorities reportedly sometimes refused admission to classes or examinations of chadored women.

Although women students played and play an important role in political demonstrations and activities, even more numerous in the demonstrations of 1978 were chadored bazaari women, who came out usually in separate ranks to participate in the mourning processions, where they had always been, but where their presence took on a new political meaning. As the threat of violence grew, women often marched bravely at the head of processions; participants recognized that this put the police and regime in a difficult position.

The size and courage of demonstrating crowds was again seen in Isfahan in July when three days of demonstrations led to numerous deaths and martial law. Aside from this there was a partial break in the pattern of escalating forty-day-interval demonstrations during June and July, and in the same period the shah made a number of promises of liberalization, including, notably, free elections with a variety of political parties to occur the following year. Westernized Iranians and foreigners present then can attest that this was a period of euphoria for Westernized liberals in Iran; they believed the liberal pressures and mass protests had sufficed to start the regime on a path of true liberalization from which it could not turn back, given the threat of renewed street action if it did. The possibility that street demonstrations might culminate in the shah's overthrow and a regime headed by Khomeini, still in exile, was scarcely discussed at this time by the new middle classes. Later in 1978 many of them were to join the revolution, but in June and July they almost universally miscalculated the situation.[11] (Those analysts who attribute the Iranian revolution to the "middle class" or "the bourgeoisie" without specifying which middle class or bourgeoisie are wide of the mark; modernized intellectuals were important to the verbal protests of 1977–78 but they and other Westernizers, aside from some of the students, were overshadowed by the active religiously oriented protests of 1978 until late in the year. Throughout 1978 most Westernizers misjudged the situation, first thinking that the shah's regime would stay in and reform, and later that the Revolution would allow them a significant postrevolutionary role.)

A lull on one summer day when demonstrations might have been expected to occur did not imply that things were quieting, as many intellectuals thought, but may have been a preparation for the holy month of Ramadan, when mass mobilization was easy. Already by early August the Shiraz International Festival, held under the auspices of the queen and considered by the religious a decadent sign of subservience to the non-Muslim West, was threatened with serious trouble and had to be canceled. Far more dramatic was the fire in the Rex Theatre in Abadan in August, in which hundreds were killed; the government tried to blame it on oppositional terrorists but the great majority of Iranians believed it to be a provocation by the shah via SAVAK. Although evidence points to gross incompetence and possible complicity by local authorities, it is highly unlikely that the shah, at a time of relative quiet which he hoped to preserve, would order an act that could only have the opposite effect. What counted, however, was what people thought, and the fire helped to rekindle active protests that would probably have occurred, if a bit later, in any case. (In 1980 a trial of one of the accused indicated that a religiously oriented group was responsible, possibly manipulated by police, and, according to some, perhaps having ties to higher clericals.)

In the face of vast protest, the shah tried to meet his problem with further concessions that still left power in his hands. He removed Amuzegar as premier and replaced him with Sharif-Emami, a longtime politician whom the shah had also used in 1960 to try to assuage the opposition. The shah allowed Sharif-Emami to widen political freedoms, but accompanied this with severe repression of active opposition. During Sharif-Emami's two-month premiership the press and majles debates became far freer, old political parties resurfaced, new ones were born, and orderly political demonstrations were allowed. A new ministry to protect religious affairs was created, casinos were closed, and the recent monarchy calendar that began with Cyrus the Great, not Mohammad's hijra, was abolished. A code to deal with royal family corruption was too little and too late. Sharif-Emami's reputation as a Freemason, a group that most Iranians associated with Western, and especially British, influence, added to his difficulties in attracting support.

In the same period repression became worse than ever. Although a peaceful demonstration that comprised over a million people occurred on September 5, three days later martial law was declared in the early morning hours, so that many did not hear of it, and on "Black Friday," September 8, those shot and killed in a massive but peaceful Tehran demonstration in Jaleh Square probably numbered from 500 to 900, though both higher and lower figures are given. This ended all real opportunity for an accommodation with the opposition, and two months later, in November, the shah ended the attempt and appointed General Gholam Reza Azhari prime minister in a new military government. (This followed riots and the burning of public buildings, which some think were caused by the army to force the shah to act.) Schools and universities were now closed, newspapers suspended, and meetings of over three persons in Tehran prohibited, although the new government was not as repressive as many had feared and did not cow the opposition. The arrest of ex-prime minister Hoveyda and ex-SAVAK head General Nasiri were widely regarded as scapegoating.

Throughout the 1977–78 period Khomeini's popularity grew. In this more than in previous revolutionary protest movements the urban poor and subproletariat were represented, and because of their large numbers they at first came out in greater strength than did factory workers and the middle classes, despite the latter's importance. For the urban poor Khomeini and his words were supreme guides, and as revolutionary anger, enthusiasm, and activity grew, Khomeini's refusal to make any compromise with the monarchy and his implication that problems could be solved by a return to Islamic ways had increasing appeal for the Muslim masses. Popular ayatollahs who stressed rather a return to full implementation of the 1906–07 constitution, whether the moderate Shariatmadari or the socially conscious Mahmud Taleqani (whose arrest and imprisonment in the summer of 1977 was a further cause of discontent), were bound to lose influence to the more uncompromising Khomeini in revolutionary circumstances.

In the fall there was the decisive entry of the industrial and salaried working classes, including the key oil workers, into the mass protest movement, and also of the new middle classes, represented chiefly by the revived coalition of some National Front elements, generally known as the National Front. Both groups, whatever the private views of some of their constituents, had little choice but to join forces with Khomeini. He, evidently in part because of Iranian pressure on Iraq, had been forced to leave Iraq and, after being refused entry to Kuwait, with permission from the shah to the French, took refuge near Paris in October 1978. This proved a foolish move by Iran's regime, as telephone, airplane, and cassette communication was easier than before, Iraqi controls on Khomeini ended, and worldwide television and press coverage of Khomeini vastly increased.

As people became increasingly fearless, enthusiastic, and aroused, even in the face of deaths in demonstrations, and as total opposition to the regime spread to new classes of people, there began the crucial stage of the revolution, with massive politico-economic strikes against the shah starting in late summer, lasting until the end of the Revolution, and virtually paralyzing the economy. In September strikes began in the Tehran oil refinery and at a large petrochemical complex at Bandar Shahpur, followed in days by a strike of NIOC workers at the main center of Ahwaz. Strikes then spread through the government and oil industry, so that by late October the production level had fallen to an average of 1.5 million barrels daily, about 28 percent of its former level. Leftist, liberal, and religious groups encouraged the strikes and discouraged acceptance of large wage settlements. By the time military government arrived few public services were functional. The military government pledged to end strikes, but instead they increased. Attempts to reimpose censorship were met by press strikes.

The return of oppositionists from abroad and the revival of protest in Iran encouraged open activity by guerilla groups, both in killing Iranian military and police leaders, and participating in oppositional demonstrations. Now the Feda'iyan and the Mojahedin were able to apply united front tactics effectively and to attract open members and followers. In the course of 1978 they became sizable movements, largely of young people, who were attracted partly by the more visible activity of these groups than of either the pro-Soviet or pro-Chinese Communist groups. (The Soviets and especially the Chinese refrained from criticizing the shah until the very end.) On the other hand, late 1978 also saw an increase in grassroots organization by the Khomeini supporters. All these groups as well as many others published newspapers, pamphlets, and posters that were widely and eagerly read and helped spread and influence revolutionary ideas.

From France, Khomeini's refusal to compromise with either the shah or the liberal constitutional monarchists, which was wholly consistent with his nature and ideology, was also just what his style of revolution needed. Karim Sanjabi visited him in the name of the National Front and emerged with a short declaration that spoke of both Islam and democracy as basic principles; once the Revolution was won, however,

Khomeini explicitly refused to put the same word, democracy, into either the title of the Republic or its constitution—a position consistent with his view that democracy was a Western import and Islam sufficed. Khomeini's statements in France convinced many secularists that he would support their rule. His indications that he did not want to rule directly were probably based on the false assumption that others would rule just as he wanted them to. The apparent democratic nationalist tone of many of his statements from France was largely due to the advice of his Western-educated entourage there—Bani Sadr, Ghotbzadeh, and Yazdi. Many revolutionaries knew only these French statements and not the theocratic ideas of his *Hokumat-e Islami.*

The Sanjabi-Khomeini visit and statements were of great importance to the outcome of the Revolution, as they brought about a Khomeini-National Front association and probably foreclosed the possibility of a solution midway between the monarchy and the Islamic Republic and sealed the later failure of Shapour Bakhtiar to implement such a solution.

The shah's failure either to win over or cow the growing opposition was shown in massive peaceful demonstrations in several cities, with probably over a million people in Tehran, on December 11, 1978, to mark Ashura, the anniversary of the death of Imam Hosain, seen as a martyred victim of autocracy. In this demonstration a resolution was passed asking Khomeini to lead Iran and calling on Iranians to struggle until the shah was overthrown. The shah tried to appease the opposition by finding a moderate oppositional prime minister and got Shapour Bakhtiar, a signer of the 1977 National Front letter for civil liberties, to agree on December 30 to form a new constitutional government, provided the shah leave Iran indefinitely and a Regency Council be set up. Bakhtiar was denounced by his National Front colleagues, now allied with Khomeini, and was not redeemed by his release of political prisoners, his announced dismantlement of SAVAK, or promised changes in the economy and foreign relations.

Until late fall top American policy makers in Washington and Tehran, misled in part by their limited Iranian contacts and their reliance on SAVAK and Iranian officials for their knowledge of the opposition, were sure the shah's regime would last. By fall some in the State Department and in Iran were changing their views, and from early November Ambassador Sullivan cabled home his doubts that the shah, and later Bakhtiar, could win out. The embassy began secret contacts with the antileftist parts of the pro-Khomeini opposition, including National Front leaders, Bazargan, and some clericals, especially Ayatollah Mohammad Beheshti, a Khomeini follower recently returned from Europe. Many American policy makers thought, on the basis of Khomeini's recent statements and political inexperience, that in the event of a revolutionary victory Khomeini might step into the background and allow moderates to rule. The State Department seems to have approved a late, abortive plan for a National Front-Clerical ruling alliance with the shah effectively to bow out. (The shah's refusal to abdicate and the opposition's refusal to settle for less was one stumbling block.) This was the probable context of Ambassador Sullivan's plan to send an American envoy to meet with Khomeini, which was apparently blocked by National Security Adviser Brzezinski, who opposed the State Department's approach and actively promoted a hard line, which he thought could keep the shah in power.

Carter followed no clear policy but did send General R. Huyser to Iran in early January 1979 to report on the state of the armed forces and work to keep them unified and intact. If either Bakhtiar or a largely moderate government won out it was seen as important to keep the army intact as a conservative, anti-Communist, and potentially pro-American force. Huyser worked to unify the generals behind Bakhtiar, with armed force or a coup as final options, but in the end key generals saw the cause was lost and did not fight. The unexpectedly rapid march of events and the continuing indecisiveness of the shah forestalled any possibility of a coup and paved the way for Khomeini's accession in February 1979. Neither the embassy nor most of Washington policy makers considered a coup a viable possibility by 1979, given the overwhelming strength of the revolutionaries. By late 1978 many in the embassy and State Department were convinced the shah could not last and were in contact with secular and religious figures who might enter a governmental coalition with which the American government could deal. American military intervention was not a serious possibility given the united strength of Iran's revolutionary movement, not to mention American post-Vietnam wariness of dubious military adventures.

American contacts with the opposition and lack of intervention for the shah made many anti-Khomeini Iranians believe that the United States was responsible for Khomeini's victory. It appears rather that the State Department was trying to make the best of what it saw as a bad situation; near the end there was no feasible way to stop the Khomeini movement, and so Americans tried to contact it and encourage its moderates in the hope of lessening its anti-American tone. No aid was given to the opposition, and apart from one late statement by Carter indicating uncertainty that the shah's rule would last, verbal and moral support for the shah, including regular counsel from Ambassador Sullivan, continued until the end. Brzezinski's hawkish proshah policies could not succeed, given the shah's lack of internal support and his objections to using massive force at a time he feared he would not live long and thought his young son should not inherit after a bloodbath.[12]

It seems unlikely that a different American policy in 1978–79 could have significantly changed the course of events. Neither of the two sides that alternately influenced Carter had much chance of influencing the Revolution: there was no practical way to save the shah, nor is there reason to think that Sullivan's people could have achieved their ends had they increased American contact with Khomeini and his coalition. Probably only a very different set of policies over the previous twenty-seven years could have led to different results.

As to the shah's vacillating carrot-and-stick behavior during the crisis it may first be said that, as in the case of United States attitudes and policy, there is no proof that different behavior in 1978 would have maintained his throne. Iranians had in the past heard many words and promises regarding freedom and especially economic betterment, and were now so resentful about autocracy, corruption, jailings, torture, and terrorization (which went far beyond those plotting against the regime), that they were unlikely to be impressed by promised concessions. This was all the more so in that palpable concessions by the shah in 1978 did not include sharing political power with the populace or even choosing a prime minister with a large popular base and freedom of action. The opposition feared that concessions like the promised future free elections could always be withdrawn as long as the shah remained anything more than a Western type of constitutional ruler, as envisaged in the 1906–07 constitution. The shah's concessions were always a step or more behind popular demands, and at the end the constitutional monarchy favored by some of the opposition was no longer acceptable to its pro-Khomeini majority. The shah did show himself weaker and more indecisive than most people expected. This was not only due to cancer and drugs, but echoed his weakness until 1953, which later remained hidden only when he was sure he was in command. Megalomania and insecurity went together, as with many similar ruling figures. His insecurity and suspicion extended to the United States, and he was unsure of American support, particularly if he should opt for harsh policies.

The possibility of the shah's using more military force throughout also posed several problems. First, before fall it would have seemed extreme, whereas by fall soldiers were refusing to fire on crowds and some even fraternized with them, especially conscripts and others who revered Khomeini and identified with the protestors; the shah did not want to risk more of this. Second (and this affected more than the military sphere), it seems likely that the shah long believed much of his own propaganda and also his toadying aides who assured him he was vastly popular and that the demonstrators were a minority of agitators who had misled people; he therefore long retained hope of regaining popularity by concessions, and did not wish to alienate more people by massacres. Third, the shah wished history to regard him as a great ruler who had beneficially transformed Iran, and massive slaughters (although one such was allowed in September) could only tarnish this image and make his son's succession, which he expected to be near, more difficult. Fourth, the shah's massive armed forces and secret police were not well trained for the situation they faced; they were designed on the one hand to give Iran the posture of an international great power, able to police areas beyond its borders, and on the other, in the case of the secret police, to infiltrate and hunt down small numbers of oppositionists. Weapons and training for crowd control had not been given priority—another sign of the shah's misreading his people. In a sense the shah was caught in the same situation as his American official sponsors; while it might at one time have been possible to suppress demonstrations and strikes by military force (though probably not without American aid), this would result in a government far more unpopular and repressive than that which began in 1953, given the far greater scope, revolutionary devotion, and unity of different political parties and groups in 1978 than in 1953.

The shah's growing megalomaniac self-confidence in the 1970s did not equip him to deal in a new and flexible way with unanticipated mass opposition, while his cancer, the drugs he was taking, and probably his doubts about American and British intentions, added to his tendency to withdraw and collapse in face of opposition, seeking his salvation from frequent advisory sessions with the American and British ambassadors rather than taking a strong and firm-sounding stand of any sort. The recent deaths of confidants Asadollah Alam and Manuchehr Eqbal added to his confusion.[13] The shah's turn to the American and British ambassadors indicates how much the system he had built had deprived him of supporters whose words he trusted and suggests his dependence on outside powers.

The new premier, Bakhtiar, to effect the kind of transition the moderates preferred, negotiated the shah's "temporary" departure on January 16, with a regency council of which he was a member. He ordered the release of all political prisoners and the dismantlement of SAVAK, began a review of all important foreign contracts, refused oil sales to Israel and South Africa, and declared he would make major cuts in military and nuclear-plant expenditures. None of this won him opposition support, however, not even from the National Front, which had expelled him as a traitor.

Khomeini's followers were clamoring for his return from Paris; Bakhtiar stalled by closing the Tehran airport, but soon had to allow Khomeini's return to a massive welcome, on February 1, 1979. Four days later Khomeini appointed Mehdi Bazargan as the "real" prime minister, creating a situation known in some other revolutions as "dual power." For several days there was a standoff; according to some sources, Bazargan was secretly negotiating on behalf of Khomeini with the United States, SAVAK, and the army chiefs for an orderly transition of power. A showdown, however, began on the evening of February 9 when units of the elite Imperial Guard tried to suppress a Tehran rebellion of pro-revolutionary air-force cadets and technicians (*homafars*), who resisted strongly. When word of the struggle reached the Feda'iyan and Mojahedin, as well as some other armed groups, they mobilized, distributed guns among members and sympathizers, and moved to support the struggling cadets and technicians. Successfully fending off the Imperial Guards, the fighters spent February 10 and 11 opening up prisons, police stations, armories, and Tehran's major military bases. Similar events occurred in the provinces. Hundreds of lives were lost but in two days power was effectively transferred. Guerillas and homafars, with the aid of religiously led groups, had routed the elite Imperial Guard. The crucial role of the guerillas was noted both in the Western and Iranian press.[14]

Robert Graham mentions "numerous mullah-led local committees" in the movement "led by the main guerilla groups,"[15] and oral sources also note molla-led groups, but there seems no doubt (despite occasional denials) that the leftist guerilla groups were of major importance in the military victory, as were the homafars themselves. This brought the transfer of power on February 11, 1979, to the coalition of Khomeini and his followers, including clericals, lay religious figures led by Barzagan, and, for a time, a few lay National Front and other ministers, notably Dr. Karim Sanjabi.

Numerous eyewitnesses have commented on the almost universal enthusiasm, discipline, mutual cooperation, and organization which not only added to the esprit and extent of the last months of the revolution and distributed supplies and heating oil during the revolutionary strikes, but helped make it impossible to break off one group from the others. Spontaneous or directed councils and committees to organize revolutionary guards, urban quarters, factories, and other institutions began in this period, and many continued after February when, however, prerevolutionary unity increasingly broke down.

10

Politics and Economics under Khomeini: 1979–1989

The Iranian Revolution of 1978–79, like many revolutions, united several groups, classes, and parties with disparate ideas who were against the old regime. As in many revolutions, the coalition did not long outlast victory. Iran's revolution also had distinctive features, especially the unique leading role of clerics. Some revolutions have had religious ideologies, but clerical rule after a revolution was new. Most nonclerics in the opposition underestimated both the probability of clerical rule and the ability of the clergy to rule—this was true of Khomeini's Islamic but nonclerical Paris advisers, of various liberal and leftist groups, and also of the oppositionists who fled Iran, all of whom thought they could come out on top as clerical incompetence was manifested. Opposition groups that might have united against the drive toward a clerical monopoly with its strict version of Islam did not do so. This was partly because in the early stages of the revolution Khomeini indicated that he and clerics would not rule directly. Khomeini and his followers in 1978–79 kept out of circulation Khomeini's treatise *Islamic Government,* also known as *Velayat-e faqih* (guardianship of the jurisprudent), which endorsed with novel Shi'i arguments great power for a single *faqih,* and spread instead the more liberal views of his Paris entourage.[1] Whether sincerely or not, Khomeini made several publicly recorded statements that neither he nor the ulama would hold direct power in a new government, and he never before or shortly after coming to power referred to velayat-e faqih. According to Abolhasan Bani Sadr and others, even privately he indicated he had renounced the ideas in his *Islamic Government,* and in the initial period of his rule he gave the same impression in both word and deed.[2]

Khomeini's appointment of the nonclerical Mehdi Bazargan as prime minister and support of Bani Sadr in the first presidential elections seemed to support Khomeini's statements that he and the clergy would not rule directly. At the same time, however, Khomeini and his followers took steps to increase clerical power. As events evolved from 1979 through 1983 the clerical forces won out and enforced their program. Some oppositional Iranians then said Khomeini had "hijacked" the revolution, some tying this to the earlier conspiracy view that the United States supported him—showing an underestimation of the organizational ability and mass support of the Khomeinists.[3] The strength of forces that opposed and worked against a clerical monopoly of power from 1979 through 1982 was greater than it may appear in retrospect, so they were not entirely unreasonable in expecting a different outcome. The ultimate triumph of the Khomeinists was not only due to domestic factors but was aided by the impetus for national unity provided by the United States hostage crisis of 1979–81 and the Iran–Iraq war of 1980–88.

The decade of Khomeini's rule was marked by the ever-growing power of his followers and elimination, often by violence and despite resistance, of opposition groups, and by increasing enforcement of ideological and behavioral controls on the population. Widespread desires for greater freedom and social equity were not fulfilled, although there were some successful social programs. The decade also saw splits among the Khomeinists, based in part on the divide between his popular class followers and richer bazaaris, and events of the first decade produced widespread disillusionment both with Khomeinism and with various leftist alternatives. The experience of isolation in the Iran–Iraq war made many see the need for having good relations even with formerly excoriated countries, while the ideal of spreading Islamic revolution was mortally wounded by the decade's end.

In the four years between 1979 and 1983 Khomeini's forces took power from what had been a multiparty revolution and state. Although Khomeini appointed a largely secular provisional government under Bazargan, he simultaneously built up more powerful clerical institutions. He early made use of his power to appoint each city's Friday prayer leaders, who became the chief purveyors of his line to the population, and also used his powers in governmental and party organizations and in clerical groups and theological seminaries. He was helped by several of his ex-students, including Ayatollahs Hosain Ali Montazeri and Mohammad Beheshti. He also built up a kind of parallel government in the

Council of the Islamic Revolution, under the direction of his close clerical followers, whose membership was long kept secret. Several groups and parties resisted this trend, and their resistance, continued opposition to single-party rule, the multiplication of governing institutions, and disagreements among proclerical groups helped keep the system from becoming a dictatorship. The Khomeinists were not unanimous in their views and had autonomous leaders in several powerful institutions, some of them elected. Iran never became a dictatorship but always had a complex variety of power centers and experienced more compromises than the outside world realized.[4] Some might characterize it as an authoritarian state, although it was unusual in its inclusion of democratic elements, such as a popularly elected parliament and presidency, which often clashed with the clerical authoritarians. The contradiction between clerical-authoritarian and popular rule was, and remains, embedded in the constitution of the Islamic Republic. Also, even clerical power centers held autonomous powers and sometimes expressed separate policies. The right of qualified ayatollahs to issue independent rulings that were binding on their followers was never abrogated, despite the priority given to Khomeini's rulings.

Upon the victory of the revolution in early 1979 there were many groups with widely varying programs, some of which were allowed in the government, while the leftists, despite their importance in the revolution, were not. The parties included the liberal Islamic nationalist Freedom Movement (FM) and the Muslim People's Republican Party (MPRP). The FM was strong in 1979, having its leader Mehdi Bazargan as prime minister and over a third of the ministers in the Provisional Revolutionary Government (PRG). The MPRP was strongest in Azerbaijan, among the followers of Ayatollah Shariatmadari (who was not a member) and others who wanted greater decentralization and rights for ethnic nationalities. Both parties stood for democracy, Muslim-oriented nationalism, and the ulama as guides, not rulers. Both had support among the modern and traditional middle classes and some of the ulama. Both favored relations with the West and were often called moderates.[5] Bazargan and many moderates (as well as many clerics) opposed the radical socioeconomic reforms directed mainly at helping the poor and advocated not only by the non-Khomeinist left but also by many in the Khomeinist left.

Secular liberal nationalists in the National Front (NF) were based in the professional middle classes and advocated Western-style democracy.

The NF had a third of the ministers in the provisional government. After the revolution, younger, more left-leaning members dissatisfied with the NF, led by Hedayatollah Matin-Daftari, Mosaddeq's grandson, created the National Democratic Front (NDF) in March 1979, with a leftist program and a stress on human rights. The emigration of hundreds of thousands of largely modern middle-class Iranians reduced the NF and NDF constituencies.

The Muslim non-Khomeinist left included the armed and disciplined Mojahedin-e Khalq (MK). Decimated by executions under the shah, they grew rapidly during and after the revolution, and in 1979 organized large rallies in the major cities. They, like the Marxist Feda'iyan-e Khalq, were partly responsible for the revolution's victory. The MK called for rule by peasants and workers, the nationalization of industries, an end to ties with the West, and close relations with the third world and Eastern Europe. They had a radical interpretation of Islam.[6] The secular left ranged from Stalinists to Maoists and Trotskyists. The largest were the Soviet-oriented Tudeh and the Feda'iyan-e Khalq, while the Maoist Peykar came from the secular wing of the MK. Secular left programs were similar to that of the MK minus Islam. Their parties were largely composed of high school and university students, with some intellectuals and workers. Khomeini refused to meet with leftist parties and excluded them from government.

There was no unity among leftist groups. The Feda'iyan at first tried to work both with the Khomeini forces and with the Tudeh, which led to splits, the most important being into Majority (pro-Tudeh) and Minority groups in 1980. Leftists followed contradictory strategies, with the Feda'iyan Majority and the Tudeh backing Khomeini, while others supported the moderates, and many criticized both. The left had contributed importantly to the revolution but often used terms most Iranians did not understand, lacked a good analysis of Iran, and were sometimes blinded by anti-imperialist rhetoric. The influence of Soviet policy on the Tudeh and Feda'iyan Majority was a deterrent to their developing appropriate programs for Iran. Also, the left had no significant source of economic support, unlike the clerics, who were heavily supported by bazaaris and old and new foundations.[7]

The Khomeinists centered in the Islamic Republic Party (IRP), created with Khomeini's approval in February 1979. Ayatollah Mohammad Beheshti was its main figure; he had a Ph.D. in religious studies from Tehran University, spoke English and German, and had been sent by the shah's government to head the Islamic Center in Hamburg in the seventies. The IRP was created to increase clerical and Khomeinist power to support Islamic government and comprised various Islamic groups. The IRP included opposing interests of merchants and the lower classes, but Khomeini's popularity and the desire for strength against the opposition kept it viable as long as opposition groups were allowed to exist and could be seen as a threat to Khomeinist power. It had ties to armed paralegal forces like the Revolutionary Guard (Pasdaran), created by Khomeini in May 1979, and the violent groups called *hezbollah*. These groups disrupted demonstrations and attacked dissidents. Khomeini appointed IRP-endorsed ulama as Friday prayer leaders in nearly all cities and as his representatives in government bodies. The IRP got support from the traditional middle class and from the often-migrant poor. A conservative religious group in the first period who did not support Khomeini's idea of rule by the jurist, velayat-e faqih, was the *hojjatiyeh* society, which began before 1978 as an anti-Baha'i group. Khomeinists severely criticized it in 1983, after which the term virtually disappeared.[8] Another term current in the early period was *maktabi,* adopted by Khomeinists to contrast with the hojjatiyeh and other non-Khomeinists.

Khomeini was popular because of his uncompromising attitude to the shah, his anti-imperialist and populist rhetoric, his simple lifestyle and language, and his religious status. Although he made Bazargan prime minister, he chose many key administrative personnel from clerics and others in his camp. He then kept mostly divorced from direct administration, except to intervene pro or con when other bodies had acted, and hence shielded himself from much criticism for bad policies.

Both nationalists and ulama respected Bazargan. When he took over, government authority was almost nonexistent, and some ethnic groups (Kurds, Turkomans) and leftists were in revolt. Thousands of trained persons had fled, oil production was low, strikes continued, major industries were shut down, and unemployment and inflation were high. The government had to restore order and supervise a referendum, an election, and a constituent assembly. Despite accomplishing these tasks, the provisional government soon had far less power than the Khomeinists and their organizations.

Regional autonomist movements in non-Persian-speaking areas were important in these early years, with some risings among the Turkomans and armed struggles by the Kurds, backed by the National Democratic Party and some of the leftist parties, from 1979 through 1981. Some

Azerbaijanis also put forth autonomist demands, and opponents of the new constitution, led by MPRP activists, took control of Tabriz in a December 1979 rising with nationwide ambitions that was suppressed by the Khomeinists. All ethnic or partially ethnic risings were defeated. They may have strengthened the willingness of those whose first language was Persian to acquiesce in measures to strengthen the central government, but their defeat did not end disillusionment with the center among the ethnic minorities, especially as publication and broadcasting in local languages, as promised in the constitution, while often permitted, became increasingly controlled by the government.

In the early period there was agreement between Khomeinists and much of the left around issues like the nationalization of major enterprises and anti-imperialism, directed mainly at the United States. Both the leftist parties and the Khomeinists often opposed middle-class liberals or moderates, who were considered too Western or even tools of the West. Many saw the PRG gradualist approach as too slow, of too little help to the poor, and too small a break with the past, so its popularity fell while that of the Khomeinists and the leftist parties grew.

Khomeinists dominated what could be called the parallel Islamic government, especially the Council of the Islamic Revolution (CIR), which passed laws and competed with the PRG on many matters, though they worked together to defeat rebellious ethnic minorities and to impose financial order by nationalizing major industries and banks. Ayatollah Motahhari was assassinated in May 1979, and the death of Ayatollah Taleqani in September was a blow to moderation and progressive thought. Karim Sanjabi, the NF foreign minister, felt compelled to resign in April and was replaced by Ibrahim Yazdi of the FM. The IRP aimed at taking over the government but found the liberals temporarily useful.

Khomeinists came to dominate most new institutions. The *komitehs* (from the French *comité*) were at first autonomous organizations dating back to late 1978, when they coordinated strikes and demonstrations and sprang up everywhere. The PRG and many moderates opposed them. Many of them were true grassroots and workers' organizations, and some in the left worked to make them evolve into workers' councils. The Khomeinists, however, brought them under control via regulations and purges.[9]

Khomeinists also monopolized the judiciary, which brought in a codified sharia (Islamic law). There were secret trials of enemies of the revolution without defense lawyers, and summary executions. Sadeq

Khalkhali was the notorious "hanging judge," and hundreds of men associated with the old regime, including ex–prime minister Hoveyda, were executed.[10] Moderates, including Bazargan and some leading clerics like Shariatmadari, protested the revolutionary courts and executions, to little avail, though Khomeini ordered summary executions temporarily halted in March. A committee led by Ayatollah Hosain Ali Montazeri established rules of conduct for revolutionary courts, after which they resumed somewhat reduced activities.

Khomeinists led the Pasdaran. Khomeini's representatives were also spread throughout the armed forces. Some army, police, and gendarmerie officers were executed or imprisoned, thousands fled, and purges of the armed forces only stopped with Iraq's September 1980 invasion. The Pasdaran remained loyal to Khomeini; they mainly came from the popular classes and were an effective counterweight to the less ideological armed forces.

The new Foundation for the Dispossessed (*Bonyad-e Mosta'zefin*) received the fortunes of the Pahlavi Foundation and other confiscated properties, including hundreds of companies, factories, housing units, agricultural lands, and substantial holdings in the West. The Khomeinists used this massive economic unit to recruit popular class workers and loyal managers. The *Jehad-e Sazandegi* (Reconstruction Jihad) mobilized youth by sending them to rural areas to aid the poor with cheap or free housing and sanctioned some seizures of urban homes and rural lands by the poor. The complex of institutions created or expanded in 1979 was used as a weapon to consolidate IRP power, destroy the opposition, promote Shi'i populism, and help purge the bureaucracy. All these Khomeinist and clerically led or guided institutions kept the PRG from having significant power. The left helped to weaken the PRG, which they considered an organ of pro-Western liberals, and this facilitated the rise of the Khomeinists. The Feda'iyan and the Tudeh often attacked the PRG and its members as representatives of capitalists, landlords, and the United States, noting accurately that the PRG did not try to implement major social reforms and was willing to deal with the United States. The NDF was also hostile to the PRG. Although in retrospect this hostility may seem an error, it partly reflected a realistic assessment of possible PRG acquiescence in future United States measures to control Iran and its oil, and also PRG reluctance to take decisive steps to help the poor that many on the left advocated.

Khomeini insisted on an early referendum allowing people to vote only for or against setting up an Islamic Republic. The NDF, the Feda'iyan, and the Democratic Party of Kurdistan were the only groups to boycott the referendum, while other secular groups were misled by IRP statements that gave a democratic interpretation of the future Islamic Republic. A 98 percent positive vote was announced. The next job was to draft a constitution. The original draft by an appointed committee was far more democratic than the final constitution and was very like the 1906–07 constitution without the constitutional monarch. It did not mention velayat-e faqih and gave no powers to the clergy beyond a constitutional commission similar to that included in the 1906–07 constitution (though never created). Khomeini was at first inclined to submit this constitution to a referendum, but both secular and religious groups pushed for further discussion of the draft, with the secularists not foreseeing that clerics would control revisions and create a less democratic constitution. The final draft was assigned to a seventy-three-member elected assembly of experts. During the election campaign velayat-e faqih first became a national issue, and electoral procedures were rigged to favor the clerical party, who began to reveal their true colors. The NF, NDF, and several ethnic and leftist groups boycotted the elections, whose results greatly boosted the Khomeinists. Fifty-five seats were won by clerics, many of them IRP members, and only a few secularists won. One of them, Abdol Rahman Qasemlu, the leader of the Democratic Party of Iranian Kurdistan, was not allowed to take his seat.[11]

Before the assembly met, the PRG passed new press laws forbidding collaborators of the old regime to publish newspapers and setting penalties for insulting the ulama or principles of the revolution. The paper *Ayandegan* was the first victim: accused of receiving contributions from SAVAK and Israel, its offices were ransacked by Hezbollah, who also attacked the headquarters of the NDF and violently forced the Feda'iyan, Mojahedin, and Tudeh out of their Tehran offices. Over forty newspapers were shut; and by September the largest remaining papers, *Kayhan* and *Ettela'at,* were turned over to the Mostaz'efin Foundation.

The elected Assembly of Experts wrote a far more clerically oriented and potentially authoritarian constitution than the draft. It included a provision on velayat-e faqih that gave extraordinary powers to Khomeini. Article 4 says the faqih has divine authority to rule and is accountable only to God. Later articles list his powers, which include control of the army and Pasdaran, the right to disqualify presidential candidates and to dismiss the president if the high court or majles find him incompetent. The power of the majles is restricted by the Guardian Council, which can reject legislation it finds incompatible with Islam or the constitution. The Guardian Council was a twelve-member body with six ulama appointed by the faqih and six jurists selected by the majles from a list prepared by the supreme judicial council, most of whose members were appointed by the faqih. Based on its view of the sharia, the supreme judicial council prepared bills on all judicial matters and appointed, dismissed, promoted, and demoted all judges. Khomeini was made faqih for life. On his death, an elected clerical Assembly of Experts would either nominate a faqih or set up a three- to five-member Leadership Council. The constitution includes some provisions protecting citizens' rights, requires free education for all up to middle school, and contains a number of provisions for the eradication of poverty and prevention of foreign economic or political domination. These rights were, however, expressed in general terms, whereas the numerous provisions that added to the power of the clergy and created a dominant faqih, or leader, were more specific. Women were not given equal status or rights, and the constitution stressed their role in the home. The constitution, before its 1989 amendment, also included a prime minister, so that there were two ruling officials below the faqih, who held the most power to the extent he wished to use it.[12] Although many among the left, the liberals, and also senior clerics opposed giving such powers to the faqih, they did not unite to form an effective opposition, which in any case would probably have had only a marginal effect.

The Bazargan government worked to improve political and economic relations with the United States, which in many ways reciprocated. But when influential Americans convinced President Carter to allow the ex-shah to come to the United States from Mexico for cancer treatment despite the provisional government's warnings, the situation changed dramatically. The Iranian right and left launched campaigns against the United States, and when Bazargan and Yazdi met with U.S. National Security Adviser Zbigniew Brzezinski in Algeria in October they were widely excoriated. On November 4, 1979, the "Students Following the Line of the Imam" (SFLI) attacked and seized the U.S. embassy in Tehran. They took embassy personnel hostage and confiscated documents. The takeover, like an earlier one, would have been brief had it not got the support of Khomeini, who saw in it a chance to get rid of the liberal government, radicalize the revolution, and increase his power.

After the SFLI refused Bazargan's order to evacuate the embassy, his government resigned.

The Khomeinists prolonged the crisis in order to weaken moderates and non-Khomeinist senior ulama, pass the constitution, and consolidate power. Debate on the constitution was undermined by claims that such debate was now treacherous. A selective release of U.S. embassy documents defamed the moderates, the only ones who were shown as meeting with Americans, though senior Khomeinists had also done so. The left, including the Mojahedin, joined this attack. The MPRP led the only effective anticonstitution forces, and its patron, Ayatollah Shariatmadari, issued a fatwa against the constitution, which led to violent clashes in several cities. When the constitutional referendum was held on December 2–3, 1979, it was boycotted by the NF, MPRP, and Kurdish and Azerbaijani groups, and, with a lowered total vote, won with a claimed *no* vote of only thirty-one thousand.

Groups in Azerbaijan, partly inspired by the opposition of Shariatmadari to government policies, continued to demonstrate, and violent clashes ensued, culminating in an uprising in Tabriz that captured the radio-television stations. Khomeinists regained power by promising Azerbaijan some autonomy, but Shariatmadari said this promise was broken, and there were more bloody risings in Tabriz, which Shariatmadari refused to support. The Pasdaran occupied MPRP headquarters, some participants in the risings were executed, the MPRP was dissolved, and Shariatmadari was silenced and put under virtual house arrest.[13]

In 1979, SAVAK was essentially reconstituted as SAVAMA, apparently with the advice of the ex-shah's friend since boyhood, the former director of the Imperial Inspectorate, Hosain Fardust. By 1980 several prominent liberals and leftists had been forced to go into hiding and later escaped the country. They included Matin-Daftari, whose NDF party was suppressed, partly owing to its support of demands being put forth in the name of Kurds, Azerbaijanis, Arabs, and Baluchis; the lay liberal lawyer Hasan Nazih, who was first made head of the National Iranian Oil Company and then fired; Rahmatollah Moqaddam Maraghe'i, a prominent liberal activist; and the popular ex–presidential candidate Admiral Madani.

Khomeini courted the support of those wary of clerical power by banning clerics from running for president in 1980. The IRP ended up supporting an obscure candidate who got only 700,000 votes, fewer than the NF's Admiral Madani, who got 2 million. Bani Sadr, running as an independent, won with 10.7 million votes out of 14 million. Bani Sadr was popular among the left for his ideas and championing of programs like the nationalization of industries. He hoped to create a kind of social democratic Islamic Iran. He seemed powerful, being not only president but also head of the armed forces and the Supreme Defense Council, but his power was undermined by the growing strength of the IRP and its general secretary, Beheshti. The majority of the new majles were IRP members, and almost half were clerics. The majority elected Ali Akbar Hashemi Rafsanjani of the IRP central committee as the majles speaker. The IRP majority rejected the credentials of some NF and pro–Bani Sadr deputies, including Admiral Madani, who fled Iran. The majles also rejected several of Bani Sadr's candidates for prime minister, and he finally chose Mohammad Ali Raja'i from a list of acceptable candidates presented by a majles committee. The IRP controlled the majles, the cabinet and, with Beheshti as president of the Supreme Court, the judiciary. Bani Sadr was the last obstacle to their total power, and the Iraqi invasion facilitated his elimination. In the disputes between Bani Sadr and the IRP, led by Beheshti, Khomeini came down sometimes on one side and sometimes on the other and often urged the two sides to compromise, but in the spring of 1981 he broke with Bani Sadr.

In 1979 and early 1980 universities were a forum for ideological debate. Khomeini supported a campaign to cleanse the universities of "subversives." Some nonuniversity leftists had, after being forced from their headquarters in the summer of 1979, taken refuge on university campuses. Inspired by Khomeini, the Council of Islamic Revolution in April 1980 gave an ultimatum to the left to leave the universities; some leftists and others were physically forced out, with a large number killed or wounded. Bani Sadr announced the start of a Cultural Revolution, which antagonized the left and the moderates; he thought he could thus manage this revolution, but in fact the Khomeinists did so. In May 1980 Khomeini established a seven-member, mostly IRP, Council of the Cultural Revolution. The komitehs dismissed many from the universities and shut them down indefinitely. This became for most of them a three-year shutdown, and many former students and professors could never return. The Cultural Revolution was a major blow to Iran's cultural and intellectual life and achievement, interrupting the education and professional livelihood of many and encouraging further emigration by students, teachers, and other professionals.

The relations of Khomeini with Iraq had deteriorated when Saddam Hussein forced him to leave Iraq in November 1978. After Bazargan's fall, Iraq claimed Iran was intervening in their affairs, and on September 22, 1980, Iraq invaded Iran. Iraq never really accepted the 1975 Iran–Iraq treaty regarding the Shatt al-Arab border, and Saddam Hussein now thought Iran was weak and vulnerable and that the (minority) Arab population of oil-rich Khuzistan would help Iraq. This was a major miscalculation, and the Iranian armed forces and volunteers, including the young new irregular Basij, fought effectively, though with great loss of life in "human wave" tactics. Iraq's invasion did the opposite of what Iraq expected, uniting Iranians, combining Shi'i and nationalist fervor, reviving the armed forces, and strengthening the Pasdaran and Khomeinists.

Iraq at first succeeded in invading southwestern Iran. Bani Sadr and the IRP favored different strategies, the IRP favoring human wave assaults by irregular forces. The IRP feared Bani Sadr's ties to the regular armed forces meant he might use them for a coup. The war strengthened the Khomeinists, who led the Basiji organization of mostly youthful war volunteers and the Pasdaran, who strengthened their position. On the pretext of wartime emergency the Khomeinists increased repression, closing the Mojahedin newspaper, for example. Owing to the war and U.S. economic sanctions goods were rationed, with the clergy put in charge of the distribution network from mosques.

A few weeks after the hostage taking Bani Sadr developed a U.S.-supported plan for a U.N. commission to investigate Iran's grievances against the shah in return for the release of the hostages. Khomeini's declaration in February 1980 that only the new majles could settle the crisis ended this plan. Nonetheless, Bani Sadr with foreign help developed another plan—to extradite the shah to Iran from Panama, where he then was—but the shah got word of it and fled to Egypt. Bani Sadr then abandoned the hostage crisis, where he could do nothing, given probable reversals of his policies by Khomeini or the majles, and focused on the war. In April 1980 the United States made an attempt to send helicopters to Iran as part of a hostage rescue plan, but the malfunction of three of the eight helicopters forced the commander to abort the plan. One helicopter collided with a transport plane, killing eight Americans. The attempt increased Khomeinist suspicions of U.S. plans for a coup. Two coup plots were exposed in June and July with arrests and executions of many officers. The NF was also accused of coup plots, and the Hezbollah took the NF headquarters and shut its newspapers. Purges of the bureaucracy and army ensued.

By the fall of 1980 Khomeinists controlled all institutions except the presidency and some important cabinet positions. But holding the hostages was costing Iran diplomatic isolation and U.S. sanctions. Khomeini now announced conditions for resolving the crisis: A pledge by the United States not to intervene in Iran's affairs; the return of Iranian assets frozen in the United States; the cancellation of U.S. claims; and the return of the shah's wealth. Soon secret negotiations between Iran and the United States began. Negotiations went quickly, but the Iranians delayed releasing the hostages, after the majles approved the accord, until just after Carter left office on January 20, 1981.[14] In the accord, reached in Algeria, the United States pledged not to intervene in Iran's affairs, promised cooperation in lawsuits in the United States to extradite Pahlavi family wealth, and released Iran's frozen assets, though the amount transferred was smaller than Iran claimed and some of that was used to pay Iran's debts to U.S. banks. A special court was set up in The Hague, which peacefully adjudicated U.S. claims against Iran. Though Iran presented the agreement as a victory, it was in fact almost wholly favorable to the United States and did not meet any of Iran's original demands. Also, the hostage affair lost Iran international support that it might have had against Iraqi aggression.

Bani Sadr attacked the IRP's handling of the hostage affair and its outcome and said he could have done better. The IRP and Speaker Rafsanjani presented the agreement as a great victory, however. When hezbollahis attacked Bani Sadr's speech at a rally in March 1981, he ordered the police to arrest them. The IRP got the prosecutor-general to investigate the arrest as a violation of law and some deputies demanded Bani Sadr's impeachment. Khomeini arranged a conciliation committee to look into the feud and ordered Bani Sadr and the IRP to stop fighting until the committee reached a conclusion. But Bani Sadr continued to denounce the Raja'i government for human rights violations, torture, and censorship and called for a referendum to settle his dispute with the IRP. In response, the government closed Bani Sadr's newspaper, and komitehs arrested some of his associates. His budget was cut, and he was made to sign bills in five days or the prime minister would do so. The majles declared Bani Sadr incompetent, and Khomeini dismissed him as the armed forces commander. After Bani Sadr wrote to Khomeini criticizing his leadership, Khomeini, invoking his constitutional right, dismissed

Bani Sadr, who, from hiding, called for an uprising. He had never tried to create a party or coalition, and he now chose to ally with the Mojahedin.

The Mojahedin from 1979 on had bad relations with the Khomeinists. The Hezbollah attacked their headquarters, which they eventually evacuated. They supported the Kurdish rebellion, opposed velayat-e faqih and boycotted the constitutional referendum. Khomeini called them Monafeqin, or hypocrites. When they rallied against Bani Sadr's impeachment in June 1981, the Hezbollah killed some of them, and they began an armed struggle against the regime. At a conference of the IRP leadership in June, a bomb killed more than seventy men, including Beheshti, four ministers, and twenty-five deputies. Soon after, the chief of Tehran's main prison was assassinated. The Mojahedin were blamed, and there was fierce repression, including ultimately thousands of executions.[15]

The IRP replaced those killed and went on with the presidential election in July 1981, with Raja'i becoming president and Mohammad Javad Bahonar prime minister. Khomeini ordered attacks on the Mojahedin. As their hoped-for mass rising did not occur, Masud Rajavi, the head of the Mojahedin, and Bani Sadr escaped to France in late July 1981 and formed the National Council of Resistance, soon joined by the NDF and the Kurdish Democratic Party. Assassinations continued in Iran, with a bomb killing, among others, President Raja'i, Prime Minister Bahonar, and the head of the national police. In a presidential election in October 1981, Hojjatoleslam Ali Khamene'i became president. The majles, which leaned toward the populist faction of the IRP that came to be called the Islamic Left, rejected Khamene'i's first choice for prime minister, the conservative Ali Akbar Velayati, and accepted the Islamic leftist Mir Hosain Musavi.

Government attacks on the Mojahedin culminated in the discovery of their main hideout in Tehran, and their top leaders were killed. Many of them now joined the Kurdish rebels, while others fled to Europe. The Mojahedin had miscalculated the government's vulnerability and their own appeal; their rising ended by strengthening the Khomeinists. From then on the Mojahedin operated mostly in the West and Iraq. Their violent pro-Iraq activities in the Iran–Iraq war caused the NDF and Bani Sadr to withdraw from the National Council of Resistance. In 1986 the French government forced them to leave Paris, and their center henceforth became Baghdad, Iraq, with which they were, until the U.S. 2003 victory in Iraq, allied.[16]

Another leftist group, the Communist League, took over the small northern city of Amol in January 1982. The government quickly retook it and captured and executed most of the league's leaders. Soon after, the government discovered the underground centers of the Feda'iyan minority, who supported Kurdish rebels, and several were executed. Some Peykar leaders were also arrested.

Several Kurdish groups, the most important of which was the left-leaning Kurdish Democratic Party (KDP), had been involved in armed struggles against the central government since 1979. Over time several non-Kurdish leftist groups joined them, and the KDP joined the Paris-based National Council of Resistance. Early efforts to reach agreements between the Kurds and the center were abortive, and in the summer of 1982 the Iranian government launched a major assault which recaptured virtually all Kurdish rebel-held territory by the end of 1983, got final victory in July 1984, and forced the KDP into Iraq.[17]

The remaining left—the Tudeh and the Feda'iyan majority—backed the government. The Tudeh, the oldest leftist party with the best-known leaders, interpreted the revolution as an anti-imperialist petty bourgeois one and a precursor to socialist revolution. Unlike the prerevolution Feda'iyan and Mojahedin, they did not, either before or after the revolution, support individual killings or guerrilla tactics. In both periods they put forth moderate "united front" programs; before the revolution they strove unsuccessfully to attain legality, and after the revolution they strove, ultimately unsuccessfully, to maintain it. The Khomeinists used Tudeh support to help put down their other opponents and to facilitate relations with Moscow. Until 1983 the Tudeh was allowed to publish and spread its influence. In early 1983 the government turned on the Tudeh, arresting over seventy members, including several from the Central Committee and the armed forces. The party was accused of spying for the Soviet Union and planning to overthrow the government. Their army officers were executed, while ideologues like Ehsan Tabari and Nureddin Kianuri were imprisoned. They then appeared on television asking for forgiveness and mercy, condemning their past, implying their party was a spy network for the Soviets, and saying that Shi'ism was superior to Marxism.[18] Some observers said the confessions, and also confessions during these years by those with non-Tudeh affiliations, were based on torture and drugs. Some of the Feda'iyan Majority were also arrested, and both parties were declared illegal in May 1983. This left the IRP and the Freedom Party the only parties allowed to function.

In April 1982 Ghotbzadeh was arrested; he confessed that he had planned to oust the government and said Shariatmadari had knowledge of the coup plot. Ghotbzadeh was executed, and Shariatmadari was condemned and put under house arrest until his death in 1986. One by one the Khomeinists had efficiently got rid of their rivals; the rivals never united, and in several cases they helped the government against one another.

With the Khomeinists secure, the universities, purged and given partially new curricula, were gradually reopened. In December 1982 an all-clerical Assembly of Experts was elected to choose Khomeini's successor as faqih. It began meeting in 1983, but not until November 1985 did it declare for Grand Ayatollah Hosain Ali Montazeri.[19] He was the leader of the Friday prayer imams, had considerable support from the bazaar and professionals, and was liked by Khomeini. Most of the senior grand ayatollahs, however, opposed velayat-e faqih and many opposed Montazeri.

The second majles, elected in May 1984, was dominated by the IRP, and President Khamene'i was reelected in March 1985. Though the new Khomeinist elite was partly united in outlook, they became increasingly factional. The factions changed over the years, and some people sided with one on some issues and with another on others, but they can be generally subsumed under three trends. Common names for them are the Islamic Left, comprising Khomeinists who stressed measures for the common people such as land reform and the nationalization of enterprises and were against better relations with the West; the Conservatives, or Islamic Right, who defended private property and religious orthodoxy and control; and later the Pragmatists, or Modern Right, who emerged from the Conservatives and stressed getting Iran's ailing economy moving after the shocks caused by revolution, war, and the flight of trained personnel and capital. Khomeini mostly stayed above the factions and tried to mediate among them.[20]

The Khomeinist elite had, however, proved to be more unified and competent than its opponents supposed and managed to build a functioning state with powerful security forces. The main support for the regime came from the popular classes, the traditional bazaar bourgeoisie, and most of the clergy. Increasingly in the postrevolution period, political and economic power was concentrated in the hands of the Khomeinist clergy and the bazaar bourgeoisie. Soon after the revolution there were land seizures by peasants in some regions, and factory strikes and workers' committees set up in urban areas, but the authorities, whether by compromise, persuasion, or force, gradually brought such movements under control. The loyalty of many of the poor was retained in part by subsidies for housing and items of mass consumption and some measures favoring villages, health, and education (discussed in chapter 12). Equally important may have been the cultural identification of many of the urban poor with the clergy and their hostility to the westernized mores of the rich. The overall decline in the economy hurt most of the poor and many in the middle classes, however, and favoring the traditional commercial bourgeoisie hurt nearly all other classes and the economy as a whole. The economy was also hit by huge capital flight, which began before the revolution and continued long after despite governmental efforts to stop or slow it.

The state and the foundations allied to it soon controlled about two-thirds of Iran's enterprises and labor force. The revolutionary era began with a vast expansion of the public sector through the nationalization of industries, banks, and other businesses, and the great expansion of clerically controlled foundations. Rationing, subsidies, price controls, redistribution of confiscated properties, and direct financial rewards based on the government's oil income helped sustain the loyalty of the lower classes. There were also many early abortive efforts by workers to take over factories and by villagers to take land. These and other oppositional attempts were suppressed, as was the independent press, and many oppositionists were silenced, jailed, or forced into exile.

The Islamic Left supported a kind of Islamic socialism, with state control over the economy. But private property was entrenched in Islamic law, many clerics owned land, and the Islamic conservatives, allied with bazaar merchants, favored a mostly private economy and disliked government controls to help the poor. The Islamic Left had majles majorities and the support of Prime Minister Musavi in the 1980s, but the conservatives in the Guardian Council often vetoed their measures. In 1981–82 the majles passed a series of land reform laws, which were first vetoed and then watered down to pass, and there were failed majles attempts to nationalize foreign trade.

After 1984, as economic problems increased with the war, including rampant inflation, oil price declines, and money shortages, pragmatists who wanted to rescue the economy with free market measures and lessened government controls gained strength. The popular militias that tended to favor the Islamic Left on economic issues were with the conservatives on enforcing what they considered Islamic values. Even after the Cultural Revolution, when universities were gradually reopened after 1982 and other controls were loosened, vigilante groups continued to operate.

The most contentious and central social questions concerned women. Women who had benefited from Pahlavi reforms were alarmed in March 1980 by Khomeini's ending the Family Protection Law (FPL) and requiring Islamic dress. Khomeini made a tactical retreat regarding dress after massive women's protests. In July, however, government employees were ordered to wear "Islamic dress," and a year later the majles required all women to do so. The return to a codified sharia brought a revival of polygamy, temporary marriage, child marriage (girls could marry at age nine, though almost none did), and an end to the FPL's equalization of women's rights in divorce and child custody. Though social trends like urbanization and female education meant that the average age of women at marriage actually rose quite steadily, to over twenty-two today,[21] women still lost substantial rights and status and, until the war required their work, were largely discouraged from working.

A main concern of the state from the first has been the regulation of behavior. Liquor and most kinds of music were outlawed, and very few Western films were allowed in. Gender segregation and dress codes were perhaps the most important part of behavioral regulation; coeducation was abolished except in universities, where men and women sat on different sides of the class. For several years women were encouraged to stay home and devote themselves to motherhood. Young zealots patrolled the streets enforcing dress codes and Islamic morality.

In August 1982 the Supreme Judicial Council declared all un-Islamic modern codes null. In August 1983 an interest-free banking bill was approved, though, as elsewhere in the Muslim world, the system then established did not bring much change. Judges were ordered to use Shi'i codified laws or fatwas from reputable ayatollahs. The majles passed the *qesas* (retribution) bill and reintroduced flogging, amputation, and stoning to death as well as capital punishment for sodomy. (In practice, while flogging has been common, the other punishments have not.) Teachers were required to purvey the state ideology. New Islamic student associations were formed with the aim of supporting the government, and textbooks were revised in accord with the new ideology. Ideological commitment to the revolution became a requirement for university admission.

The Islamic Left increased in power within the IRP and had a clear majority in the 1984–88 majles. In the foreign policy realm, after the demise of the Bazargan government, Iran's leaders tried to fulfill the Khomeinist ideology by exporting Islamic revolution to other Muslim countries, but had success in promoting Islamic revolutionary parties almost exclusively among Shi'is from Lebanon to the Persian Gulf states and Pakistan. Iran's leaders also had only very limited relations with the West and the Soviet Union. This policy, however, hindered the pursuit of the war against Iraq. In the war, Iran succeeded in retaking the occupied southwestern territory and in the summer of 1982 decided to carry the war into Iraq, expecting to get far more support from the Shi'is of the invaded land than they in fact did. Relations improved with the Soviets, who did nothing to defend the Tudeh and were willing to cooperate with Iran. The Iranians sent economic delegations to the Soviet Union and other East European countries.[22]

Regarding the West, Foreign Minister Ali Akbar Velayati tried first to move closer to Europe. But the main foreign policy event of the mideighties was the "Irangate affair," marking Iran's hope to get outside assistance for the war and the economy. Iranian arms had come heavily from the United States before the revolution, which increased the need for American supplies. Parts of the ruling elite also favored better relations with the United States. The Irangate affair on the U.S. side sprang from the desire of President Ronald Reagan to free American hostages taken in Lebanon. The United States, which was giving Iraq substantial help in the war, also worried that a weakened Iran might become subordinate to the Soviets. Israel was already helping Iran. In January 1986, Reagan authorized the CIA to purchase four thousand Tow missiles from the Defense Department and sell them to Iran via Israel. Robert McFarlane, ex–national security adviser, was sent to Iran to try to further rapprochement with so-called Iranian moderates (including Speaker Rafsanjani and his supporters), but the mission failed. The secret of United States–Iran ties was kept until early November, when a small Beirut newspaper, *ash-Shiraa*, revealed the U.S. weapon sales, and the affair was exposed to considerable public indignation in both Iran and the United States. (In the United States it was also called the Iran-Contra affair, as profits from the arms sales were used to finance the Nicaraguan Contra rebels after Congress had cut off legal finances.)[23]

The continued war with Iraq was Iran's main foreign policy issue, and it soon impacted domestic policies. Iraq responded to Iran's move into Iraqi territory with new attacks on Iranian shipping and oil and economic installations and sent missiles that hit Iranian cities. Along with a fall in oil prices and economic woes, the war's effects were becoming disastrous. Revelation of the Irangate affair also hurt Iran, as the United States now decided to take a stronger stance against Iran. Iran's installation of missiles that could attack nearby U.S. warships and its mining of the gulf to damage ships heading for Iraq provided a pretext for U.S. action. The United States agreed in March 1987 to protect Kuwaiti tankers against Iran by reflagging and escorting them. Iran's relations with Saudi Arabia deteriorated after Iran stirred up demonstrations that became violent in the July 1987 pilgrimage. Kuwait, Saudi Arabia, and the United States all helped Iraq against Iran. The United States did not object when Iraq used poison gas against Iranian troops, with devastating immediate and long-term effects and implications of further possible use. And it was subsequently revealed that U.S. companies supplied Iraq not only with arms but also with elements known to be mainly useful for manufacturing chemical and biological warfare. The United States, knowing it was untrue, also said Iran was partly responsible for chemical warfare attacks on Kurds and used this story to deflect international condemnation of Iraq.[24]

In July 1987 the U.N. Security Council passed Resolution 598 calling for a cease-fire; Iraq accepted, but Iran did not respond. From September 1987 through April 1988 the United States destroyed a number of Iranian ships and oil platforms, partly in response to Iranian attacks on United States–flagged ships. On July 3 an American cruiser, the *Vincennes*, mistakenly, but recklessly in view of the information available to the captain, shot down a civilian Iranian airliner, killing 290. In Iran pressure was growing to end the war. Khomeini transferred command of the armed forces from Khamene'i to Rafsanjani, who was becoming known as the leading pragmatist. The economy was collapsing, enthusiasm for the war was gone, and the United States was increasing its support for Iraq. Backed by Khamene'i and majles leaders, Rafsanjani said there was no choice but to accept Resolution 598. Khomeini had to agree, saying on July 20, 1988, that the decision was for him "more deadly than poison" but was needed to save the revolution.[25]

In the late 1980s there were several important internal high-level changes. In the late 1980s, factionalism in the IRP had intensified, the major issues being the war, opening up to foreign countries, and economic policies. Khomeini kept the various factions in a certain balance, possibly in order not to risk losing the support of any of them. Internal disputes in the IRP, especially between Islamic Left and the conservatives, became so acute that they were one reason Khomeini in 1987 chose to dissolve the party, which by then had hardly any role. IRP leaders had requested the dissolution, partly because the party did almost nothing and had little incentive to when it had no rivals. The dissolution led to a 1988 split within the main clerical organization into two groups with similar names: the original Combatant Clergy Society came to be controlled by the conservatives, and the breakoff Combatant Clerics Association was led by members of the Islamic Left. These two groups were the leading organizers of much subsequent factional politics.

In 1988–89, Khomeini took several important steps to weaken potential opponents and strengthen the state and his followers, especially as his death could not be far distant. Ayatollah Montazeri, whom the Assembly of Experts chose as Khomeini's successor in 1985, became increasingly controversial. Mehdi Hashemi, who ran an organization out of Montazeri's office to export the revolution, was blamed for leaking the information on Iran's relations with United States and Israel. Hashemi and others were arrested on charges of counterrevolutionary activities and executed in 1987. In addition, Montazeri called for open assessment of failures, protested to Khomeini the sudden execution of thousands of dissidents in 1988, and, in a change of views, ceased supporting the export of revolution. He said Iran should only be an example, and the best way was to reduce state interference in the economy and lift barriers to free speech. In February 1988, Khomeini criticized Montazeri and in March called a meeting of the Assembly of Experts to discuss him and then essentially told Montazeri his resignation was accepted. Montazeri gave up his office and returned to teaching in Qom, where he was later put under house arrest. He, however, continued in various ways to speak, publish, and have contact with students, several of whom became important reformers in the 1990s.

In January 1988 Khomeini, responding to an interpretation of his words by Khamene'i, made the startling and unprecedented statement that the needs of the Islamic state outweighed Islamic law, including such basic commandments as prayer. In February he established the Expediency Council to resolve the constant and crippling differences between the majles and the Guardian Council. In April 1989 Khomeini ordered Khamene'i to direct a revision of the constitution. A constitutional committee, partly appointed by Khomeini and partly elected by the majles, was created. Faced with a situation in which none of the grand ayatollahs fully accepted velayat-e faqih, Khomeini and others were led to change the constitution's stress on the religious qualifications of the faqih. The revised constitution increased the political and decreased the religious nature of the faqih, saying that preference for the faqih should be based on his public support and knowledge of social and political issues as well as knowledge of Islamic jurisprudence. The faqih's powers were defined with greater specificity and included commanding the armed forces, declaring war and peace, and controlling appointments to the Guardian Council, military and security forces, the judiciary, and state radio and television. The revisions made the faqih's qualifications mainly political and formalized his control over most state powers, thus strengthening his position vis-à-vis the president and majles. Without explicit authorization he also controls the major private foundations and the selection of Friday prayer imams. This does not mean that he is an absolute dictator, as Khamene'i, like Khomeini before him, has had several times to compromise or even bow to the will of other institutions or demonstrators. The proposed revision also abolished the post of prime minister and put the Expediency Council in the constitution to arbitrate majles legislation rejected by the Guardian Council.

These changes, as well as a few rulings by Khomeini that favored the Islamic Left, temporarily strengthened the left, but their real import was to strengthen and partially rationalize the central government and increase and politicize the constitutional nature and powers of the faqih. This soon strengthened the pragmatist Modern Right and the conservatives, who were favored by the next faqih and president. Khomeini died on June 3, 1989, and the Assembly of Experts, without waiting for the electorate's ratification of the constitutional changes, named Khamene'i as faqih on June 5. As Khamene'i could not stay as president, the Guardian Council authorized presidential elections at the end of July. Rafsanjani, with only one opponent, won overwhelmingly, and the constitutional amendments were approved.

Khamene'i's religious credentials were weak, though he was speedily given the title of ayatollah. He had great influence with the Pasdaran and similar groups, and his brother-in-law headed the Foundation for the Dispossessed. Khomeini's January statement that the interests of the Islamic Republic took precedence over Islamic law gave the faqih authorization to ignore the views of those with greater religious credentials, although the state never dared break with Shi'i tradition to the point of invalidating the independent fatwas of senior ayatollahs, which were binding on their followers. Many Shi'is inside and outside Iran openly or silently rejected Khamene'i as such a "source of emulation." Khamene'i did not press the question of religious authority but concentrated on building up his real power over the years.

Efforts to promote Khamene'i to grand ayatollah were rejected by much of the clerical establishment in Qom. The gap between Khamene'i's religious stature and that of rivals like Montazeri and other distinguished grand ayatollahs who rejected Khomeini's version of velayat-e faqih remained. The secret Special Court for Clergy, created in 1987, and vigilante gangs were increasingly used to intimidate clerics who might threaten Khamene'i. The continued contrast between the original religious theory of the office of faqih and its actual occupant have contributed to internal disputes.

Also in 1988–89, when Khamene'i and Rafsanjani were trying to rescue the economy by renewing economic ties abroad, Khomeini undermined their effort. In September 1988, the Indian-born British subject Salman Rushdie published the novel *The Satanic Verses,* which many Muslims considered a blasphemous insult to Islam. Demonstrations, often violent, began in India and Pakistan and among South Asian Muslims in Britain. On February 14, 1989, Khomeini issued a statement, which was soon referred to as a fatwa. Based on the principle that apostates from Islam were subject to death, Khomeini wrote to inform the world's Muslims that "the author of *The Satanic Verses,* which is against Islam, the Prophet, and the Koran, and all those involved in its publication who were aware of its content, are sentenced to death." The head of the important 15th of Khordad Foundation offered a $2.6 million reward to Rushdie's killer. Rushdie went into hiding, protected by British security forces, but other persons tied to the publication and sale of the book were shot and killed or wounded.[26]

Many Muslims questioned the legitimacy of a decree issued by a Shi'i cleric against a Sunni citizen of a foreign country. Khomeini, fresh from failures in Iraq, was, however, trying to revive his role as the leader of militant Islam. The decree ended efforts to improve relations with the United Kingdom and other Western countries. The image of Iran in non-Muslim countries was greatly damaged. Khomeini's death in June 1989, left Iran with a relatively strong government but with huge economic, social, and international problems.[27]

11

Politics and Economics in Post-Khomeini Iran

The post-Khomeini era can be divided into two major periods: From mid-1989 to spring 1997 President Hashemi Rafsanjani, generally allied with Leader (also called faqih) Khamene'i, led a government that achieved some economic reconstruction and improved Iran's foreign relations. It was not, however, able or willing to attempt changes that would have dramatically improved Iran's domestic and foreign situation or significantly decreased controls on personal behavior. From 1997 the reformist Mohammad Khatami and other reformists won several elections with huge majorities and instituted increased freedom of the press and in other cultural matters and some reforms, but there was a powerful conservative backlash, reassertion of many controls on speech, writing, and behavior, and then widespread disillusionment. The struggle for power continues, and most Iranians, as expressed in their votes and words, would like to see significant change.

In August 1989 in national presidential elections the "pragmatist" Hashemi Rafsanjani was elected, and Mehdi Karrubi replaced Rafsanjani as speaker of the majles, which was then controlled by the Islamic Left. Khamene'i and Rafsanjani allied on most issues. Khamene'i, whose clerical title was raised from hojjatolislam to ayatollah, though many did not recognize his right to this religious title, concentrated on building a network of supporters in the government and revolutionary institutions, in which he was generally successful.

The eight-year Iran-Iraq war and continued economic decline and crisis caused widespread public discontent. President Rafsanjani promised reconstruction and also to reverse the economic policies of the Islamic Left, who for most of the 1980s had pursued policies that increased state control of the economy. Rafsanjani led a drive for market-based economic change and a less confrontational foreign policy. The Islamic Left noted that the new economic policies benefited the rich and hurt the poor and opposed Rafsanjani's reforms. They said his openings to the West would bring renewed Western domination. Many in the Islamic Left preferred Montazeri to Khamene'i. The Islamic Left's political positions contributed to lessening their power.[1]

Iran faced huge problems with major war damage, the destruction of its main port, Khorramshahr, and the virtual ruin of many industries, including the Abadan refinery and the Kharg loading facilities. Per capita income had dropped at least 40 percent since the revolution, and many wartime shortages continued. Ongoing disagreements among factions, with the Left still strong in the majles, hurt possibilities for a coherent economic plan. Problems like inflation, unemployment, deficit spending, overwhelming dependence on oil, and declining agricultural self-sufficiency were worse than ever.

President Rafsanjani was seen as a pragmatist, and he tried to promote technocrats. He sponsored two successive five-year plans aiming to repair war damage, improve infrastructure, and increase production and growth via private and foreign investment. With this aim, the Tehran stock exchange was revived, shares in some government enterprises were sold, and some government assets like mines privatized. The government created free trade zones on the Gulf islands of Kish and Qeshm, started construction projects, encouraged expatriates to return, devalued the currency, instituted export incentives, and lowered some barriers to foreign investment.

By 1989 many in the government and also faqih Khamene'i supported President Rafsanjani's reconstruction program, including his attempts to favor new enterprises and a market economy. As part of reforms largely designed to get a loan from the International Monetary Fund, the Rafsanjani government introduced a liberalization package that proposed reducing government subsidies and multiple exchange rates, devaluing the currency, promoting exports, and privatizing nationalized industries. In agriculture, it called for removing import subsidies, reducing the public sector's role, and putting more emphasis on profitability, the private sector, research, and extension. The first five-year plan, 1988–93, stressed privatization. Despite these liberalization policies, problems including factional rivalries and ideological differences led to the abandonment or basic modification of many of them.

The privatization of over a thousand public enterprises was begun in 1993 but was suspended a year later largely because of the widespread scandals and corruption that had accompanied the sales of state enterprises with the privatization program. The majles then passed guidelines making the government give privileged access to share buyers who had sacrificed for the revolution. A cabinet committee drew up privatization bylaws in January 1995, but the program was delayed and partial. Massive imports and the rise of short-term foreign debt to about $20 billion reached unprecedented levels. The situation worsened when President Clinton imposed an economic embargo in May 1995.

The reforms had some results, including shifting from inward-looking development based on agriculture to industrial growth based on export promotion and liberal trade policies and the lessening of obstacles to private business. The agricultural sector improved in performance after the introduction of the market liberalization policies. However, after liberalization money flowed more into real estate and construction of luxury apartments in Tehran than into productive investment. There was also a buildup of large foreign debts. This necessitated new financial restrictions in order to pay off the debts.

After abortive and mostly rhetorical attempts to free Iran from its dependence on oil, Iran's rulers recognized its continued centrality to the economy and the nation. With the forced departure of foreign companies from Iran in 1979 and the abandonment of technical measures to keep up wells, oil productive capacity had fallen disastrously in the 1980s. Despite efforts by the National Iranian Oil Company after 1989, which led to some increase in production, oil production was insufficient to meet the needs of Iranians and to pay off the large foreign debt of post-1989 years. The government had to appeal to international companies.

In May 1993 the Clinton administration announced dual containment, including partial economic sanctions, against Iran and Iraq. Some U.S. companies could still do business with Iran, but when Conoco announced a billion-dollar deal to develop Iran's offshore oil the Clinton administration, under pressure from Congress and the pro-Israeli lobby, announced a total embargo on dealings with Iran in April 1995. Trade with the United States, which had climbed after the war, virtually ended. The U.S. Congress passed the Iran-Libya Sanctions Act in 1996, which threatened even non-U.S. countries making large investments in energy. The act was denounced by the European Union as null and void, but it still blocked some needed investment, though some foreign companies did invest, thus improving production. As internal consumption needs grew, Iran could not export as much oil as before. But Iran remains one of the world's top oil exporters and has huge natural gas reserves.

Iran took moderate or neutral positions in the Kuwait crisis and Gulf War of 1991–92, which facilitated the restoration of relations with several Arab states, which had been cut off in the Iran-Iraq war. Iraq's desire to preserve Iranian neutrality in the Gulf War made it give up what it had gained in the Iran-Iraq war and revert to the 1975 pro-Iranian definition of the Shatt al-Arab border. International animosity toward Iraq led to its being declared the aggressor in the Iran-Iraq war and hence liable for reparations. The Gulf War thus helped Iran, though Iran disliked the vastly increased U.S. presence in the Gulf.

By 1992 economic progress had occurred in many areas, helped by a temporary jump in oil prices due to the Gulf War. There was, however, no real increase in political freedoms. Though political parties were authorized in a 1981 law, no application to form a political party was approved. The Guardian Council disqualified more than 1,000 of 3,150 candidates for the fourth majles elections in 1992. Many of the disqualified were from the Islamic Left, including the Association of Combatant Clerics. Among those pushed out were prominent revolutionaries like Sadeq Khalkhali, Behzad Nabavi, Mehdi Karrubi, Ali-Akbar Mohtashemi, and Mohammad Khoeniha. Some denounced these disqualifications as dictatorship. Even the leftists who ran did not do well in the elections, however, and the Islamic Left lost control of the majles to the pragmatists and conservatives. The fourth majles strengthened the conservative bazaar-backed Combatant Clergy Society, one of whom, Hojjatoleslam Ali Akbar Nateq Nuri, was elected speaker. From 1992 to 1996 the conservatives gained further in power, getting some support from Khamene'i, and got control of important ministries of intelligence, culture and Islamic guidance, interior, and state media.

After they lost power, many Islamic leftists underwent an intellectual and political transformation, influenced not only by events in Iran but also by dramatic events in Eastern Europe and the Soviet Union, which undermined ideas of state-centered economic planning and strict ideological controls. Many of them, including persons involved in the U.S. embassy hostage taking like Abbas Abdi and Massoumeh Ebtekar (the English language spokesperson, "Mary"), became advocates of greater democracy, human and civil rights, and better relations with the world, and opponents of existing governmental controls. Some returned to higher education as students or teachers, some who were clergy benefited from the introduction of modern Western philosophy in higher religious schools, and some became journalists, writers, filmmakers, or artists. At the same time, a rising number of educated female and male students, professionals, and others were beginning to discuss issues of human and women's rights, greater freedoms, and governmental transparency after the traumatic experiences of revolution and war, disillusionment with governmental controls, and continued economic hardship. Many of them expressed and acted on their new views, especially beginning in 1997.

In 1993 Rafsanjani won a second presidential term, but with a small majority and far fewer who bothered to vote. He faced many difficulties, including criticisms from both Left and Right. As oil prices slumped, foreign debt rose from ca. $9 billion in 1991 to $34 billion in 1993, inflation was over 30 percent per annum, in one year reaching 49 percent, and the value of the rial fell disastrously. Declining living standards brought workers' riots in several large cities in 1992, which were brutally repressed, but more occurred in 1994 and 1995.

As new majles elections approached in 1996, Rafsanjani ended his alliance with the conservatives, probably fearing that a victory by the conservative Ali Akbar Nateq Nuri in the 1997 presidential race would push the country too far to the right. Rafsanjani backed the Servants of Construction, a small group of technocrats who favored economic reconstruction and played an important political role. The Guardian Council in 1996 disqualified 40 percent of the applicants for candidacy in elections to the new majles, including many on the Left. No faction got a majority in the elections; Nateq Nuri remained speaker but with a low majority. The Conservative-Pragmatist alliance ended, and in the presidential elections the Left and the Pragmatists became strange bedfellows.

Abroad, Rafsanjani at first improved relations with Europe and the Arab world but faced an increasingly hostile United States between 1992 and 1997. The main issues cited against Iran by the Clinton government were its hostility to the then-active Arab-Israeli peace process, Iranian support for "international terrorism," and its pursuit of nuclear energy, which the United States thought was aimed at development of a nuclear bomb. These issues, which are seen very differently by Iran and by many other countries than they are by the United States, have remained major concerns of the United States and also of Israel. Since 2001 persons with ties to these governments have cited them as possible justifications for attacking Iran.[2]

The degree of official Iranian support for killings outside Iran is impossible to know exactly, but it almost certainly existed through the early 1990s, while several analysts say there has not been official support for killings more recently. The term *terrorism,* now in vogue, fails to make distinctions. Iran carried out raids and assassinations against the MK in retaliation for deadly MK attacks inside Iran. It also supported anti-Israeli groups like Hamas and especially the Lebanese Hizbollah, who were seen not only in Iran but also in much of the Third World as fighters for the liberation of Lebanon and Palestine from Israeli occupation using means available to a weak side against a militarily overwhelming one—means similar to some used in past anticolonial fights in Israel, South Africa, Algeria, and elsewhere. This view is not shared by those who are horrified by the killing of civilians, except perhaps when it is done by states in wars. Before 1997 Iran also supported some murders of Iranian oppositionists abroad. Besides the killings that resulted from the Rushdie decree, several prominent opponents of the government were killed abroad, among them the Kurdish leader Abdol Rahman Qasemlu in 1989 and Shapour Bakhtiar in 1991. In 1992 four Iranian Kurdish oppositionists were killed at Mykonos Restaurant in Berlin. German investigations traced the killings to high Iranian officials. One man was indicted and accused of ordering the killing on behalf of a group that included Khamene'i and Rafsanjani. Iran denounced the trial, but in April 1997 a German court said Khamene'i, Rafsanjani, and other officials were responsible. Germany recalled its ambassador, as did the other EU countries, and attempts to restore relations were unsuccessful as long as the Rushdie affair continued. There is, however, disagreement about how much the leaders of Iran were involved in all of the above incidents, and even more about how much if at all Iran has been involved in killings abroad since the early 1990s.[3] A recent Argentine report ties Iran via Hizbollah to the March 1992 bombing of the Israeli embassy in Buenos Aires, in which twenty-nine people were killed, and to the July 1994 bombing of the city's Jewish community center, in which eighty-five were killed. Some Israelis have tied this to vaguer reports on more recent activities and use this as one reason to urge the United States to go to war with Iran after Iraq.[4]

The constitution limited presidents to two terms, so Rafsanjani could not run in 1997, and in mid-1996 he confirmed he would step down. Khamene'i named him head of the Expediency Council. There was great interest in the 1997 elections; two hundred candidates applied to run, including nine women, who were screened out by the Council of Guardians, as were all but four of the applicants. The four final candidates included the conservative majles speaker Ali-Akbar Nateq Nuri, Mohammad Khatami, and two others who soon appeared to have no chance. Nateq Nuri had been one of the activist clergy since 1963, was elected to the majles in 1986, and became majles speaker after the victory of the conservatives in 1992. He often tangled with Rafsanjani. Khamene'i made known his preference for Nateq Nuri, who got the most time on television and radio. The commander of the Pasdaran issued written orders to vote for Nateq Nuri, and the other organized vigilante groups were behind him. Nateq Nuri had a long list of influential individuals and organizations behind him and appeared to be a sure winner. But Nateq Nuri's strength made the pragmatists fear that his victory would give the conservatives absolute power. This brought about an unusual electoral alliance between the pragmatists, led by the pro-Rafsanjani group, the Servants of Construction, who backed Khatami, and the Islamic Left, many of whom now held liberal reformist views. Polls showed most people expected Nateq Nuri to win.

Khatami began as a Khomeinist, and after the revolution he took Beheshti's place as director of the Islamic Center in Hamburg. His background also included editorship of the newspaper *Kayhan* and election to the first majles in 1980. He held various posts and in 1983 became minister of culture and Islamic guidance, a post he held for nine years under varying governments. His policies toward intellectuals and artists included subsidies and other encouragement to the newly important film industry. He eased censorship on printed material, encouraging a rising number and variety of publications. He became popular among intellectuals for relaxing censorship. But his ministry became controversial when it tried unsuccessfully to defend a journalist tried by the Special Court for the Clergy. Khatami resigned in 1992 and was sent to head the National Library.[5] He was known as an intellectual and had written two books, one of which criticized the stagnation of political thought in Iran after the tenth century, while the West made huge strides in knowledge. He tried to reconcile Islam and liberal democracy.[6]

In his campaign Khatami promised his Islamic government would follow and serve popular desires, including those for greater freedom.

He advocated greater rights for women, Sunnis, and other minorities and emphasized civil society, a term he explicated and popularized in his speeches. He organized trips throughout the country and met with people face to face without the usual security precautions. Nateq Nuri, in contrast, had a status quo platform and approach. Khatami's platform, with its call for greater freedoms, the rule of law, strengthening of civil society, economic development with equity, and a moderate foreign policy was especially popular among the youth and students, women, the new middle class, and minorities, including the neglected Sunni Muslims. He presented a friendly, smiling, populist image. He won an amazing victory; a record number of eligible voters voted, and Khatami got 69 percent of the vote. Analysis of the vote showed that women and young people especially voted for him. Nateq Nuri got only 7 million votes to Khatami's 29.7 million.

Khatami's landslide election in May 1997 made many believe Iran was entering a period of fundamental reform. Some hoped a democratic regime would emerge. The reformist camp comprised centrist pragmatists, Islamic liberals, and secularists. The centrist Servants of Construction, who wanted free market reforms, backed Khatami, and several of its leaders were named to high positions in his first government, though the 2000 elections were to show that their popular support was weak. Islamic leftists who had gradually abandoned radical positions and embraced democracy were probably the most important part of Khatami's coalition. After his election some of them established the Islamic Iran Participation Front, which became the major reformist organization. A pro-reform coalition named Second of Khordad (the date of Khatami's election) was formed and included Left Islamic groups, the centrist Servants of Construction, and others. Khatami's cabinet, which even the conservative-dominated majles approved, included both the Islamic Left and centrists. Perhaps afraid to try to get majles approval, he did not try to appoint any women ministers but did appoint Massoumeh Ebtekar vice president. He was forced to accept the conservative candidate for the important Intelligence Ministry, and Khamene'i decided to keep crucial control over the security forces.

The conservatives, after initial confusion, pulled together to give effective support to Khamene'i, who had more power than Khatami. The conservatives and especially Khamene'i controlled virtually all the major institutions except the presidency and cabinet. Recognizing the power of the conservatives, Khatami concentrated on opening political discourse and taking his case to the people. Minister of Culture Ataollah Mohajerani eased restrictions on the press, allowing many reformist newspapers to open. These became the center for extensive debates about civil society, tolerance, the rule of law, the position of women, and possible different interpretations of, or approaches to, velayat-e faqih. In the absence of political parties, the press became the center of political debate.[7]

Khatami's first term had a mixed record, but he was effective in improving relations with the West and with Arab countries, particularly those in the Gulf who had conflicts with revolutionary Iran. His success in foreign relations was possible, as even Khamene'i and those around him saw that bad relations with Western and Middle Eastern countries hurt Iran economically and politically. Iran's economy still suffered from low investment in industry, high unemployment, and overwhelming dependence on oil income, and opening foreign ties could be of some help, though it could not solve Iran's structural and legal obstacles to development.

Khatami carried further Rafsanjani's efforts to strengthen ties with Islamic countries. One success was the holding of the Organization of the Islamic Conference in Tehran in December 1997 despite the U.S.'s failed attempt to organize a rival meeting in Qatar. Nearly all OIC members came to Tehran, even enemies like Iraq and the PLO (disliked for accepting the Oslo accords). This was followed by a thaw in Saudi-Iranian relations; their ideological rivalry was played down as both wanted to stabilize the region and oil policy. They signed a formal cooperation agreement in May 1998. The Saudis had some success in improving Iran's relations with the United Arab Emirates and Egypt, though the UAE still protested the occupation of the islands of Tunbs and Abu Musa, begun by the shah, and the Egyptians unsuccessfully pressed Iran to rename a street named after Anwar Sadat's assassin.

Tensions with Iraq, Afghanistan, and Turkey, by contrast, continued. Iraq allowed the Mojahedin-e Khalq to make border attacks on Iran, while Iran provided the base for the anti-Saddam Hussein Supreme Council of the Islamic Revolution in Iraq (SCIRI). Relations with Afghanistan deteriorated when the Taliban took control, as Iran opposed them and backed the Northern Alliance. In September 1998, after several Iranian officials were murdered in the Afghan city of Mazar-e Sharif, Iran mobilized but did not attack. Relations with Turkey were clouded by Turkey's military ties to the United States and Israel and by U.S. advocacy of an oil pipeline from ex-Soviet lands to a Turkish port instead of a more direct line that would go through Iran. In 1999 Iran protested Turkish prime minister Bulent Ecevit's support of Iran's student protest, while Turkey protested what it considered Iranian support for Turkish Islamists.

Khatami became the first Iranian president to visit several foreign capitals, including Rome and Paris, and reopened relations with Italy, France, and other European countries. In September 1999 he said, without disagreement from Khamene'i, that the Iranian government would no longer target Salman Rushdie or others associated with his novel, and that for Iran the case was "completely finished." Despite the vocal disagreement of some clerics and the reiteration of the private reward for Rushdie's killer, Britain accepted this and restored relations at the ambassadorial level. Helpful trade, loan, and investment agreements from Europe followed, though constitutional provisions on foreign investment continued to limit such investments.

Less successful was Khatami's attempt to improve relations with the United States, highlighted by his famous January 1998 CNN interview in which he proclaimed his admiration for American political traditions and called for a "Dialogue of Civilizations." His friendly words were answered by conciliatory words from the U.S. secretary of state, Madeleine Albright. There followed an exchange of wrestling teams, freer travel to and from the United States, and an end to the embargo on just two items—carpets and pistachios. Although the Dialogue of Civilizations became a UN slogan for 2001, relations with the United States foundered both on hostility from Iran's conservatives and on U.S. insistence on changes in Iranian policy on Israel, nuclear weapons, and support of terrorism as preconditions for discussions. Khamene'i and various conservatives have continued to denounce the United States, and the issue of normalizing U.S.–Iran relations has become deeply entangled in Iran's power struggle, which hurts any real progress. A pragmatic improvement in relations as the United States sought Iranian help in its Iraq policies in early 2003 may or may not bring a long-term change. Regarding the improvement of relations with Europe and with Iran's neighbors, including Russia and ex-Soviet states, Khamene'i has supported Khatami's initiatives, which have been fruitful. In addition to the general increase in economic relations and trade with Europe and Russia, Russia supplies Iran with arms and with technology for nuclear energy, which both Russia and Iran say is for peaceful use; Iran has recently invited inspections.[8]

In the economy, basic reforms remained largely stymied after Kha-tami's 1997 victory. The ruling elite, who represent an alliance between the commercial bazaar bourgeoisie and conservative clerics, resists giving up their economic privileges as they do their political ones. Constitutional restrictions still make it difficult for foreigners to invest in Iranian enterprises, although some changes in these rules are under way. The constitution forbids foreigners to own concessions, operate oil products, or enter production-sharing agreements. Some ways around these restrictions has been found , and an improved foreign investment law was passed in 2002. Almost all the big international oil companies have a presence in Iran but they object to obstacles stemming from Iran's constitution. Khatami and many others oppose a convention to change the constitution because a convention with restricted candidates might worsen the constitution. The alternative is to allow further laws that reinterpret the constitution, but here the obstacle remains the conservative judiciary, allied with commercial bazaar merchants with little interest in foreign investments.

Those in government and foundations who control businesses discourage competition. Merchants who support the status quo and oppose change are still favored by the conservative clerics who control major governmental and judicial institutions. Nonetheless, the Khatami government took some steps to improve the economy. Khatami backed a five-year plan for 2000–05, much of which is devoted to promoting the rule of law, non-oil exports, privatization, and deregulation. But relatively little has come of it, as most of these reforms would weaken the ruling clerics or their allied bazaaris. About 60 percent of the economy is still controlled and planned by the state, and another 10–20 percent by five large foundations that are also tied to the Leader. They have preferential access to credit, foreign exchange, and licenses and contracts, which makes it difficult for others to compete. There has been some private initiative in banking. Khatami has also taken some steps to tax the untaxed, reduce dependence on oil, and further liberalize exchange rates to bring them in line with international market rates; a unified single exchange rate was achieved in 2002. Those with capital still prefer to invest it in import-export and domestic trade or in real estate, not in long-term investment in industrial production.

Unlicensed small enterprises in the "free" economy continue to grow and add to the GDP. They avoid taxes and social legislation and also go unreported in statistics.[9] Iran still has low wages and high unemployment, even among the educated. Faced with the needs and support of the poor, Khatami turned away from neoliberalism in some matters, refusing to privatize various public services and retaining subsidies on necessities. He also raised the wages of public employees, some of whom, like teachers, were paid below the official poverty level.

Under both Rafsanjani and Khatami there has been some significant economic recovery, including a buildup of industries, and many manufactured products are produced under customs protection, but Iran still has no export markets for industrial products. It remains more profitable and less risky to speculate in currency or real estate. Hence, despite recovery from war damage, the economy remains overwhelmingly dependent on government-controlled oil income. The per capita GDP is still substantially below its prerevolution levels despite recent rises. According to World Bank figures, which take 1974 as 100, per capita GDP went from a high of 115 in 1976 to a low of 60 in 1988, the year war with Iraq ended. It has since recovered, reaching almost 90 today, with significant real growth in the past three years.[10] Although oil no longer accounts for as high a percentage of the national revenue as it did thirty years ago, it still provides a 40–50 percent direct share of government revenue, ca. 65 percent if its indirect share is included, and 80 pecent of export earnings.[11] While its impressive health and education record give Iran a respectable place in the UN's human development index, the rise in unemployed, educated youth, and continued population growth as young people have babies have created an explosive economic situation.[12] Strict limits on foreign investment, a weak legal framework, the majority economic role of corrupt governmental institutions and foundations, and the dearth of productive investment by the bazaar bourgeoisie create obstacles to economic reform and development. Iran remains overwhelmingly dependent on fluctuating oil income.

Domestically, hard-liners began to attack Khatami's allies soon after his victory. They denounced statements by Grand Ayatollah Montazeri, who in November 1997 called for a sharp reduction in the powers of the Leader, saying that the occupant of this position should "supervise, not rule." He was placed under house arrest but continued to make critical statements. In April 1998 the judiciary brought charges of corruption against Tehran's reformist mayor, Gholam Hosein Karbaschi, and several of his deputies. Karbaschi had become highly popular mainly through his notable publicly useful building achievements in Tehran—parks and green space, cultural centers in poor areas, roads and highways, housing and public buildings. The police attacked student-led demonstrations in Karbaschi's behalf. Karbaschi's trial was broadcast on television, which popularized his attacks on the conservatives and the judicial system. He was convicted and given a long prison sentence. Conservatives also led the June 1998 parliamentary impeachment of Interior Minister Abdollah Nuri. In the summer of 1998, the conservative judiciary began closing reformist newspapers and arresting editors and journalists.

Khatami's modest measures met with a harsh response from Iran's conservatives, including Nateq Nuri, who was still speaker of the majles, Mohammad Yazdi, the head of the judiciary, and the heads of the Council of Guardians and the Assembly of Experts. The Council of Guardians threw out over half the candidates for election to the Assembly of Experts in 1998, which resulted in a small turnout and victory for the conservatives.

The vigilante groups—Pasdaran, Basij, and various street gangs—often raided newspaper offices and attacked demonstrators. The head of the judiciary, Yazdi, said in July 1998 that the press was abusing freedom, and he was backed by Khamene'i. There was a wave of newspaper closures, though closed newspapers often reopened under new names. The majles passed a bill in September 1998 calling for journalists who criticize Islamic principles to be charged with threatening national security, and the judiciary set up a press court to try journalists.

In the first year and a half of Khatami's presidency at least nine dissident writers or activists were murdered, died under suspicious circumstances, or disappeared, and many others were attacked or arrested. The long-time Persian nationalist Daryush Foruhar, age seventy, and his wife were stabbed to death in November 1998. Two days later the body of a journalist was discovered, and soon another writer was found strangled. Prominent intellectuals wrote an open letter to Khamene'i and Khatami, who set up a task force to bring the cases to justice. In mid-September suspects were arrested. The authorities tried to blame nongovernmental groups, but when some persons cited evidence that high officials were involved, the Ministry of Intelligence felt compelled to admit that some "rogue elements" in the ministry were responsible. It seems likely that they had approval from higher officials. In the ensuing uproar Montazeri and others called for a thorough investigation and a purge of the ministry. The investigating committee's report in January 1999 absolved the ministry of guilt. Khamene'i urged that disputes over the murders end. Investigations were secret, and ten unidentified suspects were arrested, only some of whom were later named.

These events shocked Iranians, forcing conservative leaders to denounce the killings and producing demands that the security forces be purged. The conservative intelligence minister Ghorban Ali Dorri Najafabadi soon resigned and was replaced with a reformer. In the following months rumors continued that leading conservatives had ordered the murders. These rumors were given credence in June 1999 when a leading suspect died mysteriously in prison, in what many allege was an attempt to cover up the involvement of top officials. Also in June the security forces arrested thirteen Iranian Jews on charges of spying for Israel, in what was widely seen as an attempt to undermine Khatami's program for improved relations with the West. Several were sentenced to jail, though in early 2003 those still in jail were released.

The reformist interior minister authorized political parties, and several reformist and centrist parties registered. Khatami succeeded in holding the first elections to local and municipal councils in February 1999, as foreseen in the constitution. Reformists saw elected local councils as a step toward decentralizing power and as a training ground for democratic politicians. There were several thousand candidates, including many women and independents, with a large number identified either as conservatives or as reformists. The reformists again scored a major victory, and in nearly every major city at least one woman was elected. The Council of Guardians has no control over candidates for local elections, so anyone could run, and their attempts to disqualify many victors in Tehran and elsewhere were strongly resisted and mostly failed. The local councils have relatively little power, though many thought they could be a first step toward decentralization. A new local council election in early 2003, however, showed that most people were disillusioned with the limits imposed on local councils and with the failure of the political process to produce significant reform, as very few voted, especially in the big cities, and hence conservatives scored victories.

Four student leaders were arrested in late May 1999, and in early July the majles approved a bill sharply restricting freedom of the press. Judicial authorities closed down the newspaper *Salam* for publishing a story that linked the press bill to the serial killings. On July 8, 1999, many Tehran University students staged peaceful protests against the press bill and the closure of *Salam*. That night police violently attacked a student dormitory, killing one student and injuring and arresting many. Khatami and other officials denounced this, and students organized large protest demonstrations that continued for days and spread to Tabriz and other cities, with continued violence. The protestors increased their demands, calling for freedom of the press and democracy. They also clashed repeatedly with the police and pressure groups, possibly encouraged to violence by *agents provocateurs* in their ranks. To restore order, the government on July 12 announced a ban on demonstrations. Many ignored the ban and were attacked by police and vigilantes, producing brutal battles in central Tehran. Facing threats from the Pasdaran, Khatami was forced to denounce the protestors. Dozens were injured and some 1,400 were arrested. Conservatives then organized a large counterdemonstration, and the students were forced to give up their protests. These events left Iran tense and polarized. Many students and other reformers were very bitter, both at the hard-liners' brutal actions and at Khatami's lack of support for the protestors.

Chastened by these events, both the Khatami and the Khamene'i camps tried for a time to be more conciliatory. Most protestors were released, though some were tried and given stiff sentences. Nearly one hundred policemen were tried for the dormitory attack, which, along with the trials for the political murders, showed that officials perpetrating illegal violence were not immune from punishment. Parliament put off the press bill. Khamene'i replaced the hard-line head of the judiciary, Yazdi, with a reputed pragmatic conservative, Ayatollah Mahmoud Hashemi Shahrudi.

In the period before the first round of majles elections in February 2000, however, Abdollah Nuri, a leading reform candidate who might have become speaker, was arrested and given a five-year prison sentence, making him ineligible to run. Several more reform newspapers were closed. Rafsanjani decided to run, hoping to become speaker of parliament again, and the centrist Servants of Construction and the conservatives backed him. The Islamic Left attacked him, exacerbating a split between them and the center. The Council of Guardians, contrary to expectations, vetoed only a few candidates, probably realizing the reformers would win in any case. This helped reformers to have a huge victory, taking 71 percent of the seats decided in the first round. Rafsanjani, now identified with the Right, came out thirtieth among thirty Tehran winners. His daughter and women's rights activist Faezeh Hashemi, who was easily elected in 1996, lost, as did many conservative and centrist incumbents. The break of most of Rafsanjani's centrists from the

reformists, however, weakened possibilities for reform and further polarized Iran.

In March 2000 Said Hajjarian, the leading reform strategist, was shot
and severely wounded. Although several men without political ties were
convicted of the crime, it was widely believed that powerful conservatives were responsible. After the reformist victory in the first round of
majles elections, conservatives, who continued to control the majles until
the runoffs, passed an amendment to the press law saying that banned
periodicals could no longer reappear with different names, and that writers who had worked for banned periodicals could not be hired by others.
The conservatives were encouraged by Khamene'i's strong criticism of
reformist newspapers. (The new reformist parliament later tried to re-
peal these amendments, but Khamene'i stopped them.) The press court
closed most reformist newspapers, and more journalists were arrested.

Reformist victories were confirmed in the runoff elections in May
2000. The press law, newspaper closures, arrests, and efforts of the
Guardian Council to nullify many election results sparked demonstrations throughout Iran, with Khatami appealing for calm. When the
Guardian Council nullified Tehran's vote, Khamene'i, fearing unrest,
ordered it to certify the elections, which it did while raising Rafsanjani's
vote. He, however, realizing he could not be elected speaker, resigned.

The new majles opened on May 27, 2000. A moderate reformer,
Mehdi Karrubi, was elected speaker, and two reformers, Behzad Nabavi
and Mohammad Reza Khatami, became deputy speakers. In July students staged peaceful demonstrations in several cities to commemorate
the 1999 riots and were violently attacked in Tehran. Nearly all the remaining reformist papers were closed, and several more journalists were
arrested. There was little the reformists could do. Parliament passed
a number of reform bills, but the Council of Guardians blocked most
of them.

Minister of Culture Mohajerani resigned in December 2000 after
being pursued by hard-liners. Other reformers were imprisoned, and in
March and April 2001 over sixty members of the Liberation Movement
were arrested on dubious charges. Reformers decided to avoid provoca-
tive acts, but Khatami failed to get concessions, thus frustrating many
supporters, especially among the youth. While some agreed with his
nonconfrontational policy, others disagreed or thought Khatami had not
exhausted nonviolent alternatives.

From the spring of 2000 there were a number of violent attacks on reformers. Iranian reformists attended a conference in Berlin run by the Heinrich Böll Foundation, which was disrupted by foreign-based Iranian opposition groups, one man stripping and a woman dancing in the aisles. State television repeatedly aired edited tape of the conference, and eighteen participants were arrested, including two prominent women—the publisher Shahla Lahiji and the human rights lawyer Mehrangiz Kar—and prominent male reformers. They were charged with acting against national security and collaborating with counterrevolutionaries, and some received harsh sentences.[13] Waves of arrests involved journalists, professionals, students, clerics, and politicians. Some were given long sentences, and others were held in secret confinement. Akbar Ganji, the most popular of the reformist journalists, who had spoken and written denouncing "Islamic fascism," was sentenced to prison after his latest book named ayatollahs whom he accused of organizing about a hundred assassinations in the past decade.

Previously tolerated figures with anti-Shah credentials, like Ezzetollah Sahabi and religious nationalists of the Freedom Movement, were arrested, and the latter accused of plotting to overthrow the regime. The leader of the Movement of Muslim Militants, Habibollah Peyman was arrested, and Ibrahim Yazdi, leader of the Freedom Movement, was charged in absentia while in the United States for cancer treatment. Continuing repression is led by the all-powerful judiciary, which is accountable only to Khamene'i and has its own intelligence and police services.

Contributing to political discontent is economic unrest. The continued power of those who profit from the status quo blocks many, though not all, attempts at economic reform. Unemployment, officially ca. 14 percent, is often estimated at closer to 30 percent, and especially hits the young, and inflation continues. Young people in particular show signs of depression and alienation, with cheap drugs from Afghanistan taking an increasing toll. While many young people continue to be politically engaged and interested, others are concerned mainly about their immediate, often consumer-oriented, satisfactions; their politics are limited to a desire to behave as they wish, and they reject what the regime is for and favor what it opposes.

Women are continuing the struggle to expand their rights that characterized the nineties, while also entering the general reform movement. The new reformist parliament, ironically, has fewer women deputies than its predecessor, and many women activists face the familiar problem of their male colleagues' urging them to postpone women's demands.

The reformist parliament did pass several laws aimed at reducing discrimination against women in marriage, divorce, and inheritance. The Guardian Council, however, vetoed them. Khatami has tried to forward women's causes: he has created in each ministry a department to look out for women's interests and financed dozens of women's NGOs and involved them in the formulation of his five-year plan.

Khatami ran for reelection in the June 2001 presidential elections and got an increased majority despite Iran's economic and other woes. He has been unable to make significant dents in Khamene'i's power, which is backed by his judiciary, intelligence, and armed forces. Khatami is unable even to exercise all the powers given him by the constitution, as he has publicly noted. He has opposed attempts to change the constitution as inevitably being controlled by conservatives and has also opposed public actions that might lead to violence. It is not surprising that more and more people have given up on him as a leader of meaningful reform.

Optimists point to the proliferation of NGOs and other organizations of civil society, a term popularized by Khatami and other reformers. They note that the first local and municipal elections saw reformist victories and allowed the decentralization of some functions. New ideas expressed in film, literature, and even from the pulpit have led to a widespread discourse favoring human rights, legal reform, and pluralism. Women have gained ever-increasing roles in education and society, even if they have achieved few legal reforms. Ridding the ministry of information of several assassins is another achievement.

Probably Khatami's greatest achievement has been to help to popularize the idea of democracy and to make the government somewhat more open. Many varied books are published, and the expanded media and public debate has brought many discussions about the rule of law, civil society, and a variety of interpretations and rejections of velayat-e faqih. Some secular and religious intellectuals had already been discussing such things, but Khatami reached a much larger national audience. He changed a former debate about "American Islam" versus "authentic Islam" to one distinguishing a peaceful, compassionate Islam from a violent, regressive one.

After the severe repression of the student-led movement of 1999 there was less reformist protest until 2002. Then, on November 6 a death sentence was passed on the history professor Hashem Aghajari for a June speech rejecting the doctrine that all Shi'is should follow a leading cleric and saying that imitation was for monkeys while people could themselves see the meaning of Islam. Throughout November, the sentence gave rise to a large and lengthy student-led protest movement. President Khatami announced as a result that the death sentence was inappropriate and would not be applied, while Khamene'i told the courts to reconsider and revise it.

The leaders of today's reform movement include many former radicals and members of the Islamic Left, including Akbar Ganji, Abbas Abdi, and others. Many have become wary about revolution and attempts for change that might provoke governmental crackdowns. Hence some current movements try to steer a course between doing nothing and provoking the Islamic Right. Yet a radicalization of reformers and a spread of protests has occurred, mainly owing to the Right's unwillingness to follow the will of the people, who voted overwhelmingly for reform in four elections.

In fall 2002, the reformist majles passed two bills to expand the powers of the elected president and limit the Guardian Council's powers to veto legislation—bills that the Guardian Council would have to approve or reject. Reaction by the Right began with the arrest of authorized public opinion researchers, whose polls showed that 74 percent of respondents favored negotiating with the United States and 64 percent favored opening relations with it. Abbas Abdi, Hossein-Ali Ghazian, and Behrooz Geranpayeh were arrested and sentenced to several years in prison as a result.[14] An even more devastating poll showed 94 percent of respondents saying Iran was in urgent need of reform and 71 percent backing a referendum to choose a new form of government.[15] The death sentence handed down to Aghajari was part of a new wave of right-wing backlash. Several Iranian intellectuals have spoken out boldly, as in open letters to the Leader and in a manifesto of republicanism by Ganji. (Oppositional lay and clerical writings are discussed in the next chapter.)

The reform movement is in transition and its members are learning and changing. Khatami never claimed to want to bring about a Western-style secular democracy but has talked about Islamic democracy, without clarifying its meaning. Since he came in, despite the newspaper closings and trials that get the most publicity in the West, people still speak out far more, publish new ideas, and in the arts and personal conduct repression is far less severe than it was. Khatami's tenure has opened space to talk and voice alternatives to the ruling elite's approach. Also, Khatami has helped to keep the opposition nonviolent, which has split the conservative camp. Among conservatives some now talk about competing with the reform movement and others about eliminating it. Only time will tell how important this split is.[16]

Many of the nongovernmental reformers, particularly among the youth, have lost faith in Khatami and other governmental reformers and think only a popular movement can bring results. This group is sometimes called the third force to distinguish it from governmental reformers. They consider the current reformist-conservative struggle in the government as an insider power struggle among elites that are part of the system. Those in the third force want the reformers to go much further and do not share all the governmental reformers' viewpoints. Many of them argue for a secular democracy, whereas the governmental reformers and those who support them are calling for evolutionary change in the system rather than a new system. To some degree this is a difference in aims, but with many people it is mainly a difference in what is considered possible—some who might prefer secular democracy think an evolutionary and gradual approach is the only way to avoid more serious crackdowns and defeat.

There is no unanimity among either Iranian or foreign experts as to whether the current complex situation, with the numerous major domestic and foreign questions still pending in early 2003, should lead to optimism or pessimism about Iran's short-term future. A January 2003 survey in *The Economist* saw political deadlock between conservatives and reformers as prolonging economic deadlock:

> political deadlock means economic deadlock. . . . The clerics dare not abandon their control over the state enterprises and *bonyads*. They dare not antagonize their supporters in the bazaars with a programme of privatization, deregulation and freer trade. Nor do they dare risk a mass uprising by reforming the subsidy system . . . [even though it] helps the better-off much more than the poor. Iran cries out for a proper welfare system, directed at those most in need. . . . Meanwhile, it may be asked, who will provide the jobs for the burgeoning number of young people? . . . with job-creation lagging behind the increase in the labour force . . . and registered unemployment of 16% (probably five points below the true figure), the number of people out of work can only rise.[17]

A recent analysis by Jahangir Amuzegar is more optimistic about the economy, while stressing the virtual universality of discontent:

> A recent study leaked from Iran's Interior Ministry revealed that nearly 90 percent of the public is dissatisfied with the present government. Of this total, 28 percent wants "fundamental" changes in the regime's struc-

ture, and 66 percent desires "gradual reforms." Less than 11 percent—most probably those on the government dole—is satisfied with the status quo. Other private polls show an even greater degree of unhappiness with the government.

The combination of these two phenomena—the bankruptcy of Iran's ideology and the failure of its economy—now confronts the Islamic Republic with the worst challenge to its legitimacy yet. The public and the press now openly question the role of Islam—and especially the concept of the *velayat-e faqih*—in a society where people want greater freedom and the rule of law.[18]

Amuzegar sees some recent positive economic developments, partly brought on by pressure from international economic institutions whose help Iran needs, although several of those changes he lists were, when he listed them, plans rather than current realities. Amuzegar thinks that economic reform may continue and, by undermining the elite's power, will help the growing political opposition movement to take power.[19] Some, though far from all, persons who have been to Iran recently note the rise in GDP over the past few years (mainly because of high oil prices) and stress the positive elements of economic changes that have occurred since the revolution.[20]

One positive note in early 2003 was the authorities' lifting of the house arrest of Grand Ayatollah Montazeri after five years. Montazeri had been confined to his home in Qom, since November 1997, when he said Iran's supreme leader, Khamene'i, was not competent to issue religious rulings. He has been in deteriorating health and calls increased in January 2003 to lift the house arrest—even in hard-line newspapers. More than one hundred Iranian legislators had called on President Khatami as the head of the Supreme National Security Council to lift the restrictions on Montazeri.[21] Some think the authorities did not want to risk popular reaction to his dying while under house arrest. After being freed, Montazeri resumed his strong verbal attacks on the ruling elite. Other positive changes reported in February 2003 were an end to stoning as a (rare) punishment and the pardoning of those jailed Jews who had not already been freed.[22]

Complicating Iran's internal problems are new foreign relations realities that began after September 11, 2001. Iran helped the United States, especially in Afghanistan, where Iran backed the Northern Alliance, aided in the installation of Hamid Karzai, reined in some of Iran's Shi'i supporters, and strongly opposed the Taliban. Iranians were therefore

shocked when President George W. Bush in January 2002 linked Iran
with Iraq and North Korea as part of an "axis of evil," based largely
on its supposed pursuit of nuclear weapons, though there were also U.S.
allegations of ties to terrorism. Iran says it is not pursuing nuclear
weapons, is open to inspection, and is opposed to terrorism, and it has
turned over al-Qaeda members to Saudi Arabia for trial. It regards pro-
Palestinian groups like Lebanon's Hizbollah as fighters against Israeli
occupation of Palestinian land who are using the only weapons available
to nongovernmental groups, not as terrorists.

Iran by early 2003 had limited cooperation with the United States,
having allowed the Shi'i Iraqi group based in Iran to meet and cooperate
with the Iraqi opposition abroad, and, in January 2003, allowing Iraqi
exile oppositionists to come into Iran and meet with Iraqi oppositionists
in Iran and with Khamene'i's people.[23] Iran, however, fears a further
growth of U.S. power on its borders and believes it could be the next target of U.S. attack, supported by Israel. In late March, U.S. Secretary of
Defense Donald Rumsfeld warned Iran against allowing anti-Saddam
Iraqis in Iran to fight. Hostile U.S. statements, including several by various prominent Americans, that the United States expects the current
Iranian regime to fall soon have had the opposite effect from what they
intended—they strengthen the hard-liners and create suspicion of those
who want better relations with the United States. Even though polls indicate that most Iranians want such relations, too much should not be made
of such sentiments. In the Muslim world today, as in Eastern Europe
during the Cold War, Americans are most popular in countries where the
United States has little or no presence. This popularity is unlikely to
continue during or after an aggressive war or bombing of suspected
nuclear facilities, or even after a long Iraq occupation. Nor is the Iranian
government necessarily as close to collapse or fundamental change as
either the United States or many Iranians wish. The situation is too
complex for anyone reliably to predict its outcome, and continued U.S.
sanctions, statements of support of those who want to overthrow the
government, and new U.S. intervention are all likely to be unhelpful.[24]
Many Iranians think that they are next on the U.S. attack list, and some
statements by U.S. government figures give support to this idea.[25] Iranians should be allowed to work out their future for themselves, and both
social and political developments suggest that in the long term popular
forces will gain enough strength to bring about significant change.

12

Society, Gender, Culture, and Intellectual Life

Many social and cultural changes have taken place in Iran since the revolution, several of which have influenced or been influenced by the political and economic changes discussed in chapters 10 and 11. Some areas of society, culture, and gender relations contrast with the often negative picture of political and economic trends described in those chapters, though nearly all embody contradictions and do not mitigate disillusionment with the regime. These more positive developments have several aspects: some are due to largely successful government programs in rural development, health, family planning, and education, including the unanticipated consequences of such programs, while others owe more to struggles by women, young people, professionals, ethnic minorities, and some in the popular classes. In all areas change has been partial, and dissatisfaction continues and has even been fanned by change.

Society, Education, Health

Some important social changes have occurred in the largely successful efforts to improve the lives of rural populations through technology and health care and to expand all levels of education for both genders to the entire country. Two other major changes have been the rapid pace of urbanization, so that the great majority of the population now lives in a variety of urban areas, and an unusually dramatic demographic transition, changing from rapid population increase until the late 1980s to a dramatic lowering of birthrates since then. Urbanization and education, despite the religious limits on curricula, have engendered wide dissatisfaction with the strict social controls posed by the clerical government, to which poor economic performance has also contributed. In recent years a cultural and intellectual explosion has given voice to many new ideas in the arts and in political and religious discourse. These trends have been felt to varying degrees in different areas, and here there will be less space than the topics deserve to deal with important differences, especially among nomadic tribes, among ethnic and religious minorities, and among social classes.

The social organization of the economy changed significantly after the revolution, and a few areas showed improvement. One resulted from a new emphasis on improving rural conditions. The Reconstruction Jihad (*jehad-e sazandegi*) began as a movement of volunteers to help with the 1979 harvest but soon took on a broader, more official role and carried out, with the help of local populations, programs that included road building, piped water, electrification, clinics, schools, and irrigation canals. The lack of radical land reform meant that few lands were distributed to the peasants, but in other ways rural life generally improved.

Two other areas in which the Islamic Republic has had an impressive record are education and public health. Achievements have been notable in rural and impoverished areas and have been especially felt by women and children. In the field of education, schools received substantial governmental funding, including school construction in villages and poor neighborhoods. The accessibility of schools made it easier for girls to attend, as did the enforcement of single-sex primary and secondary schools (which had been dominant even before) and religious leaders' endorsement of girls' education. Though education before university level remains mostly rote memorization and includes some religious emphasis, most of the curriculum remains secular. Under the new regime not only did literacy among young males and females approach universality, but also the percentage of females among university admissions continually rose, until they were about 66 percent by 2003. Possible explanations for girls' greater achievement are that girls have fewer permitted activities away from home and do more homework, and that low teacher salaries mean that women who teach in girls' schools are more qualified and motivated than the men who teach in boys' schools, as women have less access to higher-paying jobs.

Following an early period during which a few subjects were barred or had quotas, today nearly all university subjects are open to women. Almost every village has a school. Female literacy rose from 36 percent in 1976 to 72 percent in 1996—a level comparable to Turkey and over double that in Pakistan—and is still rising. Although textbooks mostly show women in traditional family roles, there has been some reform in such depictions.[1] There is also an effective adult literacy program.

While universities were closed and purged for three years, with great losses of students, teachers, and intellectual life, they have in recent years gradually become freer, and some classes cover liberal Western thinkers and even Marx. At first, women were barred from several subjects, and men could not study gynecology, though existing male gynecologists continued to practice. The effective campaign to lift these restrictions in the late 1980s was spearheaded by Zahra Rahnavard, the wife of ex–prime minister Mir-Hosain Musavi. Al-Zahra University for women, based on a prerevolutionary institute, is now a serious university-level institution, led by the same Zahra Rahnavard. Despite great advances in university education, both male and female graduates face high levels of unemployment. Also, the shortage of facilities and teachers at all levels as well as low pay, which leads university teachers especially to hold several jobs, means that the quality of education has generally fallen. Ideological indoctrination has been largely unsuccessful, judging from surveys of high school and university students and from student protests.

At the time of the revolution, health care was a major problem and particularly affected women and children. Poverty, lack of services, and early and frequent childbearing contributed to high maternal and infant mortality rates. Successive governments channeled impressive resources into health programs, especially in remote, deprived areas. A key program was the creation of a grassroots primary health care network that has transformed access to health care in many areas. From 1985 to 1997 maternal mortality rates dropped from 140 deaths per 100,000 live births to 37.[2] Infant mortality rates were also slashed.

Regarding family planning the government did an amazing U-turn at the end of the 1980s. Although birth control was never outlawed, the emphasis of the Islamic Republic from 1979 to 1988 was on population growth. As mortality rates declined, however, population skyrocketed, with no employment in sight for many. There was an abrupt turnaround in policies in 1988–89 so that, by learning from other countries and adding the endorsement of most leading Muslim clergy, Iran developed one of the world's most effective programs. With the help of many involved in prerevolutionary family planning programs, the new program took off once Khomeini authorized it. Free family planning was reintroduced, and shortly thereafter sterilization was again permitted. Benefits for children were cut off after the first three.

The government says every couple should attend premarital classes, in which men and women are separately counseled on family planning and other issues.[3] Abortion is an emotional issue. Before the revolution it was allowed under certain conditions, but this was abolished. For the next twenty years it was allowed only if there was a risk to the mother's life, after which Khamene'i said it could be done if the unborn child had a severe disease. Illegal abortions continue, though their prevalence is unknown.

Iran's uniquely rapid success in lowering birthrates from the late 1980s had several causes: rapid urbanization always brings smaller families; health programs and lowered infant mortality meant couples knew most children would survive; the rise in female education contributed to rising marriage ages and greater women's initiative in family planning. Also important were the commitment of governmental and religious leaders; increasing economic difficulties that delay marriage and the desire to have children; and the preexistence of the primary health care networks providing a variety of services, to which the official birth control programs were wisely tied. In most villages health care began in the 1980s with a male and a female worker, usually a couple, who ran a health house. Both were trained for two years in care of mothers and children, family planning, and other health matters and then sent back to the village. By now most rural health clinics have trained doctors and nurses. All new doctors must repay their free medical education by serving for up to five years in village clinics before moving to a city. Pregnant women get free checkups. People know the doctors or health workers, who distribute condoms, pills, and even Norplant injections. They also visit schools and check children's health and record births, diseases, and deaths. Birthrates have fallen from among the highest in the Middle East to among the lowest. New births are slightly below replacement rates, while population growth, which reflects immigration and the babies born to earlier baby boom couples, is down to 1.2 percent.[4] Iran should continue to experience population growth while the large group of people born in the 1980s have children, but population should then level off and decline if current trends continue.

A rural health worker, Zinat Darya'i, became the subject of a dramatized documentary. She is from the Persian Gulf island of Qeshm, a poor and conservative region. She tells how her life changed when she abandoned the Gulf-Arab-style facemask, the *borqa* (the same word as the Afghan burqa, but a different garment). After working with foreign doctors as a girl, she went to Bandar Abbas to train, When she returned without a mask she was ostracized, but years later when she saved the life of a child she became a local heroine. Other stories of rural and urban health workers indicate similar evolutions from seclusion to health work and to public activity.[5]

While the urban primary health care system and that in remote rural areas have problems, Iran's primary health care system has numerous achievements. Every year the government mobilizes up to half a million volunteers in a mass immunization campaign. Less impressive are problems arising from drugs. While AIDS is a taboo subject, one doctor estimates the number of cases at twenty to thirty thousand. It is spread primarily among intravenous drug users, especially in jail. Authorities now include information about AIDS in their antidrug literature.

Drugs, from the traditional opium to processed heroin, are a major problem. In 1999 the government admitted there were more than a million addicts. Drug use is especially widespread among young people and is tied to the overall cynicism found among many who are not poor. According to researchers at the University of Tehran's Faculty of Social Science who have done extensive field research among drug users in Tehran, Qazvin, and Kerman, drugs are common among upper-class youth (who prefer the "recreational" drugs popular in Europe) and working-class youth (who prefer the traditional, cheaper opium), and less common among middle-class youth, whose parents are the most worried.[6] Nongovernmental organizations (NGOs), which have flourished since Khatami's election in 1997, have helped provide treatment and narcotics anonymous programs for a limited number of addicts.[7] In recent years Iran has become more open about its drug problem and willing to learn from the experience of other countries in combating it.

The conservative majles, after Khatami's 1997 election, pushed through a controversial 1998 bill segregating all health services for men and women, and saying that women should not be treated by men. Thousands of doctors and medical students signed a petition against it, so it was changed to give women the right to demand female doctors where possible. The Guardian Council sent it back to parliament as too expensive, but after the Ministry of Health gave funds it was passed. The students at an all-women's medical college in Qom protested against a segregation that meant they could have no male teachers, staff, or patients. Most of them transferred to coeducational medical schools elsewhere.

Important strides have thus been made in education and in primary health care. Improvements at grassroots level in water, sanitation, hygiene, and nutrition have especially helped the popular class and rural women and children. Nevertheless, continuing government support for laws and practices that institutionalize male supremacy, controls on the lives of women and young people, and continued economic crisis and hardship has made the positive changes in education and health only part of a less impressive total picture.

In the sphere of culture and behavior, the regime has often tried to impose its image of an Islamic society, based largely on the practices and beliefs of its most puritanical followers. In the first years of the revolution many cinemas were burned or closed, Iranian and Western pop music was forbidden (though not Iranian or Western classical music or Iranian folk music), the sexes were rigidly separated in all public places, dress codes were applied to both men and women, with those on women far more strict and limiting, and censorship was applied rigorously. Schools were made to give a central place to religious instruction, with recognized religious minorities allowed to add their own religion. In the Cultural Revolution of 1980–83, in great part a war against Western culture, many professors were dismissed, students expelled, cultural and scientific figures publicly denounced, and Iranian radio and television broadcast only religious and official programs. The Cultural Revolution was one reason many teachers and trained persons left Iran. One part of the program was to unite the theological schools of Qom with the universities, making secular teachers go for a time to Qom. This experiment had the unexpected effect of opening many students in Qom to Western thought, and today one finds clerics and teachers of theology who know something of contemporary Western thought and philosophy. In general, however, the Cultural Revolution greatly weakened Iran in the science and technology needed for development. Only students judged ideologically sound were sent abroad during the Cultural Revolution. Families with money who did not emigrate often sent their children abroad to study, and most of them remained abroad, as most still do. When the universities were reopened, war veterans and others tied to official religious politics got priority admission.

In 1982, with Rafsanjani's encouragement, the private Islamic Free University was established. It tried to reconcile religious and scientific education and also spread higher education into many towns and cities; its branches covered many more areas than did the few state universities. This theoretically Islamic university, which paid better salaries than the state universities, became less ideological than the state universities and also more appealing to many students, especially young women whose families might not want them to travel far from their homes. State universities also spread. The level of instruction is often low, as teachers must have several jobs to make ends meet, and there is little time for research. In the pragmatic trend that followed the Iran–Iraq war, the government emphasized science and technology and supported the building of universities and also sent students abroad. Although large numbers of students continued to study abroad, many have not returned.[8] Unemployment and unsuitable employment remain a major problem among the educated. Also, there are still to some extent "two cultures," the clerical and the modernized/westernized. The former is the domain of clerics, bazaaris, and some of the urban poor, and the latter of the growing educated middle and professional classes and most students. There is among the educated, however, more blending and compromise between the two than before, with many clerics studying Western thinkers and many reformers coming to terms with new interpretations of Islam.

Contrary to a widespread impression, young people are not much more numerous in Iran than in nearby countries, but they have a much more important political role, especially since voting rights begin at age fifteen. Partly because of the lack of recreational facilities, universities and also arts classes have taken the central place in the lives of many young people. There are more than 2 million annual applicants for the 150,000 places at the state universities. Private foreign language, arts, and computer courses are also very popular, as are many sports. Young people are often impatient and have many causes for despair with current conditions. Faced with this, the government has for the most part stopped cracking down hard on behavior: women can wear shorter coats and makeup and show more hair; boys and girls in big cities can be seen together, even holding hands. Certain gathering spots and walks in the mountains are places for the sexes to be together, while home parties and liquor can usually be managed with bribes. Intermittent crackdowns, however, create a climate of apprehension and discontent. Between forbidden television satellites, widely available tapes of all kinds, and the Internet, people are acutely aware of the contrast between restrictions on their lives and the freedoms in many other countries.

Women and the Family

The situation of women shows all the contradictions of the revolution. It was central to the clerical revolutionaries, who abrogated the Family Protection Law before any other law and reestablished sharia law. Despite the great limits on women's rights enforced in the first years of the revolution, several factors led to a partial comeback. Women reacted against the annulment of prerevolutionary reforms and their loss of jobs, especially public sphere jobs. Many women went to work in the private sphere and some became entrepreneurs and professionals. Even Islamist women became conscious of the need to change people's thought and behavior if women were to have the most elementary rights. In the Iran–Iraq war the government called on women to contribute. The war showed up major contradictions. According to Islamic law, war widows had to give custody of their children to their husbands' families. Protests against such injustices became effective, and this law and some other legal practices were reformed. Groups that were formerly opposed have united around specific issues. Men and women, secular and Islamic, from both sides of the cultural divide have worked together to achieve several goals, many of them women-oriented.

The groups that cooperated in the 1978–79 revolution thought women's issues could soon be solved if their own party took power, without any need for separate feminist efforts. The active participation of women in revolutionary politics, however, awakened the consciousness of many popular-class women about their political potential, and middle-class women increasingly acted to promote women's rights. Khomeini and his associates insisted on women's political mobilization, encouraged girls' education, and also supported women's activities during the Iran–Iraq war. At the same time they enforced many laws and practices unfavorable to women, barred the judiciary to women, and dismissed many professional women from their government jobs. Many middle-class women responded by entering the private sphere in novel ways and by going into areas open to them, like teaching, medicine, and the arts.[9]

Increasingly vocal opposition to policies that sanctioned polygamy, temporary marriage, free divorce for men, and child custody to fathers and their families came from women, especially in the women's press. Women majles deputies and others made similar arguments. For example, women produced Islamic arguments to limit polygamy strictly.

Women's magazines featured stories of the suffering women experienced under despotic husbands, such as wife-beatings, suicides, and loss of children. Publicity and activism brought some legal remedies in the 1980s, such as limits on a husband's right to stop his wife from taking a job. A new marriage contract was introduced that spelled out husbands' behavior that would give the wife the right to divorce. These and later changes moved in the direction of restoring aspects of the annulled Family Protection Law.[10] The reformed provisions in marriage contracts were, however, valid only if the groom signed them. Judges became more sensitive to women's rights as a result of struggles, and when reforms did not make it through the legislative process the government tried to mitigate some injustices by instructions to the courts.

After struggles, a limited divorce reform bill passed parliament in 1989, saying divorces had to have court permission before being registered, though studies suggest that male applications were almost never denied.[11] Sometimes provisions once denounced by clerics as secular heresies passed parliament as Islamic reforms, and even when reform was limited the climate of publicity and struggle favored better treatment of women.

A novel trend of women interpreting Islam in more gender-egalitarian ways became important with the entry of more religious women into the public sphere and the limitation of discourse to Islamic parameters. Many women felt the shock of being deprived of rights after the revocation of the Family Protection Law, and many were hurt by the imposition of severe controls and punishments regarding behavior. Some women mastered technical forms of Islamic argumentation after the government opened higher religious education to women. More girls were being educated, which made them more sensitive to their loss of rights. The few Islamist women elected to the first parliament were unable to get even timid proposals for women's rights passed. But there soon developed a new group of Islamist women, some related to major political figures, who pressed women's causes more effectively. Many women became successful entrepreneurs, and others entered highly visible professions. The women's press became both a profession and a rallying point.

The new women's press, begun in the 1980s, developed and flourished especially in the 1990s, as an important part of press liberalization. The prerevolutionary magazine *Zan-e Ruz,* which changed its tone after the revolution, became a platform for opposing family laws and practices with new interpretations of Islam and included discussion of several women's demands. Following a disagreement with others in *Zan-e Ruz,* editor Shahla Sherkat quit it and launched the monthly *Zanan* in February 1992, which became notable for its gender-egalitarian stance and for including articles by men and women, Islamic and secular, including secular Iranian women living abroad. The prominent secular lawyer Mehrangiz Kar was a frequent contributor. It also carried articles by the reformist cleric Hojjat ol-Islam Saidzadeh. Many of the arguments in *Zanan* included reinterpretations of Islam. They stressed the egalitarian spirit of those Quranic verses that address both men and women and interpreted inegalitarian verses, such as those allowing polygamy, as due to temporary circumstances. They say authentic Islam is gender-egalitarian, and inegalitarian laws are deviations caused by prejudice.

Articles in *Zanan* defending women's right to be judges were followed by some doing the same on other grounds in the more conservative journal of the Islamic Center in Qom, *Payam-e Zan.* Despite a press and political campaign, women cannot be regular judges, but a 1995 modification of the law allows them to be consulting judges, especially in matters regarding the family and minors, and in practice they often make judicial decisions.

Advancement of women's causes, primarily due to cooperation between secular and Islamic women, has also seen the growing involvement both of secular men and of reformist clerics. They are a minority and must choose their words carefully in a clerical context still dominated by conservatism. These current allies have compromised in order to work together. As stated in an interview by the prominent secular lawyer Mehrangiz Kar in 1996, "The revolution gave women confidence in themselves. With all the sacrifices they made, Iranian women know how much their current and future rulers owe them and that egalitarian rights are part of what is due to them. This demand is no longer that of a group of women; it is a nationwide one. The Islamic government cannot escape it without risking a brutal separation of the state and religion."[12]

Reformist interpretations of Islam are not new in the Muslim world, but in the Middle East they have not hitherto been adopted by so many traditionally educated clerics or by so many women from a great variety of social backgrounds. Combined with the salience of reform leaders in Iran's government and public sphere, the Iranian women's movement is beginning to have an impact beyond Iran's borders in addition to the transformations it is bringing to Iran. There has been unprecedented gender solidarity among Islamic and secular activists, with, for example, secularists like Mehrangiz Kar, the jurist Shirin Ebadi, and the film director Tahmineh Milani contributing to women's magazines with a theoretically Islamic orientation.[13]

Iran's census, like many in the Global South, seriously undercounts women's work. Its low figures for women's work in rural and nomadic contexts have little meaning. Nomadic women usually work more than men—this includes caring for animals and plants, gathering food, and doing all the weaving of knotted carpets and flat weave items, many of which are sold and contribute to family income. In Gilan and Mazanderan rural women work in the fields, and elsewhere do important work in or close to home; in many areas they take part in harvesting. Rural and tribal women are usually not counted as part of the labor force. In urban areas small commodity producers and both male and female workers who are employed by medium or small private enterprises are often not declared as being in the workforce, in order to evade paying tax and insurance.[14]

Cultural attitudes and home workloads still limit the number of working-class women who work in a now-predominantly urban Iran. In the years right after 1979 many factories closed and the number of working-class women declined, but in recent years economic pressures and the growth of consumerism have intensified the felt need for two incomes, and increasing numbers of men have accepted a working wife. Many middle- and upper-class women work. Women who lost jobs or found themselves shut out after the revolution were often more resourceful than men in carving out new working lives. They went in unprecedented numbers into business and the professions, including medicine and law and also into writing and the arts, including a significant presence in filmmaking. The proportion of women employed is higher than the figures in the low teens that are often cited. A women-endorsed measure to allow part-time work without loss of benefits has encouraged this trend.

With the continued rapid growth of female education and urbanization, two factors that correlate dramatically with falling birthrates worldwide, birthrates can be expected to fall even further, and low birthrates may ease burdens on women and bring more into the labor force. In the meantime, however, the current large number of children and youths, along with a "child-centered" trend also known elsewhere, of parents' having to take children to special classes and activities and supervise their homework, have increased burdens for many middle-class women.[15]

The story of women in sports is a dramatic area of advance and successful women's struggles and now involves far more women and girls than in the prerevolutionary period. The scene has been transformed from one in which the government successfully discouraged women's sports to one in which a growing numbers of girls and women pursue team and individual sports. Sports are "Islamically" legitimized by allowing sports that involve showing the body to be played where only women are present. Although their participation has aroused some opposition, women also increasingly take part in sports where they are seen by men, including skiing, waterskiing, and bicycling, however encumbering the clothing they must wear.[16] Women, barred from being spectators at men's soccer matches, broke through into a stadium in a politically significant 1997 event, and in early 2003 one soccer club announced it would admit female spectators.

The terrain of women's rights is one of unprecedented cooperation among disparate groups on the one hand and severe ideological and political struggles on the other. Ties with women in other countries via international conferences, travel, and the press and media have helped to promote reform.[17] Some secular reformers criticize other secularists' cooperation with Islamic reformists. They note that most of the sharia-based inegalitarian laws are still in force, including the need for a father's permission for a first marriage, polygamy, temporary marriage, and de facto free divorce for men. They say the achievements of reform to date should not be exaggerated, and the task of getting an egalitarian interpretation of the sharia enacted may prove impossible. To this, others respond that pressing for reform within the Islamic framework has accomplished some important changes and may be the only way to progress in Iran today, although the recent growth of secular arguments may open up new channels.

It is possible, as some say, that no regime that styles itself Islamic and bases its law on the sharia can become truly gender-egalitarian. But the possibility of evolution to something parallel to Christian democracy, a largely secular and democratic form of rule, should not be ruled out. This is what is advocated by the reformist thinker Abdol Karim Soroush, who says that true Islam is unknowable, and so we must work with varying interpretations of it.

Many women are deeply conscious of social injustice toward them. A few dare to take unprecedented protests, notably that on International Women's Day, March 8, 2003, calling for women's equality and an end to Guardian Council vetoes of measures to end discrimination that have been approved by the majles.

Other social changes affecting women and families have been confirmed by recent research. Among them is a change in the affective life in cities, including even clerically dominated Qom. Most fathers are no longer the remote patriarchal figures they once were, and sons and daughters no longer consider their fathers inflexible lawgivers. Fathers' statements can be questioned, and they have become more empathetic. This is paralleled by Khatami's image as a charismatic brother, whereas Khomeini was seen as a superfather or grandfather. Urban families of many classes have been modernized since 1979, with change particularly noticeable among girls, who with their greatly increased access to modern education and to the universities no longer accept everything that their fathers want for them.[18]

Urban marriage patterns have also changed. Before 1979 most Iranian young people, with exceptions among modernized classes, accepted arranged marriages. Marriage has now become a matter of negotiation between parents and children. It is still often not an issue of personal choice, but it is no longer simply imposed; girls discuss marriage with their parents and play an active role in it. Marriages after the first one have long been more products of individual choice.

The Arts: Especially Film

The early revolutionary rulers put strict limits on the arts, outlawing some forms of music and artistic representations of uncovered bodies and censoring printed works and the media. These limits, like the prohibition of alcohol and dress rules, were widely flouted in private homes, and increasingly in more public places. There were also distinctions among them; printed works could and still can often publish ideas that would not be tolerated elsewhere, and many varied foreign books were allowed in and even translated. Mohammad Khatami, minister of culture and Islamic guidance from 1983 to 1992, encouraged the easing of censorship rules and the expansion of Iranian cinema. Although cinema is only one of the many arts that have flourished in recent years, it is the best known and is studied worldwide and hence will be emphasized here. The trends seen in film, toward increasing freedom and sophistication, are also found in the other arts.

Cinema in Iran has a history going back to the early twentieth century, but the first "world-class" films are generally considered to be two 1969 works by New Wave directors, Dariush Mehrju'i's *The Cow* and Mas'ud Kimia'i's *Qeisar*. There were other good films in this realistic genre until the mid-1970s. There was also much clerical and religious hostility to cinema, which resulted in many theaters being closed or even burned down in the revolutionary period. From 1979 to 1982 most existing Iranian and foreign films were banned, and there was almost no support for new films. To support a revival of filmmaking with approved content, the cabinet in June 1982 issued new regulations, charging the Ministry of Culture and Islamic Guidance (MCIG) to carry them out. All films and videos needed an exhibition permit. Among the grounds for denying a permit were various forms of insult to Islam, to other recognized religions, and to the Islamic Republic; encouraging prostitution, addiction, or bad behavior like smuggling; negating people's equality regardless of color, language, and belief; hurting Iran in the interest of foreigners; or showing details of violence and torture. Women were to be chaste, good mothers, but also have a useful social role and not used to arouse sexual desire.[19] They also had to be "Islamically" dressed, even in the home.

Until 1989 all film ideas had to undergo five stages at the MCIG to be shown: it reviewed the synopsis, approved the screenplay, issued a production permit, reviewed the completed film, and then issued the permit. Many scripts were disallowed, and many films were made but not released. In December 1987 Khomeini lightened morality codes, in April 1989 some previously banned films were released, and then approval for screenplays was dropped. From the mid-1980s various measures improved the financing of film. Films were produced by a variety of public, semipublic, and private institutions. Ideologically approved films, often with social content and stressing ethics, were made by several groups, including the Foundation for the Dispossessed and the Jihad (later Ministry) for Reconstruction. Many women entered the film industry in all capacities, including numerous directors.

The first important films dealing with real people and, as became common, without any religious themes were Amir Naderi's *The Runner* (1986), Mehrju'i's *The Tenants* (1986), and Bahram Beyza'i's, *Bashu, The Little Stranger* (1988). Mehrju'i's film was a popular social satire, while the other two films had elements that typified many later Iranian art films—children as leading characters and locations and persons far from Tehran, sometimes featuring non-Persian ethnic groups. Children were partly chosen as their lives could be treated holistically, without the restrictions on intergender contact or adult discourse that limited realistic depiction of adults. Adult themes played an increasing role, however.

Iranian films began to appear at international festivals, win numerous prizes, and become earners of needed hard currency.[20] Though the serious films known abroad were less popular at home than more commercial films or than the foreign films that entered in various legal and illegal ways, they remained important to Iranian cultural and intellectual discourse. As Richard Tapper notes, many questions dealt with in contemporary film are core questions of modern Iranian identity:

> Iran as homeland and Persian as dominant language and culture, modernity ... and Shi'a Islam ... In the twentieth century, extreme versions of all three original elements of *iraniyat* have been tried and have failed: Iranian nationalism/Persian chauvinism; westernization/top-down modernization; Islamic fundamentalism. There is now a widely perceived imperative to negotiate an acceptable balance ... together with a strong movement, massively supported by the youth and women ... to reject the traditional politics of monopolization of power, control, secrecy and violence, in favour of democracy, transparency and political, religious and ethnic pluralism.
>
> Cinema has become a major focus and arena for these discussions and debates.[21]

Continuing censorship means that political questions are usually broached in films only implicitly and symbolically, but many films show realistically the problems of women, of the poor, and of remote regions and ethnic minorities.

Many directors have made important films, only a few of which can be mentioned. The best-known internationally is Abbas Kiarostami, whose films include three about a region of northern Iran made before and soon after a major earthquake: *Where Is the Friend's House?* (1987), about a small boy's struggle to return a school homework notebook to a friend; *Life and Nothing Else,* which shows the devastating effects of the earthquake, and *Through the Olive Trees* (1994), about casting a film in the region; it depicts a cross-class relationship between teenagers and the active role of women in filmmaking. His *The Taste of Cherry* (1997), about a Tehran man who picks up men from various classes and ethnic groups to help him in a planned suicide, won the highest prize at the Cannes Film Festival. His new *Ten* concerns a divorcee and the passengers she picks up while driving around Tehran. Kiarostami is known for apparently simple, realistic stories with humanistic themes.

Also well known is Mohsen Makhmalbaf, who started as a fiercely committed Islamist but later changed his views and made a wide variety of films, among them *The Cyclist* (1989), about a poor man who must exhaust himself by riding a bicycle in circles for twenty-four hours to feed himself and his small daughter, and *Gabbeh* (1995), a lyrical, romantic, and visually spectacular view of the Qashqa'i nomads. Makhmalbaf also formed a kind of home film school, and his young daughter Samireh Makhmalbaf has directed *The Apple* (1998) from a true story of young girls who were literally never allowed outside the house, and *Black-boards* (1999), which won the jury prize at Cannes. Makhmalbaf's wife, Marzieh Meshkini, directed the imaginative three-episode film, *The Day I Became a Woman* (2000), set in the Gulf island Qeshm, with its many African-Iranian inhabitants.

Other important women directors include Rakhshan Bani-Etemad and Tahmineh Milani, whose strongly feminist and critical *Two Women* (1999) created much controversy. Popular directors especially of films featuring children include Majid Majidi, with *Children of Heaven* (1997) and *The Color of Paradise* (1999), and Jafar Panahi, with *The White Balloon* (1995).

There have also been several important documentaries and films that combine documentary footage with reenactments. One documentary is *Divorce Iranian Style* (1998) by the London-based Ziba Mir-Hosseini and the British filmmaker Kim Longinotto. It shows the efforts of several determined and articulate Iranian women in court to try to get divorces. Although one woman had a good legal case she had to compromise by giving up the delayed dower due her under Islamic law in return for a quick divorce, while another's efforts to circumvent the Islamic law giving fathers custody of even young children in the event of his ex-wife's remarriage were futile.

Despite bans since 1994 on television satellites they remain common, and every sort of video is easily available, as is every kind of recorded music. After Khatami's election some previously banned films were released. Among them Davud Mirbaqeri's *The Snowman,* which dealt with banned themes like transvestism, unveiled women, homosexuality, and drinking, brought physical attacks on the theaters showing it. In Khatami's presidential years some previous film taboos were broken. *Under the Moonlight* (2001) by Seyyed Reza Mir-Karimi, which won the Critics' Week Prize at Cannes, deals with a young cleric-in-training who, during a crisis of faith, joins homeless men living under a bridge in Tehran and encounters poverty, prostitution, and drugs. Ebrahim Hatamikia's *Low Heights* (2002) shows a reality-based story of a jobless man from war-ravaged Khuzistan who hijacks a plane in the hope of getting employment outside Iran. Hatamikia is known for films depicting the Iran–Iraq war's impact on Iran.

A filmmaker who began work in the 1970s New Wave with films including *Prince Ehtejab* is Bahman Farmanara, whose 1978 film *Tall Shadows in the Wind* was banned under both the shah and Khomeini. When the censors finally relented regarding his proposed films in 2000 he triumphed with the prizewinning *Smell of Camphor, Fragrance of Jasmine,* a black comedy in which he plays a filmmaker obsessed with making a documentary about his own funeral. His *A House Built on Water* (2002), showing a drunken doctor who deals with young drug addicts and seekers of abortion and restored virginity, has played internationally but, as of early 2003, had not been approved for Iranian release.

Iranian cinema has ironically benefited as well as suffered from government controls because if foreign films were allowed in freely Iranian films could lose much of their domestic audience. Also, in many parts of the world, such as China, pre-1990 Eastern Europe, and Iran, where censorship limits the direct expression of ideas, film becomes a center for the best minds, themes, and ideas.

Long sections could equally have been presented here about several other arts. There has been a flowering, especially in the past decade, of novels, short stories, and poetry, many of them, as in prerevolutionary years, written by women and often, like films, expressing views of contemporary problems. Many young people are studying the fine arts and music, and this has resulted in significant production. In the early postrevolutionary years visual art was mostly a clerical version of "socialist realism," but now it has a great range of styles, from re-creations of traditional miniatures and calligraphy, to paintings and sculpture that use traditional elements in new ways or combined with modern ones, to varieties of modern art. Often far more of a woman is shown in pictures or sculptures than can be seen on the street. Restrictions on music have been relaxed and at least in big cities there are many concerts of traditional art and folk music, both Persian and of other ethnic groups, and of Western classical music, many of them of high quality.[22] Western pop music is available on cassettes and influences music played in homes and in some concerts.

Intellectual Trends: Lay and Clerical

In recent years there has been a flowering of new religious and political ideas. There are many who hold largely secular views and combine in different degrees various forms of nationalism, feminism, and social democracy; these views cannot always be safely expressed in their entirety in print and are often rather similar to their Western counterparts, although many secularists may feel it more necessary to speak of Islam than most secularists do of Christianity in today's West.

Although it is critics of the political and religious status quo and governing system who get the most attention in discussions of Iranian intellectual life (including those in this volume), there are other intellectual developments, some supported by the government, that contribute to the spread of knowledge and debate. Great attention, for example, is given to serious studies of history, notably the history of the Qajar period, with countless memoirs and travelogues from that period being edited and published. Documents from the Pahlavi and earlier periods have been gathered and made available to scholars. Regional and local history is also stressed, with local histories written for almost every town. There are numerous high quality academic journals on topics including architecture, Iran's cultural heritage, and history and regional interests. The government promotes and subsidizes such projects, as it does many international conferences, and even offers book prizes to foreign works on Iranian topics. While this may in part be seen as propaganda (as is also true of many government-supported cultural efforts in other countries) it is notable in welcoming international, chiefly Western, contributions to the study of Iran more than they were welcomed before the revolution or than such studies are welcomed in many other countries. Cooperative research projects, especially in the social sciences, with French and other European and Japanese scholars, have resulted in important publications. This all reflects changes in governmental and nongovernmental attitudes toward the West, which had focused overwhelmingly on damages caused by imperialism, and toward Iranian history, which in the 1980s and beyond had been overwhelmingly manipulated to create a past in which clerics were almost the only positive leaders.[23] This change is also seen in university and even seminary teaching of modern Western philosophers, including many with views far distant from those of Iran's rulers. Numerous books about Iran with views far from official clericalism are quickly translated and published and often become the focus of discussion, while books and articles published in Iran continue to raise critical arguments.[24]

Regarding more critical trends, the press, whose women's branch was discussed above, has been a major force in intellectual and political development, especially since 1989, and in many ways took the place of political parties and their platforms and debates. Some semi-oppositional periodicals began even before Khatami's opening of the press, and many more newspapers and periodicals followed. They published a variety of critical views and discussed with extensive freedom and originality most of the important social, cultural, and intellectual issues of the day. Serious crackdowns on the press began after the government's attack on reformists following the spring 2000 conference in Berlin. For a time, however, once a newspaper was closed it could open again with a new name and the same staff and profile. As noted in chapter 11, the conservatives who controlled the majles until the spring of 2000 amended the press law to say that banned periodicals could no longer reappear with different names. The press court closed most reformist newspapers, and several journalists have been arrested, though critical press articles, periodicals, and newspapers have not been completely quashed.

Some journalists voiced views similar to those of the main clerical and nonclerical writers of books and treatises containing theoretical critiques of Iran's religio-political system, and some journalists went further. Notable is the journalist Akbar Ganji, who in a 1997 lecture called conservative advocates of totalitarian Islam fascists and explicated that term. The lecture's publication brought his arrest. Several of his articles were published in January 2000 as a book titled *The Fascist Interpretation of Religion and Government: Pathology of Transition to the Democratic*

and Development-Oriented State. Its preface favored rationalist and
mystic readings of Islam and not "the reduction of religion to its husk
and to dry customs, and the violent imposition of the jurisprudential
reading on humankind." Ganji also alleged that high-ranking clerics
were involved in the murders of about one hundred dissidents during
1989–97. He was twice imprisoned—first for a year and then, in 2002, on
a six-year sentence—but his book continued to be reprinted and widely
discussed.[25] His latest treatise, known as the "Manifesto of Republicanism" (2002), written in prison, criticizes even Khomeini and also the
ineffectiveness of governmental reformers. He calls for a separation of
religion and state and for liberal democracy.

Serious intellectual writings and discussions involving secularists, religious liberals, and reformist clerics have grown since the early 1990s,
and even when their outlets in the periodical press were restricted, books
and treatises could still be published. Lively and passionate debates cover
a variety of issues, only a few of which can be dealt with here. Thinkers
who have written since 1990 are generally more sophisticated and more
knowledgeable about a variety of Western and Islamic sources than were
their intellectual predecessors. These predecessors, like their contemporaries in many parts of the world, if they were politically oriented,
tended to have ideological views that emphasized one factor as central to
solving Iran's problems—whether class, economics, and socialism for the
Marxists, science, nationalism, or racism for many modernizers, or varying interpretations of Islam for both Islamic modernists and Islamic conservatives. (Similar simplifications were also characteristic of many intellectuals elsewhere.) Nearly all tended to stress foreign imperialist evils far
more than internal reasons for Iran's problems. Reformists who stressed
Islam usually took the path known as Islamic modernism—basically the
claim that all the positive values they had seen in the West—science,
representative government, a better position for women, and so forth—
were found in Islam if it were rightly understood. The Mojahedin-e
Khalq, Shariati, and Khomeini had different views of Islam, but all were
ideological and convinced that their path would solve the problems of the
world. The popularity in the Pahlavi period of ideological views, especially Marxism-Leninism and nationalism, helped encourage competing
political-ideological constructions of Islam, the most influential being
those of Shariati and Khomeini (see chapter 8). Thinkers of the 1990s
were more complex and sophisticated; they broke with ideologies that
implied that ideological correctness could bring about an ideal society.

They also considered Western ideas to be complex and varied, not a solution to all problems (as had some earlier Iranian nationalists), not simple extensions of ideas already present in Islam or Iran, and not, alternatively, simply dangerous aspects of imperialism. Several of the new thinkers are well acquainted with both Western and Islamic thought, and, unlike many of their ideological predecessors, do not think huge social advances can be attained suddenly if people act in favor of a particular ideology. There has been a new stress on freedom of thought, including of religion, which earlier thinkers had tended to subordinate to anti-imperialism or other values, and also on the importance of democracy, greater gender equality, and new and fair laws. There have also been a variety of strong criticisms of clerical rule.

Probaby the most influential thinker of the past decade is Abdol-karim Soroush, a lay professional with an extensive knowledge of both Islamic and Western thought. Born in 1945 in Tehran, he attended a religious secondary school, Tehran University, and the University of London, where he apparently did not finish his doctorate in pharmacology. In the immediate postrevolution years he was seen as a proregime ideologist, writing against Marxism and becoming a member of the High Council of the Cultural Revolution in the early 1980s. Sources differ on how responsible he was for Cultural Revolution policies, but this history is still held against him by some intellectuals. Many of Iran's leading reformers, however, have emerged from similar backgrounds, having been transformed from young enthusiasts of the revolution to effective opponents of policies and politics of the postrevolution regime.

When, soon after Khomeini's death, various new periodicals opened the door to debate on public issues, the bimonthly *Kiyan*, launched in 1991 and featuring lead articles by Soroush, was especially significant. It translated articles by a variety of Western thinkers. Soroush stood out by his intelligence, command of Western and Islamic knowledge, and ability to write and speak on either a popular or elite level. Though his writings, which, like those of Shariati, are often transcribed lectures, include contradictions and differences over time, a few summary points may be made about them. Among Islamic thinkers he early favored mystics like the poet Rumi and Persian philosophers who combined rationalism and mysticism, like the Safavid philosopher Molla Sadra, thus differentiating himself from the legalist interpretation and from current clerical emphasis on external behavior. Later he stressed the centrality of science and wrote against both mysticism and relativist postmodernism.

According to Afshin Matin-asgari, "This focus on rational and critical philosophy, as opposed to metaphysics, mysticism, and nihilistic relativism, is central to Soroush's contribution to the secularization of Islamic thought and a significant step toward bridging the gap between religious and secular intellectuals."[26] As against Shariati, he argued that Islam is open to different interpretations and should not be made ideological.

Entering more directly political ground, by 1995 Soroush endorsed as key features of Western development tolerance, free expression, women's rights, and democracy. He argues that the separation of church and state protects religion by freeing it from political interests. He criticizes the West for hedonism and imperialism but also notes that Iranian attacks on the West are oversimplified and confused. Soroush argues for a "democratic religious government" but rejects any single interpretation of religion or privileged role for a clergy. Central to his view of religion in government and society is his repeated insistence that although a true Islam exists, it is unknowable by humans, whose interpretation of religion necessarily changes with historical and other circumstances. Therefore, no one interpretation of religion should be enforced. Although some think his democratic religious government is a contradiction in terms, it may be compared to contemporary European Christian Democracy, in which Christian Democratic governments generally make no attempt to enforce Catholic doctrines not accepted by a majority of the population.

Most controversially, in 1995 Soroush proposed that interpreters of religion should not be paid but should have to make their living in other ways, an idea attacked by Khamene'i. This led to disruptions of his lectures and a physical attack, followed by his defenders' leading the largest demonstration at Tehran University since the first years of the revolution. From 1996 on, however, Soroush was forbidden to teach, and, like a number of reformers, has been abroad in recent years. Despite this and the closing of *Kiyan*, his influence continues strong, though there are now other similarly influential thinkers, some of them clerics and others more unequivocal secularizers than Soroush.[27]

Unique to Iran—as the only state that has embodied clerical rule with populist republican elements, full of contradictions that soon came to be widely felt—are numerous writings by clerics that try to deal with the contradictions. Some clerical writers come down on the conservative side of most questions, but more original are clerical thinkers who adopt novel views, the best known of whom are Mohammad Shabestari and Mohsen Kadivar.

Mohammad Mojtahed Shabestari's long career started before the revolution. Now a professor of theology at Tehran University, he was born in Tabriz in 1936, spent the 1970s at the Islamic Center in Hamburg, and knows German intellectual writings and theories. His work stresses interpretation, including interpretations that are not derived only from the Quran and tradition. In his books and articles he says that only general principles are eternal, while specific rules and practices must change. For contemporary life the general principles of the sharia must be supplemented by the human and social sciences, which have wrongly been left out of seminaries. He cites the diversity of approaches to Islam of Ash'arites, Mu'tazilites, Islamic philosophers, and mystics in arguing for freedom of thought and free will. He stresses that the spiritual support religion can provide during modernization is totally different from having religion manage society, though he avoids overt polemics with the conservatives.

Shabestari distinguishes himself both from those who say people must adapt completely to the Quran and *sunna* and those who reject any such adaptation, and says that only the general values of government and society are tied to religion. Implicitly, unlike Khomeini and many Islamists who believe what is passed by parliaments is not truly legislation but only an extension of Islamic law, Shabestari alludes subtly to human legislation. His God is a font of ethical principles, while laws are not sacred. He in effect leaves open to humans the regulation of the family, social relations, politics, the state, the judiciary, and punishments. He says external critics of religion like Marx and Feuerbach can help the faithful to refine their concepts. He says there must be institutional guarantees of freedom; and, in what seems a veiled criticism of velayat-e faqih, he says Islam has no single form of polity; and that faith flourishes in states with institutional guarantees of freedom, checks and balances, a means for peaceful transitions of power; and a good parliament, judiciary, and economy. He denies that only the ulama are capable of knowing if a polity is compatible with Islam. He indicates that political institutions are civil, not religious. He does, however, retain conservative views on some personal matters and, unlike Kadivar and some others, does not directly criticize velayat-e faqih.[28]

Among clerical writers, a critique of velayat-e faqih is found especially in Mohsen Kadivar. Born in 1959, he received his early education in Shiraz. When the revolution came, he switched from engineering at Shiraz University to a seminary. In 1981 he went to a seminary in Qom, while concurrently doing university study aimed at a doctorate. He began writing, and in 1999 was sentenced to prison for his writings by the Special Court for the Clergy. Ironically, his arrest and eighteen-month prison term resulted in the dissemination of the writings and ideas of this previously little-known cleric.

Kadivar's writings make their points via exegesis of Shi'i thinkers, especially those who expounded Mu'tazilite theology or philosophers like Mulla Sadra, to support a view of the harmony of reason and revelation. He says if the externals of religion seem to contradict reason the externals need reinterpretation. Jurisprudence, *fiqh,* is in need of revision, which requires profound knowledge both of fiqh and of contemporary natural and human sciences. We must distinguish between universal principles and those meant for particular times and places. Like Shabestari, he concludes that humans may derive from religion general principles and values, but practical affairs are more in the domain of human experience (which implies secular norms). Different political and economic systems are needed in different periods, and complex industrial society is very different from past societies.

In talks Kadivar deals with other issues central to democracy. One of them, after analysis of Islamic sources, concludes, "Even though the popular interpretation of Islam in many cases does not reflect the freedom of religion and belief yet the other interpretation of Islam that is based on the original rules of Islam is in concord with the freedom of religion and belief that has been mentioned in the Universal Declaration of the Human Rights."[29]

In his two books Kadiver sees velayat-e faqih as a main problem. The first analyzes and criticizes different relevant Shi'i views. The second, *Hokumat-e velayi,* also discusses different views and indicates the lack of Quranic or rational need for velayat-e faqih, and the lack of evidence to support it in the Traditions of the infallible imams. He notes that Shi'i theology does not discuss what type of government there should be in the absence of imams. Velayat (guardianship) in Islam is over those who are not fully competent to make decisions, while in fiqh the principle is that everyone manages their own affairs, disposes of their property, determines whom and whether to marry, what to wear, where to live, and how to behave. He tries to demonstrate that neither the Quran, the

Prophet, Shi'i Tradition, nor rational inquiry supports velayat-e faqih. He contrasts velayat with republicanism, saying that in a republican state people are equal and considered competent, and leaders must heed the views of their constituency. He believes democracy and velayat-e faqih are irreconcilable; there must either be a faqih appointed by God or an elected leadership. In his view, God has delegated political management to the people, who should elect leaders and have a constitution compatible with religion. In his first book his arguments are often implicit, coming from the examination of theories of other thinkers, such as Montazeri, who has become increasingly critical of seeing the faqih as a ruler and who notes that in Shi'i theory, divine appointment of rulers is suspended pending the return of the Hidden Imam. Montazeri is cited as saying that today rule must be based on popular elections. In his second book Kadivar declares his positions more directly. Like Shabestari, Kadivar stresses that Islamic elements should be restricted to general principles and values, while practical issues and social programing should be based on current human experience.[30]

In a talk in the United States in 2002, Kadivar tied rejection of velayat-e faqih to endorsement of democracy:

> Velayat-e faqih has no credible foundation in Islamic jurisprudence. It is a notion that is formed in the minds of a group of honorable jurists through a specific reading of a handful of Islamic passages. Refuting velayat-e faqih does not in any way undermine any of the Islamic teachings, requirements or obligations. I believe democracy is the least erroneous approach to the politics of the world. (Please note that least erroneous does not mean perfect, or even error free.) Democracy is a product of reason, and the fact that it has first been put to use in the West does not preclude its utility in other cultures—reason extends beyond geographical boundaries. One must adopt a correct approach, regardless of who came up with the idea; "look into what is being said, not at who says it."[31]

In January 2003 Kadivar left the United States in the middle of a Harvard fellowship and returned to Iran to join the current struggle. He immediately began making a number of important speeches in Iran calling for reform and predicting the downfall of the regime if reform is blocked. He called on Khatami to fulfill his pledge to resign if the two major reform bills are blocked. He also said the separation of religion and state is inevitable and a must.[32]

In today's climate, when large numbers of Iranians are pressing for human rights, the discourses of Soroush, Shabestari, and Kadivar have been important in pointing a way to reconcile democratic government with a liberal view of religion that endorses essentially secular politics. As is the case with theorists who concentrate on the position of women, there are also secular thinkers who do not discuss Islam, and both groups have often cooperated in many ways—in the press, in the majles, and in demonstrations. A number of clerics have taken strongly reformist or democratic positions, with some attacking any privileged political position for the clergy, and among nonclerics appeals for secular government are increasing even more.

While Shabestari and other clerical reformers are clearly influenced by Western thought, we should take seriously their references to different trends within Islam. The Mu'tazilites, Islamic philosophers, and Sufis were, in different ways, more open to ideas like free will, natural law, and less strict observance of externalities of the law than were the strict legists, and even within the legal tradition there is much more difference and flexibility than is often thought. The formerly important Akhbari school of Shi'ism said that each individual could interpret the Traditions of the Prophet and imams, without need of an ulama. More recently, most of the top ayatollahs in Iran have either rejected velayat-e faqih as currently practiced, most strongly in the case of Montazeri, or stood aloof from politics, as did many of their predecessors. In part, contemporary clerical reformers are drawing on traditions that were strong in Iran or are following clerics who are outside the official sphere.[33]

By 2002–03 dissatisfaction with clerical rule had spread even among clerics, at every level from clerical student through ayatollah. In the summer of 2002 Ayatollah Jalal ed-Din Taheri, the Friday prayer leader in Isfahan, resigned with a scathing statement attacking the clerical government,[34] and some months later he called on clerics to join one hundred majles deputies and others in defending Ayatollah Montazeri from house arrest and other indignities. His letter appeared on several reformist Internet news sites, which have become substitutes for about ninety publications that have been shut down.[35] Audio cassettes by Montazeri and other critical clerics circulate widely. Another grand ayatollah, Yusef Sane'i, has issued enlightened fatwas especially on women's rights and also on human rights and ethnic and sexual discrimination;[36] Hojjat ol-Islam Yusefi Eshkevari is still in prison owing to his participation in the Berlin Conference and to his liberal statements on Islam, especially those opposing mandatory veiling. Clerics of all levels are reacting to a growing public disaffection that is increasingly reflected in hostility toward them, from the well-known refusal of most taxi drivers to pick them up to the hostile reception they get if they speak at universities. More clerics are listening to the arguments of religious reformers, many of whom were students of Montazeri. Some note that Shi'i leaders before Khomeini did not advocate clerical rule. Some favor the separation of religion from politics and are open to an Islam that incorporates some modern ideas and behavior patterns regarding gender and other questions. Open expression of such views can bring arrests and punishment by the special court for the clergy, but some are letting their views be publicly known.[37]

Growing Internet use generally and especially by the opposition parallels previous use of contemporary communications technology for oppositional purposes—the telegraph was central in the tobacco protest and the constitutional revolution, and audio cassettes in the 1978–79 revolution. The Internet and satellite television keep many Iranians, even those who only hear about them, aware of international developments, especially those that concern Iran, and the Internet is also used for internal dissident communication.

Minority Populations

The situation of religious and ethnic minorities in Iran is a highly controversial subject on which not nearly enough research has been done and on which scholars and observers inside and outside Iran have very different opinions, often based on few locally verifiable facts. Hence, much of what is said below is tentative. It is not surprising that minority questions are controversial: As elsewhere, those who identify with minority demands for change tend to stress grievances, whereas those more concerned with Iran's territorial integrity or with its national or Shi'i identity often play down such grievances. There is concern that not only neighboring states and ethnic groups but also the United States could be using ethnic and religious grievances to undermine the unity and territorial integrity of Iran, and this concern goes beyond supporters of the Islamic Republic. In recent years there has been increasing recognition by the government that some grievances are genuine, and that it is in Iran's interest to try to address them.

While the constitution guarantees equal rights to ethnic minorities and recognized religions, including rights to worship and to use local languages, these rights are not always fully realized in practice. The

situation for minorities has, however, improved in recent years, especially under Khatami. Non-Islamic "people of the book"—Christians,
Jews, Zoroastrians, and Sabeans (a small group near the Iraq border)—
are recognized in the constitution. The first three have seats in the majles,
and in theory and partly in practice are protected; but there has been
some popular reversion to older Iranian Shi'i views of non-Muslims as
unclean persons whose touch and contact are to be avoided. Jews have
suffered from being associated with Israel, and the great majority of
prerevolutionary Iranian Jews have migrated to Israel or the United
States, while many thousands remain in Iran. The position of minorities
who adhere to unrecognized religions is more difficult. The Baha'is, who
may number as high as three hundred thousand, continue to be seen as
apostates from Islam and as such underwent a period of severe repression, including executions, until 1985, with a decline and then an apparent end of executions thereafter. Baha'is and Jews, as before the revolution, are still sometimes seen as agents of foreign powers, though some in
the reformist movement reject such views. Discrimination against them
is partly based on this perception.[38]

There are also minorities that follow non-Twelver Shi'i versions of
Islam—by far the largest are Sunni Muslims—and there are also some
Isma'ili Shi'a and sects like the Ahl-e Haqq. Sunnism is found chiefly
among ethnic minorities outside the Iranian plateau and bordering on
conationals abroad—Turkomans in the north, Baluchis in the southwest,
most Kurds in the west,[39] and a minority of Arabs, who are overwhelmingly Shi'i. Some of these groups participated in uprisings after the revolution, based as much on ethnic and economic demands as on religious
differences. Sunnis continue to be discriminated against, de facto, as they
are not a recognized category, and there is an official pretense that Islam
is one, while Sunnis have been disfavored in mosque building, representation, and other ways, partly owing to the economic underdevelopment
of their regions and their cross-border ties. Khatami spoke and acted
against such discrimination and got especially high vote percentages in
Sunni areas. His popularity in these areas is also due to his work for
decentralization via local councils and for more independent publishing
in local languages.

The constitution speaks of equal rights for all ethnic groups and says
that regional and ethnic languages can be used in the press and media and
their literature can be taught in the schools. This has been partially real-

ized in practice, though some in the central government continue to fear that greater freedom for Sunni worship and for uncontrolled local language use might strengthen the ties of these groups with their cross-border co-ethnics and possibly encourage separatism. State broadcasting has programs in Kurdish, Azerbaijani Turkish, Turkmen, Baluchi, and Arabic, but some in these areas find their quantity and quality inadequate and would like more independent local broadcasting and publishing.[40]

The Islamic Republic has clearly broken with the Pahlavi practice of disallowing use of regional languages. One can purchase newspapers, books, music tapes, and videos in Azerbaijani Turkish and Kurdish, and there are radio and television stations in ethnic areas that broadcast news and entertainment programs in even more languages. Nevertheless, in several Arab, Azerbaijani, Kurdish, and Baluchi cities, one frequently hears charges of "Persian chauvinism" from members of ethnic minority groups. Many Persians do have stereotyped views not only of minorities who live in underdeveloped regions but even of Turks who do not. Prior to 1992, there was no public discussion of ethnic minority issues, but since that time scholarly journals, the media, and even committee hearings in the majles have been addressing various aspects of the issue, including cultural grievances, and the influence of cross-border nationalities (especially the efforts of Azeri Turks in the Republic of Azerbaijan to appeal to "our brothers and sisters in southern Azerbaijan").

The Kurds have been particularly active in voicing political, cultural, and economic demands. Some Kurds believe that Khatami, despite his appointment of the first postrevolution Kurdish governor of Kurdistan and his work with local Kurdish groups and for further use of Kurdish, has not fulfilled all his campaign promises toward ethnic minorities. Those Kurds who are Sunni are the most prone to identify with Kurds in Iraq and Turkey. The Kurds are of particular concern to the central government. Any Kurdish move that could be seen as promoting separatism or as undermining government power has been resisted by all Iranian central governments, whether monarchical or IRI, conservative or reformist. Khatami has taken steps toward meeting some Kurdish grievances and allowing Kurds to have a greater say in their own rule.[41]

Baluchistan, the most underdeveloped and impoverished region of Iran, has been the scene of complaints of anti-Sunni and anti-Baluchi discrimination and of some lethal Sunni–Shi'i and other violence, though much of it has been between Afghan refugees, who make up a large majority in the capital city, Zahedan. Iran has also taken in, at its own expense, some two million Afghan refugees, partly Sunnis, some of whom have gone home, but others remain in Iran.

To the Shi'i Arabs of Khuzistan province there now must be added a large and rapidly reproducing number of Shi'i Arab refugees from Iraq, who the Iranians hope will go home, as a number of them did during and after the United States war with Iraq. While the local Arabs identify as Iranians, the refugees do not, even though many want to stay in Iran.[42]

The largest non-Persian ethnic group by far is the Azerbaijani Turks, who comprise about a quarter of the total population and are numerous in Tehran and elsewhere outside Azerbaijan. The Azerbaijanis mostly occupy the plateau, have close economic and cultural ties with Persian-speakers, and, perhaps most important, are Shi'is. Hence, despite past autonomist movements centering on greater local power and use of Azerbaijani Turkish, it seems most unlikely that they will break with Iran, despite propaganda in this direction from some Iranian Azerbaijanis abroad and from the ex-Soviet Republic of Azerbaijan. As before the revolution, some Azerbaijanis identify mainly as Iranian or Shi'i Muslim, some as mainly Azerbaijani, and some as two or all three of the above. Antiseparatist Azerbaijanis have included not only several prominent early Iranian nationalists like Taqizadeh and Kasravi, recent dissidents like Ayatollah Shariatmadari, Mehdi Bazargan, and some leaders of the left, but also several pillars of the regime, including Khamene'i. Many Azerbaijanis may be feeling increased ethnic identity, as well as resentment of Persian stereotypes of "Turks" as being dull or having other undesirable qualities.[43]

Other important ethnic minorities include the major inland tribal confederations, notably the Turkic Qashqa'i and Shahsevan and the Luri Bakhtiaris and Lurs, all in the west. Only a minority of these groups continues their annual migrations, while most have followed the trend toward settlement. The border ethnic regions also include nomadic or recently nomadic tribes. Although tribal peoples have been subject to religious restrictions on things like dress, music, and dancing, the major changes in the lifestyles of nomadic or formerly nomadic rural people have been more due to socioeconomic trends than to religious controls.[44] The central government has publicized economic and other measures for the tribes, but the resources devoted to them have been small.

Some of Khatami's supporters distributed election materials in the

Azerbaijani and Kurdish languages in 1997, and Khatami has continued to appeal both to ethnic and local groups through his work for two provisions in the Iranian constitution, for elected local councils and for increased recognition of freer linguistic rights of minorities. The Iranian state has some genuine concerns regarding foreign exploitation of minority grievances and, regarding some Kurds and a few Azerbaijanis, having separatist ideas. Governments of whatever ideology are fearful and react strongly regarding separatism. Yet, failing to carry further than has been done to date programs to meet the cultural and economic grievances of minorities can only add to their disaffection and to the potential of separatist feelings and movements. It is wrong, however, to discount current governmental efforts regarding ethnic minorities, which have been significant.

Overall, most of the demands put forth by minorities are congruent with more general reformist demands for greater democracy, local control, economic progress and reform, and an end to clerical controls over law and behavior. Although there are disagreements within the all-Iranian reform movement, and also between the views of some minority reformers and some in Tehran, such divergences may not be insuperable if efforts to enforce Shi'i Islam are abandoned and the government grants more autonomy, targeted economic programs, and freer use of local languages than Iran has seen to date.

On balance the question of minorities, like many social, intellectual, and cultural questions, is one that has seen important changes since the revolution—changes that in recent years have gone some way to meeting minorities' demands. In nearly all these areas, Iran today appears to be in a period of transition, where trends toward urbanization, education, and some modernization of the economy and society have contributed to the spread of ideas and demands that are in conflict with vested governmental and clerical-bazaari interests.

Conclusion

Iran since the revolution is a prime example of a country whose political and social policies had unforeseen consequences, some of them undesired by those who initiated the policies. The increase in public health and encouragement of births in the revolution's first decade brought a fall in the death rate and a population explosion of those now aged thirteen to twenty-three. This is the very group who are feeling most strongly restrictions on behavior, unemployment, and alienation from the regime and are protesting in various ways. The spread of education and urbanization has helped create a more critical spirit and the concentration of people in cities where they are most easily reached by a variety of new ideas. The enforcement of legal and behavioral restrictions on women has resulted in a more significant and active women's movement than ever before. The experience of breaking with the West has undermined the tendency to blame all problems on Western imperialists and has encouraged the development of more complex political analyses. Even those with clerical educations are increasingly inclined to question what the leading political clerics say and do. Perhaps most important, the actual experience of clerical rule and sharia laws has greatly undermined belief that Islamic government, in any but some completely transformed interpretation of it, can solve human and social problems. Secular ideas are probably stronger in Iran than anywhere else in the Muslim world. In many Muslim countries autocratic and mainly secular rule is encouraging the kind of Islamist reaction that Iran experienced in the 1970s, and it seems unlikely that most of these countries will learn from Iran's experience that Islamist rule is not solving many basic problems. In Iran, Islamist rulers undertook a number of policies that in the end encouraged the development of a healthier, better-educated, and (inadvertently from their viewpoint) more sophisticated society, but their policies accomplished this at a huge cost in lost exiles and capital, economic decline, the enforcement of second-class citizenship for women, and major, sometimes brutal, limits on human rights. Iran has emerged from the worst of postrevolutionary times, and it is to be hoped that it can carry further advances in education, health, and intellectual and cultural sophistication and also move toward a more democratic political regime, but this will not occur without further struggles.

Conclusion

Beginning in the nineteenth century and continuing with far greater rapidity since the time of Reza Shah, Iran has seen a process of modernization that, like all such processes, has had both positive and negative aspects in terms of the welfare of the general population. It has opened up possibilities for richer and freer lives for many people, but these possibilities have often either gone unrealized or been realized in partial and contradictory ways. Contrary to a widespread view, the process of modernization of society and culture has continued under the Islamic Republic, especially in such aspects as the spread of education and health care, urbanization, and changes in family relations. Under most Iranian governments, whether monarchical or clerical, there has, however, been a gap between the authoritarian means employed by governments and what most of the people see as in their best interests. Governments, whether monarchical or clerical, however popular or tolerated they may have been initially, have over time shown themselves in most matters to favor the interests of a narrow group in society rather than the interests of the great majority of the population. In addition, they have taken advantage of increasingly modern means of governmental coercion and control. This is hardly unique to Iran, and what is special is the propensity of Iranians to mount mass movements that challenge, often successfully, the powers that be. This book has tried to describe and explain these developments and to present and analyze the special features of Iran.

To point up a few elements important to modern Iranian history: Iran's aridity, ecological decline over the centuries, and the large presence of nomadic tribes, including the rule since the eleventh century C.E.

by tribal leaders in both the central government and in large, essentially autonomous regions, created a premodern situation in which effective central government was difficult and rarely attained. To keep power rulers had to meet the demands of local tribal leaders, landlords, and ulama, and often had little relation to local populations beyond taking part of the taxes from those who collected them. While means of rule were often autocratic and arbitrary, the direct power of rulers over distant provinces was usually small. In a situation of varying government power and frequent tribal unrest or warfare with little long-term stability, it was impossible for anything like a capitalist system or the legal framework that might encourage it to develop.

The Safavid period was notable, first, for giving Iran for the first time relative unity within boundaries that, although shifting, approximated those of today and, second, for converting most of the population from Sunni to Shi'i Islam. These accomplishments were important for Iran's future identity and territorial integrity. The Qajars reestablished a unified Iran without great difficulty after its 1722–96 period of division and internal warfare and, despite a few losses to the Russians and British, Iran retained the great majority of the Safavid territory. The importance to Iranian unity of its being, after the Safavids, over 90 percent Shi'a, is rarely noted. Even though Iran has numerous ethnic groups whose first language is not Persian and has seen several autonomist movements, the common Shi'i heritage has been a significant social glue except in the few border areas where Sunnis predominate. This common Shi'i heritage as well as the importance numerically and culturally of the Persian language, premodern ideas of Iranian identity, and a predominant history of unity since 1501 has made Iran less subject to ethnic division than neighbors like Iraq or Afghanistan.

Iran's modern history has also been influenced by the evolution of Twelver Shi'ism, in which Iranian clerics have played a leading role. In both Sunnism and Shi'ism the ulama, meaning those with a religious education, had a role in some ways broader than the considerable role of the Catholic clergy in the West, even though they, unlike either Catholic or Orthodox Christians, could not set a doctrine that all believers were expected to follow. It has been said with much justice that in Islam the law is central, and Islamic law and custom were upheld by the ulama. In addition, the evolution of Shi'ism into a system in which leading ulama's rulings carried unusual weight with their followers as well as the strong ties down to today between the ulama and Iran's urban bazaar classes created a situation where the bazaar-ulama alliance could form one basis for revolt against the government, as happened in 1890–91, 1905–11, and 1978–79.

The current importance in contemporary Iran and the Muslim world of Islamist politics should not make people forget the great importance in Iran's modern history of secular ideas and forces, which are reappearing in Iran with great strength. Iran has experienced strong secular trends of different varieties. Nationalists from Mirza Aqa Khan Kermani on disdained Islam and the Arabs and looked to a constructed and partly invented pre-Islamic Iranian past for the modern values they favored. Many of them were politically on the left, but nationalist ideas were appropriated by the Pahlavi shahs and lost some of their appeal after Mohammad Reza Shah combined them not only with dictatorship, but also with new attacks on customs considered Islamic, rash economic policies, brutality toward opposition, and dependence on the U.S. Iran also has a long tradition of leftist and socialist politics, beginning as early as the 1905–11 revolution and becoming particularly strong during and after World War II, with the Tudeh Party and other leftist groups. The Left was partly discredited by its association with Communist countries that sought accommodation first with the Pahlavis and then with the Islamic Republic; it was also violently suppressed by the Pahlavis, and it lost credit with the fall of the Soviet Union. The rise of Islamic politics in the 1970s was largely in reaction to the failures of nationalism and communism as foci of opposition. Iranian Islamism incorporated some ideas, practices, and class support from prior Marxist and nationalist movements and initially combined the popular classes, intellectuals and students, and the bazaar bourgeoisie. Since 1979 the divergent interests of these groups and classes have broken down even the Islamist part of the revolutionary coalition, while the autocratic and ideological methods used by clerical rulers, economic difficulties, and clerical controls on behavior, felt especially by women and young people, have discredited clerical rule with most people. A more positive feature of recent years, with the spread of education and disillusionment with absolutist ideologies, has been the development of ideas that would retain Islamic identity while advocating secular government, attempting to overcome the divide between those who follow traditional Islamic customs and those who want modern freedoms. While not all educated people hold such views, their salience is a hopeful sign for a future Iran that may not be as divided into mutually uncomprehending and hostile "two cultures" as it has been since Pahlavi times.

Part of Iran's modern history can be explained by the role of outside powers, first motivated by Iran's strategic position for the British Empire and for Russia, and later also by its oil. Before the rise of Reza Shah, Britain and Russia had great influence on Iran's government, while under the Pahlavis influences were more indirect and emanated increasingly from the U.S. While Mohammad Reza Shah was never the simple tool of the U.S. that his enemies proclaimed, he saw his own interests as tied to U.S. policy and support, and this support not only brought him back to power by overthrowing the popular Mosaddeq government in 1953 but helped him build up a dictatorial and repressive government, especially after 1963.

In each stage of modern history, popular movements have reacted against the ideology and practices of those in power. Faced with a traditional Qajar government that was complaisant to Britain and Russia, Iranians saw the best hope for independence and self-strengthening in a Western-style parliamentary constitution in 1905–11. When the ensuing governments were too weak to fend off foreign incursions, many Iranians initially supported the rule of a strong man, Reza Shah. In reaction to the continued power of the British and their oil company, most Iranians backed Mosaddeq's nationalist movement in 1951–53. After Mosaddeq was overthrown with U.S. help, oppositional feeling was directed at the increasingly dictatorial shah. When nationalist and leftist opposition were suppressed and lost some popularity, there was a turn in the 1970s toward the Islamic opposition, which got strength from the association of secularism, Westernization, and U.S. control with the increasingly unpopular shah. Today, with the personal controls and often brutal punishments enforced by the Islamic regime, along with economic difficulties, people are seeking a variety of contrasting solutions, some of which try to combine social democracy with new interpretations of Islam, while others are overtly or covertly secular, and some, with typical nostalgia, even have hopes from those formerly reviled—whether constitutional monarchy or U.S. intervention.

Most politicized groups in Iran now concentrate on internal change, not salvation from abroad, however. There is not a simple division among reformers and hard-liners. Among clerics and their supporters several groups may be distinguished, ranging from the most conservative through those who, backed by the bazaar and some business interests, want strict interpretations of Islam in sociocultural and judicial affairs, but welcome modern business and science, to left-leaning Islamist moderates and a large group of younger theologians or seminarian rebels in Qom and elsewhere who think clerical government is spoiling the good name of Islam and depriving them of respect and their livelihood. They, along with a number of grand ayatollahs, challenge the ruling concept of velayat-e faqih as an innovation, if not a heresy, and believe the clergy should not rule.

Nonclerical thinkers are similarly divided and include those who favor an Islamic state but believe it must be based on fresh interpretations of the Quran and Islam, those who speak in favor of an Islamic identity but want to leave the government to nonclerics under an "Islamic democracy;" and secular groups who advocate a Western-type democratic system in which Islam and other faiths will all be treated as personal choices and protected as part of civil liberties and human rights. It seems probable that secularism, though without the insults to Islamic practices experienced under the Pahlavis, is more popular than it appears under current limits on free speech, which result in considerable self-censorship of views that might bring jail sentences. Most of the above groups want major changes in the current system in the direction of greater democracy and freedom, including an economy less controlled by a few favored interests and greatly increased rights for women, whatever the differences in their ideas and ultimate aims.

The largely negative experience of clerical government summarized in this book has created a change, or even reversal, of former attitudes among many Iranians. From being popular, clerics have become unpopular. From being unpopular, the U.S. has become popular with many Iranians. From being hated, the Pahlavis are now looked on nostalgically by some, and the broadcasts favoring Reza Pahlavi beamed in by satellite from Iranian diaspora stations in the U.S. get some attention. Pahlavi's program speaks of mass civil disobedience to topple the government, followed by a popular referendum to decide the form of government—a program unobjectionable even to many Iranians suspicious of his aims and allies. Some in the U.S. government favor giving aid to the opposition or even the forcible overthrow of the current regime in the name of helping Iran's reformers, after which a regime friendly to the U.S. would be installed. Many think this program is one for Pahlavi restoration via U.S. intervention. While U.S. popularity with many Iranians has risen in the past decade, during which there was no U.S. presence in Iran, there is no guarantee, in view of Iran's mobilizations against foreign control for more than a century, that this popularity will be sustained if there are increased steps toward U.S. intervention and control. The president's listing of Iran as part of an "axis of evil" increased the strength of the hard-liners, and the conservative swing in the 2003 municipal elections may reflect in part the same trend.

Writing in early 2003, I am struck by a partial reversal in the foreign policy images of Iran and the U.S. in the eyes of most of the world. In the 1980s Iran was under a highly ideological ruler who wanted to spread his ideology to the point of controlling other governments—a goal that was essentially lost in the Iran-Iraq war and never had a real chance of success. Since then Iran's foreign policy has become increasingly pragmatic and realistic, and it is not known to what degree the central government was responsible for a few recent incidents that seem to break with this pragmatism. Since 2001, by contrast, U.S. foreign policy has become increasingly ideological and threatening to those whom its leaders target verbally. Iran, because of its oil and strategic position as well as the publicly stated U.S. concerns over Iran's nuclear program and support for groups like Hizbollah, could be a target of another U.S. "preventive" military attack or of attempts to overthrow the government and install one more friendly to the U.S.

While political predictions are usually wrong and the current Iranian situation is so complex both internally and externally that very little can be predicted with confidence, past Iranian experience indicates that Iranians are unlikely in the long run either to tolerate a vastly unpopular government or to let foreigners control Iran's destiny. Iran's history of increasing modernization, comprising industrialization, urbanization, the great spread of modern education and health systems and of awareness of a variety of ideas, and new independence for girls and women despite external controls, along with Iran's extraordinary modern history of effective popular movements, give reason for hope that better government is in Iran's future. U.S. intervention would risk tainting internal processes that should be given time to play out. Even if the U.S. could succeed in getting popular support to overthrow the current government, the long-term effects of heavy interference in Iran's affairs would probably be no better than they were in the 1970s. The creativity and proven oppositional abilities of the Iranian people give reason to hope that they will be able to change the existing system for the better without any outside intervention.

Notes

Chapter 1. Religion and Society to 1800

1. See W. Montgomery Watt, *Muhammad at Mecca* (Oxford, 1953) and *Muhammad at Medina* (Oxford, 1956); Maxime Rodinson, "The Life of Muhammad and the Sociological Problem of the Beginnings of Islam," *Diogenes* 20 (Winter 1957): 28–51, and *Mohammad*, trans. A. Carter (London, 1971). These interpretations have been challenged in some more recent work.

2. On Shi'i history, see A. Bausani, *Religion in Iran: From Zoroaster to Baha'u'llah*, trans. J. M. Marchesi (New York: Bibliotheca Persica, 2000); M. G. S. Hodgson, *The Order of Assassins* (The Hague, 1955); Yann Richard, *L'Islam Chi'ite* (Paris, 1991); Moojan Momen, *An Introduction to Shi'i Islam: The History and Doctrines of Twelver Shi'ism* (New Haven, 1985); L. Clarke, ed. and trans., *Shi'ite Heritage: Essays on Classical and Modern Traditions* (Binghamton, N.Y., 2001); W. M. Watt, *Islam and the Integration of Society* (London, 1961).

3. W. M. Watt, "The Reappraisal of Abbasid Shi'ism," in G. Makdisi, ed., *Arabic and Islamic Studies in Honour of Hamilton A. R. Gibb* (Leiden, 1965).

4. Watt, "Reappraisal," 653.

5. On these groups, see especially John K. Birge, *The Bektashi Order of Dervishes* (London, 1937); C. Huart, *Textes persans relatifs a la secte des Houroufis* (Leiden, 1909); Michel M. Mazzaoui, *The Origins of the Safawids* (Wiesbaden, 1972); V. Minorsky, *Notes sur la secte des Ahle-Haqq* (Paris, 1921); and C. Cahen, "Le problème du shi'isme dans l'Asie Mineure turque préottomane," in *Le Shi'isme imamite* (Paris, 1970).

6. Hasan-i-Rumlu, *Ahsanu't-Tawarikh*. C. N. Seddon, trans. (Baroda, India, 1934), 27.

7. (In order): Hanna Sohrweide, "Der Sieg der Safaviden in Persien und seine Rückwirkungen auf die Schiiten Anatoliens im 16. Jahrhundert," *Der Islam* 41 (1965): 106–09; C. Grey, ed. and trans., *A Narrative of Italian Travels in Persia, in the Fifteenth and Sixteenth Centuries* (London, 1873), accounts by C. Zeno, 59, an Anonymous Merchant, 172, and V. d'Alessandri, 223; J. Chardin, *Voyages de Monsieur le Chevalier Chardin en Perse et autres lieux de l'Orient* (Amsterdam, 1711), 2:52, 275–81.

8. See E. G. Browne, *A Literary History of Persia* (1928; reprinted Cambridge, 1953), 4:73–78.

9. See Grey, ed., *Italian Travels*, 206–23, and Z. V. Togan, "Sur l'origine des Safavides," in *Mélanges Louis Massignon* (Damascus, 1957): 3:345–57.

10. As some scholars have maintained that political claims by the mujtahids are very recent, it is worth repeating at some length what Chardin says in the late seventeenth century: "many of them [mujtahids) maintain that it is not at all true that the Succession of Imams was lost, and that there is nobody today who has at least part of the charge; and that it is even impossible that this occur, but one must believe on the contrary that the succession of Imams continues always and that there is always someone who has the charge of Lieutenant of God on earth. . . . They teach that the *Imam* should be sought particularly among the . . . Mujtahid(s)" (*Voyages,* 2:337). And "The People of the church . . . and all those who profess the strict observation of religion, hold that in the absence of the Imam, the royal place should be filled by a Mujtahid. . . . 'How is it possible,' say the people of the Church, 'that these impious . . . Kings, drinkers of wine, consumed by passion, be the vicars of God, and that they have communication with heaven? . . . Our kings being iniquitous and unjust men, their domination is a tyranny, to which God has subjected us to punish us, after having taken from the world the legitimate successor of his Prophet. The supreme throne of the universe belongs only to a mujtahid, or man who possesses sanctity and science above most people. It is true that since the mujtahid is holy, and consequently a man of peace, there must be a king who carries a sword for the exercise of justice, but he must be only like his minister and dependent on him" (*Voyages,* 2:207–08). Playing down the ulama's premodern political claims are J. Eliash, "Misconceptions Regarding the Juridical Status of the Iranian 'Ulama,'" *International Journal of Middle East Studies* 10:1 (1979): 9–25; and S. A. Arjomand, "Political Action and Legitimate Domination in Shi'ite Iran: Fourteenth to Eighteenth Centuries A.D.," *Archives Européennes de Sociologie* 20:1 (1979): 59–109.

11. The Twelver Creed by al-Allama al-Hilli, *al-Babu'l-Hadi 'Ashar,* trans. W. M. Miller (London, 1928), praises the Mu'tazilites, stresses the rationality and comprehensible justice of God, and says that men have free will and that certain things are incumbent on God. See also W. Madelung, "Imamism and Mu'tazilite Theology," in *Le Shi'isme imamite* (Paris, 1970). Thanks to N. Keddie's 1979–80 graduate seminar, especially to J. Cole and T. Shimamoto, for aiding in this analysis.

12. See Comte Arthur de Gobineau, *Religions et philosophies dans l' Asie Centrale* (Paris, 1957), 35–39.

Chapter 2. Foundations of Nineteenth-Centry Iran

1. On the contrasting centralizing role of cannons and decentralizing role of good handguns, see H. Inalcik, "The Socio-Political Effects of the Diffusion of Firearms in the Middle East," in V. Parry and M. Yapp, eds., *War, Technology, and Society in the Middle East* (London and New York, 1975). The point on the importance of rifles to the resurgence of tribes in eighteenth-century Iran was suggested to me by Robert McDaniel. Among the works showing significant eighteenth-century socioeconomic change are T. Naff and R. Owen, eds., *Studies in Eighteenth-Century Islamic History* (Carbondale, Ill., 1977); N. Berkes, *The Development of Secularism*

in Turkey (Montreal, 1964); and A. Hourani, "The Changing Face of the Fertile Crescent in the Eighteenth Century," *Studia Islamica* 8 (1957): 89–122.

2. The estimates are by C. Issawi, ed., *The Economic History of Iran: 1800–1914* (Chicago, 1971), 20. A detailed study of a shorter period is G. G. Gilbar, "Demographic Developments in Late Qajar Persia, 1810–1906," *Asian and African Studies* 11:2 (1976): 125–56.

3. More detailed analyses of the role of tribes in Iran and the Middle East are found in N. R. Keddie, "Is There a Middle East?" *International Journal of Middle East Studies* 4:3 (1973): 255–71; "Socio-Economic Change in the Middle East since 1800: A Comparative Analysis," in A. Udovitch, ed., *The Islamic Middle East, 700–1900: Studies in Social and Economic History* (Princeton: Darwin Press, 1981). There is a large literature on Iranian tribes by authors including G. R. Garthwaite and J. P. Digard on the Bakhtiaris; L. G. Beck and P. Oberling on the Qashqa'i; W. Irons on the Turkomans; P. Saltzman and B. Spooner on the Baluchis; R. and N. Tapper on the Shahsevan; G. Chaliand and M. van Bruinessen on the Kurds; and D. Bradburd and L. Helfgott on theoretical questions. The best analyses of the role of tribes are by Thomas J. Barfield in "Turk, Persian, and Arab: Changing Relationships between Tribes and State in Iran and along its Frontiers," in N. R. Keddie and R. Matthee, eds., *Iran and the Surrounding World: Interactions in Culture and Cultural Politics* (Seattle, 2002), and "Tribe and State Relations: The Inner Asian Perspective," in Philip Khoury and Joseph Kostiner, eds., *Tribes and State Formation in the Middle East* (Berkeley, 1991).

4. On the Qajar bureaucracy, see the article by A. R. Sheikholeslami in A. Banani, ed., *State and Society in Iran* (special issue of *Iranian Studies*, 1978) and his *The Structure of Central Authority in Qajar Iran, 1871–1896* (Atlanta: Scholars Press, 1997) and S. Bakhash, *Iran: Monarchy, Bureaucracy, and Reform under the Qajars, 1858–1896* (London, 1978). In the literature important men are known either by their given names, often preceded by the honorific "Mirza" and followed by the honorific "Khan," or by titles, which may change, or (as here) by the name followed by the title. In the latter case we italicize the title to distinguish it from the name. Most titles were abolished under Reza Shah, who also introduced family names. (The word "Mirza" *before* a name means an educated man; *after* a name it keeps its original meaning of a royal prince.)

5. On the disruptive economic impact of opium, see the important article by Roger Olson in M. Bonine and N. Keddie, eds., *Modern Iran: The Dialectics of Continuity and Change* (paperback, *Continuity and Change in Modern Iran*) (Albany, 1981). Overviews of nineteenth- and twentieth-century agricultural changes are in N. R. Keddie, "Stratification, Social Control, and Capitalism in Iranian Villages, before and after Land Reform," *Rural Politics and Social Change in the Middle East*, ed. R. Antoun and I. Harik (Bloomington, Ind., 1972), reprinted in N. R. Keddie, *Iran: Religion, Politics and Society* (London, 1980), and A. K. S. Lambton, *Landlord and Peasant in Persia* (1953; reprinted London, 1969).

6. This is suggested to us by the studies of leading families in Maragheh by M. J. Good and in Shiraz by Wm. Royce in M. Bonine and N. Keddie, eds., *Modern Iran*, which suggest considerable long-term continuity until at least the Reza Shah period, as does the study of mobility in various social strata in Shiraz by Ahmad Ashraf and Ali Banuazizi. This contrasts to the high mobility in Tehran elite families, most

of whom came from elsewhere, as shown in the unpublished work of Constance Cronin on Tehran.

7. There has yet to be a book-length study of women's religious lives or women mollas, although there are several articles that touch upon it, and several scholars including myself have witnessed women's ceremonies. Research in Iran was largely inspired by the first Western work to deal extensively with Shi'i women's religious ceremonies and mollas, E. W. Fernea's enthralling account of life in a Iraqi village, *Guests of the Sheik* (Garden City, N.Y., 1965).

8. On the harem as a center of useful work and management, see A. L. Marsot, "The Revolutionary Gentlewomen in Egypt," in L. Beck and N. Keddie, eds., *Women in the Muslim World* (Cambridge, Mass., 1978).

9. J. Atkinson, trans., *Customs and Manners of the Women of Persia* (1832; reprinted New York, 1971); A. Chodzko, "Code de la femme chez les persans," unidentified offprint at the Institut Nationale des Langues Orientales Vivantes in Paris.

Chapter 3. Continuity and Change Under the Qajars: 1796–1890

1. G. Curzon, *Persia and the Persian Question*, 2:470–71 (London, 1892): "Formerly, the Crown only, claimed one-tenth; but this proportion was doubled by Fath Ali Shah. In practice it is found that the assessment frequently amounts to 30 percent, and 25 percent may perhaps be taken as a fair average. The system, however, varies absolutely in different parts of the country, and even in different parts of the same province."

2. See N. R. Keddie, "Stratification, Social Control, and Capitalism in Iranian Villages, before and after Land Reform," *Rural Politics and Social Change in the Middle East*, ed. R. Antoun and I. Harik (Bloomington, Ind., 1972), reprinted in N. R. Keddie, *Iran: Religion, Politics and Society* (London, 1980).

3. Mid-nineteenth-century appeals by merchants to the government to limit or prohibit European imports are noted in various sources, among them one reported by a British consul in 1844, cited in C. Issawi, ed., *The Economic History of Iran, 1800–1914* (Chicago, 1971), 76. By the late nineteenth and early twentieth centuries merchants and nationalists were forming companies to boycott Western goods and promote Iranian ones. Even merchants who profited from foreign trade often saw opportunities for greater profit if European privileges were ended.

4. See the account in H. Algar, *Religion and State in Iran 1785–1906* (Berkeley and Los Angeles, 1969), 94–99, which challenges standard Western accounts.

5. See H. Algar, "The Revolt of Agha Khan Mahallati and the Transference of the Isma'ili Imamate to India," *Studia Islamica* 29 (1969): 55–81.

6. See N. R. Keddie, "Religion and Irreligion in Early Iranian Nationalism," *Comparative Studies in Society and History* 4:3 (1962): 265–95, and the sources cited therein (reprinted in N. R. Keddie, *Iran: Religion, Politics and Society* [London, 1980]). On Shaikhism and Babism, see M. Bayat, *Mysticism and Dissent: Socioreligious Thought in Qajar Iran* (Syracuse, 1982), and Abbas Amanat, *Resurrection and Renewal: The Making of the Babi Movement in Iran, 1844–1850* (Ithaca, 1989).

7. See Roger Olson, "Persian Gulf Trade and the Agricultural Economy of Southern Iran," in M. Bonine and N. Keddie, eds., *Modern Iran: The Dialectics of*

Continuity and Change (Albany, 1981). G. Gilbar, "Persian Agriculture in the Late Qajar Period, 1860–1906," *Asian and African Studies* 12:3 (1978): 363, while noting price rises in basic foodstuffs, speaks of a more diversified peasant diet but cites only sugar, tea, opium, and tobacco. His article is, however, factually informative. Nineteenth-century economic decline is argued in H. Katouzian, *The Political Economy of Modern Iran* (London, 1981), chap. 3.

8. A partial translation of this work is found in W. M. Floor's mimeographed Ph.D. thesis, "The Guilds in Qajar Persia," (Leiden, 1971).

9. There is now controversy over the helpful or harmful impact of Western trade on Iranian nineteenth-century living standards. The primarily optimistic views represented by papers presented by Gad Gilbar and Guity Nashat at a 1978 congress in Babolsar, Iran, and Gilbar, "Persian Agriculture," seem based too heavily on assumptions found in pro-British documentation, while V. Nowshirvani's paper at Babolsar was more balanced. W. Floor spoke at a 1980 congress at Harvard of general nineteenth-century immiserization, a view supported by H. Katouzian, *Political Economy*. Olson, "Persian Gulf Trade," indicates that the commercialization of agriculture concentrated wealth in the hands of a few while leaving the majority more vulnerable. When one looks at similar long controversies about prerevolutionary France or post–industrial revolution England it seems clear that not even the unearthing of better statistics and more sophisticated arguments is likely to solve this question to everyone's satisfaction.

10. Curzon, *Persia*, 1:480.

11. On Mirza Hosain Khan, see A. Karny, "Mirza Hosein Khan Moshir od-Dowle and His Attempts at Reform in Iran, 1871–1873" (Ph.D. diss., UCLA, Los Angeles, 1973), and G. Nashat, *The Beginning of Modern Reform in Iran* (Urbana, 1981).

12. See F. Kazemzadeh, *Russia and Britain in Persia. 1864–1914* (New Haven, 1968), chaps. 2–3: L. E. Frechtling, "The Reuter Concession in Persia," *Asiatic Review* 34 (1938); E. Taimuri, *Asr-e bikhabari ya tarikh-e emtiyazat dar Iran* (Tehran, Eqbal, 1953–54).

13. Kazemzadeh, *Russia and Britain,* and Denis Wright, *The English amongst the Persians* (London, 1977).

Chapter 4. Protest and Revolution: 1890–1914

1. On Malkom Khan, see H. Algar, *Mirza Malkum Khan: A Study in the History of Iranian Modernism* (Berkeley and Los Angeles, 1973), the newspaper *Qanun,* and M. Tabataba'i, *Majmu'eh-ye asar-e Mirza Malkam Khan* (Tehran, 1948–49). *Qanun* has been reprinted as a book in Iran.

2. On Afghani, see N. R. Keddie, *Sayyid Jamal ad-Din "al-Afghani": A Political Biography* (Berkeley, 1972), and *An Islamic Response to Imperialism: Political and Religious Writings of Sayyid Jamal ad-Din "al-Afghani"* (Berkeley, 1968); and H. Pakdaman, *Djamal-ed-Din Assad Abadi dit Afghani* (Paris, 1969), and the Persian and Arabic works referred to therein.

3. N. R. Keddie, *Religion and Rebellion in Iran: The Tobacco Protest of 1891–1892* (London, 1966), and the sources in several languages referred to therein.

4. On the late nineteenth century, see E. G. Browne, *The Persian Revolution of*

1905–1909 (Cambridge, 1910); C. Issawi, ed., *The Economic History of Iran: 1800–1914* (Chicago, 1971); and S. Bakhash, *Iran: Monarchy, Bureaucracy and Reform under the Qajars* (London, 1978).

5. See N. R. Keddie, "The Origins of the Religious-Radical Alliance in Iran," *Past and Present* 34 (July 1966): 70–80, and "Religion and Irreligion in Early Iranian Nationalism," in N. R. Keddie, *Iran: Religion, Politics and Society* (London, 1980).

6. On the British and Russian role in these years, see F. Kazemzadeh, *Russia and Britain in Persia, 1864–1914* (New Haven, 1968); N. R. Keddie, "British Policy and the Iranian Opposition 1901–1907, *Journal of Modern History* 39:3 (1967): 266–82, and "Iranian Politics 1900–1905: Background to Revolution," *Middle Eastern Studies* 5:1, 2, 3 (1969): 3–31, 151–67, 234–50.

7. On prerevolutionary oppositional writing, see H. Kamshad, *Modern Persian Prose Literature* (Cambridge, 1966), and E. G. Browne, *The Press and Poetry of Modern Persia* (Cambridge, 1914). I have consulted the Persian books and newspapers mentioned in the latter work.

8. On the probable participation of both the shah and leftists in the Atabak's assassination, see N. R. Keddie, "The Assassination of the Amin as-Sultan (Atabak-i A'zam), 31 August 1907," in C. E. Bosworth, ed., *Iran and Islam* (Edinburgh, 1971).

9. On the revolution, see Janet Afary, *The Iranian Constitutional Revolution, 1906–1911: Grassroots Democracy, Social Democracy, and the Origins of Feminism* (New York, 1996); Mangol Bayat, *Iran's First Revolution: Shi'ism and the Constitutional Revolution of 1905–1909* (New York, 1991); Vanessa Martin, *Iran's First Revolution: Shi'ism and the Constitutional Revolution of 1905–1909* (London, 1989); Houri Berberian, *Armenians and the Iranian Constitutional Revolution of 1905–1911: "The Love for Freedom Has No Fatherland"* (Boulder, Colo., 2001); Browne, *Persian Revolution;* W. M. Shuster, *The Strangling of Persia* (New York, 1912). Among the best Persian books on the revolution are Nazem ol-Eslam Kermani, *Tarikh-e bidari-ye Iranian,* 2d ed. (Tehran, 1332/1944); A. Kasravi, *Tarikh-e mashruteh-ye Iran,* 12th ed. (Tehran, 2535/1977); M. Malekzadeh, *Tarikh-e enqelab-e mashrutiyat-e Iran,* 7 vols. (Tehran, 1328–32/1949–53); and Sayyed Hasan Taqizadeh, *Tarikh-e avva'el-e enqelab-e mashrutiyat-e Iran* (Tehran, 1338/1959–60) A vast literature and documentation exists on the subject, in Persian and English especially.

10. See M. Bayat-Philipp, "Women and Revolution in Iran, 1905–1911," in L. Beck and N. Keddie, eds., *Women in the Muslim World* (Cambridge, Mass., 1978).

11. On the Bakhtiaris and their relations with the British, see Gene R. Garthwaite, *Khans and Shahs: A Documentary Analysis of the Bakhtiyari in Iran* (Cambridge, 1983), Garthwaite's chapter in M. Bonine and N. Keddie, eds., *Modern Iran: The Dialectics of Continuity and Change* (Albany, 1981), and his "The Bakhtiyari Khans, the Government of Iran, and the British, 1846–1915," *International Journal of Middle East Studies* 3:1 (1972): 24–44.

Chapter 5. War and Reza Shah, 1914–1941

1. See F. S. Cocks, ed., *The Secret Treaties and Understandings* 2d ed. (London, 1918), 15–25.

2. See the discussions of these movements in R. W. Cottam, *Nationalism in Iran: Updated Through 1978,* 2d ed. (Pittsburgh, 1979).

3. J. M. Balfour, *Recent Happenings in Persia* (Edinburgh and London, 1922), 3.

4. J. C. Hurewitz, ed., *The Middle East and North Africa in World Politics: A Documentary Record,* 2d ed. (New Haven and London, 1979), 2:182–83.

5. United States, Department of State, *Papers Relating to the Foreign Relations of the United States,* Caldwell to Lansing, August 16, 1919; 1919 (Washington, D.C., 1934), 2:699 (henceforth called U.S. *Papers*).

6. Colby to Caldwell, August 16, 1920, U.S. *Papers,* 1920 (Washington, D.C., 1936), 3:354.

7. F. A. C. Forbes-Leith, *Checkmate: Fighting Tradition in Central Persia* (London, 1927), 44.

8. For discussions of this period and Ironside's key role, see Michael P. Zirinsky, "Imperial Power and Dictatorship: Britain and the Rise of Reza Shah, 1921–1926," *International Journal of Middle East Studies* 24, 4 (November 1992): 639–63; Cyrus Ghani, *Iran and the Rise of Reza Shah: From Qajar Collapse to Pahlavi Rule* (London: I. B. Tauris, 2000); R. H. Ullman, *Anglo-Soviet Relations 1917–1921,* (Princeton, 1972), vol. 3, chap. 9; D. Wright, *The English amongst the Persians* (London, 1977), 180–84. On the (underreported) role of the Democrat-oriented gendarmerie from 1911 on, see Stephanie Cronin, *The Army and the Creation of the Pahlavi State in Iran, 1910–1926* (London: I. B. Tauris, 1997).

9. Hurewitz, *Middle East,* 244.

10. Ibid., 242–43.

11. On these postwar movements, see especially Cottam, *Nationalism.* On Lahuti see Cronin, *The Army,* 47 ff.

12. On Taqizadeh, Iranshahr, and the influence of European pro-"Aryan" racial theories on Iranian intellectual and official nationalism, see especially Afshin Marashi, "Nationalizing Iran: Culture, Power, and the State, 1870–1941" (Ph.D. diss., University of California at Los Angeles, 2003).

13. See the documents in U.S. *Papers,* 1927 (Washington, D.C., 1942), 3:523–24.

14. On Millspaugh's mission, see, in addition to the secondary works covering the period, A. C. Millspaugh, *The Financial and Economic Situation of Persia, 1926* (New York, 1926).

15. On the Sinclair negotiations and their ultimate failure, see U.S. *Papers,* 1923 (Washington, D.C., 1938), 2:711–36, and 1924 (Washington, D.C., 1939), 2:539–52.

16. The 1921–25 events, as well as those of earlier and later periods, are covered in Nikki R. Keddie, *Qajar Iran and the Rise of Reza Khan 1796–1925* (Costa Mesa, Calif., 1999), and Jean-Pierre Digard, Bernard Hourcade, and Yann Richard, *L'Iran au XXe siècle* (Paris, 1996). See also Cronin, *The Army.*

17. V. Sheean, *The New Persia* (London, 1927), 231–32.

18. R. N. Gupta, *Oil in the Modern World* (Westport, Conn., 1976; reprint of Allahabad: Kitab Mahal, 1949), gives production figures, 60.

19. L. P. Elwell-Sutton, *Modern Iran* (London, 1941), 13, 1–33.

20. Badr ol-Molk Bamdad, *From Darkness into Light: Women's Emancipation in Iran,* ed. and trans. F. R. C. Bagley (Hicksville, N.Y., 1977); Jasamin Rostam-Kolayi, "Foreign Education, the Women's Press, and the Discourse of Scientific Domesticity in Early Twentieth Century Iran," in Nikki R. Keddie and Rudi Matthee, eds., *Iran and the Surrounding World: Interactions in Culture and Cultural Politics* (Seattle: University of Washington Press, 2002); Keddie, *Qajar Iran,* 85.

21. More optimistic interpretations are found in A. Banani, *The Modernization of Iran, 1921–1941* (Stanford, 1961), in various writings by D. Wilber, and L. P. Elwell-Sutton, "Reza Shah the Great: Founder of the Pahlavi Dynasty," in G. Lenczowski, ed., *Iran under the Pahlavis* (Stanford, 1978). More critical interpretations are in H. Katouzian, *The Political Economy of Modern Iran* (London, 1981), Ervand Abrahamian, *Iran between Two Revolutions* (Princeton: Princeton University Press, 1982), and John Foran, *Fragile Resistance: Social Transformation in Iran from 1500 to the Revolution* (Boulder, Col.: Westview Press, 1993).

22. Mohammad H. Faghfoory, "The Impact of Modernization on the Ulama in Iran, 1925–1941," *Iranian Studies* 26:3–4 (Summer/Fall 1993): 277–312; Banani, *Modernization*, 70–84.

23. A. K. S. Lambton, *Landlord and Peasant in Persia* (reprinted London, 1969), 189.

24. Ibid., 197.

25. Ibid., 209.

26. Rudi Matthee, "Transforming Dangerous Nomads into Useful Artisans, Technicians, Agriculturists: Education in the Reza Shah Period," *Iranian Studies* 26:3–4 (Summer/Fall 1993): 325; Banani, *Modernization*, 108. See also I. Sadiq, *Modern Persia and Her Educational System* (New York, 1931).

27. Bamdad, *From Darkness into Light*.

28. Banani, *Modernization*, 80–84.

29. D. N. Wilber, *Iran: Past and Present* (Princeton, 1948), 143–44, R. N. Gupta, *Iran, an Economic Study* (New Delhi, 1947); and with different details, Bharier, *Economic Development*, 194–98.

30. Banani, *Modernization*, 133–35, 75–78; Bharier, *Economic Development*, 202–07.

31. Patrick Clawson, "Knitting Iran Together: The Land Transport Revolution, 1920–1940," *Iranian Studies* 26:3–4 (Summer/Fall 1993): 236–50. See also Elwell-Sutton, *Modern Iran*, 93–94, and Wilber, *Iran*, 147.

32. Wilber, *Iran*, 132. Bharier, *Economic Development*, 172–80, gives official figures that are divided somewhat differently.

33. Wilber, *Iran*, 132–33.

34. Bank Melli Iran, *Bulletin de la Banque Mellie Iran* 12 (June 1937): 43–49.

35. Bank Melli Iran, *Bulletin* 55 (Dec. 1941–Jan. 1942): 12.

36. Elwell-Sutton, *Modern Iran*, 115–16.

37. Bharier, *Economic Development*, 65–66, using official figures for expenditures by ministries.

38. Elwell-Sutton, *Modern Iran.*, 117, gives budgets for two years, 1940–41 and 1941–42. See also the ministry budgets 1928–48 in Bharier, *Economic Development*, 65–66.

39. K. Sandjabi, *Essai sur l'économie rurale et le régime agraire de la Perse* (Paris, 1934), which also contains the information below.

40. Lambton, *Landlord*, 246–49.

41. R. W. Davenport, "Soviet Economic Relations with Iran, 1917–1930" (Ph.D. diss., Columbia University, 1953), 141. See also the text and tables on trade in Bharier, *Economic Development*, 102–16.

42. Great Britain, Department of Overseas Trade, *Economic Conditions in Persia* (London, 1930), 13–14.

43. A. Amini, *L'institution du monopole du commerce exterieur en Perse* (Paris, 1932), 144–47. On exchange controls, see Bharier, *Economic Development,* 123–26.

44. Bank Melli Iran, *Bulletin* 2 (March 1934): 3; Wilber, *Iran,* 136.

45. Bank Melli Iran, *Bulletin* 55 (Dec. 1941–Jan. 1942): 326.

46. Elwell-Sutton, *Modern Iran,* 142; on other aspects of education, see Matthee, "Transforming Dangerous Nomads."

47. H. E. Chehabi, "The Banning of the Veil and Its Consequences," and Jasamin Rostam-Kolayi," Expanding Agendas for the 'New' Iranian Woman: Family Law, Work, and Unveiling," both forthcoming in Stephanie Cronin, ed., *Reza Shah's Iran;* H. E. Chehabi, "Staging the Emperor's New Clothes: Dress Codes and Nation-Building under Reza Shah," *Iranian Studies* 26:3–4 (Summer/Fall 1993): 209–33.

48. M. W. Thornburg, "An Economic Study of the Near East with Particular Reference to Oil Revenues (unpublished study, 1944), 25–29.

49. Vanessa Martin, *Creating an Islamic State: Khomeini and the Making of a New Iran* (London: I. B. Tauris, 2000), 13.

Chapter 6. World War II and Mosaddeq: 1941–1953

1. G. Lenczowski, *Russia and the West in Iran, 1918–1948* (Ithaca, 1949), 168.

2. Ibid., 175.

3. A. Millspaugh, *Americans in Persia* (Washington, D.C., 1946), 85–86.

4. Bank Melli Iran, *Bulletin* 56 (Feb.–March 1942): 470.

5. Millspaugh, *Americans,* 47. On American wartime and postwar relations with and interests in Iran, see James A. Bill, *The Eagle and the Lion: The Tragedy of American-Iranian Relations* (New Haven, 1988); Mark J. Gasiorowski, *U.S. Foreign Policy and the Shah: Building a Client State in Iran* (Ithaca, 1991); Barry Rubin, *Paved with Good Intentions* (New York, 1980); and B. Kuniholm, *The Origins of the Cold War in the Middle East* (Princeton, 1980).

6. Millspaugh, *Americans,* 61, 83.

7. On the Tudeh, see Ervand Abrahamian, *Iran between Two Revolutions* (Princeton, 1982); Maziar Behrooz, *Rebels with a Cause: The Failure of the Left in Iran,* (London, 1999); S. Zabih, *The Communist Movement in Iran* (Berkeley, 1966).

8. Zabih, *Communist Movement,* chap. 3, and L. P. Elwell-Sutton, "Political Parties in Iran: 1941–1948," *Middle East Journal* 3:1 (1949): 48.

9. E. Abrahamian, "The Strengths and Weaknesses of the Labor Movement in Iran, 1941–53," in M. Bonine and N. Keddie, eds., *Modern Iran: The Dialectics of Continuity and Change* (Albany, 1981).

10. Millspaugh, *Americans,* 45, and Elwell-Sutton, "Political Parties," 50.

11. Lenczowski, *Russia,* 250–53.

12. Millspaugh, *Americans,* 113, 152.

13. Ibid., 96–152.

14. United States, Department of State, *Treaties and other International Agreements of the United States of America 1776–1949,* 8, "Military Mission with Iranian Gendarmerie" (Washington, D.C., U.S.G.P.O., 1971), 1286–89.

15. R N. Frye, *Iran* (New York, 1953), 113–14. On Allied contributions to inflation, see H. Katouzian, *The Political Economy of Modern Iran* (London, 1981), 142–43.

16. United Nations, Department of Economic Affairs, *Public Finance Information Papers: Iran* (New York, 1951), 21.

17. Great Britain, Department of Overseas Trade, *Persia: Review of Commercial Conditions* (London, 1945), 21–29.

18. Lenczowski, *Russia,* 246, and interviews with Sayyed Zia and others, 1960.

19. Of the several works on the politics of Iranian oil, probably the best is L. P. Elwell-Sutton, *Persian Oil: A Study in Power Politics* (London, 1955). Among works with further information are F. Fesharaki, *Development of the Iranian Oil Industry* (New York, 1976); A. Sampson, *The Seven Sisters* (New York, 1975); M. W. Thornburg, "An Economic Study of the Near East with Particular Reference to Oil Revenues" (unpublished, 1944); and J. M. Blair, *The Control of Oil* (New York, 1976).

20. T. C. Young, "The National and International Relations of Iran," in T. C. Young, ed., *Near Eastern Culture and Society* (Princeton, 1951), 202.

21. Zabih, *Communist Movement,* chap 3; Lenczowski, *Russia,* 195.

22. E. Abrahamian, "Communism and Communalism in Iran: The *Tudah* and the *Firqah-i Dimukrat,*" *International Journal of Middle Eastern Studies* 1:4 (1970): 291–316; Zabih, *Communist Movement,* chap. 3.

23. Zabih, *Communist Movement,* chap. 3.

24. William Eagleton, Jr., *The Kurdish Republic of 1946* (London, 1963), and M. M. Karadaghi, "The Kurdish Question" (unpublished thesis, Berkeley, 1955), 137–54.

25. Terms in Lenczowski, *Russia,* 302.

26. Iran, Ministère du Travail, *La Loi du travail* (Tehran, 1946).

27. International Labour Office, *Labour Conditions in the Oil Industry in Iran* (Geneva, 1950), 28–29.

28. Lenczowski, *Russia,* 308.

29. M. Thornburg, "Communism (Persia)" (unpublished, n.d.), 3.

30. Lenczowski, *Russia,* 313–14. Colonel Schwarzkopf, superintendent of the New Jersey State Police during the Lindbergh kidnapping case of the 1930s, whom I as a child used to hear on a program called "Junior G-Men," was the father of the 1991 Gulf War's General Norman Schwarzkopf, who spent some childhood years in Iran.

31. A. K. S. Lambton, *Landlord and Peasant in Persia* (London, 1953), 379–81.

32. Overseas Consultants, Inc., *Report on Seven Year Development Plan for the Plan Organization of the Imperial Government of Iran* (New York, 1949), 3:8.

33. L. J. Hayden, "Living Standards in Rural Iran: A Case Study," *Middle East Journal* 3:2 (1949): 143. An unpublished Iranian study funded partly with Ford Foundation aid showed very low incomes but also income variation from the relatively prosperous northwest to the incredibly impoverished southeast; it also indicated income and status variation within each village. See N. R. Keddie, "The Iranian Village before and after Land Reform," *Journal of Contemporary History* 3:3 (1968): 69–91, reprinted in H. Bernstein, ed., *Underdevelopment and Development: The Third World Today,* (Harmondsworth, 1973); and N. R. Keddie, "Stratification, Social Control and Capitalism in Iranian Villages, before and after Land Reform," in I. Harik and R. Antoun, eds., *Rural Politics and Social Change in the Middle East* (Bloomington, Ind., 1972), reprinted in N. R. Keddie, *Iran: Religion, Politics and Society* (London, 1980).

34. OCI, *Report,* 3:13; and R. N. Gupta, *Iran: An Economic Study* (New Delhi, 1947), 45.

35. United Nations, *Public Finance Information Papers: Iran* (New York, 1951); and M. Thornburg, "Rising Prices, High Cost of Living, and Fall in Value of the Rial" (unpublished, 1948), 5–6. Sometimes customs duties are listed separately from indirect taxation, but in effect they were a form of indirect taxation, hitting especially items of mass consumption.

36. Thornburg, "Rising Prices," 4.

37. A. Moarefi, *The Iranian Seven Year Plan and Its Monetary Effects* (Washington, D.C., 1950), pt. 3, 85.

38. Lambton, *Landlord*, 244.

39. Ibid., 289.

40. Ibid., 262–63.

41. OCI, *Report*, 1:47.

42. M. Thornburg, "Conversation with Agha Firoughzadeh" (unpublished, Tehran, 1949), 103.

43. United Nations, Department of Economic Affairs, *Review of Economic Conditions in the Middle East, 1951–1952* (New York, 1953), 40.

44. OCI, *Report*, 4:8.

45. Ibid., 18.

46. Ibid., 149, 189.

47. See T. C. Young, "The Social Support of Current Iranian Policy," *Middle East Journal* 6:2 (1952): 125–43.

48. Ibid., 130–31.

49. On working-class and trade-union activity, see especially Abrahamian, "The Strengths and Weaknesses of the Labor Movement in Iran"; see also Gupta, *Iran*, 83.

50. OCI, *Report*, 1:35–38.

51. M. Naficy, "Preliminary Report on the Persian Seven Year Plan" (unpublished, Tehran, 1947), 3.

52. Quoted in Moarefi, *Seven Year Plan*, pt. 6, 2.

53. M. Thornburg, "The Seven Year Plan" (unpublished speech, Tehran, October 19, 1947), 3.

54. OCI, *Report*, 1:5.

55. Moarefi, *Seven Year Plan*, pt. 3, 87.

56. Thornburg, "The First Year of the Plan" (unpublished speech, Tehran, April 5, 1950), 4.

57. Thornburg, "Statement on behalf of O.C.I." (unpublished, June 24, 1950), 3–6.

58. See *Middle East Economist* 5 (May 1951): 8.

59. On Iranian grievances, see especially Elwell-Sutton, *Persian Oil*, chaps. 13–14.

60. Among the sources for this is J. Kimche, *Seven Fallen Pillars: The Middle East 1945–1952* (London, 1953), 341, 348, 354.

61. Elwell-Sutton, *Persian Oil*, chaps. 17–20.

62. *Middle East Economist* 6 (September 1952): 8. On Mosaddeq, see James A. Bill and William Roger Louis, eds., *Musaddiq, Iranian Nationalism and Oil* (Austin, 1988); Homa Katouzian, *Musaddiq and the Struggle for Power in Iran* (London, 1991); R. W. Cottam, *Nationalism in Iran: Updated through 1978* (Pittsburgh, 1979).

63. As early as July 1951, Max Thornburg recommended to Secretary of State Dean Acheson a "bold course" supported by the United States to establish a

"responsible" government that would reach an oil settlement. Thornburg, "Notes for Discussion with Dean Acheson: 5 July, 1951, Washington, D.C." (unpublished).

64. United Nations, Department of Economic Affairs, *Summary of Recent Economic Developments in the Middle East 1952–1953* (New York, 1954), 25. For the dramatic improvement in exports and the balance of trade, see the official statistics reproduced in Katouzian, *Political Economy*, 184.

65. United Nations, *Summary*, 32.

66. Max W. Thornburg to Clare Booth Luce (unpublished, Rome, May 7, 1953). Luce's zeal in pressuring the Italians about buying Iranian oil was brought up against her in the Senate when she was confirmed as ambassador to Brazil.

67. Harry N. Howard, "The Development of United States Policy in the Near East, South Asia, and Africa during 1953: Part I" *Department of State Bulletin* 30:765 (February 22, 1954): 279.

68. Kermit Roosevelt, *Countercoup: The Struggle for the Control of Iran* (New York, 1980). This work was reportedly approved both by the then-shah, to whom Roosevelt represented that it was better to tell the true story than to have false or partly false stories believed, and by the CIA. After publication in the fall of 1979, it was recalled from bookstores in early November, and all copies that the publisher (McGraw-Hill) had or recovered were destroyed. According to reliable sources, British Petroleum (BP, ex-AIOC) objected because British secret service activities were attributed to it. (Internal evidence in the book shows the author often uses false names and identifications without warning the reader.) There has also been speculation that the Carter administration, having decided to let the ex-shah into the United States for medical treatment and knowing it might cause trouble, did not want further publicity given to America's role in the 1953 coup. Clearly proud of his Iran activity, Roosevelt represents Iran as threatened by Russia and communism, and the majority of Iranians as behind the shah, not Mosaddeq. A 1980 edition corrects the point on BP. Various oral sources state that Roosevelt was not as much in charge of the Iranian operation as he says and that he misstates some facts, such as the sum of money spent and his description of the Iranians involved.

69. Gasiorowski, *U.S. Foreign Policy*, 78, based on interviews with five retired CIA officers, gives further details: "This 'fake' Tudeh crowd, paid for with fifty thousand dollars a CIA officer had given 'was designed to provoke fears of a Tudeh takeover and thus to rally support for Zahedi'. The crowd was soon joined by real Tudeh members'. The combined crowd attacked the Reza Shah mausoleum and several mosques and tore down statues of the shah and his father. These demonstrations continued the next day, leading Ambassador Henderson to demand that they be broken up by the police, who were still in their barracks. In what was to be a fateful decision, Mosaddeq acquiesced. The Tudeh retailiated by ordering its cadres off the street. On Wednesday, August 19, most of the Tehran police were to turn against Mosaddeq, while Tudeh crowds remained off the streets."

70. Loy Henderson's statement is in Amin Saikhal, *The Rise and Fall of the Shah* (Princeton, 1980), 215n70. My 1980 interviews with involved parties confirm a figure of several million dollars.

71. For further information on Mosaddeq's overthrow see Gasiorowski, *U.S. Foreign Policy*, chap. 3, Zabih, *Communist Movement*, 199–207. Andrew Tully, *C.I.A: The Inside Story* (New York, 1962), chap. 7, and D. Wise and T. B. Ross, *The Invisible Government* (New York, 1964), 110–13, gave the essence of the story before

Roosevelt's detailed account. R. W. Cottam, *Nationalism in Iran*, stresses internal Iranian forces in the overthrow, but in Cottam's more recent "The Imperial Regime of Iran: Why it Collapsed?" in *L'Iran d'hier et de demain* (Quebec, 1980), he says, "As Dr. Mossadeq had been informed by Soviet Intelligence, his dismissal was the first act of a coup d'état organized by the American CIA and British MI-6 to make General Fazlollah Zehedi prime minister and dictator in Iran." He goes on to say, "The western governments provided the money and direction of eliminating Mossadeq. The purchase of mercenary mob support proved to be the critical element in achieving success on August 19, 1953." This account may be presumed to supersede Cottam's better known earlier one. The detail about Soviet intelligence may come from inside information, although a reliable oral source speaks rather of a Tudeh military officer who was to participate in the coup as having warned Mosaddeq. Gasiorowski's authoritative account is partly based on interviews with CIA participants. See also the new works at the end of this book's bibliography.

Chapter 7. Royal Dictatorship: 1953–1977

1. R. W. Cottam, *Nationalism in Iran. Updated Through 1978* (Pittsburgh, 1979), chap. 16. For details and analysis of the whole post-1953 period, see E. Abrahamian, *Iran between Two Revolutions* (Princeton, 1982), H. Katouzian, *The Political Economy of Modern Iran* (London, 1981), and B. Rubin, *Paved with Good Intentions* (New, York, 1980).

2. On the shah's security methods, see especially M. Zonis, *The Political Elite of Iran* (Princeton, 1971), chaps. 3, 4, and passim.

3. Statistics from Bank Melli *Bulletin* cited in John Marlowe, *Iran: A Short Political Guide* (London, 1963), chap. 7, especially 107.

4. This was discovered in interviews with officials involved in a Ford Foundation–sponsored village survey in Iran in the 1950s, some of whose unpublished written work is reported in N. R. Keddie, "The Iranian Village before and after Land Reform," *Journal of Contemporary History* 3:3 (1968): 69–91, reprinted in H. Bernstein, ed., *Underdevelopment and Development: Third World Today* (Harmondsworth, 1973).

5. Ibid.; A. K. S. Lambton, *The Persian Land Reform 1962–1966* (Oxford, 1969), chap. 2; W. Floor, "The Revolutionary Character of the Iranian Ulama" *International Journal of Middle East Studies* 12:4 (1981): 501–24.

6. On political events in 1960–63 and the Kennedy administration's encouragement of reform to forestall revolution, see James A. Bill, *The Eagle and the Lion: The Tragedy of American-Iranian Relations* (New Haven: Yale University Press, 1988), chap. 4, and Gasiorowski, *U.S. Foreign Policy and the Shah*, 175–187, which says on pages 185–87 that the White Revolution initially increased the shah's popularity, destroyed much of the traditional upper landed class, contributed to swelling the ranks of urban migrants, important in the revolution, and increased clerical opposition to the shah, and that 1963 can be seen as the year "in which a highly autonomous state was finally established in Iran."

7. H. Algar, "The Oppositional Role of the Ulama in Twentieth-Century Iran," in N. R. Keddie, ed., *Scholars, Saints, and Sufis* (Berkeley and Los Angeles, 1972), 246, lists four "real targets of Khumayni's criticism of the regime in 1963," two of which are "the proposal to grant capitulatory rights to American advisors and

military personnel in Iran and their dependents; [and] the contracting of a $200 million loan from the United States for the purchase of military equipment," and on 249 speaks of Khomeini as having been exiled in June 1963. In fact, however, as is documented both in Floor, "Iranian Ulama," and in Zonis, *Political Elite,* chap. 3, both the immunity bill and the loan were passed in late 1964 (although there was earlier discussion of the former), and Khomeini, who was not exiled in 1963 but twice imprisoned up to May 1964, attacked the above-mentioned bills late in 1964, after which he was exiled. Although Algar is correct in saying Khomeini opposed the two bills, this was mainly in 1964, not 1963 as he says.

8. Floor, "Iranian Ulama," gives ulama writings on land reform and woman suffrage; Khomeini and Shariatmadari seem not to have written against land reform, but opposition by several other important ulama is documented by Floor. A recent book quotes a written statement from Khomeini opposing land reform, but Eric Hooglund assures me that none of the anti-Khomeini agrarian specialists in Iran has been able to find any authentic statement by Khomeini against land reform. The cited statement, even if genuine, was not known either at the time or before the 1990s. Khomeini, concerned about mass support, seems to have avoided taking a position on land reform.

9. On Khomeini's life, thought, and political role, see Vanessa Martin, *Creating an Islamic State: Khomeini and the Making of a New Iran* (London: I. B. Tauris, 2000), and Baqer Moin, *Khomeini: Life of the Ayatollah.* (London: I. B. Tauris, 2000).

10. Quoted in Algar, "Oppositional Role," 247.

11. On capitalism in Iran, see especially Fred Halliday, *Iran: Dictatorship and Development* (New York, 1979), chaps. 5ff. On the shah's use of reforms to strengthen his political power, see J. A. Bill, *The Politics of Iran: Groups, Classes and Modernization* (Columbus, Ohio, 1972), chap. 6.

12. See especially R. Looney, *The Economic Development of Iran* (New York, 1973).

13. This policy was proposed by, among others, Hossein Mahdavy in an unpublished paper delivered at Harvard in 1965.

14. See the calculations in Keddie, "The Iranian Village."

15. See the calculations from Plan Organization and Central Bank data in J. and A. Carey, "Iranian Agriculture and Its Development: 1952–1973," *IJMES* 7:3 (1976): 359–82. On land reform and its results, see, in addition to the works cited in notes 4, 5, and 11–14 above, and 16–18 below, M. G. Weinbaum, "Agricultural Policy and Development Politics in Iran," *Middle East Journal* 31:4 (1977); Paul Vieille, *La Féodalité et l'état en Iran* (Paris, 1975); T. Brun and R. Dumont, "Iran: Imperial Pretensions and Agricultural Dependence," *MERIP Reports* 71 (1978); A. K. S. Lambton, "Land Reform and the Rural Cooperative Societies," in E. Yar-Shater, ed., *Iran Faces the Seventies* (New York, 1971); and N. R. Keddie, "Oil, Economic Policy and Social Conflict in Iran," *Race and Class* 21:1 (1979): 13–29. E. J. Hooglund has done extensive field study of the Iranian land reform over a period of years, the results of which have been given in several articles and in *Reform and Revolution in Rural Iran* (Austin, 1982).

16. M. A. Katouzian, "Oil versus Agriculture: A Case of Dual Resource Depletion in Iran," *Journal of Peasant Studies* 5:3 (1978): 347–69, and the cited Oxford University dissertation by Fatemah Etemad Moghadam, "The Effects of Farm Size and Management System on Agricultural Production in Iran," Somerville College, 1978.

17. Calculations from official figures in J. and A. Carey, "Iranian Agriculture," 359, and Halliday, *Iran*, 130. The Careys' statement that over 8 percent of Iran's total population went from rural to urban areas in 1972–73 can be reconciled with the fact of rising rural population only if 1972–73 was an exceptional year. Both statements are based on official statistics, but these are often in error, as noted in T. Walton, "Economic Development and Revolutionary Upheavals in Iran," *Cambridge Journal of Economics* 4:3 (1980), where the increase in rural-urban migration in the 1966–76 census period is analyzed. The migration figures in Halliday, *Iran*, for 1956–76 are compatible with the slight increase in those employed in agriculture that he cites; clearly the migration rate was higher in the 1970s than before.

18. See Lois Beck, "Economic Transformations among the Qashqa'i Nomads, 1962–1977," in M. Bonine and N. Keddie, eds., *Modern Iran: The Dialectics of Continuity and Change* (Albany, 1981); and Dan Morgan, *Merchants of Grain* (New York, 1979).

19. G. B. Baldwin, *Planning and Development in Iran* (Baltimore, 1967).

20. Much of the above analysis is based on private conversations or unpublished reports by Iranian and international organizations. Among the most useful published works are R. Looney, *Economic Development*; International Labour Organization, *Employment and Income Policies for Iran* (Geneva, 1973); D. Housego, "Quiet Thee Now and Rest," *The Economist*, August 28, 1976; R. Graham, *Iran: The Illusion of Power*, rev. ed. (London, 1979), and Halliday, *Iran*. A more recent summary is in Gasiorowski, *U.S. Foreign Policy and the Shah*, which notes, 207, "The decadence, corruption, and Westernized outlook of the upper class and royal family clashed sharply with the values and social customs of the traditional middle and lower classes, creating growing cultural dualism. The traditional middle and lower classes increasingly regarded the royal family and the upper class as immoral and un-Islamic and blamed the shah and his policies for this moral degeneration. Moreover, the growing gap between the values and social customs of the modern and traditional sectors of society largely paralleled the gap between the living standards of the upper and lower classes."

21. M. H. Pesaran and F. Gahvary, "Growth and Income Distribution in Iran," in R. Stone and W. Peterson, eds., *Econometric Contributions to Public Policy* (London, 1978). Pesaran has done excellent studies on income distribution, as has F. Mehran; most of the latter were distributed in mimeo by the ILO. On income distribution, see also Looney, *Economic Development*, and his *Income Distribution Policies and Economic Growth in Semiindustrialized Countries* (New York, 1975), and ILO *Employment*.

22. Graham, *Illusion of Power*, chap. 5.

23. See Keddie, "Oil, Economic Policy and Social Conflict."

24. See A. Sampson, *The Arms Bazaar: From Lebanon to Lockheed* (New York, 1977), chap. 14, "The Arming of the Shah." On the 1960s, see J. C. Hurewitz, *Middle East Politics: The Military Dimension* (New York, 1969), chap. 15, "An American Client: Iran."

25. On Iranian women 1960–77, see the introduction and articles by L. Beck, M. Fischer, M. Good, J. and M. Gulick, B. Pakizegi, N. Tapper, and P. Vieille, in L. Beck and N. Keddie, eds., *Women in the Muslim World* (Cambridge, Mass., 1978).

26. On the secular opposition, see Halliday, *Iran*, chap. 8. *MERIP Reports* 86 (Mar.–Apr. 1980) is entitled "The Left Forces in Iran," and in addition to articles and

interviews by Fred Halliday, contains a major article by E. Abrahamian, "The Guerrilla Movement in Iran, 1963–1977," 3–15. See also Abrahamian, *Iran.*

27. See M. Fischer, *Iran: From Religious Dispute to Revolution* (Cambridge, Mass., 1980), chap. 6, and S. Akhavi, *Religion and Politics in Contemporary Iran* (Albany, 1980), chaps. 5–6.

Chapter 8. Modern Iranian Political Thought

1. On ta'ziyeh, see P. J. Chelkowski, *Ta'ziyeh: Ritual and Drama in Iran* (New York, 1979). Women's ceremonies have been witnessed by the author in Isfahan, 1977, and elsewhere.

2. On popular theater, see W. Beeman, "A Full Arena: The Development and Cultural Meaning of Popular Performance Traditions in Iran," in M. Bonine and N. Keddie, eds., *Modern Iran: The Dialectics of Continuity and Change* (Albany, 1981). I saw versions of several of these plays at the Shiraz Festival in 1976.

3. This is based on oral presentations by Kaveh Safa Esfahani on Iranian women's theater games.

4. See especially the discussion of the dissident tradition since Safavid times by Mangol Bayat-Philipp, "Tradition and Change in Iranian Socio-Religious Thought," in Bonine and Keddie, *Modern Iran.*

5. See N. R. Keddie, *Sayyid Jamal ad-Din "al-Afghani": A Political Biography* (Berkeley and Los Angeles, 1972,) and Keddie, *An Islamic Response to Imperialism: Political and Religious Writings of Sayyid Jamal ad-Din "al-Afghani."* (Berkeley and Los Angeles, 1968). On other thinkers, see H. Algar, *Mirza Malkum Khan: A Study, in the History of Iranian Modernism* (Berkeley and Los Angeles, 1973); E. G. Browne, *The Persian Revolution of 1905–1909* (Cambridge, 1910) and *The Press and Poetry of Modern Persia* (Cambridge, 1914); M. Bayat, *Mysticism and Dissent, Socio-religious Thought in Qajar Iran* (Syracuse, 1982).

6. In addition to the above works, see H. Kamshad, *Modern Persian Prose Literature* (Cambridge, 1966).

7. Interview with Mohammad Ali Jamalzadeh, Geneva, summer, 1961; discussed also in N. R. Keddie, "Religion and Irreligion in Early Iranian Nationalism," reprinted in N. R. Keddie, *Iran: Religion, Politics and Society,* (London, 1980).

8. See Keddie, "Religion and Irreligion," and E. G. Browne, *Materials for the Study of the Babi Religion* (Cambridge, 1918), 221. Confirmation of those listed by Browne as men who were reputed to be Azali Babis (for at least a large part of their lifetime) was given me orally by Sayyed Hasan Taqizadeh in 1960, although he did not want to be listed as a source during his lifetime: the most important were Mirza Aqa Khan Kermani; Shaikh Ahmad Ruhi (and his brothers); Malek al-Motakallemin; and Mirza Jahangir Khan.

9. See H. Algar, "The Oppositional Role of the Ulama in Twentieth-Century Iran," in N. R. Keddie, ed., *Scholars, Saints, and Sufis* (Berkeley and Los Angeles, 1972), and A.-H. Hairi, *Shi'ism and Constitutionalism in Iran* (Leiden, 1977).

10. See M. C. Hillmann, "Furugh Farrukhzad, Modern Iranian Poet," in E. W. Fernea and B. Q. Bezirgan, eds., *Middle Eastern Muslim Women Speak* (Austin, 1976). Farzaneh Milani has written a UCLA dissertation on Farrukhzad.

11. See Kamshad, *Modern Persian Prose,* pt. 2, and Sadeq Hedayat, *Haji Agha,* trans. G. W. Wickens, introduction by Lois Beck (Austin, 1979).

12. Kamshad, *Modern Persian Prose*, chap. 12.

13. See S. Behrangi, *The Little Black Fish and Other Modern Persian Stories*, trans. E. and M. Hooglund (Washington, D.C., 1976); R. Baraheni, *The Crowned Cannibals: Writings on Repression in Iran* (New York, 1977); "Iran: Contemporary Persian Literature," special issue of *Literary Review*, ed. T. M. Ricks, vol. 18, no. 1 (1974).

14. See E. Abrahamian, "Kasravi: The Integrative Nationalist of Iran," in E. Kedourie and S, G. Haim, eds., *Towards a Modern Iran* (London, 1980), and the sources cited therein.

15. See Jalal Al-e Ahmad, *Khasi dar miqat* (Tehran, 1977) and the discussion of it in Brad Hanson "The 'Westoxication' of Iran: Depictions and Reactions of Behrangi, Al-e Ahmad, and Shariati," *International Journal of Middle East Studies* 15:1 (Feb. 1983): 1–23. See also the discussion of Shariati in S. Akhavi, *Religion and Politics in Contemporary Iran* (Albany, 1980), and M. Bayat-Philipp, "Shi'ism in Contemporary Iranian Politics: The Case of Ali Shari'ati," in Kedourie and Haim, eds., *Towards a Modern Iran*.

16. On Khalil Maleki and Iranian political ideas and programs in the Pahlavi period, see H. Katouzian, *The Political Economy of Modern Iran* (London, 1981).

17. See M. Rodinson, *Marxisme et monde musulman* (Paris, 1972).

18. See A. Abdel-Malek, "Political Islam—Positions," unpublished text, Round Table on Socialism in the World, 1978, Cavtat, September, 1978.

19. The phrase "Gharbzadegi" was popularized by Al-e Ahmad, but he borrowed it from Ahmad Fardid; see J. Al-e Ahmad, *Gharbzadegi*, 2d ed. (Tehran, 1979), 16.

20. The best biography of Al-e Ahmad is that which he himself wrote in 1967–68, "Masalan sharh-e ahvalat," *Jahan-e Nau* 26:3 (Tehran, 1348/1969): 4–8.

21. Hanson, "The Westoxication of Iran," notes that in his pilgrimage diary, *Khasi dar miqat*, Al-e Ahmad tries to be a Muslim but observes what is around him at Mecca with a very detached and critical eye.

22. Al-e Ahmad wrote, after citing Shariati at length, that in January 1969 he "had the honor to meet two or three times the great Ali Shariati while I was in Mashhad, and I was impressed. We spoke at length on the subject of intellectuals in our society, and I am happy that on these questions we walk on the same path." (*Dar khedmat va khiyanat-e raushanfekran*, 3d ed. [Tehran, 1977–78], 51n1).

23. See n. 19, above.

24. Fazlollah Nuri has generally been considered by historians as a reactionary, so Al-e Ahmad's view was shocking to many.

25. Naraghi, a sociologist known in the West, was for some years with UNESCO. He was particularly concerned with problems of cultural colonialism and the flight of intellectuals. Born into a family of Kashan ulama, Naraghi speaks of Islam as an institution, a spiritual tradition defending national identity against materialist leveling. Religion, however, is not central to his cultural sociology. See E. Naraghi, *L'Orient et la crise de L'Occident*, trans. B. Simon (Paris, 1977), 167–85. He was imprisoned after the revolution and wrote a book from France recounting his prison experiences.

26. See M. Fashkhami, *Talkhisi az zendegi-ye qa'ed-e a'zam Emam Khomeini* (Tehran, 1357/1978), 13–15.

27. Ruhollah Khomeini, *Kashf al-asrar* (n.p., 1323/1944), 2.

28. Ibid., 185–86, 222.

29. W. G. Millward, "The Islamic Political Theory and Vocabulary of Ayatullah Khumayni, 1941–1963," unpublished paper, presented to MESA, Salt Lake City, 1979.

30. Ruhollah Khomeini, *Hokumat-e eslami* (Najaf, 1971), 13. There are several recent editions, sometimes as *Velayat-e faqih.*

31. *Hokumat-e eslami,* 33.

32. Ibid., 53.

33. Ibid., 60.

34. Ibid., 177.

35. *Jehad-e akbar,* published together with *Hokumat-e eslami.* It is undated but must come from the years of exile in Najaf.

36. As leader of the great outdoor prayers at Tehran University, Ramadan, 1979, he attacked the Kurdish and Arab autonomy movements as inspired by outside leftists, but in his last statement in September 1979 he restated his former sympathy with minority desires. Possibly he feared Iran might fall apart, which caused him for some months to mute his criticisms of the government.

37. See M. Taleqani, *Tarjomeh va sharh-e Nahj al-balagha* (n.p., n.d.); Taleqani, *Partovi az Qor'an,* 4 vols. (reprinted, Tehran).

38. M. H. Na'ini, *Tanbih al-omma va tanzih al-mella; ya hokumat az nazar-e Eslam,* introduction, notes, and commentary by M. Taleqani (n.p., 1955). On this book, see A. Hairi, *Shi'ism and Constitutionalism in Iran* (Leiden, 1977).

39. M. Taleqani, *Eslam va malekiyat dar moqayeseh ba nezamha-ye eqtesadi-ye gharb* (n.p., n.d.). The mention of "gharbzadegi" (167) suggests that this book may date from the 1960s.

40. Ibid., 282, 297, 141, 283.

41. See Taleqani's article in *Bahsi dar bareh-ye marja'iyat va ruhaniyat* (Tehran, 1341/1962), and A. K. S. Lambton, "A Reconsideration of the Position of the *marja' al-taqlid* and the Religious Institution," *Studia Islamica* 20 (1964): 125ff. Taleqani was the sole religious leader who openly approved of Shariati; see his speech of 26 Ordibehesht (1358/1979) in *Majmu'eh-ye chand sokhanrani dar Daneshgah-e Tehran be monasebat-e ruz-e Shariati* (n.p., n.d.).

42. See M. Bazargan, "Peragmatizm dar Eslam," in *Bi-nehayat kuchekha* (Tehran, 1357/1978).

43. See the "portrait" of Bazargan in *Le Monde,* February 7, 1979.

44. See M. Bazargan, *Marz bain-e din va siyasat,* speech of September 12, 1962 (n.p., n.d.), 8.

45. Ibid., 46.

46. *Mazhab dar Orupa,* lecture of 1942, ed. and notes by M. Khosraushahi, recent reedition (Tehran, n.d.).

47. *Kar dar Eslam va dar Iran,* lecture, April 1946 (Qom, 1347/1968).

48. See, for example, *Bad va baran dar Qor'an* (Qom, 1344/1965).

49. M. Bazargan, "Entezar-e mardom az maraje'," in *Bahsi dar bareh-ye marja'iyat,* 126ff.

50. The existing short biographies of Shariati disagree about dates. See "Zistnameh-ye Doktor Shari'ati," in *Yadnameh-ye Doktor 'Ali Shari'ati be monasebat-e chehelom-e u* (Tehran, 2536 shah/1977); "Salnameh-ye zendegi va asar-e Doktor 'Ali Shari'ati," *Yadnameh-ye salgard-e hejrat-e "Abu Zarr-e zaman" Os-*

tad Doktor 'Ali Shari'ati (Tehran, 1978). Shariati's doctoral dissertation at the Sorbonne, which both authors of this book have seen, was a philological one under the direction of Professor G. Lazard: an edition, translation, and introduction to a classical Persian text, the *Faza'el-e Balkh.*

51. A preliminary bibliography of Shariati by Y. R[ichard] is in *Abstracta Iranica,* 1 and 2 (Tehran-Leiden, 1978, 1979). Hamid Algar has translated some texts in *On the Sociology of Islam* (Berkeley, 1979). These are among the least specifically Shi'i texts of Shariati. Other translations include *Hajj* by A. Behzadnia and N. Denny (Bedford, 1978), and several booklets in English published in Tehran by the Hosainiyeh Ershad, the Shariati Foundation, and the Hamdani Foundation. The oratorical style of Shariati and the rapid analyses he sometimes made before his enthusiastic public render translation difficult.

52. A. Shariati, *Tashayyo'-e 'alavi va tashayyo'-e safavi* (n.p., n.d.), 320ff. An independent translation is in Shahrough Akhavi, *Religion and Politics in Contemporary Iran* (Albany, 1980), 231–33. Akhavi's book appeared after this section was written; it contains additional useful information about the men and trends discussed herein.

53. A. Shariati, *Fatima Fatima ast,* lecture delivered in 1350/1971, recently reprinted.

54. A. Shariati, *Ommat va emamat* (n.p., n.d.), 179–80.

55. A series of fatwas has recently been reproduced in Qom without a title page, but with the original handwriting photocopied to prove authenticity, containing condemnations and warnings of leading mujtahids against Shariati. Included are Ayatollah Khomeini, who never names Shariati but points to his ideas in decrees of 1964, 1977, 1978, and 1979; Ayatollah Shariatmadari, Ayatollahs Najafi, Kho'i, Qomi, Milani, Esfahani, Abdollah Shirazi, Mar'ashi, and others. Khomeini almost surely did not direct a 1964 decree against the then-unknown Shariati, but it may have been included to indicate that Khomeini was the first to see the danger of one who wished to divide the ulama. (Shariati was in France during Khomeini's 1962–64 political activities, and his works do not refer to Khomeini, whereas Al-e Ahmad praises Khomeini and reproduces his speech against capitulations in October 1964 in his *Dar Khedmat,* 7ff.)

56. *Yadnameh-ye salgard-e hejrat.*

57. A. Shariati, *Tashayyo'-e 'alavi,* 273–74.

58. A. Bani Sadr, *Mauqe'iyat-e Iran va naqsh-e Modarres,* vol. 1 (n.p., 1356/1977); and *Monafeqin az didgah-e ma,* reprinted (n.p., n.d.); and *Kish-e shakhsiyat* (n.p., 1355/1976).

59. *Eqtesad-e tauhidi* (Tehran, 1357/1978).

60. A. Bani Sadr, *Bayaniyeh-ye jomhuri-ye eslami* (Tehran, 1358/1979), xi. On the ties between Shariati and Bani Sadr, see the three texts of Bani Sadr in the collection *Vizhenameh (-ye Shari'ati), yekomin salgard* (n.p., n.d.). Through his favorable reflections on Shariati's work one may discern Bani Sadr's position—more subtle than that of his predecessor but very close, notably on the problem of the place of theologians in society. He writes, "We must not expect anything from the 'traditional' masters who are the guardians of cultural institutions. In two centuries they have been deprived of the foundations of thought and action, and this deprivation continues. Sometimes they make a little formal protest before submitting. Among them, it is true, have been found Sayyed Jamal ('Afghani'), Modarres,

Khomeini, and Taleqani. But these same traditional masters have kept these persons from conquering their enemies" (131–32).

61. A. Bani Sadr, *Osul-e payeh va zabeteha-ye hokumat-e eslami* (n.p., 1975).

62. Ibid., 51–52.

63. Critical studies of recent Islamic thought in Iran are found in articles by W. Floor, H. Katouzian, and others in *Mardomnameh* (Berlin, 1981). Other critical studies include N. Keddie, "L'Ayatollah, est-il integriste?" *Le Monde*, August 22, 1980, and "Islamic Revival as Third Worldism," reprinted in N. R. Keddie, *Iran and the Muslim World: Resistance and Revolution* (New York, 1995). Translations from the writings of Bani Sadr and selections from his French writings are in Abol-Hassan Banisadr, *Quelle révolution pour l'Iran?* (Paris, 1980). A survey of traditional and modern Shi'i thought is Y. Richard, *Le Shi'isme en Iran* (Paris, 1980).

Chapter 9. The Revolution

1. Many of the above conclusions about the shah's illness and its political effect are based on my own observations and newspaper reading in Iran in the summers of 1977 and 1978 and on interviews 1978–81. The role of the shah's cancer in weakening him in 1978 is discussed in M. A. Ledeen and W. H. Lewis, "Carter and the Fall of the Shah: The Inside Story," *Washington Quarterly* 3:2 (1980): 3–40. Conclusions on the role of the human rights program are based on observations and interviews, and on B. Rubin, *Paved with Good Intentions* (New York, 1980), chap. 7, and R. Cottam, "Goodbye to America's Shah," *Foreign Policy* 34 (Spring 1979): 3–14.

2. R. Graham, *Iran, The Illusion of Power,* rev. ed. (London, 1979), has good brief coverage of the revolution in chapter 12, which ends in March 1979. In addition to books and articles specifically mentioned below, for the Revolution and its background I have used numerous interviews, regular newspaper reading, especially of *Le Monde*, the *New York Times*, the *Washington Post*, and the *Los Angeles Times*, as well as regular reading of magazines and journals, including the 1979 Iranian journal *The Iranian* and many others. See also M. Fischer, *Iran: From Religious Dispute to Revolution* (Cambridge, Mass., 1980), esp. chap. 6.

3. Graham, *Iran,* 212, and newspaper coverage at the time.

4. E. Abrahamian, "The Guerrilla Movement in Iran, 1963–1977," *MERIP Reports* 86 (Mar.–Apr. 1980): 3–21.

5. Ibid., 9–10.

6. Ibid., 11.

7. This has been reported in several sources, but the most interesting may be Fereydoun Hoveyda, *The Fall of the Shah,* trans. Roger Liddell (New York, 1980). Although apologetic and often inaccurate about himself and his brother, Hoveyda has some good information about the 1970s. On pages 84–85, after discussing Amuzegar's abrupt credit squeeze, Hoveyda says, "In his relentless drive to cut spending, Amuzegar abruptly canceled the funding that my brother had made available for religious purposes, amounting to about eleven million dollars a year. This money, charged against the secret budget of the Prime Minister, was used to finance the upkeep of the country's mosques and Koranic schools as well as for various other expenses. . . . These grants were for the benefit of all the clergy, including the supporters of Khomeini." Hoveyda goes on to note Amuzegar's announcement of the plan to extend the Tehran north-south expressway to go through the bazaar,

giving rise to "rumors that the shah wanted to destroy their tradespeople's shops and disperse them. After the Amuzegar government's drastic cuts and the announcement of this plan, discontent spread among religious circles, the middle classes, and the tradesmen in the bazaars." Hoveyda's views are, however, contested by a few Iranians interviewed, who feel that the acts described were the fault of the shah rather than Amuzegar.

8. Ruhollah Khomeini, *Nehzat-e Eslami 3: Tazadd-e Eslam va shahanshahan va rezhim-e shahanshahan* (n.d., n.p.). (The text of a talk given on June 22, 1971, in Najaf directed against the shah's celebration of the 2,500th anniversary of the Persian monarchy).

9. R. Graham, *Iran,* 224.

10. See E. Hooglund, "Rural Participation in the Revolution," *MERIP Reports* 87 (May 1980): 3–6.

11. This is based on extensive interviewing of Iranian liberals in Iran in June and July 1978 and subsequently.

12. On the above points, aside from newspapers see Rubin, *Paved with Good Intentions*; W. Sullivan, "Dateline Iran: The Road Not Taken," *Foreign Policy* 40 (Fall 1980); M. Ledeen and W. Lewis, "Carter and the Fall of the Shah"; and R. Shaplen, "The Eye of the Storm," *New Yorker*, pts. 1 and 2, June 2 and 9, 1980.

13. The above conclusions are based on my analysis of numerous sources, including those mentioned in note 12, above, and on interviews with several involved parties.

14. Abrahamian, "Guerrilla," 13.

15. Graham, *Iran,* 240.

Chapter 10. Politics and Economics Under Khomeini

1. When I cited in talks in 1978 Khomeini's treatise (which I had read under the title *Hokumat-e Islami* in 1973 in the library of the School of Oriental and African Studies) Iranian students accused me of falsifying his views, and there was a similar reaction when English translations of several passages of the work were published late in 1978 in the *New York Times*.

2. Asghar Schirazi, *The Constitution of Iran: Politics and the State in the Islamic Republic,* trans. John O'Kane (London: I. B. Tauris, 1997), 24–26.

3. Mohsen M. Milani, *The Making of Iran's Islamic Revolution: From Monarchy to Islamic Republic* (Boulder: Westview Press, 1988), 324. Vanessa Martin, *Creating an Islamic State: Khomeini and the Making of a New Iran* (London: I. B. Tauris, 2000), shows how well the Khomeinists were organized before and after the revolution.

4. For the first years of the revolution, see Shaul Bakhash, *The Reign of the Ayatollahs: Iran and the Islamic Revolution,* rev. ed. (New York: Basic Books, 1989). A useful work analyzing Iran's many centers of power is Wilfried Buchta, *Who Rules Iran? The Structure of Power in the Islamic Republic* (Washington, D.C.: Washington Institute for Near East Policy, 2000).

5. On the Freedom Movement, see H. E. Chehabi, *Iranian Politics and Religious Modernism: The Liberation Movement of Iran under the Shah and Khomeini* (Ithaca: Cornell University Press, 1990).

6. For a complete history of this group until 1986, see Ervand Abrahamian, *The Iranian Mojahedin* (New Haven: Yale University Press, 1989).

7. The best book on the secular left is Maziar Behrooz, *Rebels with a Cause: The Failure of the Left in Iran* (London: I. B. Tauris, 1999).

8. David Menashri, *Iran: A Decade of War and Revolution* (New York: Holmes and Meier, 1990), 268–71.

9. For a firsthand account of workers' councils, see Asef Bayat, *Workers and Revolution in Iran: A Third World Experience of Workers' Control* (London: Zed Books, 1987).

10. On Khalkhali and Hoveyda's trial and execution, see Abbas Milani, *Persian Sphinx: Amir Abbas Hoveyda and the Riddle of the Iranian Revolution* (Washington, D.C.: Mage Publishers, 2000). On execution statistics, Ervand Abrahamian, *Tortured Confessions: Prisons and Public Recantations in Modern Iran* (Berkeley: University of California Press, 1999), says that from February 1979 through June 1981, 757 persons were executed. This includes 260 persons executed as drug dealers, murderers, robbers, and "sexual offenders." It does not include those killed in fighting in Kurdistan, Baluchistan, and Khuzistan. Most of the executed were royalists.

11. Schirazi, *The Constitution of Iran,* 25–32.

12. On all phases of the constitution, see ibid.

13. See Bakhash, *Reign of the Ayatollahs,* chap. 4.

14. On the hostage crisis, see especially Gary Sick, *All Fall Down: America's Tragic Encounter with Iran* (New York: Random House, 1985).

15. According to Abrahamian, *Tortured Confessions,* 129–32, from June 1981 through July 1988 there were 7,943 persons executed, of whom 6,472 were Mojahedin, 350 Feda'iyan, 255 Paykar, and 101 Kurdish Democrat Party. There was also an unknown number on both sides killed in armed fights. Of the 7,943 the largest group were from the Mojahedin-e Khalq, and the rest from different leftist groups.

16. How unthinkingly many prominent persons in the West, including parliamentarians and congresspersons, will sign anything opposed to the IRI is shown by the fact that the Mojahedin have continued to get support, mainly in the form of signatures to their statements, in the United States and in European countries, despite the United States having listed them since the 1990s as a terrorist group and their long alliance with Iraq.

17. David McDowall, *A Modern History of the Kurds,* rev. ed. (London: I. B. Tauris, 2000), chap. 13.

18. Ervand Abrahamian has written me that these confessions were less categorical than they are often made to seem.

19. Menashri, *Iran,* 266–68, 347–50.

20. On factions, see Mehdi Moslem, *Factional Politics in Post-Khomeini Iran* (Syracuse: Syracuse University Press, 2002); Bahman Baktiari, *Parliamentary Politics in Revolutionary Iran: The Institutionalization of Factional Politics* (Gainesville, Fla.: University Press of Florida, 1996).

21. Most recent works give the average age of women at marriage as twenty-two or twenty-three and rising, but *The Economist* January 19, 2003, *Survey: Iran* "The Curse of Westoxification," gives the figure of twenty-six, which seems high, unless it includes marriages subsequent to first marriages and the other works do not.

22. On Iran's international policies in these years, see especially R. K. Ramazani,

Revolutionary Iran: Challenge and Response in the Middle East (Baltimore: Johns Hopkins University Press, 1986).

23. On this and prior aspects of United States–Iran relations, see James A. Bill, *The Eagle and the Lion: The Tragedy of American-Iranian Relations* (New Haven: Yale University Press, 1988).

24. See Joost R. Hiltermann in the *International Herald Tribune*, January 17, 2003: "Analysis of thousands of captured Iraqi secret police documents and declassified United States government documents, as well as interviews with scores of Kurdish survivors, senior Iraqi defectors and retired United States intelligence officers, show . . . that the United States, fully aware it was Iraq, accused Iran . . . of being partly responsible for the [Halabja poison gas] attack. The State Department instructed its diplomats to say that Iran was partly to blame. The result . . . was that the international community failed to muster the will to condemn Iraq strongly. . . . This was at a time when Iraq was launching what proved to be the final battles of the war against Iran. Its wholesale use of poison gas against Iranian troops and Iranian Kurdish towns, and its threat to place chemical warheads on the missiles it was lobbing at Tehran, brought Iran to its knees. The deliberate American prevarication on Halabja was the logical . . . outcome of a pronounced six-year tilt toward Iraq. . . . The United States began the tilt after Iraq, the aggressor in the war, was expelled from Iranian territory by a resurgent Iran. . . . Sealed by National Security Decision Directive 114 in 1983, the tilt included billions of dollars in loan guarantees and other credits to Iraq. Sensing correctly that it had carte blanche, Saddam's regime escalated its resort to gas warfare, graduating to ever more lethal agents. Because of the strong Western animus against Iran, few paid heed. Then came Halabja. Unfortunately for Iraq's sponsors, Iran rushed Western reporters to the blighted town. . . . In response, the United States launched the "Iran too" gambit. The story was cooked up in the Pentagon, interviews with the principals show. A newly declassified State Department document demonstrates that United States diplomats received instructions to press this line with United States allies. . . . The UN Security Council['s] . . . choice of neutral language (condemning the 'continued use of chemical weapons in the conflict between the Islamic Republic of Iran and Iraq,' and calling on 'both sides to refrain from the future use of chemical weapons') diffused the effect of its belated move. Iraq proceeded to step up its use of gas until the end of the war and even afterward. . . . Some of those who engineered the tilt today are back in power in the Bush administration. They have yet to account for their judgment that it was Iran, not Iraq, that posed the primary threat to the Gulf; for building up Iraq so that it thought it could invade Kuwait and get away with it; for encouraging Iraq's weapons of mass destruction programs by giving the regime a de facto green light on chemical weapons use; and for turning a blind eye to Iraq's worst atrocities, and then lying about it." Stephen Pelletiere revived the charge that Iran was responsible for gassing Halabja in an op-ed in the *New York Times*, Jan. 31, 2003, a charge that was effectively refuted by subsequent letters from several informed specialists in the *New York Times*. Hiltermann expands on this subject in a forthcoming book on the aftermath of the Iran–Iraq war, ed. Lawrence Potter and Gary Sick.

25. On the war, see Shahram Chubin and Charles R. Tripp, *Iran and Iraq at War* (London: I. B. Tauris, 1988), and Dilip Hiro, *The Longest War: The Iran-Iraq Military Conflict* (New York: Routledge, 1991). In 1988, the last year of the war,

Amnesty International estimates that about 2,500 persons were executed. See Abrahamian, *Tortured Confessions,* 209–19. This would bring total political executions since 1979 to ca. 11,000, the largest number coming not right after the revolution but at times of a virtual civil war with the MK and war with Iraq. Although these are grim and indefensible figures, they pale in comparison with the "great" revolutions in France, Russia, and China and with executions tied to civil wars, coups, and dictatorships in Latin America, Indonesia, and Africa, not to mention genocidal killings in several continents.

26. There are several books on the Rushdie affair, among them Malise Ruthven, *A Satanic Affair: Salman Rushdie and the Rage of Islam* (London: Chatto and Windus, 1990).

27. The basic events of the period since 1979 are well summarized in Elton L. Daniel, *The History of Iran* (Westport, Conn.: Greenwood Press, 2001), though I do not always agree with his emphases or conclusions.

Chapter 11. Post-Khomeini Iran

1. For an analysis of the differing policies of the Khamene'i-Rafsanjani pro-capitalist leadership and the populist Islamic Left, see Ervand Abrahamian, *Khomeinism: Essays on the Islamic Republic* (Berkeley: University of California Press, 1993), Epilogue. For details, see Mehdi Moslem, *Factional Politics in Post-Khomeini Iran* (Syracuse: Syracuse University Press, 2002), and Bahman Baktiari, *Parliamentary Politics in Revolutionary Iran: The Institutionalization of Factional Politics* (Gainesville: University Press of Florida, 1996).

2. Among several statements by Israelis and by some pro-Israeli Americans, see *Haaretz,* March 20, 2003: "Could the American people still be facing years of war . . . The issue was raised in Israel well before the assault began, prompted by remarks earlier this week by former prime minister Shimon Peres. 'The war in Iraq is just the beginning,' Peres told Israel Channel One Television. 'Problems of the first magnitude can be expected thereafter, as well: Iran, North Korea, and Libya. The problem is, can you simply abandon the world to dictators, to weapons of mass destruction?' Asked if that meant America might then be facing as many as five or six years of war at this point, Peres replied, 'That is very possible. I don't know how long it will take, but the problem is a global one, and it will not end in Iraq, even if a new regime is instituted.' "

3. Discussing Iran's involvement in terrorism on the Gulf 2000 website, specialists expressed every view from no proven involvement to likely extensive involvement. At my request, Giandomenico Picco wrote me expanding his view there: "I was personally involved in . . . the operation that led to the release of 11 Western hostages from Lebanon in 1991, including Terry Anderson and Terry Waite. What I can offer as a comment is as follows: 'There is no question that Iran made a major contribution in the liberation of the Hostages in Lebanon at the end of the civil war in that country. I worked directly with the Iranian government to achieve that end. Both operationally and politically I could not have done it without their assistance.

It seems to me that the Iranian Revolution did have at the outset a wing that wanted to export their brand of Islamic system and used all kind of instruments to do so. It would appear that the[y] . . . began to lose ground by the mid-nineties at the latest. . . . In any case major international terrorist operations attributable, rightly or wrongly, to an Iranian connection, after 1997 do not seem to appear on any radar screen. it is an open secret that "official Iran" contributed to Hezbollah's decision in Lebanon not to open a second front after the beginning of the Intifadah during the last two years. The link between Hezbollah and Iran remains, in my opinion, still strong. But Hezbollah today is quite different from what it was twelve years ago. Is Hezbollah becoming more like the IRA? with two wings, one political and one military, necessarily not always in full agreement?' "

4. See, among several related items in the Israeli newspaper *Haaretz*, the March 23, 2003, article, "Corridors of Power: Who would give the go-ahead?" by Uzi Benziman, whose final subhead is "Next target Iran," and which ends, "After the war in Iraq, Israel will try to convince the U.S. to direct its war on terror at Iran, Damascus and Beirut. Senior defense establishment officials say that initial contacts in this direction have already been made in recent months, and that there is a good chance that America will be swayed by the Israeli argument."

5. Nayereh Tohidi writes me that his letter of resignation was originally cited by intellectuals to his credit for speaking out against censorship and resigning when he was pressured to do things that went against his principles. Later, however, some people used that resignation against him, saying that he was weak under pressure and has a tendency to resign rather than stay and fight. Recently, there have been a series of rumors about his possible resignation from the presidency, with some favoring it and others saying he should prove he is not a quitter and will stay and fight.

6. Mohsen M. Milani, "Reform and Resistance in the Islamic Republic of Iran," in John L. Esposito and R. K. Ramazani, eds., *Iran at the Crossroads* (New York: Palgrave, 2001), 38, includes a key translation from Sayyed Mohammad Khatami, *Az donya-ye shahr ta shahr-e donya* (Tehran: Nay Press, 1994).

7. On Khatami and other political questions, see, in Joseph A. Kechichian, ed., *Iran, Iraq, and the Arab Gulf States* (New York: Palgrave, 2001), Olivier Roy, "Tensions and Options among the Iranian Clerical Establishment," Shaul Bakhash, "Reformists, Conservatives and Iran's Parliamentary Elections," and Ahmed S. Hashim, "Civil-Military Relations in the Islamic Republic of Iran."

8. On Iran's international relations, see the chapters by Jalil Roshandel, Eric Rouleau, and Eric Hooglund in Eric Hooglund, ed., *Twenty Years of Islamic Revolution: Political and Social Transition in Iran since 1979* (Syracuse: Syracuse University Press, 2002), chapters by Mohiaddin Mesbahi, Fred Halliday, Gary Sick, and R. K. Ramazani in Esposito and Ramazani, *Iran at the Crossroads,* and those by Wilfried Buchta, Asef Bayat and Bahman Baktiari, Vali Nasr, and Gary Sick in Nikki R. Keddie and Rudi Matthee, eds., *Iran and the Surrounding World: Interactions in Culture and Cultural Politics* (Seattle: University of Washington Press, 2002).

9. Maryam Poya, *Women, Work and Islamism: Ideology and Resistance in Iran* (London: Zed Books, 1999), and other surveys in urban and rural areas show, for example, that many more women work than is officially reported, and Poya notes this especially for small enterprises.

10. *The Economist,* Jan. 19, 2003, *Survey: Iran,* "Stunted and Distorted," chart from the World Bank.

11. Ibid. Many thanks to Jahangir Amuzegar for reading over this chapter and suggesting several additions or changes—here he added oil's indirect share in the budget.

12. This situation is well summarized in Bernard Hourcade, *Iran: Nouvelles*

identités d'une république (Paris: Editions Belin, 2002), and in *The Economist,* Jan. 19, 2003, *Survey: Iran.*

13. See Jane Howard, *Inside Iran: Women's Lives* (Washington, D.C.: Mage Publishers, 2002), Epilogue.

14. *New York Times,* Feb. 3, 2003.

15. *The Economist,* Jan. 19, 2003, *Survey: Iran* "A Secular Democracy-in-Waiting."

16. Thanks to written communications from Maziar Behrooz and Mark Gasiorowski in December 2002 for contributing to this assessment of the current state of reform, which is also informed by my discussions with Afshin Matin, Nayereh Tohidi, and Ervand Abrahamian.

17. *The Economist,* Jan. 19, 2003, "Stunted and Distorted."

18. Jahangir Amuzegar, "Iran's Crumbling Revolution," *Foreign Affairs* 82: 1 (January/February 2003), 44–57, 52.

19. Ibid. After reading this summary of his views and what I say in note 23 below, Amuzegar wrote me on March 22, 2003, "My 'enthusiasm' about the economy is predicated upon a series of further reforms and events (including membership in WTO)—many of which appear to be less and less certain now. . . . In the same article I have not ruled out temporary reversals of the reformers' fortunes, and possible increases in repression before the ultimate implosion."

20. Eric Hooglund wrote me in January 2003, "Changes . . . have doubled the size of the middle class and eliminated the worst forms of poverty . . . and even among the lower income and poor, there is fairly universal access to adequate food, shelter, and health care. Redistribution of wealth was an aim of the revolutionaries in the early years, and that has been achieved." This is contrary to the view of Jahangir Amuzegar, "Iran's Theocracy Under Siege," *Middle East Policy* 10:1 (Spring 2003) 135–53, that income distribution is highly inequitable and that despite "23 years of pursuing 'Islamic social justice,' adopting harsh . . . measures such as arbitrary appropriation of both tangible and intangible property from their lawful owners, forced distribution of land, generous subsidies, price controls, and tens of government-created 'charitable' organizations to help the poor, the regime admits its failure to improve domestic income distribution." Amuzegar writes me that "data on income distribution in most of the developing countries are virtually non-existent. My own information is based on tens of different private and public statements and reports, none of which can reveal the whole story. Iran certainly has a very unequal distribution of income" (149).

21. "Iran Lifts House Arrest of Top Dissident," *New York Times,* January 27, 2003.

22. *New York Times,* Feb. 22, 2003, reported that Khamene'i pardoned five Jews jailed on charges of spying for Israel. They were the last of a group of eleven Jews and two Muslims to be released: "They were arrested in 1999 and tried behind closed doors in . . . Shiraz in 2000. Three of them were acquitted, and the rest received jail sentences of up to 13 years, which were later reduced in an appeals court. Three of them were pardoned in October and two were released after they served their jail terms. There were 100,000 Jews in Iran before the Islamic revolution in 1979, but the number has dropped to 25,000 since then. Iran still has the largest Jewish community in the Middle East outside Israel."

23. *New York Times,* Jan. 26, 2003, reports a visit of Iraqi opposition figures (including Ahmad Chalabi and Kanan Makiya) to Iran for meetings with Iraqi Shi'i oppositionists and senior (conservative) Iranian figures in a U.S.-funded building. Iran officially opposed the U.S. attack on Iraq but wanted to protect itself whatever the outcome. See Elaine Sciolino, "Iraqi Opponent Says He's Leaving Iran to Plan Takeover," and "Iran Veers Between Admiration and Resentment of American Power," *New York Times,* January 28, January 30, 2003. These events and others are discussed in Jon Lee Anderson, "Letter from Iran: Dreaming of Baghdad," *New Yorker,* Feb. 10, 2003, 58–69.

24. Amuzegar, "Iran's Crumbling Revolution," voices the view of most Iran scholars in opposing U.S. spoken or active intervention in Iran, although his conclusion is more optimistic than are the private views of those specialists who think that, partly as a result of U.S. policies, things may get worse in the short term. Amuzegar concludes: "These developments should not suggest . . . that Washington can determine or even affect the outcome of Iran's political ferment. Events within Iran will dictate the U.S. posture rather than the other way around. Clerical dogmatism cannot be defeated from afar—particularly given Iranians' profound mistrust of outside meddling.

"If the U.S. truly wishes to see a modern, democratic, and peaceful Iran, Washington must follow a calculated 'wait and see' policy. Neither Bush's anger, nor his empathy, nor even his promise of friendship with democratic forces will be enough to change Iran. Thus as long as U.S. vital national interests are not seriously threatened and Iran is not clearly implicated in anti-American terrorist acts, the U.S. should refrain from both unsubstantiated accusations and implied threats against the Islamic Republic. Washington would be best served by letting the currently accelerating process of democratization run its course. The theocracy's days are numbered—Iran's own internal currents assure this" (57).

25. Paul Krugman, *New York Times,* March 18, 2003, citing such statements, says, "It's a matter of public record that this war with Iraq is largely the brainchild of a group of neoconservative intellectuals, who view it as a pilot project. In August a British official close to the Bush team told *Newsweek:* 'Everyone wants to go to Baghdad. Real men want to go to Tehran.' In February 2003, according to *Ha'aretz,* an Israeli newspaper, Under Secretary of State John Bolton told Israeli officials that after defeating Iraq the United States would 'deal with' Iran, Syria and North Korea. Will Iraq really be the first of many? It seems all too likely—and not only because the 'Bush doctrine' seems to call for a series of wars. Regimes that have been targeted, or think they may have been targeted, aren't likely to sit quietly and wait their turn." I may add that world opinion and events after the U.S. military victory in Iraq may help determine whether and how this plan is undertaken.

Chapter 12. Society, Gender, Culture, and Intellectual Life

1. Jane Howard, *Inside Iran: Women's Lives* (Washington, D.C.: Mage Publishers, 2002), 89. Golnar Mehran has written widely on education and textbooks: see her "The Presentation of the 'Self' and the 'Other' in Postrevolutionary Iranian School Textbooks," in Nikki R. Keddie and Rudi Matthee, eds., *Iran and the Surrounding World* (Seattle: University of Washington Press, 2002).

2. Howard, *Inside Iran,* 102.

3. A Persian-speaking American friend who visited a male class was amazed at the frank discussion of female anatomy and how to satisfy one's wife.

4. Basic statistics are on the Population Reference Bureau website *www.prb .org.* It includes a summary article by Farzaneh Roudi-Fahimi, "Iran's Family Planning Program: Responding to a Nation's Needs," which cites some of the important works I have read on the subject done in Iran by Amir H. Mehryar, who kindly sent me several papers, and Akbar Aghajanian. See Amir H. Mehryar, ed., *Integrated Approach to Reproductive Health and Family Planning in the Islamic Republic of Iran* (Tehran: Institute for Research on Planning and Development, 2001). Marie Ladier-Fouladi has written important articles and a new book on Iranian demography, but I disagree with her attribution of the decline in births almost entirely to factors other than the birth control program.

5. Howard, *Inside Iran,* 102–08; Homa Hoodfar, *Volunteer Health Workers in Iran as Social Activists: Can "Governmental Non-governmental Organisations" be Agents of Democratisation?* Women Living under Muslim Laws Occasional Paper no. 10, 1998, n.p.

6. Information from Eric Hooglund, who has extensive contact with Iran and its scholars.

7. On AIDS and drugs, see Howard, *Inside Iran,* 112–13, 117.

8. On education, see Bernard Hourcade, *Iran: Nouvelles identités d'une république* (Paris: Éditions Belin, 2002), and Farhad Khosrokhavar and Olivier Roy, *Iran: Comment sortir d'une revolution religieuse* (Paris: Editions de Seuil, 1999), and numerous articles by Golnar Mehran.

9. Haleh Esfandiari, *Reconstructed Lives: Women and Iran's Islamic Revolution* (Washington, D.C.: Woodrow Wilson Center Press, 1997) analyzes the lives and words of several professional women, based on extensive interviews in Iran.

10. Parvin Paidar, *Women and the Political Process in Twentieth-Century Iran* (Cambridge: Cambridge University Press, 1995), 282–84.

11. Ziba Mir-Hosseini, *Marriage on Trial: A Study of Islamic Family Law: Iran and Morocco Compared* (London: I. B. Tauris, 1993).

12. Nouchine Yavari-d'Hellencourt, "Discours islamiques, actrices socials et rapports sociaux de sexe," in Nouchine Yavari-d'Hellencourt, ed., *Les femmes en Iran: Pressions sociales et strategies identitaires* (Paris: L'Harmattan, 1998), 226.

13. See Nayereh Tohidi, "International Connections of the Iranian Women's Movement," in Keddie and Matthee, *Iran and the Surrounding World.*

14. Maryam Poya, *Women, Work and Islamism: Ideology and Resistance in Iran* (London: Zed Books, 1999), 19.

15. Azadeh Kian-Thiébaut, *Les femmes iraniennes entre Islam, état et famille* (Paris: Maisonneuve et Larose, 2002), chap. 5.

16. Elaine Sciolino, *Persian Mirrors: The Elusive Face of Iran* (New York: Free Press, 2000), chaps. 5–7, has much firsthand information on women, and on pages 118–20 discusses women's sports and the leadership in them of Faezeh Hashemi, a daughter of Rafsanjani.

17. Tohidi, "International Connections of the Iranian Women's Movement."

18. Farhad Khosrokhavar, "L'Iran, la démocratie et la nouvelle citoyenneté," *Cahiers internationaux de Sociologie* 101 (2001), 291–317, and "Le mouvement des femmes en Iran," *Cahiers de Genre* 33 (2002), 137–54.

19. For a complete list and analysis, see Hamid Naficy, "Islamizing Film Culture in Iran," in Richard Tapper, ed., *The New Iranian Cinema: Politics, Representation and Identity* (London: I. B. Tauris, 2002), 36–37, 46 ff.

20. Hamid Naficy "Cinematic Exchange Relations: Iran and the West," in Keddie and Matthee, *Iran and the Surrounding World.*

21. Richard Tapper, "Introduction," in Richard Tapper, ed., *The New Iranian Cinema*, 20.

22. At an awards dinner in 2002 I sat next to an assistant conductor of the Los Angeles Symphony, who told me he spent some weeks each year conducting the Tehran Symphony, which he said was of very good quality, well attended, and has more women than the Los Angeles Symphony.

23. See Ervand Abrahamian, *Khomeinism: Essays on the Islamic Republic* (Berkeley: University of California Press. 1993), chaps. 4, 5.

24. To give personal examples: My works received mostly negative reviews in Iran before the revolution and in the early postrevolution years—coming first from Iranian nationalists who disliked my attention to oppositional ulama, and later from IRI supporters. When *Roots of Revolution* was translated a few years ago, however, it quickly became the object of positive discussion regarding what it said about Iran's modern development and problems. Books by my ex-students Maziar Behrooz on the Iranian left and Afshin Matin-asgari on the international Iranian student movement were published in Persian and elicited much interest and discussion. The book by another ex-student, Rudi Matthee, on Safavid silk trade, won one of several prizes for foreign works on Iran at an international conference in 2002. Other scholars have had similar experiences. (Full book references are in the bibliography.)

25. Said Amir Arjomand, "The Reform Movement and the Debate on Modernity and Tradition in Contemporary Iran," IJMES 34 (2002): 719–31. This article discusses key writings by Kadivar, Khatami, Mojtehed-Shabestari, and Soroush. The murder allegation is noted in *The Economist, Survey: Iran,* Jan. 19, 2003, "The Trials of Everyday Life." Its inclusion of Rafsanjani among the accused and the changes in Ganji's sentence by different courts from ten years to six months to six years are in *New York Times,* July 17, 2002.

26. Afshin Matin-asgari, " 'Abdolkarim Soroush and the Secularization of Islamic Thought in Iran," *Iranian Studies* 30:1–2 (Winter/Spring 1997): 95–115, 103.

27. On Soroush, see especially Matin-asgari, "Abdolkarim Soroush," Farzin Vahdat, *God and Juggernaut: Iran's Intellectual Encounter with Modernity* (Syracuse: Syracuse University Press, 2002), Arjomand, "The Reform Movement," and Abdolkarim Soroush, *Reason, Freedom, and Democracy in Islam: Essential Writings of Abdolkarim Soroush,* ed. Ahmad Sadr, trans. Mahmoud Sadri (New York: Oxford University Press, 2000). I have heard Soroush express his views in two lectures.

28. Farzin Vahdat, "Post-revolutionary Discourses of Mohammad Mojtahed Shabestari and Mohsen Kadivar: Reconciling the Terms of Mediated Subjectivity. Part I: Mojtahed Shabestari," *Critique: Journal for Critical Studies of the Middle East* 16 (Spring 2000): 31–54.

29. *http://www.kadivar.com/Htm/English/Papers/HumanRights.htm*. This is from Kadivar's web page, which includes several of his talks, in English and Persian.

30. Vahdat, "Post-revolutionary Discourses of Mohammad Mojtahed Shabestari and Mohsen Kadivar: Reconciling the Terms of Mediated Subjectivity. Part II: Mohsen Kadivar," *Critique* 17 (Fall 2000).

31. *http://www.kadivar.com/Htm/English/Papers/Velayat-e%2oFaghih.htm.*
I heard this talk, expressing his current views on velayat-e faqih, at the Middle East
Studies Association meeting in Washington, D.C., November 2002.

32. Communication from Nayereh Tohidi; see the interview with Kadivar on-
line in Persian in *Iran Emrooz,* and his description of these events in Persian on
his website, *http://www.iran-emrooz.de/khabar/kadivar811107.html.* While noting the important reformist positions of the men discussed here, Ziba Mir-Hosseini,
Islam and Gender: The Religious Debate in Contemporary Iran (Princeton: Princeton University Press, 1999). 213, wrote a few years ago, "Nearly twenty years into
the Islamic Republic, no influential male Modernist—whether cleric or layman—has
yet seriously addressed the issue of gender in Islam. If the Neo-Traditionalists are
still under the spell of Motahhari's text . . . Modernists seem to be equally mes-
merized by Shari'ati's seminal *Fatemeh Fatemeh ast.*" Not everyone would say that
this is still true.

33. See this volume, pp. 19–21 [oo–oo].

34. Ayatollah Taheri spoke out against "despair, unemployment, inflation and
high prices, the hellish gap between poverty and wealth, the deep and daily growing
distance between the classes, the stagnation and decline of national revenue, a sick
economy, bureaucratic corruption, desperately weak administrators, the growing
flaws in the country's political structure, embezzlement, bribery and addiction" and
castigated "those who are astride the unruly camel of power . . . society's dregs and
fascists who consist of a concoction of ignorance and madness, whose umbilical
cords are attached to the centers of power." Quoted in *The Economist,* Jan. 19, 2003,
"The Surreal World of Iranian Politics."

35. "Iranian Cleric Denounces Action Against a Dissident," *New York Times,*
January 20, 2003.

36. Nazila Fathi, "Liberal Ayatollah Tugs at Ties Constricting Iran's Women,"
New York Times, July 29, 2001. After listing a series of important issues concerning
women on which Sane'i says current law should be changed, Fathi adds, "Ayatollah
Saanei was once very much a part of the religious establishment in the early days of
the revolution. He was on the 12-member Guardian Council that drafted the Constitution. Later he was appointed chief prosecutor, and he was part of the religious
establishment that replaced the secular legal code with Islamic law. . . . Since with-
drawing from the government in 1984, Ayatollah Saanei has devoted his career to
clarifying his position that men and women enjoy equal rights in the Koran. He has
also moderated some of his views, with his most liberal rulings coming in the last
several years, since the rise of the reformist president, Mohammad Khatami. . . .
Today, his views have become increasingly important to the aspirations of the reform
movement. 'His willingness and courage to say things against the traditional main-
stream is what makes him different from other clerics,' said one secular feminist."
Sane'i's views a few years ago are discussed in Ziba Mir-Hosseini, *Islam and Gender,*
passim.

37. Nazila Fathi, "Political Fervor of Iranian Clerics Begins to Ebb," *New York
Times,* January 17, 2003, says "many clerics here [in Qom] are openly questioning
the wisdom of that earlier generation. The foray into politics, they say, has stained
the image of the Shiite clergy. It will not be restored, they insist, until the clergy
withdraws from government. . . . 'The political performance of clerics in the past two
decades has caused a lot of problems for all clerics,' said Abolfazl Moussavian, 47, a

middle-ranking cleric who teaches at Mofid University in Qum. 'First of all, those in power do not tolerate any ideas other than their own. Secondly, people have become skeptical toward clerics and blame them and religion for the current problems.' " For the slower change among some clerics regarding gender questions, see Ziba Mir-Hosseini, *Islam and Gender.*

38. On the non-Islamic religious minorities, see Eliz Sanasarian, *Religious Minorities in Iran* (Cambridge: Cambridge University Press, 2000). On all minorities, see Nikki R. Keddie, "The Minorities Question in Iran," in Shaheen Ayubi and Shirin Tahir-Kheli, eds., *The Iran-Iraq War: New Weapons, Old Conflicts* (New York: Praeger, 1983), reprinted in Nikki R. Keddie, *Iran and the Muslim World: Resistance and Revolution* (London: Macmillan, 1995).

39. Most works say that the majority of Iran's Kurds are Sunni, Eric Hooglund disagrees and wrote me, Jan. 30, 2003, "only about one-third of Kurds in Iran are Sunni Muslims; another one-third are Shi'i and one-third more are Ahl-e Haqq ... there also are communities of Yazidi Kurds, mostly in Ilam province."

40. As noted above, the degree of ethnic discontent is a controversial subject on which not enough research has been done to make definitive statements. Works published in the West tend to stress it, while Hooglund has cited to me several studies done in Iran that indicate it is less prevalent than these Western studies suggest and has summarized some of their findings.

41. For basic facts since 1979–99, see David McDowall, *A Modern History of the Kurds,* rev. ed. (London: I. B. Tauris, 2000), chap. 13. For background, see Martin van Bruinessen, *Agha, Shaikh and State: The Social and Political Structures of Kurdistan* (London: Zed Books, 1992).

42. See Jon Lee Anderson, "Letter from Iran: Dreaming of Baghdad," *New Yorker,* Feb. 10, 2003, 58–69.

43. Brenda Shaffer, *Borders and Brethren: Iran and the Challenge of Azerbaijani Identity* (MIT Press, 2002), contains important information and analyses, but some scholars of contemporary Iran, including Azerbaijanis, have cited to me several assertions about Iranian Azerbaijanis that cannot be based on knowledge, as she has, as she points out, not been to Iran. On Iranian Azerbaijan they prefer the analyses by Touraj Atabaki, *Azerbaijan: Ethnicity and Autonomy in Twentieth-Century Iran* (London: British Academy Press, 1993), though this book stops in 1946.

44. Two U.S.-based anthropologists, Lois Beck, who studies the Qashqa'i, and Erika Friedl, who studies a settled tribal group, have returned several times since the revolution to continue their important work on tribal and rural areas. See, e.g., Erika Friedl "The Dynamics of Women's Spheres of Action in Rural Iran," in Nikki R. Keddie and Beth Baron, eds., *Women in Middle Eastern History: Shifting Boundaries in Sex and Gender* (New Haven: Yale University Press, 1991), and Lois Beck, "Local Histories: A Longitudinal Study of a Qashqa'i Subtribe in Iran," in Rudi Matthee and Beth Baron, eds., *Iran and Beyond: Essays in Middle Eastern History in Honor of Nikki R. Keddie* (Costa Mesa, Calif.: Mazda Publishers, 2000).

Select Bibliography of Books in English

(For books that cross time periods, the predominant period is chosen.)

GENERAL

Alexander, Yonah, and Allan Nanes, eds. *The United States and Iran: A Documentary History*. Frederick Md.: University Publications of America, 1980.

Arjomand, Said Amir. *The Shadow of God and the Hidden Imam: Religion, Political Order and Societal Change in Shi'ite Iran from the Beginning to 1890*. Chicago: University of Chicago Press, 1984.

Banani, Amin, ed. *State and Society in Iran. Iranian Studies*. Special issue, vol. 11 (1978).

Bausani, Alessandro. *The Persians: From the Earliest Days to the Twentieth Century*. Translated by J. B. Donne. London: Elek Books, 1971.

———. *Religion in Iran: From Zoroaster to Baha'u'llah*. Translated by J. M. Marchesi. New York: Bibliotheca Persica, 2000.

Bosworth, C. E., ed. *Iran and Islam: In Memory of the late Vladimir Minorsky*. Edinburgh: Edinburgh University Press, 1971.

The Cambridge History of Iran. Cambridge: Cambridge University Press, 1968–75.

Vol. 1: *The Land of Iran*. Edited by William B. Fisher,

Vol. 2: *The Median and Achaemenian Periods*. Edited by Ilya Gershevitch

Vol. 3: *The Seleucid, Parthian, and Sasanian Periods*. Edited by Ehsan Yarshater (2 pts.)

Vol. 4: *The Period from the Arab Invasions to the Saljuqs* Edited by Richard N. Frye.

Vol. 5: *The Saljuq and Mongol Periods*. Edited by John A. Boyle.

Vol. 6: *The Timurid and Safavid Periods*. Edited by Peter Jackson and Laurence Lockhart.

Vol. 7: *From Nadir Shah to the Islamic Republic*. Edited by Peter Avery, Gavin Hambly, and Charles Melville.

Chaliand, Gerard, ed. *People Without a Country: The Kurds and Kurdistan.* Translated by Michael Pallis. London: Zed Press, 1980.

Cottam, Richard W. *Nationalism in Iran: Updated through 1978.* 2d ed. Pittsburgh: University of Pittsburgh Press, 1979.

Daniel, Elton L. *The History of Iran.* Westport, Conn.: Greenwood Press, 2001.

Encyclopædia Iranica. Edited by Ehsan Yarshater. See especially the general articles by Ahmad Ashraf, Ali Banuazizi, and others.

Foran, John. *Fragile Resistance: Social Transformation in Iran from 1500 to the Revolution.* Boulder, Colo.: Westview Press, 1993.

Frye, Richard Nelson. *Iran.* New York: Holt, 1953. Revised ed.: London: Allen and Unwin, 1968.

Halm, Heinz. *Shi'a Islam: From Religion to Revolution.* Translated by Allison Brown. Princeton: Markus Wiener, 1996.

Keddie, Nikki. *Iran: Religion, Politics and Society.* London and Totowa, N.J.: Frank Cass, 1980.

——, ed. *Scholars, Saints and Sufis: Muslim Religious Institutions Since 1500.* Berkeley and Los Angeles: University of California Press, 1972.

Lambton, Ann K. S. *Landlord and Peasant in Persia: A Study of Land Tenure and Land Revenue Administration.* 1953. Reprint London and New York: Oxford University Press, 1969.

Matthee, Rudi, and Beth Baron. *Iran and Beyond: Essays in Middle Eastern History in Honor of Nikki R. Keddie.* Costa Mesa, Calif.: Mazda Publishers, 2000.

Momen, Moojan. *An Introduction to Shi'i Islam: The History and Doctrines of Twelver Shi'ism.* New Haven: Yale University Press, 1985.

Ramazani, Rouhollah K. *The Foreign Policy of Iran: A Developing Nation in World Affairs, 1500–1941.* Charlottesville: University Press of Virginia, 1966.

Upton, Joseph M. *The History of Modern Iran: An Interpretation, Harvard Middle Eastern Monographs 2.* Cambridge: Harvard University Press, 1960.

Watt, W. Montgomery. *Islam and the Integration of Society.* London: Routledge and Kegan Paul, 1961.

Wilber, Donald. *Iran: Past and Present.* 8th ed. 1948. Revised ed.: Princeton: Princeton University Press, 1978.

Wright, Denis. *The English Amongst the Persians.* London: Heinemann, 1977.

Iran: 1400–1796

Grey, Charles, ed. and trans. *A Narrative of Italian Travels in Persia, in the Fifteenth and Sixteenth Centuries.* Hakluyt Society Series, no. 49, pt. 2. London: Hakluyt Society, 1873.

Hanway, Jonas. *An Historical Account of the British Trade over the Caspian Sea.* 4 vols. London: Dodsley, 1753.

——. *The Revolutions of Persia.* London: Dodsley, 1753.

Holod, Renata, ed. *Studies on Isfahan: Proceedings of the Isfahan Colloquium.* Iranian Studies, special issue, vol. 7 (1974).

Lockhart, Laurence. *The Fall of the Safavi Dynasty and the Afghan Occupation of Persia.* Cambridge: Cambridge University Press, 1958.

——. *Nadir Shah: A Critical Study Based Mainly upon Contemporary Sources.* London: Luzac, 1938.

Matthee, Rudolph P. *The Politics of Trade in Safavid Iran: Silk for Silver, 1600–1730.* Cambridge: Cambridge University Press, 1999.

Mazzaoui, Michel M. *The Origins of the Safawids: Si'ism, Sufism, and the Gulat.* Wiesbaden: F. Steiner, 1972.

Minorsky, Vladimir, ed. and trans. *Tadhkirat al-Muluk: A Manual of Safavid Administration.* London: Luzac, 1943.

Perry, John R. *Karim Khan Zand: A History of Iran, 1747–1779.* Chicago: University of Chicago Press, 1979.

Ross, Edward D. *Sir Anthony Sherley and His Persian Adventure.* London: Routledge and Sons, 1933.

Savory, Roger M. *Iran under the Safavids.* Cambridge: Cambridge University Press, 1980.

Woods, John. *The Aqquyunlu: Clan, Confederation, Empire.* Minneapolis: Bibliotheca Islamica, 1976.

The Qajar Period: 1796–1925

Afary, Janet. *The Iranian Constitutional Revolution, 1906–1911: Grassroots Democracy, Social Democracy, and the Origins of Feminism.* New York: Columbia University Press, 1996.

Algar, Hamid. *Mirza Malkum Khan: A Study in the History of Iranian Modernism.* Berkeley and Los Angeles: University of California Press, 1973.

——. *Religion and State in Iran, 1785–1906.* Berkeley and Los Angeles: University of California Press, 1969.

Amanat, Abbas. *Pivot of the Universe: Nasir al-Din Shah Qajar and the Iranian Monarchy, 1831–1896.* Berkeley: University of California Press, 1997.

Bakhash, Shaul. *Iran: Monarchy, Bureaucracy, and Reform under the Qajars, 1858–1896.* London: Ithaca Press for the Middle East Centre, St. Antony's College,1978.

Bayat, Mangol. *Mysticism and Dissent: Socioreligious Thought in Qajar Iran.* Syracuse: Syracuse University Press, 1982.

——. *Iran's First Revolution: Shi'ism and the Constitutional Revolution of 1905–1909.* New York: Oxford University Press, 1991.

Berberian, Houri. *Armenians and the Iranian Constitutional Revolution of 1905–1911: "The Love for Freedom Has No Fatherland."* Boulder, Colo.: Westview Press, 2001.

Browne, Edward G. *Materials for the Study of the Babi Religion.* Cambridge: Cambridge University Press, 1918.

——. *The Persian Revolution of 1905–1909.* 1910. Reprint Washington, D.C.: Mage Publishers, 1995.

Curzon, George N. *Persia and the Persian Question*. 2 vols. London: Frank Cass, 1969.

Entner, Marvin L. *Russo-Persian Commercial Relations, 1828–1914*. Gainesville: University of Florida Press, 1965.

Floor, Willem M. *Agriculture in Qajar Iran*. Washington, D.C.: Mage, 2003.

———. *Traditional Crafts in Qajar Iran, 1800–1925*. Costa Mesa, Calif.: Mazda Publishers, 2003.

Forbes-Leith, F. A. C. *Checkmate: Fighting Tradition in Central Persia*. London: Harrap, 1927.

Garthwaite, Gene. *Khans and Shahs: A Documentary Analysis of the Bakhtiyari in Iran*. Cambridge: Cambridge University Press, 1983.

Issawi, Charles, ed. *The Economic History of Iran: 1800–1914*. Chicago: University of Chicago Press, 1971.

Kashani-Sabet, Firoozeh. *Frontier Fictions: Shaping the Iranian Nation, 1804–1946*. Princeton: Princeton University Press, 1999.

Kazemzadeh, Firuz. *Russia and Britain in Persia, 1864–1914: A Study in Imperialism*. New Haven: Yale University Press, 1968.

Keddie, Nikki R. *An Islamic Response to Imperialism: Political and Religious Writings of Sayyid Jamal ad-Din "al-Afghani."* Berkeley and Los Angeles: University of California Press, 1968.

———. *Religion and Rebellion in Iran: The Tobacco Protest of 1891–1892*. London: Frank Cass, 1966.

———. *Sayyid Jamal ad-Din "al-Afghani": A Political Biography*. Berkeley and Los Angeles: University of California Press, 1972.

———. *Qajar Iran and the Rise of Reza Khan 1796–1925*. Costa Mesa, Calif.: Mazda Publishers, 1999.

———. *Iran: Religion, Politics and Society: Collected Essays*. London: Frank Cass, 1980.

Lambton, Ann K.S. *Qajar Persia*. Austin: University of Texas Press, 1998.

McDaniel, Robert A. *The Shuster Mission and the Persian Constitutional Revolution*. Minneapolis and Chicago: Bibliotheca Islamica, 1974.

Mahdavi, Shireen. *For God, Mammon and Country: A Nineteenth-Century Persian Merchant, Hajj Muhammad Hasan , Amin al-Zarb (1834–1898)*. Boulder, Colo.: Westview Press, 1999.

Malcolm, Sir John. *The History of Persia*. 2 vols. London: J. Murray, 1815.

———. *Sketches of Persia: From the Journals of a Traveller in the East*. 2 vols. London: J. Murray, 1827.

Martin, Vanessa. *Iran's First Revolution: Shi'ism and the Constitutional Revolution of 1905–1909*. London: I. B. Tauris, 1989.

Najmabadi, Afsaneh. *The Story of the Daughters of Quchan: Gender and National Memory in Iranian History*. Syracuse: Syracuse University Press, 1998.

Ringer, Monica M. *Education, Religion, and the Discourse of Cultural Reform in Qajar Iran*. Costa Mesa, Calif.: Mazda Publishers, 2000.

Shuster, William Morgan. *The Strangling of Persia*. New York: Century Company, 1912.

Sykes, Christopher. *Wassmuss, "The German Lawrence."* London: Longmans, Green, 1936.

Watson, Robert G. *A History of Persia from the Beginning of the Nineteenth Century to the Year 1858*. London: Smith, Elder, 1866.

Werner, Christoph. *An Iranian Town in Transition: A Social and Economic History of the Elites of Tabriz, 1747–1848* Wiesbaden: Harrassowitz, 2000.

Yeselson, Abraham. *United States-Persian Diplomatic Relations: 1883–1921*. New Brunswick: Rutgers University Press, 1956.

The Pahlavi Period: 1925–1979

Abrahamian, Ervand. *Iran between Two Revolutions*. Princeton: Princeton University Press, 1982.

——. *The Iranian Mojahedin*. New Haven: Yale University Press, 1989.

Akhavi, Shahrough. *Religion and Politics in Contemporary Iran: Clergy-State Relations in the Pahlavi Period*. Albany: SUNY Press, 1980.

Amin, Camron Michael. *The Making of the Modern Iranian Woman: Gender, State Policy, and Popular Culture, 1865–1946*. Gainesville: Florida University Press, 2002.

Amirsadeghi, Hossein, and R. W. Ferrier, eds. *Twentieth-Century Iran*. London: Heinemann, 1977.

Amuzegar, Jahangir, and M. Ali Fekrat. *Iran: Economic Development under Dualistic Conditions*. Chicago: University of Chicago Press, 1971.

Arfa, Hassan. *Under Five Shahs*. London: John Murray, 1964.

Azimi, Fakhreddin. *Iran: the Crisis of Democracy*. London: I. B. Tauris, 1989.

Baldwin, George B. *Planning and Development in Iran*. Baltimore: Johns Hopkins University Press, 1967.

Bamdad, Badr ol-Moluk. *From Darkness into Light: Women's Emancipation in Iran*. Edited and translated by F. R. C. Bagley. Hicksville, N.Y.: Exposition Press, 1977.

Banani, Amin. *The Modernization of Iran, 1921–1941*. Stanford: Stanford University Press, 1961.

Barth, Fredrik. *Nomads of South Persia: The Basseri Tribe of the Khamseh Confederacy*. Oslo: University Press; London: Allen and Unwin, 1961.

Bashiriyeh, Hossein. *The State and Revolution in Iran: 1962–1982*. London: Croom Helm, 1984.

Bayne, Edward A. *Persian Kingship in Transition: Conversations with a Monarch Whose Office Is Traditional and Whose Goal Is Modernization*. New York: American Universities Field Staff, 1968.

Beck, Lois. *The Qashqa'i of Iran*. New Haven: Yale University Press, 1986.

Beck, Lois, and Nikki Keddie, eds. *Women in the Muslim World*. Cambridge: Harvard University Press, 1978.

Benedick, Richard Elliot. *Industrial Finance in Iran: A Study of Financial Practice in an Underdeveloped Economy*. Boston: Division of Research, Graduate School of Business Administration, Harvard University, 1964.

Bharier, Julian. *Economic Development in Iran, 1900–1970*. New York: Oxford University Press, 1971.

Bill, James Alban. *The Politics of Iran: Groups, Classes and Modernization*. Columbus, Ohio: Charles E. Merrill, 1972.

——. *The Eagle and the Lion: The Tragedy of American-Iranian Relations*. New Haven: Yale University Press, 1988.

Bill, James A., and William Roger Louis, eds. *Musaddiq, Iranian Nationalism and Oil*. Austin: University of Texas Press, 1988.

Binder, Leonard. *Iran: Political Development in a Changing Society*. Berkeley and Los Angeles: University of California Press, 1962.

Bonine, Michael, and Nikki R. Keddie, eds. *Modern Iran: The Dialectics of Continuity and Change*. Paperback edition, *Continuity and Change in Modern Iran*. Albany: SUNY. Press, 1981.

Behrooz, Maziar. *Rebels with a Cause: The Failure of the Left in Iran*. London: I. B. Tauris, 1999.

Chehabi, H. E. *Iranian Politics and Religious Modernism: The Liberation Movement of Iran under the Shah and Khomeini*. Ithaca Cornell University Press, 1990.

Chubin, Shahram, and Sepehr Zabih. *The Foreign Relations of Iran: A Developing State in a Zone of Great-Power Conflict*. Berkeley and Los Angeles: University of California Press, 1974.

Cronin, Stephanie, ed. *The Making of Modern Iran: State and Society under Riza Shah, 1921–1941*. London: Routledge Curzon, 2003.

Eagleton, William, Jr. *The Kurdish Republic of 1946*. London: Oxford University Press, 1963.

Elwell-Sutton, L. P. *Persian Oil: A Study in Power Politics*. London: Lawrence and Wishart, 1955.

English, Paul Ward. *City and Village in Iran: Settlement and Economy in the Kirman Basin*. Madison: University of Wisconsin Press, 1966.

Fesharaki, Fereidun. *Development of the Iranian Oil Industry: International and Domestic Aspects*. New York: Praeger, 1976.

Fischer, Michael M. J. *Iran: From Religious Dispute to Revolution*. Cambridge: Harvard University Press, 1980.

Gasiorowski, Mark J. *U.S. Foreign Policy and the Shah: Building a Client State in Iran*. Ithaca: Cornell University Press, 1991.

Ghani, Cyrus. *Iran and the Rise of Reza Shah: From Qajar Collapse to Pahlavi Rule*. London: I. B. Tauris, 2001.

Graham, Robert. *Iran: The Illusion of Power*. Revised ed.: London: Croom Helm, 1979.

Halliday, Fred. *Iran: Dictatorship and Development.* New York: Penguin, 1979.

Helfgott, Leonard M. *Ties That Bind: A Social History of the Iranian Carpet.* Washington, D.C.: Smithsonian Institution Press, 1994.

Hoveyda, Fereydoun. *The Fall of the Shah.* New York: Simon and Schuster, 1980.

International Labour Organization. *Employment and Income Policies for Iran.* Geneva, 1973.

Katouzian, Homa. *The Political Economy of Modern Iran.* London: Macmillan, 1981.

——. *Musaddiq and the Struggle for Power in Iran .* London: I. B. Tauris, 1991.

Kazemi, Farhad. *Poverty and Revolution in Iran: The Migrant Poor, Urban Marginality, and Politics.* New York: New York University Press, 1981.

Kedourie, Elie, and Sylvia Haim, eds. *Towards a Modern Iran.* London: Frank Cass, 1980.

Kuniholm, Bruce R. *The Origins of the Cold War in the Middle East: Great Power Conflict and Diplomacy in Iran, Turkey, and Greece.* Princeton: Princeton University Press, 1980.

Ladjevardi, Habib. *Labor Unions and Autocracy in Iran.* Syracuse: Syracuse University Press, 1985.

Lambton, Ann K. S. *The Persian Land Reform, 1962–1966.* Oxford: Clarendon Press, 1969.

Lenczowski, George, ed. *Iran under the Pahlavis.* Stanford: Hoover Institution, 1978.

——. *Russia and the West in Iran, 1918–1948: A Study in Big-Power Rivalry.* Ithaca: Cornell University Press, 1949.

Looney, Robert. *The Economic Development of Iran: A Recent Survey with Projections to 1981.* New York: Praeger, 1973.

——. *Income Distribution Policies and Economic Growth in Semi-industrialized Countries: A Comparative Study of Iran, Mexico, Brazil and South Korea.* New York: Praeger, 1975.

Matin-Asgari, Afshin. *Iranian Student Opposition to the Shah.* Costa Mesa, Calif.: Mazda Publishers, 2001.

Mehdevi, Anne Sinclair. *Persia Revisited.* New York: Knopf, 1964.

Milani, Abbas. *The Persian Sphinx: Amir Abbas Hoveyda and the Riddle of the Iranian Revolution.* Washington, D.C.: Mage Publishers, 2000.

Milani, Mohsen M. *The Making of Iran's Islamic Revolution: From Monarchy to Islamic Republic.* 1988. Revised ed.: Boulder, Colo.: Westview Press, 1994.

Millspaugh, Arthur Chester. *The American Task in Persia.* New York: Century Company, 1925.

——. *Americans in Persia.* Washington: Brookings Institution, 1946. Reprint: New York: Da Capo Press, 1976.

——. *The Financial and Economic Situation of Persia, 1926.* New York: Imperial Persian Government, 1926.

Mottahedeh, Roy. *The Mantle of the Prophet: Religion and Politics in Iran.* New York: Simon and Schuster, 1985.

Nirumand, Bahman. *Iran: The New Imperialism in Action.* Translated by Leonard Mins. New York and London: Monthly Review Press, 1969.

Oberling, Pierre. *The Qashqa'i Nomads of Fars.* The Hague: Mouton, 1974.

O'Donnell, Terence. *Garden of the Brave in War.* New Haven: Ticknor and Fields, 1980.

Overseas Consultants, Inc. *Report on Seven Year Development Plan for the Plan Organization of the Imperial Government of Iran.* 5 vols. New York, 1949.

Pahlavi, Mohammad Reza. *Answer to History.* Briarcliff Manor, N.Y.: Stein and Day, 1980.

——. *Mission for My Country.* New York: McGraw-Hill, 1961.

Paidar, Parvin. *Women and the Political Process in Twentieth-Century Iran.* Cambridge: Cambridge University Press, 1995.

Ramazani, Rouhollah K. *Iran's Foreign Policy 1947–1973: A Study of Foreign Policy in Modernizing Nations.* Charlottesville: University Press of Virginia, 1975.

Roosevelt, Kermit. *Countercoup: The Struggle for the Control of Iran.* New York: McGraw-Hill, 1979, 1980.

Rubin, Barry. *Paved with Good Intentions: The American Experience and Iran.* New York: Oxford University Press, 1980.

Sadiq, Issa Khan. *Modern Persia and Her Educational System.* New York: Teachers College, Columbia University, 1931.

Saikhal, Amin. *The Rise and Fall of the Shah.* Princeton: Princeton University Press, 1980.

Sampson, Anthony. *The Arms Bazaar: From Lebanon to Lockheed.* New York: Bantam Books, 1977.

——. *The Seven Sisters: The Great Oil Companies and the World They Shaped.* New York: Bantam Books, 1975.

Stork, Joe. *Middle East Oil and the Energy Crisis.* New York: Monthly Review Press, 1975.

Wilber, Donald. *Riza Shah Pahlavi: The Resurrection and Reconstruction of Iran.* Hicksville, N.Y.: Exposition Press, 1975.

Yeganegi, Esfandiar Bahram. *Recent Financial and Monetary History of Persia.* Published Ph.D. dissertation, Columbia University, 1934.

Yar-Shater, Ehsan, ed. *Iran Faces the Seventies.* New York: Praeger, 1971.

Zonis, Marvin. *The Political Elite of Iran.* Princeton: Princeton University Press, 1971.

INTELLECTUAL TRENDS: POLITICAL, RELIGIOUS, AND LITERARY

Al-e Ahmad, Jalal. *The School Principal.* Translated by John K. Newton. Minneapolis and Chicago: Bibliotheca Islamica, 1974.

Baraheni, Reza. *The Crowned Cannibals: Writings on Repression in Iran.* New York: Vintage Books, 1977.

Behrangi, Samad. *The Little Black Fish and Other Modern Persian Stories*. Translated by Eric and Mary Hooglund. Washington, D.C.: Three Continents Press, 1976.

Boroujerdi, Mehrzad. *Iranian Intellectuals and the West: The Tormented Triumph of Nativism*. Syracuse: Syracuse University Press, 1996.

Browne, Edward G. *A Literary History of Persia*. 4 vols. 2d ed. Cambridge: Cambridge University Press, 1928–29.

——. *The Press and Poetry of Modern Persia*. Cambridge: Cambridge University Press, 1914.

Chelkowski, Peter J. *Ta'ziyeh: Ritual and Drama in Iran*. New York: New York University Press, 1979.

Dabashi, Hamid. *Theology of Discontent: The Ideological Foundation of the Islamic Revolution in Iran*. New York: New York University Press, 1993.

Esfandiary, F. M. *The Day of Sacrifice*. New York: McDowell, 1959.

——. *Identity Card*. New York: Grove Press, 1966.

Gheissari, Ali. *Iranian Intellectuals in the Twentieth Century*. Austin: University of Texas Press, 1998.

Hedayat, Sadeq. *Hedayat: An Anthology of Short Stories*. Edited by Ehsan Yarshater. Boulder: Westview Press, 1979.

——. *The Blind Owl*. Translated by D. P. Costello. New York: Evergreen, 1959.

——. *Haji Agha: Portrait of an Iranian Confidence Man*. Translated by G. M. Wickens. Introduction by Lois Beck. Middle East Monographs, no. 6, Center for Middle Eastern Studies, University of Texas at Austin, Austin, Texas, 1979.

Kamshad, Hassan. *Modern Persian Prose Literature*. Cambridge: Cambridge University Press, 1966.

Karimi-Hakkak, Ahmad, comp. and trans. *An Anthology of Modern Persian Poetry*. Boulder: Westview Press, 1978.

Khomeyni, Ayatollah Ruhollah. *Islamic Government*. Springfield, Va.: National Technical Information Service, 1979.

The Literary Review. "Iran." 18, no. 1 (1974).

Literature East and West. "Major Voices in Contemporary Persian Literature." Michael C. Hillmann, ed., vol. 20 (January–December 1976), actual date of publication, June 1980.

Milani, Farzaneh. *Veils and Words: The Emerging Voices of Iranian Women Writers*. Syracuse: Syracuse University Press, 1992.

Pelly, Sir Lewis. *The Miracle Plays of Hasan and Husain*. Collected from Oral Tradition by Colonel Sir Lewis Pelly, 2 vols. Edited by Arthur N. Wollaston. London: W. H. Allen, 1879. Reprint: Farnborough (Hants.): Gregg International, 1970.

Rahman, Munibur. *Post-Revolution Persian Verse*. Aligarh: Institute of Islamic Studies, Muslim University, 1955.

Shari'ati, Ali. *Marxism and Other Western Fallacies: An Islamic Critique*. Translated by R. Campbell. Berkeley: Mizan Press, 1980.

———. On the Sociology of Islam. Translated by Hamid Algar. Berkeley: Mizan Press, 1979.

Southgate, Minoo, ed. and trans. Modern Persian Short Stories. Washington, D.C.: Three Continents Press, 1980.

Tabataba'i, M. H. Shi'ite Islam. Translated by Hossein Nasr. Albany: SUNY Press, 1975.

Tapper, Richard, ed. The New Iranian Cinema: Politics, Representation and Identity. London: I. B. Tauris, 2002.

Tavakoli-Targhi, Mohamad. Refashioning Iran: Orientalism, Occidentalism, and Historiography. New York: Palgrave. 2001.

Vahdat, Farzin. God and Juggernaut: Iran's Intellectual Encounter with Modernity. Syracuse: Syracuse University Press, 2002.

Vaughan, Leo. The Jokeman. London: Eyre and Spottiswoode, 1962.

1979–2003

Abdo, Geneive, and Jonathan Lyons. Answering Only to God: Faith and Freedom in Twenty-First-Century Iran. New York: Henry Holt, 2003.

Adelkhah, Fariba. Being Modern in Iran. Translated by Jonathan Derrick. New York: Columbia University Press, 2000.

Abrahamian, Ervand. Khomeinism: Essays on the Islamic Republic. Berkeley: University of California Press, 1993.

———. Tortured Confessions: Prisons and Public Recantations in Modern Iran. Berkeley: University of California Press, 1999.

Afkhami, Mahnaz, and Erika Friedl, eds. In the Eye of the Storm: Women in Post-Revolutionary Iran. Syracuse: Syracuse University Press, 1994.

Afshari, Reza. Human Rights in Iran: The Abuse of Cultural Relativism. Philadelphia: University of Pennsylvania Press, 2001.

Albert, David H., ed. Tell the American People: Perspectives on the Iranian Revolution. Philadelphia: Movement for a New Society, 1980.

Arjomand, Said Amir. The Turban for the Crown: The Islamic Revolution in Iran. New York: Oxford University Press, 1988.

Bakhash, Shaul. The Reign of the Ayatollahs: Iran and the Islamic Revolution. Revised ed.: New York: Basic Books, 1989.

Baktiari, Bahman. Parliamentary Politics in Revolutionary Iran: The Institutionalization of Factional Politics. Gainesville: University Press of Florida, 1996.

Bayat, Asef. Workers and Revolution in Iran. London: Zed Books, 1987.

Brumberg, Daniel. Reinventing Khomeini: The Struggle for Reform in Iran. Chicago: University of Chicago Press, 2001.

Buchta, Wilfried. Who Rules Iran? The Structure of Power in the Islamic Republic. Washington, D.C.: Washington Institute for Near Eastern Policy, 2000.

Chubin, Shahram, and Charles R. Tripp. Iran and Iraq at War. London: I. B. Tauris, 1988.

Dorman, William A., and Mansour Farhang. The U.S. Press and Iran: Foreign Policy and the Journalism of Deference. Berkeley: University of California Press, 1987.

Ehteshami, Anoushirvan. *After Khomeini: The Iranian Second Republic*. London: Routledge, 1995.

Esfandiari, Haleh. *Reconstructed Lives: Women and Iran's Islamic Revolution*. Washington, D.C.: Woodrow Wilson Center Press, 1997.

Esposito, John L., and R. K. Ramazani, eds. *Iran at the Crossroads*. New York: Palgrave, 2001.

Farhi, Farideh. *States and Urban-Based Revolutions: Iran and Nicaragua*. Urbana: University of Illinois Press, 1990.

Hiro, Dilip. *The Longest War: The Iran-Iraq Military Conflict*. New York: Routledge, 1991.

Hooglund, Eric, ed. *Twenty Years of Islamic Revolution: Political and Social Transition in Iran since 1979*. Syracuse: Syracuse University Press, 1984.

Howard, Jane. *Inside Iran: Women's Lives*. Washington, D.C.: Mage Publishers, 2002.

Hunter, Shireen T. *Iran and the World: Continuity in a Revolutionary Decade*. Bloomington: Indiana University Press, 1990.

Iran since the Revolution. Social Research 67: 2 (Summer 2000).

Kazemi, Farhad. *Poverty and Revolution in Iran: The Migrant Poor, Urban Marginality, and Politics*. New York: New York University Press, 1981.

——, ed. *Iranian Revolution in Perspective. Iranian Studies*, 13:1–4, 1980.

Kechichian, Joseph A., ed. *Iran, Iraq, and the Arab Gulf States*. New York: Palgrave, 2001.

Keddie, Nikki R. *Iran and the Muslim World: Resistance and Revolution*. London: Macmillan, 1995.

——, ed. *Religion and Politics in Iran*. New Haven and London: Yale University Press, 1983.

Keddie, Nikki R., and Rudi Matthee, eds. *Iran and the Surrounding World: Interactions in Culture and Cultural Politics*. Seattle: University of Washington Press, 2002.

Martin, Vanessa. *Creating an Islamic State: Khomeini and the Making of a New Iran*. London: I. B. Tauris, 2000.

Menashri, David. *Post-Revolutionary Politics in Iran: Religion, Society and Power*. London: Frank Cass, 2001.

Mir-Hosseini, Ziba. *Marriage on Trial: A Study of Islamic Family Law in Iran and Morocco*. London: I. B. Tauris, 1993.

——. *Islam and Gender: The Religious Debate in Contemporary Iran*. Princeton: Princeton University Press, 1999.

Moaddel, Mansoor. *Class, Politics, and Ideology in the Iranian Revolution*. New York: Columbia University Press, 1992.

Moghissi, Haideh. *Populism and Feminism in Iran: Women's Struggle in a Male-Defined Revolutionary Movement*. New York: St. Martin's Press, 1996.

——. *Feminism and Islamic Fundamentalism: The Limits of Postmodern Analysis*. London: Zed Books, 1999.

Molavi, Afshin. *Persian Pilgrimages: Journeys across Iran*. New York: W. W. Norton, 2002.

Moslem, Mehdi. *Factional Politics in Post-Khomeini Iran*. Syracuse: Syracuse University Press, 2002.

Munson, Henry, Jr. *Islam and Revolution in the Middle East*. New Haven: Yale University Press, 1988.

Nobari, Ali-Reza, ed. *Iran Erupts*. Stanford, Calif.: Iran-America Documentation Group, 1978.

Parsa, Misagh. *The Social Origins of the Iranian Revolution*. NewBrunswick, N.J.: Rutgers University Press, 1989.

Poya, Maryam. *Women, Work and Islamism: Ideology and Resistance in Iran*. London: Zed Books, 1999.

Race & Class. Special Issue on the Iranian Revolution. Vol. 21 (Summer 1979).

Said, Edward. *Covering Islam*. New York: Pantheon, 1981.

Salinger, Pierre. *America Held Hostage: The Secret Negotiations*. New York: Doubleday, 1981.

Schirazi, Asghar. *The Constitution of Iran: Politics and State in the Islamic Republic*. Translated by John O'Kane. London: I. B. Tauris, 1998.

Sanasarian, Eliz. *Religious Minorities in Iran*. Cambridge: Cambridge University Press, 2000.

Sciolino, Elaine. *Persian Mirrors: The Elusive Face of Iran*. New York: Free Press, 2000.

Sick, Gary. *All Fall Down: America's Tragic Encounter with Iran*. New York: Random House, 1985.

Sullivan, William H. *Mission to Iran*. New York: Norton, 1981.

Stempel, John D. *Inside the Iranian Revolution*. Bloomington: Indiana University Press, 1981.

Weiner, Myron, and Ali Banuazizi. *The Politics of Social Transformation in Afghanistan, Iran, and Pakistan*. Syracuse: Syracuse University Press, 1994.

Wright, Robin. *The Last Great Revolution: Turmoil and Transformation in Iran*. New York: Alfred A. Knopf, 2000.

Supplement

Gasiorowski, Mark J., and Malcolm Byrne, eds. *Mohammad Mosaddeq and the 1953 Coup in Iran*. Syracuse: Syracuse University Press, 2004.

Kinzer, Stephen. *All the Shah's Men: The Hidden Story of the CIA's Coup in Iran*. Hoboken, N.J.: John Wiley and Sons, 2003.

Sarshar, Houman, ed. *Esther's Children: A Portrait of Iranian Jews*. Beverly Hills, Calif.: Center for Iranian Jewish Oral History, 2002.

Index

Abadan, 231, 264
Abbas, Shah, 12
Abbasid movement, 6–7, 8, 10
Abbas Mirza, 27, 40–41, 43–44, 173
Abdi, Abbas, 265, 281
Abdülhamid, Sultan, 62–63, 64, 177
abortion, 288
Abrahamian, E., 219, 220
Achemenian dynasty, 2
Acheson, Dean, 131
'adalat (justice), 193
adalatkhaneh, 67
Afghanistan, Afghans, 2, 11, 12, 18, 36, 69,
    160, 176, 271, 279, 283, 314
Afkhami, Mahnaz, 223
Aghajari, Hashem, 280, 281
Agha Khan, 7, 44–45
Agha Mohammad Khan, 37, 39
AGIP, 139
agribusiness, 154–55
agriculture, 49, 79, 86; Iranian history shaped
    by, 1; nomadic, 24; export crops, 26, 40, 51;
    backward structure of, 96, 102; loans for,
    97; technological improvements in, 121,
    122, 151–55; import subsidies in, 264; mar-
    ket liberalization and, 265
Ahl-e Haqq, 21, 312
Ahmad Shah, 70, 74
Ahmadiya, 46
Ahsa'i, Ahmad, Shaikh, 45
Ahwaz, 233
AIDS, 289
Ain ad-Dauleh, 66–68

AIOC (Anglo-Iranian Oil Company; British
    Petroleum), 110, 112, 113, 119, 123–26,
    129, 131, 132, 136, 139
akhbaris, 19–20, 310
Akhtar (newspaper), 59, 61, 62, 174
Ala, Hosain, 83, 124
Alam, Asadollah, 140, 145, 166, 237
Alavi, Bozorg, 184
Alborz (mountain range), 2
Albright, Madeleine, 272
Al-e Ahmad, Jalal, 184, 186, 187, 188, 189–
    90, 201
Alexander, Tsar, 38
al-Farabi, 17
Algeria, 268
Ali, Muhammad, 27, 41, 44
Ali (Mohammad's son-in-law), 4–5, 6, 13,
    47, 171, 196, 202, 205
Ali Asghar Khan, *Amin as-Soltan* (Atabak),
    25, 58, 59, 60, 62, 63, 64, 65, 66, 69,
    174
Allen, George V., 113, 114
al-Qaeda, 284
al-'Urwa al-Wuthqa (newspaper), 60
Amin ad-Dauleh, 56, 59, 60, 64–65, 140, 173,
    174
Amin az-Zarb, 60, 176
Amini, Ali, 140, 142–45, 166
Amir Kabir, Mirza Taqi Khan, 25, 29, 48–50,
    58, 59, 173
Amnesty International, 215, 216
Amol, 254
Amuzegar, Jahangir, 282–83

Amuzegar, Jamshid, 144, 164, 217, 231, 217, 223, 231
Anatolia. *See* Turkey
Anglo-Iranian Oil Company (AIOC; British Petroleum), 110, 112, 113, 119, 123–26, 129, 131, 132, 136, 139
Anglo-Persian Oil Company (APOC), 72, 83–84, 101
Anglo-Persian Treaty (1919), 76–77, 78, 79, 81
Anglo-Russian Entente (1907), 69–70, 71, 131
Anis ad-Dauleh, 55
anjomans, 68, 71, 72
Anouar 'Abd al-Malek, 188
APOC (Anglo-Persian Oil Company), 72, 83–84, 101
Apple, The (S. Makhmalbaf), 300
Arab-Israeli War (1973), 163
Arabs, 5, 20, 24, 249, 251, 312, 313, 314
Armenia, Armenians, 2, 20–21, 33, 5
arms purchases, 163, 165
arranged marriage, 297
Arsanjani, Hasan, 143, 147, 149–50, 152
arts, 297–302
Aryans, 2
Ash'arites, 18, 307
Ashraf, Hamid, 219
Ashraf, Princess, 142, 159, 167
ash-Shiraa (newspaper), 258
Ashtiyani, Jalal ad-Din, 185
"Assassins," 7, 44
Assembly of Experts, 247–48, 255, 260, 275
Association of Combatant Clerics, 260, 266
Atabak (Ali Asghar Khan, *Amin as-Soltan*), 25, 58, 59, 60, 62, 63, 64, 65, 66, 69, 174
Atatürk (Mustafa Kemal), 85, 92
Averroes, 17
Avicenna, 17, 60
Ayandegan (newspaper), 247
Azali Babis, 62, 177, 179
Azerbaijan (region): Sufism in, 10; nomadism in, 24; governance of, 25, 114; military forces in, 27, 40; in Constitutional Revolution, 69; in World War I, 73, 75; rebellion in, 78, 82; economic reforms in, 79; autonomy and leftist movements in, 85, 107, 109, 111, 112, 113, 193, 229, 245, 314, 315; MPRP in, 242, 249
Azerbaijan (republic), 2, 313, 314
Azhari, Gholam Reza, 232

"Bab" (Sayyed Ali Mohammad), 45–48
Babism, 21, 45–48, 62, 173, 177, 179, 180, 190

Baghdad Pact, 139
Baha'is, 33, 45, 48, 86, 190, 224, 312
Baha'ollah, 48
Bahonar, Mohammad Javad, 253
Bakhtiar, Shapour, 216, 234, 235, 238, 268
Bakhtiar, Taimur, 143–44
Bakhtiari, Sardar As'ad, 88
Bakhtiaris, 24, 70, 71, 72, 85, 314
Baluchis, 20, 24, 249, 312, 313–14
Bandar Shahpur, 233
Bani-Etemad, Rakhshan, 300
Bani Sadr, Abolhasan, 188, 208–12, 219, 222, 240–41; Western training of, 198, 234; in Iran–Iraq war, 251; Khomeini's break with, 250, 252–53
Bank Markazi (Central Bank), 141
banks, 57, 95, 108, 159, 165, 257, 273
Bank Saderat, 228
Baqer Khan, 70
Baraheni, Reza, 184
Bashu, The Little Stranger (Beyza'i), 299
Basiji, 251, 275
Bayan, 46
bazaaris: taxes collected from, 16, 51; ulama ties with, 30, 42; Western trade and, 53–54; in Tobacco Protest, 62; under Reza Shah's regime, 102; in post–World War II period, 118, 119–20; Mohammad Reza Shah opposed by, 168; Westernization resented by, 189; in Revolution of 1978–79, 226–28; economic reforms opposed by, 273
Bazargan, Mehdi, 195, 198–200: in National Front, 145, 220; Bani Sadr's defense of, 209; in Revolution of 1978–79, 222, 235, 23, 239; as prime minister, 238, 241, 242, 244; as moderate, 246, 314; pro-American sympathies of, 248–49; fall of, 249, 251, 258
Behbehani, Sayyed Abdollah, 69, 70–71, 130, 180
Beheshti, Ayatollah Mohammad, 235, 241, 243–44, 250, 253, 269
Behrangi, Samad, 184
Bektashi order, 10, 13
Belgium, 65, 66
Beyza'i, Bahram, 299
birthrates, 285, 287, 288, 295
Blackboards (S. Makhmalbaf), 300
"Black Friday," 232
Blind Owl, The (Hedayat), 183
Boir Ahmadi, 155
Bolsheviks, 74, 75, 76, 77

Bonyad-e Mosta'zefin (Foundation for the Dispossessed), 246
Borujerdi, Ayatollah Hosain, 139, 146, 147, 186, 192, 194
bread, price of, 107
British Petroleum (Anglo-Iranian Oil Company), 110, 112, 113, 119, 123–26, 129, 131, 132, 136, 139
broadcasting, 142, 313
Brzezinski, Zbigniew, 235, 236, 248
Bush, George W., 284, 322
Bushehr (port), 50, 60
Buyids, 8, 23
Byzantine empire, 5, 12, 193

Carmathians, 7, 8
carpet trade, 32, 52–53, 58, 87, 95, 118, 151, 227–28
Carter, Jimmy, 165, 214–15, 216, 217, 235, 236, 248
cashmere, 52
Caspian fishing concessions, 56, 81, 84
Caspian Sea, 2
caviar, 56
censorship: after Constitutional Revolution, 72; under Reza Shah, 88–89, 181, 185; under Reza Shah Pahlavi, 216, 217, 233; under Raja'i, 252; under Khatami, 269, 276, 278, 290, 298, 303
Central Bank (Bank Markazi), 141
Central Intelligence Agency (CIA), 128, 129, 130, 134
centralization, 89, 92, 99, 103
Chaldiran, Battle of, 11
Chehabi, Houchang, 100
chemical weapons, 259
children: guardianship of, 30–31, 92, 167, 292–93; as laborers, 95, 112; marriage of, 257
Children of Heaven (Majidi), 300
China, 46, 74, 168, 233, 301
Christianity, 3, 5, 6, 18, 46, 193, 199, 202, 224, 312
Churchill, Winston, 126
CIA (Central Intelligence Agency), 128, 129, 130, 134
CIR (Council of the Islamic Revolution), 242, 245, 250
civil code, 89–90, 92
civil service, 89
Clinton, Bill, 265, 267
Color of Paradise, The (Majidi), 300

Combatant Clergy Society, 260, 266
Combatant Clerics Association, 260, 266
commercial code, 89
Communist League, 254
communism, 78, 85, 88, 181, 187
Confederation of Iranian Students, 218, 219, 220
Conoco, 265
Conservatives (Islamic Right), 255, 261, 269, 281
constitutionalism, 175, 179, 185
Constitutional Revolution (1905–11), 30, 32, 48, 67–71, 131, 179–81, 187
Cossack Brigade, 28, 57, 63, 70, 78, 80
cotton, 26, 51, 52, 115, 121
Council of Guardians, 248, 256, 260, 261, 266, 267, 275, 276, 277, 278, 280, 281, 289
Council of the Islamic Revolution (CIR), 242, 245, 250
Cow, The (Mehrju'i), 298
Cow, The (Sa'edi), 184
credit cooperatives, 150–51
criminal code, 89–90
Crowned Cannibals, The (Baraheni), 184
Cult of Personality, The (Bani Sadr), 209
Cultural Revolution (1980–83), 250, 257, 290, 305
Curzon, George, 54, 76
customs duties, 35, 65, 98, 115
Cyclist, The (M. Makhmalbaf), 300
Cyrus the Great, 224

dams, 137–38
Dar al-Fonun, 49
D'Arcy, William Knox, 35, 72
Darya'i, Zinat, 288–89
Dasht-e Kavir (desert), 2
Dasht-e Lut (desert), 2
Daulatabadi, Sadeqeh, 87
Daulatabadi, Yahya, 86
Davar, Ali Akbar, 85
Day I Became a Woman, The (Meshkini), 300
Day of Sacrifice (Esfandiari), 183
Debray, Regis, 219
deforestation, 2, 151
Dehkhoda, 68, 179
Democratic party (Azerbaijan), 77, 111
Democratic party (Kurdistan), 247, 253, 254
Democratic party (national), 181, 244
Derakhshesh, Mohammad, 142
deregulation, 273

Desert (Shariati), 200
Development Plan Act (1947), 121
Dhofar (province), 164
Diba, Farah (queen), 141–42, 215
divine incarnation, 6, 10, 14
divorce, 12, 30, 31, 89, 92, 100, 167, 257, 280, 292, 293, 296
Divorce Iranian Style (Mir-Hosseini, Longinotto), 300
drinking, 257
drug abuse, 279, 289
Dulles, Allen, 129
Dulles, John Foster, 129

Ebadi, Shirin, 295
Ebtehaj, Abolhasan, 137, 138
Ebtekar, Massoumeh, 265, 270
Ecevit, Bulent, 272
Economics of Unity, The (Bani Sadr), 209
education, 29, 86, 91, 99, 119, 286–87, 317; of women, 100–101, 166; competitiveness in, 291
egalitarianism, 10, 14
Egypt, 5, 6, 7, 56, 119, 139, 173, 176, 271
Eisenhower, Dwight, 128, 129
electrification, 94, 118, 137, 286
Eqbal, Manuchehr, 140, 141, 143, 166, 237
erosion, 2, 151
Esfahani, Mirza Nasrollah (Malek al-Motakallemin), 70, 179–80
Esfandiari, Sorayya, 141
Eshkevari, Hojjat ol-Islam Yusefi, 310
Eshqi (poet), 88, 182
Eskandari, Mohtaram, 87
Eskandari, Solaiman, 87
E'temad as-Saltaneh, 60
E'tesami, Parvin, 182
Ettela'at (newspaper), 225, 247
European Union, 265
Expediency Council, 260, 261, 269
exports: carpets, 32, 52–53, 58, 87, 95, 118, 151, 227–28; crops, 26, 40, 51; metals, 50, opium, 26, 51, 52, 53, 289; cotton, 26, 51, 52, 115, 121; falling prices of, 58; Depression-era decline in, 97–98; post–World War II decline in, 118; promotion of, 264, 265
extraterritoriality, 41–42, 82

Fallaci, Oriana, 166
family planning, 287–88

Family Protection Law (1967/75), 167, 223, 257, 292, 293
famines, 75, 106, 108, 110, 113
Fanon, Frantz, 200
faqih, 248, 261
Fardust, Hosain, 249
farm corporations, 153, 154–55
Fatima (daughter of Mohammad), 200, 205
Fatima is Fatima (Shariati), 204
fatwas, 261–62
Forugh Farrokhzad, 182
Foruhar, Daryush, 275
Farmanara, Bahman, 301
Faruq, king of Egypt, 141
Fascist Interpretation of Religion and Government, The (Ganji), 303–4
Fatemi, Hosain, 130
Fath Ali Akhundzadeh, 66, 178, 179
Fath Ali Shah, 37, 38, 39, 41, 44
Fatimids, 7, 10, 45
Fawzia, Princess, 141
Feda'iyan, 70
Feda'iyan-e Islam, 120–21, 124, 185–86, 195, 254
Feda'iyan-e Khalq, 168, 219–20, 221–22, 233, 238, 243, 246, 247, 254
Feuerbach, Ludwig, 307
15th of Khordad Foundation, 262
filmmaking, 295, 298–301
fiqh, 308
Fivers (Zaidis), 7, 8
flogging, 257
FM (Freedom Movement of Iran), 195, 199, 220, 242, 254, 279
folk culture, 170, 188
folk theatre, 171, 188
foqaha (jurists), 193
foreign exchange, 138, 141, 144, 264, 273
foreign investment, 160, 161, 272, 273, 274
Foroughi, Mohammad Ali, 85
Foruhar, Daryush, 216
Foundation for the Dispossessed (Bonyad-e Mosta'zefin), 246, 261, 298
France, 34, 37–38, 76, 219, 232, 272
Freedom Movement of Iran (FM), 195, 199, 220, 242, 254, 279
Freemasons, 166, 224, 231
free trade, 42, 264
free will, 18, 310
Full Powers Law (1943), 107
Fundamental Law (1906), 68

Fundamental Principles of Islamic Government, The (Bani Sadr), 210

Gabbeh (M. Makhmalbaf), 300
Ganji, Akbar, 279, 281, 303–4
Gardane, General, 38
Georgia, 38
Geranpayeh, Behrooz, 281
Germany, 72, 73, 74, 98, 101, 105, 109, 184, 268
Ghazian, Hossein-Ali, 281
Ghefari, Abu Zarr, 201
Ghotbzadeh, Sadeq, 219, 234, 255
Gilan (province), 2, 70, 75, 77, 79, 82, 96, 295
Gobineau, Comte de, 20
Grady, Henry, 124, 131
Graham, Robert, 228, 238
grain, 115, 160, 165
Great Britain, 34–35, 43, 53–54, 176, 320; Qajar dynasty backed by, 37, 44, 50, 173; Russian efforts opposed by, 56, 62, 65–66; growing influence of, 57; German threat to, 69; oil interests of, 72, 73, 76, 86, 101, 128; in World War I, 73–75; as party to Anglo-Persian Treaty, 76–77, 78, 79, 80; southern Iranian efforts by, 84–85, 107, 109, 113; as trading partner, 97, 127; in World War II, 105, 107, 109; economic development role of, 122; in 1953 coup, 129–31; diplomatic relations restored with, 136; in Baghdad Pact, 139; Mohammad Reza Shah backed by, 163–64; Behbehani's support of, 180; Rushdie affair and, 262, 272
Great Holy War, The (Khomeini), 193
Greek philosophy, 17
Griboyedov incident, 42–43
Grumman, 164
Guardian Council, 248, 256, 260, 261, 266, 267, 275, 276, 277, 278, 280, 281, 289
guerillas, 168, 187, 219–20, 222, 229, 233, 238
Guevara, Che, 194, 219
Gulf War (1991–92), 266
guns, 23

Habl al-Matin (newspaper), 66 , 174
hadith, 9
Hafez (poet), 172
Haidar Khan Amu Oghlu, 181
Hajjarian, Said, 277
Hajji Agha (Hedayat), 183
Hajji Baba of Isfahan (Morier), 66, 179

Hakamizadeh, A. A., 191
Hamas, 268
harems, 31
Harvard University, 157
Hasan (son of Ali), 6, 205
Hashemi, Faezeh, 277
Hashemi, Mehdi, 260
Hatamikia, Ebrahim, 301
health care, 99, 287–90, 315, 317
Hedayat, Sadeq, 178, 183, 184
Henderson, Loy, 130
Herat, 43, 50
Hezbollah (Iran), 193, 244, 247, 251–52, 253
history, study of, 302
Hizbollah (Lebanon), 268, 284, 322
hojjatiyeh, 244
Hokumat-e velayi (Kadivar), 308
Homayun, Daryush, 225
Horr, 202
horsemanship, 23
Hosain (son of Ali), 6, 9, 47, 147, 169, 170–71, 193, 202, 205, 206, 234
Hosain, Shah Sultan, 18
Hosainiyeh Ershad, 200, 206
Hosain Khan, Mirza, *Moshir ad-Dauleh*, 25, 32, 54–56, 58, 59, 173
hostage crisis (1979–81), 42, 241, 246–47, 251, 252, 265
House Built on Water, A (Farmanara), 301
housing shortages, 162, 164
Hoveyda, Amir Abbas, 166, 216, 217, 232, 246
Hurufi movement, 9–10
Hussein, Saddam, 251, 271
Huyser, Robert, 235
Hypocrites from Our Viewpoint, The (Bani Sadr), 209

IBEX, 164
Identity Card, The (Esfandiari), 183
ijtihad (interpretation), 9, 208
Imamis. *See* Twelvers
Imbrie, Robert, 86
Imperial Bank of Persia, 57
Imperial Guard, 238
imports: textiles, 50; tariffs on, 41, 42, 53, 60, 76, 77, 87, 141, 158–59; Depression-era rise in, 98; post–World War II decline in, 127
income distribution, 157, 158, 161–62
India, 2, 46, 52, 54, 58, 74, 174

inflation, 94, 106, 107, 108, 110, 115, 118,
127, 138, 140, 141, 147, 163, 164, 217, 256,
264, 267, 279
intelligentsia, 119
International Commission of Jurists, 215,
216
International Court of Justice, 124
International Monetary Fund, 264
Internet, 311
Irangate affair, 258
Iranian Soviet Socialist Republic, 77–78
Iranian Women's Organization, 167, 223,
229
Iran–Iraq war (1980–88), 241, 251, 253, 258–
59, 263, 266, 292, 322
Iran–Libya Sanctions Act (1996), 265–66
Iran Novin (New Iran) party, 166
Iranshahr (newspaper), 74, 83
Iranshahr, Hosain Kazemzadeh, 83
Iran's Situation and the Role of Modarres
(Bani Sadr), 209
Iraq, 2, 6, 55, 62, 113, 253; Manichaeism
founded in, 3; pilgrimages to, 28, 224; as
oil supplier, 136; in Baghdad pact, 139;
Khomeini in, 232–33; U.S. sanctions
against, 265; tensions with, 271; in "axis of
evil" speech, 284; Kurds in, 313. *See also*
Iran–Iraq war
Ironside (general), 80
IRP (Islamic Republican Party), 243–44, 246,
247, 249, 250, 251, 252, 253, 254, 255, 259–
60
irrigation, 2, 39–40, 74, 117, 126, 137–38,
151, 154, 26
Isfahan, 18, 19, 45, 61, 70, 87, 107, 230
Islamic modernism, 304
*Islam and Property, in Comparison to the
Economic Systems of the West* (Taleqani),
196–98
Islamic Free University, 291
Islamic Government (Khomeini), 240
Islamic Iran Participation Front, 270
Islamic Left, 255, 256, 258, 260, 261, 263–64,
266, 267, 269, 270, 277, 281
Islamic Right (Conservatives), 255, 261, 269,
281
Islamic Republican Party (IRP), 243–44, 246,
247, 249, 250, 251, 252, 253, 254, 255, 259–
60
Islamic Revival, 3–4, 175
Isma'il (Safavid ruler), 10, 11, 13, 14
Isma'ilis (Seveners), 7, 8, 13, 14, 44–45, 312

Israel, 146, 147, 238, 247, 268, 272, 276, 284,
312
Istanbul, 62, 69, 73, 174
Italy, 139, 272

Ja'far as-Sadeq, 7, 147
Jahangir Khan, Mirza, 70, 180
Jamal ad-Din, Sayyed, "al-Afghani," 60–61,
62, 63, 64, 175–77, 179, 212
Jamal ad-Din Esfahani, Sayyed, 66, 67, 70,
179–80
Jamalzadeh, Mohammad Ali, 74, 179, 181,
183, 184
jangalis, 75, 78, 81
Japan, 67, 179
Jazani, Bizhan, 219
Jehad-e Sazandegi (Reconstruction Jihad),
246, 286, 298
jihad, 5, 210, 211
Jews, Judaism, 3, 6, 20, 33, 224, 276, 283, 312
Jurists Association, 216

Kadivar, Mohsen, 307–10
kadkhodas, 96
Kamran Mirza Nayeb as-Saltaneh, 63
Kar, Mehrangiz, 279, 294, 295
Karbala, 19, 45
Karbaschi, Gholam Hosein, 274–75
Karrubi, Mehdi, 263, 266, 278
Karzai, Hamid, 283
Kashan, 147
Kashani, Ayatollah, Sayyed Abol Qasem,
120, 128, 129, 130, 185–86
Kasravi, Ahmad, 178, 185, 189, 191, 314
Kaveh (newspaper), 74, 80, 181
Kayhan (newspaper), 247, 269
KDP (Kurdish Democratic Party), 247, 253,
254
Kemal, Namik, 175
Kemal, Mustafa (Atatûrk), 85, 92
Kennedy, John F., 140, 144
Kermani, Mirza Aqa Khan, 62–63, 66, 177,
178, 190, 319
Kermani, Mirza Reza, 63, 64
Khalkhali, Sadeq, 245–46
Khamene'i, Hojjatoleslam Ali, 253, 255, 259,
260, 261–62, 263–64, 266, 268, 269, 270,
271, 272, 314; in press crackdown, 275–76,
278; conciliatory moves by, 277; judiciary
controlled by, 279, 281; Khatami checked
by, 280; Montazeri's attack on, 283;
Soroush rebutted by, 306

Khan, Kuchek, 75, 77–78, 82
Khatami, Mohammad, 263, 269–84, 297–98, 312, 313, 314–15
Khatami, Mohammad Reza, 278
Khaz'al, Shaikh, 72, 85, 113
Khiabani, Shaikh Mohammad, 77, 78
Khoeniha, Mohammad, 266
Khomeini, Ahmad, 191
Khomeini, Ayatollah Ruhollah Musavi: mujtahid rule under, 17; Reza Shah Pahlavi attacked by, 146–48; exile of, 168, 192, 235–36; Muslim philosophy and, 185; writings of, 191–93; Shariatmadari vs., 194–95; Taleqani vs., 196; Bani Sadr and, 208, 209; students influenced by, 219; Mojahedin-e Khalq attacked by, 207; in Revolution of 1978–79, 222, 223–39; accession of, 235; politics and economics under, 240–62; death of, 261; family planning under, 287; unapproachable image of, 297; morality codes under, 298
Khomeini, Mostafa, 191, 225
Khorasan, 82, 193
Khorramshahr, 264
khums, 16
Khuzistan, 72, 84–85, 101, 113, 138, 154, 251, 314
Kianuri, Nureddin, 254
Kiarostami, Abbas, 299–300
Kimia'i, Mas'ud, 298
Kish, 264
Kiyan (periodical), 305, 306
komitehs, 245
Kurdish Democratic Party (KDP), 247, 253, 254
Kurdistan, 111, 112, 113
Kurds, 12, 20, 21, 24, 82, 97, 107, 109, 244, 249, 259, 312, 313, 315
Kuwait, 136, 232, 259, 266

Lahiji Shahla, 279
Lahuti (major), 82
Lambton, Ann, 90
landholding, 25–26, 40, 90; by crown, 116, 138–39; absentee, 117
land reform, 81, 90, 111, 138–39, 145, 146–47, 149–52, 156, 255, 256, 286
law courts, 29–30
Lebanon, 258, 268
legal reform, 89, 216
Lenin, Vladimir, 78
Libya, 36

licensing, 159–60
Life and Nothing Else (Kiarostami), 300
literacy, 286–87
Little Black Fish, The (Behrangi), 184
Lockheed, 164
Longinotto, Kim, 300
lottery, 59
Low Heights (Hatamikia), 301
Luce, Clare Boothe, 127
Lurs, 24, 85, 97, 314

McFarlane, Robert, 258
Madani, Admiral Ahmad, 249–50
Mahmud II, 27
Majidi, Majd, 300
majles, 67–68, 70–71, 260
Makhmalbaf, Mohsen, 300
Makhmalbaf, Samireh, 300
maktabi, 244
malaria, 117
Malcolm, John, 38
Malek al-Motakallemin (Mirza Nasrollah Esfahani), 70, 179–80
Maleki, Khalil, 187
Malekzadeh, Mehdi, 179
Malkom Khan, Mirza, 58–59, 61, 66, 174, 176, 177, 190
Mani, 3
Manichaeism, 3, 6, 178
"Manifesto of Republicanism" (Ganji), 304
Manifesto of the Islamic Republic (Bani Sadr), 209–10
Mansur, Hasan Ali, 166
Maoism, 219
Mardom (People's) party, 140
marja'-e taqlid, 139, 146, 192, 198, 211
marriage contracts, 167, 293
Martin, Vanessa, 103
martyrdom, 3
Marxism, 181, 184, 194, 196, 199, 202, 209, 211, 218, 219, 222, 307, 319
Mashhad, 61, 147, 223
mashruteh, 67
Massignon, Louis, 200, 207
Matin-asgari, Afshin, 306
Matin-Daftari, Hedayatollah, 187, 243, 249
Mazanderan (province), 47, 75, 78, 96, 295
Mazdak, 3, 178
MCIG (Ministry of Culture and Islamic Guidance), 298
Mecca, 4, 5
Medina, 4, 5

Mehrju'i, Daryush, 184, 298, 299
Melliyun (Nationalist) party, 140, 166
Meshkini, Marzieh, 300
messianism, 6, 46
Milani, Ayatollah Mohammad Hadi, 146
Milani, Tahmineh, 295, 300
military reform, 89
Millspaugh, A. C., 84, 106, 107–8, 109
minerals, 57, 127, 197
Ministry of Culture and Islamic Guidance
    (MCIG), 298
Mirbaqeri, Davud, 301
Mir Damad, 17, 185
Mir-Hosseini, Ziba, 300
Mir-Karimi, Seyyed Reza, 301
Mirza Habib Esfahani, 66, 179
Mirza Reza Kermani, 60, 63
Mission for My Country (Mohammad Reza
    Shah), 166
MK. *See* Mojahedin-e Khalq
Modarres, Hasan, 85, 86, 88
Modern Right (Pragmatists), 255, 261, 267,
    269
Mohajerani, Ataollah, 271, 278
Mohammad, Prophet, 4, 5, 25, 46–47, 205
Mohammad Ali Mirza, 64
Mohammad Ali Shah, 68, 69, 70, 180
Mohammad Mirza, 44
Mohammad Reza Shah Pahlavi: accession of,
    105–6; repressiveness of, 133, 134, 167–68,
    320; modernization pursued by, 133–34,
    135, 223; elections manipulated by, 140–
    41; Parliament dissolved by, 142–43;
    reform efforts of, 145, 148, 172; nomads
    settled by, 156; ostentation by, 167, 224;
    decline and fall of, 214–39
Mohammad Shah, 44, 47
Mohtashemi, Ali-Akbar, 266
Mojahedin, 70, 195
Mojahedin-e Khalq (MK), 218, 304; guerilla
    roots of, 168, 219; leftist orientation of,
    198, 220–22; Bani Sadr on, 209; in Revolu-
    tion of 1978–79, 225, 233, 238; under Kho-
    meini, 247, 253, 254; raids by and against,
    271
Molla Sadra, 17, 185, 305, 308
Mongols, 2, 7, 10, 13, 23, 44
monopolies, 98, 115
Montazeri, Ayatollah Hosain Ali, 241, 246,
    255, 260, 262, 264, 274, 275, 283, 309, 310,
    311
Moqaddam Maraghe'i, Rahmatollah, 249

Morier, James, 66
Morocco, 36
Morrison-Knudson, 121
Mosaddeq, Mohammad: Reza Shah opposed
    by, 86, 88, 109, 139; as prime minister, 124,
    125–26; overthrow of, 128–31, 135, 136,
    186, 320; ulama and, 146; influence of, 187,
    219; anti-imperialism of, 189, 212; allies of,
    195, 199, 200, 216
Moshir ad-Dauleh (prime minister), 78
Mossad, 134
Mostaz'efin Foundation, 247
Motahhari, Ayatollah, 245
Movement of Muslim Militants, 279
Mozaffar ad-Din Shah, 63, 64, 66, 69
mujtahids, 9, 16, 17, 20, 194, 197, 198
Musavi, Mir Hosain, 253, 256, 287
music, 302
Muslim conquest, 2
Muslim People's Republican Party (MPRP),
    242, 245, 249
Mu'tazilites, 18, 307, 308, 310
mysticism, 9–10, 190, 307

Nabavi, Behzad, 266, 278
Naderi, Amir, 299
Nahj al-Balagha, 196
Na'ini, Ayatollah Mohammad Hosain, 181,
    185, 196
Najaf, 19, 45
Najafabadi, Ghorban Ali Dorri, 276
Najmabadi, Shaikh Hadi, 60
Napoleon Bonaparte, 38
Naraghi, Ehsan, 190
Naser ad-Din Shah, 25, 32, 47, 48, 49, 53, 54,
    55, 56, 59, 60, 61, 63–64, 173
Naser al-Molk, 70, 71
Nasiri (general), 232
Nasser, Gamal Abdul, 133, 139
Nateq Nuri, Hojjatoleslam Ali Akbar, 266,
    267, 269, 270
National Bank (Bank Melli), 137
National Council of Resistance, 253, 254
National Democratic Front (NDF), 187, 243,
    246–47, 253
National Front (NF): oil agreement opposed
    by, 124; divisions within, 129, 132–33;
    Baghdad Pact opposed by, 139; Reza Shah
    Pahlavi opposed by, 140, 216; in electoral
    politics, 141–42, 143, 247, 249, 250; mem-
    bership of, 145–46, 219, 222, 232; Kho-
    meini and, 147, 234; suppression of, 168,

169, 251–52; nationalism of, 187; American overtures to, 235; Bakhtiar expelled by, 238; under Khomeini, 242–43
National Iranian Oil Company (NIOC), 125, 137, 139, 142, 249, 265
Nationalist (Melliyun) party, 140, 166
nationalization, 125–26, 137, 145, 255, 256
National Will party, 109
natural gas, 266
natural law, 18, 310
Nazih, Hasan, 249
Near East Foundation, 117
Nestorians, 20–21, 33
New Iran (Iran Novin) party, 166
newspapers, 68, 83, 107, 252, 271, 275, 278, 303, 313. *See also individual titles*
NF. *See* National Front
NGOs (nongovernmental organizations), 280, 289
NIOC (National Iranian Oil Company), 125, 137, 139, 142, 249, 265
Nixon, Richard, 163
nomads, 2, 10, 90, 317–18; political power of, 12; invasions from Turkey by, 19, 22–23; patterns of, 24; women's role among, 31, 295; modernization obstructed by, 35–36; forced settlement of, 91, 156; peasants vs., 116
nongovernmental organizations (NGOs), 280, 289
North Korea, 284
North Yemen, 7
nuclear capability, 272, 284
Nuri, Abdollah, 275, 277
Nuri, Shaikh Fazlollah, 190

OCI (Overseas Consultants, Inc.), 121–22
occultation, 7–8, 208
OIC (Organization of the Islamic Conference), 271
oil, oil industry: discovery of, 70, 72; Standard Oil of New Jersey concession, 83–84; early growth of, 86; centrality of, 95, 162–63, 165, 265, 271, 274; in World War II, 110; employment in, 118; strikes in, 120, 233; crisis in, 123–31; international consortium and, 136–37
Oman, 163
Omar Khayyam, 21
On the Loyalty and Betrayal of the Intellectuals (Al-e Ahmad), 189–90
opium, 26, 51, 52, 53, 289

Organization of Petroleum Exporting Countries (OPEC), 133, 163
Organization of the Islamic Conference (OIC), 271
Ottoman Empire, 10, 11, 12, 23, 49, 56, 73, 175
Overseas Consultants, Inc. (OCI), 121–22

Pahlavi Foundation, 165, 246
Pakistan, 2, 6, 46, 139, 258, 287
Palestine, 268
Palestine Liberation Organization (PLO), 271
Panahi, Jafar, 300
pan-Islamic movement, 175–77
Parvaresh (newspaper), 66, 174
Pasdaran (Revolutionary Guard), 244, 246, 249, 251, 261, 269, 275, 277
passion play (ta'ziyeh), 170–71, 188, 202
Payam-e Zan (journal), 294
Peace of Paris (1857), 50
Peace of Tilsit (1807), 38
peasantry, 2; in post–World War II period, 113, 114–15, 116
People's (Mardom) party, 140
Persian Empire, 5
Persian Gulf, 2
Peykar group, 243, 254
Peyman, Habibollah, 279
pilgrimage, 210
Pishevari, Ja'far, 111, 112, 194
Plan Organization (PO), 137–38, 142, 157, 166
PLO (Palestine Liberation Organization), 271
Point Four, 117, 126
polygamy, 30, 31, 46, 92, 100, 257, 292, 293, 296
polytheism, 210
Pragmatists (Modern Right), 255, 261, 267, 269
prayer, 204, 210, 260
price controls, 155, 256
Prince Ehtejab (Farmanara), 301
privatization, 122, 123, 145, 264–65, 273, 274
Provisional Revolutionary Government (PRG), 242, 245, 246, 247

Qa'em Maqam, 40, 173
Qajar period, 12, 23, 24, 27, 28–36, 37–88, 302, 318, 320

qanats, 39–40, 151
Qanun (newspaper), 59, 62, 64, 174, 177
Qasemlu, Abdol Rahman, 247, 268
Qashqa'is, 24, 113, 155, 314
Qavam as-Saltaneh, 82, 112, 113, 126
Qeisar (Kimia'i), 298
Qeshm, 264
Qom, 67, 74, 103, 194, 225, 290, 321
Qorrat al-Ain, 46, 47
Qotbi, Reza, 142
Quran, 6, 9, 167, 175; women in, 12–13, 30–
    31; "allegorical" interpretations of, 17;
    Babism and, 46, 47; political ideology
    based on, 188; Khomeini on, 193

Rafsanjani, Ali Akbar Hashemi: as speaker,
    250; hostage crisis viewed by, 252; foreign
    policy of, 258, 267, 271; in Iran–Iraq war,
    259; as candidate, 261, 277–78; economic
    policies of, 262, 263–64, 274; post-
    presidential career of, 268–69; educational
    policies of, 291
Rahnavard, Zahra, 287
railroads, 35, 54, 56, 77, 85, 89, 93–94, 108,
    118
Raja'i, Mohammad Ali, 250, 252, 253
Rajavi, Masud, 253
Rastakhiz party, 166, 217, 229
Rasulzadeh, 179, 181
rationing, 256
rauzeh-khani, 171, 188
Razmara, Ali, 124
Reagan, Ronald, 258
Reconstruction Jihad (Jehad-e Sazandegi),
    246, 286, 298
Republican People's party, 194
Reuter, Julius de, 35, 54, 55–56, 57
Revival parties, 85
Revolutionary Guard (Pasdaran), 244, 246,
    249, 251, 261, 269, 275, 277
Revolution of 1978–79, 1, 32
Rex Theatre fire, 231
Reza Shah: pre-Islamic past evoked by, 2, 86,
    224, 319; military reforms of, 41, 83; acces-
    sion of, 80–86; Mohammad Reza Shah's
    emulation of, 135; modernization pursued
    by, 87–91, 133, 222–23; economic reforms
    of, 92–104; women's partial emancipation
    under, 100–101, 182; Nazi sympathies of,
    101, 105; abdication of, 105–6, 107; Kho-
    meini's attacks on, 147, 192; cultural limits
    imposed by, 172, 184, 185; leftist writings

banned by, 181; as counterweight to for-
    eign powers, 320
rial, 97–98, 267
road construction, 93, 94, 286
Roosevelt, Kermit, 129, 130
Ruhi, Shaikh Ahmad, 62–63, 177
Rumi, 305
Rumsfeld, Donald, 284
Runner, The (Naderi), 299
Rushdie, Salman, 262, 268, 272
Russia: strategic interests of, 34, 320; banking
    and railroad schemes of, 35, 56; as model,
    49; as counterweight to Britain, 54, 72;
    Qajar dynasty backed by, 37, 44, 50, 66,
    173; in territorial disputes with Iran, 41;
    Griboyedov incident and, 41–42; Reuter
    concession opposed by, 55; growing influ-
    ence of, 57, 62; Belgian ties to, 65; military
    presence of, 70, 71; in World War I, 73–74;
    reparations sought from, 76; improved
    relations with, 272
Russian Revolution (1905), 66
Russo-Iranian Treaty (1921), 81–82, 84, 112
Russo-Japanese War (1904–5), 66, 179

Sabeans, 21, 33, 312
Sabzavari (philosopher), 185
Sa'di (poet), 172
Sa'edi, Gholam Hosain, 184
Safavi, Navvab, 195
Safavids, 2, 8, 10–19, 23, 28, 44, 190, 202–4,
    318
Sahabi, Ezzetollah, 279
Sahabi, Yadollah, 195, 199
Saidzadeh, Hojjat ol-Islam, 294
Salam (newspaper), 276
Salisbury, Robert, 62
Saleh, Allahyar, 141, 142
Sane'i, Yusef, 310
Sanjabi, Karim, 216, 233, 238, 245
Saqafi, Mirza Mohammad, 191
Sartre, Jean-Paul, 200
Sasanian Empire, 2, 5, 12
Satanic Verses, The (Rushdie), 262
satellite television, 301, 311
Sattar Kahn, 70
Saudi Arabia, 36, 217, 259, 271
SAVAK, 134, 143, 147, 148, 184, 193, 196,
    217, 219, 225, 231, 234, 238, 247, 249
SAVAMA, 249
Sayyed Ali Mohammad ("Bab"), 45–48
Schwarzkopf, H. Norman, 108, 114

SCIRI (Supreme Council of the Islamic Revolution in Iraq), 271
Second of Khordad, 270
Secrets Exposed (Khomeini), 191–92
Secrets of a Thousand Years (Hakamizadeh), 191
Selim, Sultan, 11
Selim III, 27
Seljuqs, 12, 22–23
Sepahdar (prime minister), 78, 80
Servants of Construction, 267, 269, 270, 277
Seveners (Isma'ilis), 7, 8, 13, 14, 44–45, 312
Seven Year Plans, 117, 121–23, 137, 156–57
sexuality, 32, 182
SFLI ("Students Following the Line of the Imam"), 248
Shabestari, Mohammad Mojtahed, 307, 308, 309, 310
shabnamehs, 65
Shah, Nader, 20
Shah-Nameh (Firdausi), 172, 178
Shahnaz (daughter of Reza Shah Pahlavi), 141
Shahram, 159
Shahrudi, Ayatollah Mahmoud Hashemi, 277
Shahsevan, 24, 314
Shahzadeh Abd al-Azim, 63, 67
Shaikhism, 21, 45, 60, 173, 176
sharecropping, 26, 96, 114–15
sharia, 28, 89, 90, 92, 167, 180, 245, 257, 292, 296
Shariati, Ali, 165, 184, 186, 187, 188, 198, 200–208, 217, 221, 222, 225, 304, 305, 306
Shariati, Mohammad Taqi, 200
Shariatmadari, Ayatollah Kazem, 146, 193–95, 222, 224, 232, 242, 246, 249, 255, 314
Sharif-Emami, Ja'far, 141, 142, 143, 231
Sherkat, Shahla, 294
Shi'ism: origins of, 4–5; doctrinal characteristics of, 6, 47; Abbasid movement and, 6–7; divisions within, 7, 14, 20; Iran identified with, 8–9, 19, 20–21, 318; hybrids of Sunnism and, 10; ulama independence in, 15, 16–17, 19, 28, 190; Greek philosophy compatible with, 18; temporary marriage in, 32–33; Westernization challenged by, 165; family law based on, 167; contemporary currents in, 188–90; lay thinkers in, 198–212; Alid vs. Safavid, 202–4
Shiraz, 37, 45, 61, 147, 231
Shirazi, Hajj Mirza Hasan, 61

Shuster, Morgan, 71
silk, 12, 39, 52
silver, 53, 58
Sinclair Oil Company, 84
Sistan (province), 97
Smell of Camphor, Fragrance of Jasmine (Farmanara), 301
Snowman, The (Mirbaqeri), 301
Sobhh-e Azal, 48
Social Democratic party, 181
socialism, 85, 88, 187, 256
Soltanzadeh, Ahmed (Avedis), 78
Sorayya (newspaper), 66, 174
Soroush, Abdol Karim, 296–97, 305–6, 310
South Africa, 238, 268
South Persia Rifles, 74
Soviet Union: early overtures toward, 79; as trading partner, 97; in World War II, 105, 109; oil interests of, 110, 113–14; radicals encouraged by, 111, 112; Tudeh sympathy for, 126; Baghdad Pact opposed by, 139; 1960s rapprochement with, 218–19; shah tolerated by, 233; during Khomeini regime, 258; fall of, 319
Spain, 6
Special Court for the Clergy, 262, 269
sports, 296
Standard Oil of New Jersey, 83–84, 136–37
Stokes, C. B., 71
strikes, 120, 142, 143, 161, 217, 233
student activism, 218, 250, 276–77, 278, 280–81
"Students Following the Line of the Imam" (SFLI), 248
Sudan, 46
Suez Canal, 133
Sufis, 10, 11, 18, 33, 172, 185, 310
sugar, 50, 51, 53, 67, 84, 89, 94, 115, 127
Sullivan, William, 234–35, 236
sunna (tradition), 193
Sunnism, Sunnis: origins of, 4, 5; Shi'ism distinguished from, 6, 7, 8, 9, 10, 11, 13, 18, 190; family law based on, 167; Khatami and, 269, 270; discrimination against, 312; Kurdish, 313
Supreme Council of the Islamic Revolution in Iraq (SCISI), 271
Supreme National Security Council, 283
Sur-e Esrafil (newspaper), 68, 70, 179, 180
surveying of land, 150
Sykes, Percy, 74
Syria, 5, 9, 10

Tabari, Ehsan, 254

Tabataba'i, Allameh, 185

Tabataba'i, Sayyed Mohammad, 67, 69, 180

Tabriz, 10, 47, 61, 64, 68, 69, 70, 75, 194, 226, 228–29, 245, 249, 277

Taheri, Ayatollah Jalal ed-Din, 310

Tahmasp, 14

Taimurtash, Abd al-Hosain, 85, 88

Taiping Rebellion, 46

Talebzadeh (Talebof), Abd ar-Rahim, 66, 179, 190

Taleqani, Ayatollah Mahmud, 145, 181, 193, 195–98, 199, 220, 222, 224, 232, 245

Taleqani, Mojtaba, 221

Taliban, 271, 283

Tall Shadows in the Wind (Farmanara), 301

Tapper, Richard, 299

Taqizadeh, Sayyed Hasan, 69, 71, 74, 80, 86, 88, 181, 314

tariffs, 41, 42, 53, 60, 76, 77, 87, 141, 158–59

Taste of Cherry, The (Kiarostami), 300

tauhid (unity), 196

taxes: on land, 39, 89; administration of, 51, 83, 84, 126, 273; evasion of, 86; on sugar and tea, 89, 94; indirect, 95, 115; of peasants, 96, 102; of consumer goods, 98; of income, 107, 109; Seven Year Plan and, 123; regressiveess of, 158; locational inducements and, 159

ta'ziyeh (passion play), 170–71, 188, 202

tea, 50, 51, 53, 84, 89, 94, 115

Tehran: growth of, 26, 89, 95, 102; political power of, 68; in Constitutional Revolution, 70; reformism in, 75; in World War II, 105, 107; unrest in, 61, 107, 117, 232, 233, 234; teachers' strike in, 142, 143; overcentralization in, 158, 161; redevelopment plan for, 223

Tehran University, 99, 143, 195, 275

telegraphs, 54, 62, 94, 311

temporary marriage, 32–33, 92, 257, 292, 296

Ten (Kiarostami), 300

Tenants, The (Mehrju'i), 299

terrorism, 267, 268, 272, 284

textiles, 50, 51, 52, 87, 94, 123, 127

Thornburg, Max W., 121, 122, 127–28, 131

Through the Olive Trees (Kiarostami), 300

Tibet, 69

tobacco, 51, 53, 84, 94, 115

Tobacco Protest (1891–92), 30, 32, 61–62, 176, 180

trade unions, 75, 85, 94–95, 107, 112, 113, 120, 138, 217

tradition (sunna), 193

Trans-Iranian Railway, 93–94, 101, 106, 107, 118

transmigration, 6

Travelbook of Ibrahim Beg, The (Zain al-Abedin Maraghe'i), 66, 174, 179, 182

Treaty of Finkenstein (1807), 38

Treaty of Gulistan (1813), 38, 41

Treaty of Turkomanchai (1828), 41, 42

tribes, 23–24

True Dream (Jamal ad-Din Esfahani and Malek al-Molakallemin), 66

Truman, Harry, 125, 129

Tudeh party: origins of, 88, 106–7; in majles, 109; in Azerbaijan, 111; growing strength of, 112, 124, 128; Soviet oil concession backed by, 113–14; trade union support for, 120; ideology of, 126, 242, 254, 319; suppression of, 122, 136, 140, 168, 169, 247, 254; Mosaddeq abandoned by, 130; literary links of, 183, 184; propaganda of, 187; student support for, 218–19; PRG attacked by, 246

Tunisia, 56, 173

Turkey (Anatolia), Turks, 2, 55, 119, 173, 176; Twelver Shi'ism and, 9, 10, 11, 14; women in, 13, 287; nomadic invasions from, 19, 22–23; as reformist model, 58; in World War I, 73; in Baghdad Pact, 139; tensions with, 271–72; Kurds in, 313

Turkomans, 20, 24, 244, 312

Tusi, Nasir ad-Din, 17

tuyuls, 38, 49

Twelvers (Imamis), 4, 7–8, 9, 10, 11, 13, 318; Sunnism split distinguished from, 11, 13; under Safavids, 17–18

Two Women (Milani), 300

ulama, 4, 8; types of, 16; independence in Shi'ism of, 15, 16–17, 19, 28; growing power of, 19–20, 28–29, 42; reformers' hostility to, 59; in Tobacco Protest, 62; diminished role in legal matters of, 89–90; weakening under Reza Shah of, 102–4; reassertion under Mohammad Reza Shah of, 120–21; Mohammad Reza Shah opposed by, 168; in Constitutional Revolution, 179–80; Westernization resented by, 189; in political struggle, 191–212; in Revolution of 1978–79, 226

Umayyad caliphate, 5, 6, 7
Under the Moonlight (Mir-Karimi), 301
unemployment, 120, 164, 264, 271, 273–74,
  279, 287, 291, 316
United Arab Emirates, 271
United Nations, 112, 251, 259
United States: British protectorate opposed
  by, 76; Britain displaced by, 79; communism opposed by, 83, 133, 136, 144; in
  World War II, 105, 107, 108, 109–10; gendarmerie mission of, 108, 114; in post–
  World War II period, 121, 122, 125–26; as
  trading partner, 127; economic development role of, 128; in 1953 coup, 129–31; as
  dominant power in Iran, 132; Mohammad
  Reza Shah backed by, 163–64, 165–66; in
  Iran–Iraq war, 259; dual containment policy of, 265; grievances against Iran of, 267;
  normalization efforts of, 272; in Afghan
  war, 283–84; sympathy toward, 321
United States Technical Cooperation
  Administration, 126–27
unity (tauhid), 196
urbanization, 89, 95, 102, 108, 110, 117, 119,
  152–53, 162, 257, 285, 288, 316, 317
usulis (mujtahids), 9, 16, 17, 194, 197, 198;
  (mujtahidis), 20
Uzbeks, 11

Va'ez, Shaikh Mohammad, 67
vaqf, 15–16, 26, 96, 103, 152, 197
veiling, 12–13, 31, 87, 92, 100, 120, 182,
  310
velayat-e faqih, 255, 261, 271, 280, 283,
  307–9, 310, 321
Velayat-e faqih (Khomeini), 240
Velayati, Ali Akbar, 253, 258
Versailles Peace Conference, 76
videotapes, 301
Vieille, Paul, 209
Vosuq ad-Dauleh, 76, 78

Wasmuss (German agent), 73
water, 118, 151, 154, 290
Watt, W. M., 8
wells, 151, 154

Westinghouse, 164
Westoxication (Al-e Ahmad), 190, 201
"Westoxication" (Gharbzadegi), 189
wheat, 115
Where Is the Friend's House? (Kiarostami),
  299–300
White Balloon, The (Panahi), 300
White Revolution, 145, 156
Wolff, Henry Drummond, 56–57, 59, 61, 62
women: in Quran, 12–13, 30–31; in Qajar
  period, 30–33; Babi movement and, 46;
  during Constitutional Revolution, 71;
  obstacles to, 86–87; modernization program and, 91–92; dress codes for, 100,
  182–83, 257, 290; education of, 100–101,
  166; in workplace, 112, 166; suffrage for,
  145, 146; in Revolution of 1978–79, 229–
  30; under Khomeini, 248, 257, 292; under
  Khatami, 270, 279–80; in present day,
  292–97
wool, 155
World Bank, 125
World War I, 73–75
World War II, 105–10, 117–18
Wretched of the Earth, The (Fanon), 200
Writers' Guild, 216

Yazdani (banker), 228
Yazdi, Ayatollah Abdol Karim Ha'eri, 191,
  194, 219, 234, 245, 248, 277
Yazdi, Ibrahim, 279
Yazdi, Mohammad, 275
Yazid (caliph), 6, 170
Yeki bud yeki nabud (Jamalzadeh), 183

Zagros (mountain range), 2
Zahedi, Fazlollah, 109, 128, 129, 135, 180
Zaidis (Fivers), 7, 8
zakat, 16
Zanan (magazine), 294
Zands, 37
Zan-e Ruz (magazine), 294
Zell as-Soltan, 63
Zia ad-Din, Sayyed, 80, 81, 82, 109
Zionism, 193
Zoroastrians, 2–3, 21, 33, 103, 178, 312